Houghton Mifflin English

Grammar and Composition

First Course

Houghton Mifflin Company · **Boston**

Atlanta   Dallas   Geneva, Illinois
Hopewell, New Jersey   Palo Alto   Toronto

Authors

Ann Cole Brown   Former Lecturer in English composition and literature at Northern Virginia Community College in Alexandria, Virginia

Jeffrey Nilson   Teacher of English at the Wixon Middle School, South Dennis, Massachusetts, and independent computer software designer

Fran Weber Shaw   Assistant Professor of English and Coordinator of the Writing Center at the University of Connecticut, Stamford

Richard A. Weldon   Vice Principal, Associate Dean of Studies, and teacher of English at the Christian Brothers High School in Sacramento, California

Editorial Advisers

Edwin Newman   Veteran broadcast journalist, author, and chairman of the Usage Panel of the *American Heritage Dictionary of the English Language*

Robert Cotton   Vice Principal, Curriculum Director, and former chairman of the English Department at Servite High School in Anaheim, California

Special Contributors

Ernestine Sewell, University of Texas at Arlington

Luella M. Wolff, Washburn University, Topeka, Kansas

Acknowledgments

The Publisher gratefully acknowledges the cooperation of the National Council of Teachers of English for making available student writing from the Council's Achievement Awards in Writing Program.

The Publisher also wishes to thank all the students whose names appear in this textbook for granting permission to use their writing as models. The editors and the Publisher have been solely responsible for selecting the student writing used as models.

The editors have made every effort to obtain permission to use student writing. In one instance, however, it was not possible to locate a student writer.

(Acknowledgments continue on page 563.)

Printed in U.S.A.

ISBN: 0-395-31401-1

Contents

Part One

Grammar, Usage, and Mechanics

You put your thoughts into sentences in order to share them with other people. To express your thoughts clearly, you should follow the rules of English grammar, usage, and mechanics. Those rules can tell you which form of a verb to use and where to place the modifiers in a sentence. The units in Part One can also help you to decide which words state your meaning best and how to punctuate a sentence.

As you study these units, you will see that they present a description of our language today. You will learn ways of using the language to present your thoughts easily and directly. Thus, the written language will be an effective tool for you to use to communicate with others.

Nouns, Pronouns, and Verbs

Unit Preview

All the words that you use can be classified into eight groups. These groups are the eight parts of speech: nouns, pronouns, verbs, adjectives, adverbs, prepositions, conjunctions, and interjections.

Classifying words into parts of speech is similar to grouping animals by families. Scientists classify animals so that they can describe similarities and differences among the members of each group. Grammarians classify words in order to show similarities and differences in how words function in a sentence.

Each of the following passages is missing a part of speech. See whether you can tell what activities the passages describe.

PASSAGE 1

Took a from the. Then put some in the and added. Sitting down at the, he enjoyed his.

PASSAGE 2

Jim his bat to the on-deck circle. He his muscles and the bat easily. He the pitcher closely. She a sinking pitch to the batter. The batter the ball to left field for an easy out. Jim into the batter's box.

PASSAGE 3

Last Saturday Jan and climbed a cliff. Had never climbed a cliff before. Just did. Was frightened in a strange way, but sometimes has to do is afraid to do.

All the nouns have been omitted from Passage 1, all the verbs from Passage 2, and all the pronouns from Passage 3. Each passage shows how essential the missing parts of speech are to the meaning of the sentences.

For Analysis   Answer these questions about the preceding passages.

1. What everyday activity does the first passage describe? Why is it almost impossible to identify the activity without the missing nouns?
2. In Passage 2, what part of speech tells you that the passage is about baseball? Why are verbs needed?
3. Who is describing the activity in Passage 3? How would the missing pronouns help you to understand the writer's feelings about climbing the cliff?
4. Choose one of the passages and rewrite it, adding the missing part of speech. Compare your rewritten passage with those of your classmates. Did everyone add the same nouns, verbs, or pronouns?

In this unit you will learn about different kinds of nouns, pronouns, and verbs. In Unit 6 you will learn how to use these parts of speech correctly in sentences.

1.1   Nouns

A **noun** is a word that names a person, a place, a thing, or an idea.

PERSONS	PLACES	THINGS	IDEAS
Henry Aaron	town	tulip	romance
actor	British Columbia	stadium	bravery
band	Singapore	spring	goodness

Exercise 1   Nouns   On your paper, write the nouns in the following sentences. The numeral in parentheses tells how many nouns there are in the sentence.

> **SAMPLE**   The Wildcats needed to move the ball thirteen yards in order to score a touchdown.
>
> **ANSWER**   Wildcats, ball, yards, touchdown

1. Six points would tie the game with the Cougars.   (3)
2. Running in from the sideline, the quarterback tried to ignore the roar of the crowd in the stadium.   (5)
3. The coach had given Simpson two plays for the time left on the clock.   (5)
4. The players formed their huddle.   (2)
5. The quarterback drew a pattern in the mud.   (3)
6. With a shout, the players lined up facing the Cougars.   (3)
7. The center snapped the ball.   (2)
8. Simpson looked around for a receiver.   (2)
9. A split second later, two defensive tackles blasted through the wall of blockers.   (4)
10. They sprinted after the quarterback, who raced toward the sideline.   (2)
11. The defensive players grabbed the quarterback, who lofted the ball toward the receiver.   (4)
12. Suddenly, a roar exploded from the crowd; the game was tied.   (3)

1.1a   Common Nouns and Proper Nouns

All nouns are either common nouns or proper nouns. A **common noun** refers to a class of persons, places, things, or ideas. It is not capitalized unless it begins a sentence.

A **proper noun** gives the name or title of a particular person, place, thing, or idea. It always begins with a capital letter. Many proper nouns are made up of more than one word. Each important word in a proper noun begins with a capital letter: Colorado School of Mines.

	COMMON	PROPER
PERSONS	woman	Jane Addams
	teacher	Mr. Chips
PLACES	state	South Carolina
	lake	Lake George
THINGS	bridge	Golden Gate Bridge
	building	World Trade Center
IDEAS	belief	Judaism

Exercise 2   Common Nouns and Proper Nouns   On your paper, write the following nouns. Tell whether each noun is a common noun or a proper noun. For each common noun, write a related proper noun. For each proper noun, write a related common noun.

> **SAMPLE**   hero
>
> **ANSWER**   hero, common noun—Achilles

1. singer
2. Picasso
3. Harry Truman
4. cousin
5. city
6. Wyoming
7. building
8. Thanksgiving
9. street
10. park
11. author
12. mountain
13. teacher
14. Super Bowl
15. river
16. France
17. friend
18. Antioch College
19. company
20. Aunt Isabelle

1.1b   Compound Nouns

A **compound noun** is a single noun made up of two or more words. Some compound nouns consist of words that are joined. Others consist of words separated by hyphens. A third kind consists of words often used together even though they are not joined. A fourth kind of compound noun is a proper noun made up of more than one word.

SINGLE WORD	nightfall, ballplayer
HYPHENS	cave-in, daughter-in-law
SEPARATE WORDS	road hog, crepe paper, White House

Assignment 1   Compound Nouns   On your paper, use each of the following compound nouns in a sentence. If you are not sure of the meaning of a word, use your dictionary.

1. snowplow
2. shoelace
3. deadline
4. disc jockey
5. home run
6. fish story
7. brother-in-law
8. bill of sale
9. Bill of Rights
10. courtroom
11. life boat
12. walkie-talkie

1.1c   Collective Nouns

A **collective noun** is a noun that names a group or a collection of persons or things. Some frequently used collective nouns are:

army	class	flock	herd
audience	committee	troop	jury
band	crowd	group	team

Exercise 3   Collective Nouns   On your paper, write the nouns in the following sentences. Label each collective noun.

SAMPLE	A small army of women marched toward the Capitol.
ANSWER	army—collective noun; women; Capitol

1. The staff quickly responded to the alarm.
2. The audience stood up and cheered the orchestra.
3. The brigade was honored by the queen.

4. Suddenly the class became very quiet.
5. The board met last night to vote on the budget.
6. Coach Jenkins gave the team last-minute instructions.
7. The committee is sending out ballots for the election.
8. At dances, my grandparents are always the first couple on the dance floor.
9. Her family is going to Acton Park this weekend.
10. The crowd finally settled down.

Exercise 4   Nouns in a Passage   Number your paper from 1 to 10. Next to each number, list the nouns in that sentence in the following passage.

SAMPLE   A grassland is an area such as a prairie or a meadow of grass or grasslike vegetation.

ANSWER   grassland, area, prairie, meadow, grass, vegetation

(1) A large part of the world is made up of grasslands. (2) The environment in the grasslands has too much rain to make the area a desert but not enough rain to make it a forest.   (3) The prairies and the steppes in the western part of the United States are examples of two different kinds of grasslands.

(4) Prairies and steppes once covered the lowlands of the Great Plains.   (5) When the pioneers first settled the prairies of the Midwest, the grasses were tall.   (6) Soon farmlands replaced the grasslands.

(7) On the steppes, there is less rainfall than on the prairies.   (8) Dry winds and little rainfall make these areas almost arid.   (9) As a result, the steppes are the least friendly grasslands to humans.   (10) Most of this land is therefore used to graze cattle.

Assignment 2   Nouns in Newspapers   Most newspaper stories include answers to the questions *Who? Where?* and *What?* To answer these questions, the writer must use nouns that name persons, places, and things.

Find a paragraph from each of three sections of a news-paper: news, sports, and entertainment, for example. Cut the paragraphs out and tape each paragraph to the top of its own sheet of paper. Under each paragraph, list the nouns that the writer uses. Tell whether each listed noun is a common noun, a proper noun, a compound noun, or a collective noun.

Nouns in Writing

On your paper, write a common noun. The noun may refer to a person, a place, a thing, or an idea. Then write two proper nouns that are related to the common noun. Find one magazine, book, or encyclopedia article about *each* of the persons, places, things, or ideas named by your proper nouns. Read each article. Then write a paragraph explaining the differ-ences between the two persons, places, things, or ideas. You should discuss at least three differences. When you have com-pleted your paragraph, underline the nouns in your paragraph.

1.2   Pronouns

A **pronoun** is a word that takes the place of a noun. You use pronouns to refer to persons, places, things, or ideas without having to rename them.

My *uncle* likes the *roller coaster* best. **It** doesn't scare **him** one bit. [The pronoun *it* takes the place of the noun *roller coaster*. The pronoun *him* takes the place of the noun *uncle*.]

The noun that a pronoun replaces is called the **antecedent** of the pronoun.

Uncle Al bought two *tickets* for *Jimmy.* **He** gave **them** to **him.** [The noun *Uncle Al* is the antecedent of the pronoun *He. Tickets* is the antecedent of the pronoun *them. Jimmy* is the antecedent of the pronoun *him.*]

Sometimes an antecedent is not stated in the sentence, as in the following example.

Give **me your** hand.

When you speak or write, you use pronouns for two reasons. First, by using pronouns, you do not have to use the same nouns over and over.

WITHOUT PRONOUNS Mr. Peters hired John and Jane because Mr. Peters knew that John and Jane could take care of the horses.

WITH PRONOUNS Mr. Peters hired John and Jane because **he** knew that **they** could take care of the horses. [less repetitive]

Second, with pronouns you can express thoughts that are difficult or impossible to express with nouns.

What is **that?**

Has **anybody** seen a blue sweater?

Exercise 1 Pronouns as Noun Substitutes On your paper, rewrite the following sentences by replacing the words in italic type with pronouns. Choose pronouns from this list: *he, him, his, she, her, it, its, they, some.* Then underline the pronoun once and the antecedent twice.

SAMPLE Elsie planted the tomatoes so that *Elsie* would have *the tomatoes* for salads.

ANSWER Elsie planted the tomatoes so that she would have them for salads.

9

1. John sent Alice the address of the house that *John* had bought.
2. The children loved the parakeet and taught *the parakeet* tricks.
3. When the alarm rang, I turned *the alarm* off.
4. The first thing that Mrs. Lorenzo reads in the newspaper is the comic strip that *Mrs. Lorenzo* loves.
5. When Sal and Rosa came in, *Sal and Rosa* were laughing.
6. Kate sanded the chair that *Kate* had made for the bedroom.
7. Tony washed the peaches and put *the peaches* in a bowl.
8. Although the tree lost several branches in the storm, *the tree* is still relatively healthy.
9. Bud took down the screens, but he didn't have time to wash *the screens*.
10. That is the radio that Bill's parents gave *Bill* for a graduation present.

1.2a   Personal Pronouns

A **personal pronoun** is a pronoun that takes the place of a noun naming a particular person, place, thing, or idea. Personal pronouns change form to show person, number, and gender.

Person

Personal pronouns are in either the first person, the second person, or the third person. You use first-person pronouns to refer to the speaker: *I, me, my, we, us, our.* You use second-person pronouns to refer to the person being spoken to: *you, your.* You use third-person pronouns to refer to the person, place, thing, or idea spoken about: *he, him, she, her, it, they, them, their.*

FIRST PERSON   **I** repaired the clock.

SECOND PERSON   Thank **you** for the help.

THIRD PERSON   **They** tried a new route.

Number

Personal pronouns have different forms depending on whether their antecedents are singular or plural. The singular pronouns include *I, he, she,* and *it.* The plural pronouns include *we* and *they.* The personal pronoun *you* can be either singular or plural.

SINGULAR **She** rides a bike to school.

PLURAL **They** ride bikes to school.

SINGULAR Ann, will **you** put the rake away?

PLURAL Children, will **you** put the rakes away?

Gender

Personal pronouns express gender. *He, him,* and *his* indicate the masculine gender. They refer to nouns like *brother* that name males. *She, her,* and *hers* indicate the feminine gender. They refer to nouns like *sister* that name females. *It* and *its* indicate the neuter gender. They refer to places, things, and ideas.

MASCULINE The *man* packed for the vacation that **he** was taking.

FEMININE The *woman* packed for the vacation that **she** was taking.

NEUTER Is *the record* available? I want to buy **it**.

Possessive Pronouns

Personal pronouns have possessive forms to show ownership or belonging. Such pronouns are **possessive pronouns**.

This is **my** bicycle.
That bicycle is **mine**.

The following chart shows the different forms of the personal pronouns. Possessive pronouns are in parentheses.

	SINGULAR	PLURAL
FIRST PERSON	I, me (my, mine)	we, us (our, ours)
SECOND PERSON	you (your, yours)	you (your, yours)
THIRD PERSON	he, him (his)	them, they
	she, her (her, hers)	(their, theirs)
	it (its)	

Exercise 2   Personal Pronouns   On your paper, write the personal pronouns in the following sentences. Label each pronoun *First-person, Second-person,* or *Third-person.*

> **SAMPLE**   Are porpoises as intelligent as we think they are?
> **ANSWER**   we—First-person; they—Third-person

1. Some people say that porpoises are almost as smart as we are.
2. The brains of porpoises are larger than ours.
3. They certainly seem attracted to us.
4. On the last whale-watching trip that we went on, two of them played hide-and-seek with us for hours.
5. They even swam into shore and let the bathers hug them.
6. Remember the famous porpoise that the captain told you and me about?
7. He said that she would come out to greet ships heading toward shore.
8. Didn't he say that the crew called her by a pet name?
9. She used to swim in front of ocean liners as though she were guiding them to shore.
10. She became so well known to passengers around the world that a law was passed to protect her.

1.2b   Other Kinds of Pronouns

Three other kinds of pronouns are indefinite pronouns, interrogative pronouns, and demonstrative pronouns.

Indefinite Pronouns

An **indefinite pronoun** is a pronoun that does not refer to a specific person, place, thing, or idea. You can often use these pronouns without antecedents.

Somebody handed me a wrench.

Has **anybody** seen my scarf?

Suppose that we gave a party and **nobody** came?

The following list includes some frequently used indefinite pronouns:

all	each	much	other
another	either	neither	some
any	everybody	nobody	somebody
anybody	everyone	no one	someone
anyone	everything	nothing	something
anything	many	one	

Interrogative Pronouns

An **interrogative pronoun** is a pronoun that introduces a question. The most frequently used interrogative pronouns are *who, whom, which, what,* and *whose.*

Who built that snow sculpture?

What is your favorite song?

Demonstrative Pronouns

A **demonstrative pronoun** is a pronoun that points out someone or something. The four demonstrative pronouns are *this, these, that,* and *those.*

The demonstrative pronouns *this* and *these* refer to something nearby. *That* and *those* refer to something farther away. *This* and *that* are singular forms; *these* and *those* are plural.

This is a cotton shirt; **that** is a silk one.

I'll take some of **these** and some of **those**.

Exercise 3 Pronouns On your paper, write the pronouns in italic type in the following sentences. Then label each pronoun that you wrote *Indefinite pronoun, Interrogative pronoun,* or *Demonstrative pronoun.*

> **SAMPLE** *This* was one train ride that the people of Boston would never forget.
>
> **ANSWER** this—Demonstrative pronoun

1. *What* was so strange about the ride?
2. It was so strange that *someone* even wrote a song about it.
3. Long ago a train rolled into a Boston station, and *somebody* got on.
4. *Who* was he?
5. *No one* ever found out.
6. *That* is not the most curious thing, however.
7. *Everybody* saw the man get on, but *nobody* saw him get off!
8. Years later *many* thought that they saw him late at night.
9. "*That* looks like him," *someone* would say.
10. *Many* say that he still travels under the streets of Boston.
11. "*Which* is my stop?" an eerie voice cries out in the night.
12. *What* is the truth about this mysterious traveler?

Exercise 4 Different Kinds of Pronouns On your paper, rewrite the following sentences, replacing each blank with the kind of pronoun indicated in parentheses. Underline each pronoun. Some sentences have more than one correct answer.

> **SAMPLE** In 1928 Amelia Earhart was __?__ of three people to fly across the Atlantic. (indefinite pronoun)
>
> **ANSWER** In 1928 Amelia Earhart was <u>one</u> of three people to fly across the Atlantic.

1. Although Amelia Earhart flew as a passenger and standby pilot, __?__ is considered the first woman to fly the Atlantic. (personal pronoun)

2. _?_ was it about Amelia Earhart that made her want to fly the Atlantic alone? (interrogative pronoun)
3. _?_ expected her to become a doctor. (indefinite pronoun)
4. During World War I _?_ served as an army nurse in Canada. (personal pronoun)
5. _?_ is not a job everyone can do. (demonstrative pronoun)
6. One day the nurses visited a military airfield, and _?_ made Amelia Earhart go off by herself to watch the airplanes take off and land. (indefinite pronoun)
7. As _?_ watched, an airplane standing nearby suddenly started. (personal pronoun)
8. _?_ may have been the moment that she decided to make flying her life's work. (demonstrative pronoun)
9. In 1932 _?_ became the first woman to fly alone across the Atlantic. (personal pronoun)
10. _?_ can forget Amelia Earhart's contribution to aviation history? (interrogative pronoun)

1.3 Verbs

A **verb** is a word that expresses an action or a state of being. There are three kinds of verbs: action verbs, linking verbs, and auxiliary verbs.

1.3a Action Verbs

An **action verb** is a verb that expresses the action or behavior of someone or something. Some action verbs express physical actions that you can see or hear. Other action verbs express mental actions that you cannot see or hear.

PHYSICAL   The mouse **squeaked** at the cat.
The old film **flickered.**
[You can hear the mouse squeak; you can see the film flicker.]

MENTAL   Jo **dislikes** mice.
Tom **loves** old movies.
[You cannot see the actions expressed by the verbs, *dislikes* and *loves.*]

Exercise 1   Action Verbs   On your paper, write the action verbs in the following sentences. Some sentences have more than one action verb.

SAMPLE   Long before the discovery of a polio vaccine, Nurse Elizabeth Kenny developed a treatment that helped polio victims.

ANSWER   developed, helped

1. Nurse Elizabeth Kenny rushed to the bedside of a two-year-old girl.
2. The young nurse arrived at the family's hut after sundown.
3. The child had polio, which caused pain in the legs.
4. Nurse Kenny knew that heat relaxes sore muscles.
5. First she put a bag of warm salt on the child's legs.
6. Then she took a blanket and tore it into long strips.
7. She poured boiling water over the strips and wrung the water.
8. She wrapped the hot, damp wool around the child's legs.
9. Soon the pain stopped, and the child slept peacefully.
10. Later Nurse Kenny moved the child's relaxed limbs in normal patterns.
11. Many doctors condemned Nurse Kenny's treatment of polio.
12. In spite of the criticism, she developed treatment methods that today's doctors still use.
13. Nurse Kenny started her first clinic many years later.
14. She trained her nurses as physical therapists.
15. She believed that every polio patient had unused potential.

1.3b   Linking Verbs

A **linking verb** connects a noun or a pronoun with words that rename or describe the noun or pronoun.

My dog **is** a terrier. [The word *terrier* renames the noun *dog.* The linking verb, *is,* links *dog* with *terrier.*]

Most terriers **are** mischievous. [The word *mischievous* describes the noun *terriers.* The linking verb, *are,* links *terriers* with *mischievous.*]

The most frequently used linking verbs are forms of the verb *be: am, is, are, was, were, be, being, been.* The forms *be, being,* and *been* are used with auxiliary verbs (*page 19*):

am	can be	shall have been
are	could be	will have been
be	has been	could have been
being	have been	should have been
is	shall be	would have been
was	should be	
were	will be	
	would be	

In addition to *be,* other verbs may function as linking verbs. To tell whether a verb is a linking verb, replace it with a form of *be.* If the meaning of the sentence remains the same, the verb is a linking verb. The following verbs are frequently used as linking verbs:

appear	feel	smell	remain	seem
become	look	sound	stay	taste

John **became** president. [The word *president* renames the noun *John.* The linking verb, *became,* links *John* with *president.*]

The stew **smells** spicy. [The word *spicy* describes the noun *stew:* spicy stew. The linking verb, *smells,* links *stew* with *spicy.*]

Some verbs can be either action verbs or linking verbs, depending on how they are used in the sentence.

ACTION VERB   Tess **tasted** the mango.

LINKING VERB   The mango **tasted** sweet to her.

ACTION VERB   Tab **smelled** the lilac blossoms.

LINKING VERB   The lilac blossoms **smelled** fresh.

Exercise 2   Linking Verbs   On your paper, write the linking verbs in the following sentences. Then write the words that each verb links.

SAMPLE   The test will be difficult.

ANSWER   will be—test, difficult

1. The students are guests of the mayor.
2. The trains have been prompt all week.
3. This apple tastes sour.
4. The woman in white must be a doctor.
5. The witness appeared anxious.
6. Thursday will be a holiday.
7. That statement is a lie.
8. Mr. Gumbel was a teacher in Zaire.
9. The audience remained quiet during the speech.
10. That tune sounds familiar.
11. The eagle has been a symbol of power for centuries.
12. The bears became restless.

Exercise 3   Linking Verbs or Action Verbs?   On your paper, write the verbs in the following sentences. Then label each verb *Action verb* or *Linking verb.*

SAMPLE   Most of the armadillos in the United States
              inhabit Texas and Louisiana.

ANSWER   inhabit—Action verb

1. The armadillo is an interesting animal.
2. It has a protective shell on its upper body.
3. The shell feels hard and bony.
4. The armadillo uses this shell for protection.
5. The animal has strong claws.
6. It digs tunnels in the ground with its claws.
7. The armadillo's tongue appears long and narrow.
8. It eats mostly insects.
9. The adult armadillo looks about two feet long.
10. It weighs up to fifteen pounds.
11. Female armadillos bear four babies at a time.
12. Some armadillos live in the United States.

Assignment Verbs in Sentences On your paper, write an interesting sentence for each noun and verb listed below. Then tell whether the verbs in the sentences that you wrote are action verbs or linking verbs.

1. stranger—appeared
2. cook—mixed
3. doctor—operated
4. lawyer—argued
5. dancer—leaped
6. spinach—tasted
7. treasure—had been
8. train—puffed
9. singer—hummed
10. crowd—became

1.3c Auxiliary Verbs

An action verb or a linking verb sometimes needs the help of one or more other verbs. This other verb is called an **auxiliary verb.** The verb that it helps is called the **main verb.** The main verb and one or more auxiliary verbs form a **verb phrase.**

> We **will be sailing** by this time tomorrow. [The verb phrase is *will be sailing.* The main verb is *sailing.* The auxiliary verbs are *will* and *be.*]

The following list contains auxiliary verbs that are frequently used:

am, is, are, was, were, be, been
have, has, had
do, does, did
shall, should
will, would
can, could
may, might, must

Forms of *be* can be either auxiliary verbs or linking verbs. When a form of *be* is used as an auxiliary verb, it is followed by a main verb. When a form of *be* is used as a linking verb, it is the main verb.

AUXILIARY VERB	I **am going** to Hawaii. [The auxiliary verb is *am*; the main verb is *going*.]
MAIN VERB	I **am** happy. [The main verb, *am*, is a linking verb. It links *I* and *happy*.]

Forms of *have* and *do* can also be either auxiliary verbs or main verbs.

MAIN VERB	Mike **has** a new trail bike.
AUXILIARY VERB	He **has ridden** it into the mountains.
MAIN VERB	I **did** my homework.
AUXILIARY VERB	I certainly **did help** you with yours.

Auxiliary verbs always come before the main verb. Sometimes, however, the verb phrase is interrupted by another word. The words *not* and *never* may interrupt a verb phrase.

You **should** not **catch** those frogs. [The word *not* interrupts the verb phrase, *should catch*.]

In questions, the verb phrase is usually interrupted by other words.

Do frogs **cause** warts? [The word *frogs* interrupts the verb phrase, *Do cause.*]

Where **should** I **keep** my collection? [The word *I* interrupts the verb phrase, *should keep.*]

Exercise 4   Verb Phrases   On your paper, write the verb phrases in the following sentences. In each verb phrase, underline each auxiliary verb once and each main verb twice. Some sentences have more than one verb phrase.

SAMPLE   The raccoon is closely related to the panda.

ANSWER   is related

1. All kinds of wildlife are joining the rush to the suburbs.
2. The most annoying invader in our neighborhood has been the raccoon.
3. Some people have been trapping raccoons and have released them in other neighborhoods.
4. Two biologists have reported that the raccoon has discovered garbage as a source of nourishment.
5. Anyone could have told them that!
6. Another report has confirmed that raccoons have usually been too smart for humans.
7. One raccoon in my neighborhood is always outwitting me.
8. One night our sleep was interrupted by the rattle of our garbage-can lid.
9. As I was quietly approaching the driveway, I could hear noises from inside the can.
10. Suddenly the top was lifted by a large raccoon.
11. I will never forget the animal's look of contempt.
12. The raccoon ran into the woods before I could even move.
13. A raccoon does not have fingers, but it can open any so-called raccoon-proof garbage can.

14. A raccoon can easily remove rocks from the top of the can, and it can open foolproof locks.
15. I am still battling the raccoons in my neighborhood, and someday I may even win.

Exercise 5 Verbs in a Passage Number your paper from 1 to 20. *Step 1:* Next to each number, write the verb or verb phrase in that sentence. *Step 2:* Underline each auxiliary verb once and each main verb twice. *Step 3:* For each main verb, write the label *Action* or *Linking*.

SAMPLE   In December of 1776, George Washington was preparing his small army, which would soon cross the frigid Delaware River.

ANSWER   was preparing—Action; would cross—Action

(1) Washington's crossing the Delaware would lead to an important early victory in the American Revolution.
(2) Washington was faced with a difficult decision.   (3) He could wait for the Hessian attack on Philadelphia.   (4) He could also steal across the Delaware.   (5) He might take the large Hessian force by surprise.

(6) The Hessians could sense victory.   (7) The troops under Washington had suffered one defeat after another.
(8) A victory for them would be welcome.   (9) Washington seemed confident despite the odds against his troops.
(10) A successful crossing at Trenton appeared unlikely.

(11) Washington moved his forces several miles upriver.   (12) Fishermen had been gathering boats for days.   (13) The soldiers and their cannon could barely squeeze into the collection of boats.   (14) They did succeed, however.

(15) Washington's troops surprised the Hessians in the middle of a holiday banquet.   (16) A short battle followed.   (17) Hundreds of Hessians were wounded.
(18) Many others were captured.   (19) Washington's troops suffered scarcely a scratch.   (20) The battle remains an example of outstanding military tactics.

Using Action Verbs

Action verbs are often more vivid and effective than linking verbs. In your writing you should strive to use action verbs wherever possible. The four sentences that follow have linking verbs. On your paper, rewrite each sentence so that it contains an action verb rather than a linking verb. Then choose one of the sentences and use it as the topic sentence for a paragraph. In the paragraph try to use as many action verbs as you can.

1. The day was hot.
2. The kitten was playful.
3. The crowd at the football game sounded loud.
4. The sales clerk looked busy.

Unit Practice

Practice 1

A. Nouns *(pages 3–8)* On your paper, list the nouns in each of the following sentences.

1. Starlight shone through a window in my bedroom.
2. The explorers in Canada showed good sense by using snowshoes.
3. Historians believe that Hans Lippershey made the first telescope.
4. The crowd roared with enthusiasm for the celebrity.
5. The Elgin Theater will show a series of films starring Buster Keaton.

B. Pronouns *(pages 8–15)* On your paper, list the pronouns in each of the following sentences.

6. Who came to the door to sell something to us?
7. She carried nothing heavy except the suitcase.
8. I usually like horror stories, but that was too frightening.
9. What happened to everything in the cabin?
10. Are these or those the slippers that belong to Bill?

C. Pronouns *(pages 8–15)* On your paper, rewrite each of the following sentences, replacing each word in italic type with a pronoun.

11. The tourists visited Toronto, and then *the tourists* boarded a bus.
12. Does this zoo have ostriches? Where can we go to see *the ostriches*?
13. Kevin read the daily newspaper that *Kevin* bought.
14. I packed film for the camera, but I left *the film* behind at the station.
15. Did Doris and Ellen collect shells during the vacation that *Doris and Ellen* went on?

D. Verbs *(pages 15–23)*   On your paper, list the verbs and the verb phrases in each of the following sentences.

16. I thought that you would be leaving tomorrow!
17. The Golden Gate Bridge in California is a suspension bridge.
18. We were startled when an old jar dropped from the cabinet.
19. Although Lola feels tired, she will finish her work.
20. When the match ended, who was the winner?

Practice 2

On your paper, list the words in italic type in the following passage. Label each word *Noun, Pronoun,* or *Verb.*

Every   (1) *September* an exciting event   (2) *happens* in Window Rock, Arizona.   (3) *Crowds* of people leave their   (4) *towns* to travel here for the Navajo Nation Fair and Rodeo. The fair   (5) *is* a   (6) *celebration* of the harvest season, and   (7) *it* is also a reunion. Nearly seventy thousand American Indians from many tribes enjoy the (8) *activities* at this gathering. The   (9) *fairgrounds* (10) *seem* filled with food, contests,   (11) *people,* and goods.   (12) *Everyone* brings   (13) *something* to sell or trade, such as turquoise jewelry, hay, or potatoes. The main events of the fair   (14) *are* a parade, a baking contest, and   (15) *dances* that   (16) *are performed* in the traditional ceremonial manner. Finally, more than five hundred cowboys   (17) *participate* in a rodeo, and   (18) *they* compete for prizes. Whether one purchases items for sale, enjoys traditional celebrations, or observes these events, a good time   (19) *is had* by   (20) *all*!

Unit Tests

Test 1

A. Nouns *(pages 3–8)* On your paper, list the nouns in each of the following sentences.

1. Mr. Greer always buys his vegetables at this supermarket.
2. At the park, our group experienced a fright!
3. Joanne Smith took the children in the neighborhood to a play.
4. The crew wears hard hats for safety while working on the skyscraper.
5. In the moonlight, her father-in-law saw a flock of geese fly by.

B. Pronouns *(pages 8–15)* On your paper, list the pronouns in the following sentences.

6. The ceramic mug is mine, but anyone can use it.
7. Everyone came to the picnic except him.
8. What do you hope to accomplish by gathering signatures?
9. These are more popular dances; those will be forgotten.
10. Which of the clubs will let anyone in the neighborhood join?

C. Pronouns *(pages 8–15)* On your paper, rewrite each of the following sentences by replacing each word in italic type with a pronoun.

11. Many artists travel to the Painted Desert in Arizona to make paintings of *the Painted Desert.*
12. Did Sandra make that sound or was *Sandra* perfectly quiet?
13. Lorie shoveled dirt and piled *dirt* near the building.
14. I like lilies, but I rarely see *lilies* in this area.
15. Philip got the ball to take the last shot, but *Philip* lost *the ball* out of bounds.

D. Verbs *(pages 15–23)* On your paper, list the verbs and the verb phrases in the following sentences.

16. A triplane was shown at the transportation fair that we attended.

17. Although these plums taste sour, they look attractive.
18. In the winter Paul races to his house and sits by a fire.
19. We do not see our dog during storms because he hides under the bed.
20. Ms. Levine thinks that the display should not be larger.

Test 2

On your paper, list the words in italic type in the following passage. Label each word *Noun, Pronoun,* or *Verb.*

(1) *Who* would think that spiders (2) *can open* doors? It (3) *sounds* impossible—but it's absolutely true! The trap-door (4) *spider* lives underground. In order to make itself a home, (5) *it* digs a tunnel through the (6) *earth.* Then, at the top of the tunnel, the spider (7) *attaches* a door. The door (8) *is made* of mud and silk. The trap-door spider uses silk to attach (9) *this* to the tunnel. The door (10) *may be* a thin cover over the tunnel. It may also be a thick door that tightly (11) *blocks* the entrance. In this way, the trap-door spider (12) *seems* to protect itself and its (13) *young.* If (14) *anyone* travels through the (15) *West* or the (16) *Southwest* where these spiders live, (17) *he* or *she* (18) *might have* the (19) *opportunity* to see (20) *one* opening a door.

Adjectives
and Adverbs

Unit Preview

Adjectives and adverbs are modifiers. Modifiers describe, limit, or give more exact meanings to words. Modifiers also help to make sentences more alive and more interesting.

Most of the adjectives and adverbs have been omitted from the following paragraph. Read the paragraph. Then go back and make a mental note of those places where a modifier might have added to or limited the meaning of a word. For example, is the road a paved road or a dirt road? Is the house empty or is it lived in?

PARAGRAPH A

The road winds past a house that peers through a clump of trees. The house was built of blocks held in place with clay. The blocks are crumbled, and chunks of adobe lie in the grass. The windows hang from their frames. The panes have disappeared. Some shingles still curve over the boards. The loneliness of the house is eased by birds nesting in the eaves.

Now read the rewritten paragraph that follows. The added modifiers are in italic type.

PARAGRAPH B

The *dusty* road winds past a *deserted* house that peers *sadly* through a clump of *bare* trees. The house was built *long ago* of *adobe* blocks held in place with *heavy* clay. *Today* the blocks are crumbled, and chunks of *red* adobe lie in the *brown* grass. The windows hang *listlessly* from their frames. The panes have *long since* disappeared. Some *bent* shingles still curve over the *roof* boards. The loneliness of the house is eased *only* by birds nesting *precariously* in the *sagging* eaves.

For Analysis Answer the following questions about the two paragraphs that you have just read.

1. Does Paragraph A or Paragraph B create a more vivid picture in your imagination? Why?
2. In the first sentence of Paragraph B, what kind of pictures do the modifiers *deserted, sadly,* and *bare* help create?
3. Suppose the first sentence of Paragraph B read: The road winds past a *yellow* house that peers *happily* through a clump of *flowering* trees. How would the picture created in your imagination be different?
4. What does your answer to Question 3 tell you about the effect that modifiers have on other words?

In this unit you will study the adjective and the adverb. These parts of speech can change the meaning of what you write and can make your writing more interesting to read.

2.1 Adjectives

An **adjective** is a word that modifies a noun or a pronoun. The word *modify* means "to change" or "to give more information about." An adjective modifies a noun or a pronoun by describing it or by making it more exact. An adjective answers one of three questions:

1. Which?
2. What kind?
3. How many?

Each of the adjectives in the following sentences answers a different question.

Look at **those** *cobwebs.* [*Which* cobwebs? Those cobwebs.]

Stringy *cobwebs* hung from branch to branch. [*What kind* of cobwebs? Stringy cobwebs.]

Several *spiders* scurried along a branch. [*How many* spiders? Several spiders.]

More than one adjective may modify the same noun or pronoun.

Every morning **those two greedy** *squirrels* rob the bird feeder. [*Which* squirrels? Those squirrels. *How many* squirrels? Two squirrels. *What kind* of squirrels? Greedy squirrels.]

Articles

The most frequently used adjectives are the articles *a, an,* and *the.* The articles *a* and *an* are **indefinite articles** because they do not point out a particular person or thing. The article *the* is a **definite article** because it always points out a particular person or thing.

INDEFINITE   I enjoy **an** *apple* with my lunch. [any apple]

DEFINITE   **The** *apple* had a worm in it. [a particular apple]

Exercise 1 Adjectives On your paper, write the adjectives in the following sentences. Then write the noun that each adjective modifies. Do not include articles.

SAMPLE   Garlic is a tasty plant related to the onion.

ANSWER   tasty—plant

1. A garlic bulb contains small sections called cloves.
2. Cloves of garlic are used for different kinds of cooking.
3. The herb gives an unusual taste to food.
4. People have grown the spicy herb for several centuries.
5. In Europe people have used garlic since ancient times.
6. From earliest times garlic has been used for medical purposes.
7. People even used garlic to cure bad toothaches.
8. Several cloves of garlic were worn around the neck to ward off illness.
9. In some parts of the world, garlic can be a troublesome plant.
10. Cows who feed on the plant produce garlicky milk.

Placement of Adjectives

Many adjectives come directly before the nouns or pronouns that they modify.

The **tall, graceful** *dancer* leaped across **the empty** *stage*.

Adjectives may come before the nouns or pronouns that they modify and be set off with commas.

Tired and **hot,** the *children* entered the room noisily.

Black and **threatening,** the *smoke* erupted from the north face of the mountain.

Sometimes, however, adjectives appear in other places in the sentence. For example, an adjective may come after a linking verb. In this position, an adjective modifies a noun or pronoun that comes before the verb.

The *dancer* was **athletic.**

He appeared **powerful.**

Two or more adjectives may appear after the noun or pronoun that they modify. Adjectives in this position are set off with commas.

The *children,* **tired** and **hot,** entered the room noisily.

The *smoke,* **black** and **threatening,** erupted from the north face of the mountain.

Exercise 2   Adjectives   On your paper, write the adjectives in the following sentences. Write the noun or pronoun that each adjective modifies. Do not include articles.

SAMPLE   The village, remote and small, looked across a tranquil lake.

ANSWER   remote—village; small—village; tranquil—lake

1. A short distance from the village stood a small cluster of beeches.
2. Behind the trees, yellow wheat waved in the gentle breeze.
3. Brown and empty, another field spread to the south.
4. The hills behind the fields were blue and picturesque.
5. At night the low hum of crickets lulled us to sleep.
6. The air smelled sweet and grassy.
7. Every morning at four o'clock, a train, slow and noisy, would creep through the village.
8. In September a wet, cold mist promised an early autumn.
9. The lazy, hazy days of summer were about to end.
10. Busy and interesting, the summer was one that we would remember for a long time.

Exercise 3   Adjectives in a Paragraph   Number your paper from 1 to 8. Next to each number, list all the adjectives in that sentence. Do not include articles. Next to each adjective, write the noun or pronoun that it modifies.

SAMPLE In the musty attic, we discovered battered trunks with beautiful old clothes.

ANSWER musty—attic; battered—trunks; beautiful—clothes; old—clothes

(1) Huge portraits of unknown ancestors greeted us as we entered the mansion on a dark afternoon. (2) The builder of the gloomy house posed before a dusky window. (3) He leaned on a sturdy stick of ornate wood. (4) A woman, young and serious, sat in the shadow of a winding staircase. (5) She gazed at us from under a flowered bonnet. (6) Her eyes were anxious. (7) On her lap lay an open book with a bright ribbon across a worn page. (8) She seemed uncomfortable in the presence of unexpected visitors.

Proper Adjectives

A **proper adjective** is a proper noun that modifies another noun or pronoun. It always begins with a capital letter.

Do you want to go see the **John Wayne** *movie*? [*Which* movie? The John Wayne movie.]

To create many proper adjectives, you add the suffix -*n*, -*an*, -*ian*, or -*ic* to the proper noun.

PROPER NOUNS	PROPER ADJECTIVES
Asia	Asian
Rome	Roman
King Edward	Edwardian
Napoleon	Napoleonic

Exercise 4 Proper Adjectives On your paper, write each of the following word pairs so that it includes a noun modified by a proper adjective. Use a dictionary if you have trouble thinking of a proper adjective.

SAMPLE   (Africa) art
ANSWER   African art

1. (Russia) wolfhound
2. (India) sari
3. (Colombia) coffee
4. (Egypt) sculpture
5. (Europe) country

6. (America) writer
7. (Mexico) history
8. (Alaska) wilderness
9. (Tibet) culture
10. (Italy) art

Assignment 1   Proper Adjectives in Sentences   Use each proper adjective and noun that you wrote for Exercise 4 in an original sentence.

Nouns Used as Adjectives

Some nouns may function as adjectives without changing form.

I get bored halfway through **summer** *vacation*. [*What kind* of vacation? Summer vacation.]

We went to the **tennis** *matches* in Forest Hills. [*What kind* of matches? Tennis matches.]

Possessive Nouns

Nouns that show possession are used as adjectives in sentences. A **possessive noun** answers the question *Whose?* or *Which?*

You form the singular possessive of most nouns by adding -*'s*.

Alice's *grades* are improving. [*Whose* grades? Alice's grades.]

Billy's *friend* just called. [*Whose* friend? Billy's friend.]

You form the plural possessive of most nouns by adding -*s'* or -*es'* to the singular form of the noun. For further explanation of how to spell possessive nouns, see Unit 17.

The **farmers'** *group* will meet tonight. [*Which* group? The farmers' group.]

Exercise 5   Nouns as Adjectives   On your paper, write the possessive nouns and the nouns used as adjectives in the following sentences. Write the noun or pronoun that is modified by each adjective.

> **SAMPLE**   John's coat is in the hall closet.
>
> **ANSWER**   John's—coat; hall—closet

1. A beautiful autumn sun was shining.
2. The padlock on the garage door is broken.
3. Those office files belong to Sal's uncle.
4. Our science teacher gave us a test before spring vacation.
5. Please hand me the paint bucket.
6. Bentley's photographs have been displayed in art exhibits.
7. Vicki's stamina has increased since she started running.
8. Starvation during the winter months is the deer's greatest natural danger.
9. We drove Lara's parents to the bus terminal.
10. The buffalo herd stampeded through the settlers' camp.

Assignment 2   Nouns and Adjectives   On your paper, write two sentences for each word listed below. In the first sentence, use the word as a noun. In the second sentence, use the word as an adjective.

> **SAMPLE**   right
>
> **ANSWER**   Noun: It is my right to vote.
>   Adjective: You made the right decision.

1. spinach	3. glass	5. maple	7. television
2. truck	4. clay	6. country	8. banjo

Possessive Pronouns

Some **possessive pronouns*** (*page 11*) modify nouns and pronouns and therefore are used as adjectives.

I wish **my** *sister* would call. [*Whose* sister? My sister.]

He put on **his** *boots.* [*Whose* boots? His boots.]

The possessive pronouns that can function as adjectives are in the following list:

	SINGULAR	PLURAL
FIRST PERSON	my	our
SECOND PERSON	your	your
THIRD PERSON	his, her, its	their

Other Pronouns Used as Adjectives

Indefinite pronouns, demonstrative pronouns, and interrogative pronouns may also modify nouns. Here is a list of the pronouns that function most often as adjectives.

INDEFINITE   some, many, several, few

DEMONSTRATIVE this, that, these, those

INTERROGATIVE which, what, whose

Some *people* do not like sports. [*How many* people? Some people.]

Why are we going **this** *way*? [*Which* way? This way.]

Exercise 6   Adjectives   On your paper, write each noun and pronoun used as an adjective in the following sentences. Write the word that each adjective modifies. Do not include articles.

---

* Possessive pronouns that modify nouns or pronouns are sometimes called pronominal adjectives.

SAMPLE   Those laces belong to your baseball shoes.

ANSWER   Those—laces; your—shoes; baseball—shoes

1. My aunt visited several countries.
2. Her pet basked in the afternoon sun.
3. Few members like our plan for a spring festival.
4. Mother bought a huge display cabinet for her office.
5. Their dog is shedding its hair.
6. Do you like this model or that model?
7. The Scarsdale train is part of the Conrail system.
8. Which report is due before summer vacation?
9. He didn't look like a star player in that inning.
10. Several students have signed up for Mr. Brady's Saturday course in auto mechanics.

Writers Workshop

Adjectives in Advertisements

Writers of advertising copy use adjectives to make the public want the product being advertised. In an advertisement for a speaker system, for example, an advertising copywriter might describe the bass tone as the *richest, mellowest* bass tone available.

Step 1: From a newspaper or a magazine, cut out four different advertisements for the same kind of product. Underline the adjectives in each advertisement. *Step 2:* Write an advertisement for a product similar to the one for which you found advertisements in Step 1. In your advertisement use adjectives that create a favorable impression about the product. Refer to a dictionary or a thesaurus if you need help finding suitable adjectives.

2.2   Adverbs

An **adverb** is a word that modifies a verb, an adjective, or another adverb.

MODIFIES A VERB

 The pianist *played* **skillfully.**

MODIFIES AN ADJECTIVE

 She is a **very** *skillful* pianist.

MODIFIES AN ADVERB

 She plays **quite** *beautifully.*

An adverb answers one of five questions about the word or phrase that it modifies:

1. How or in what manner?
2. When?
3. Where?
4. How often?
5. To what extent or degree?

The contestants *glided* **gracefully** across the ice. [*In what manner* did the contestants glide? Gracefully.]

The contest *began* **late.** [*When* did the contest begin? Late.]

The crowd *surged* **forward.** [*Where* did the crowd surge? Forward.]

The ice machine **rarely** *works.* [*How often* does the ice machine work? Rarely.]

The contest was **very** *exciting.* [*To what degree* was the contest exciting? Very exciting.]

The words *not* and *never* are adverbs. They tell to what extent (*not at all*) and when (*never*).

The ice machine *does* **not** *work*. [*Not* modifies *does work*.]
The ice machine **never** *works*. [*Never* modifies *works*.]

Exercise 1   Adverbs   On your paper, write the adverbs that are in italic type in the following sentences. Then write what each adverb tells: *How, When, Where, How often,* or *To what degree or extent.*

SAMPLE   The strange animal hung *precariously* from a rock near the edge of the gorge.

ANSWER   precariously—How

1. We had been climbing *steadily* for days.
2. The guides had *secretly* told us about the strange animal.
3. Hill people would *occasionally* tell stories about this animal.
4. We were *quite* doubtful about the truth of these tales.
5. This mysterious animal had *never actually* been photographed.
6. Some climbers had *once* made a cast of a huge footprint.
7. The climbers had *then* sold the cast for thousands of dollars.
8. The animal's *remarkably* unusual appearance interested us.
9. People said that its face was *unbelievably* ugly.
10. The animal *carefully* pulled itself over the edge of the gorge and stared at us.

Adverbs Modifying Verbs

The most common function of an adverb is to modify a verb. An adverb that modifies a verb modifies the entire verb phrase, which includes the main verb and its auxiliary verbs.

The driver *was honking* his horn **desperately.** [The adverb, *desperately,* modifies the verb phrase, *was honking.*]

An adverb that modifies a verb does not always appear next to the verb in the sentence.

NEXT TO VERB   The police **suddenly** *arrived* at the scene.

AT BEGINNING   **Suddenly** the police *arrived* at the scene.

AT END   The police *arrived* at the scene **suddenly.**

An adverb sometimes interrupts a verb phrase. An adverb in this position modifies all parts of the verb phrase.

The man *was* **desperately** *honking* his horn.

Exercise 2   Adverbs Modifying Verbs   *Step 1:* On your paper, write all the adverbs in the following sentences. *Step 2:* Write the verb or verb phrase that each adverb modifies. *Step 3:* Write what each adverb tells: *How, When, Where, How often,* or *To what degree or extent.*

SAMPLE   Two sheep dogs loafed nearby.

ANSWER   nearby—loafed, Where

1. The assignment thoroughly confused us.
2. The pirates carefully hid their treasure.
3. The cows were grazing quietly in the meadow.
4. The truck finally reached the top of the narrow trail.
5. Sailors sometimes sang sea chanteys.
6. My grandparents came here from Puerto Rico in 1950.
7. A shipment of rare birds recently arrived at the zoo.
8. The anniversary party completely surprised my parents.
9. In the pictures, a mother giraffe is courageously guarding her infant from a pride of lions.
10. Please leave now and close the door quietly.

Exercise 3   Position of Adverbs   On your paper, rewrite each of the following sentences so that the adverb is in a different position. You may move other words as well, but do not add or remove any words. Underline the adverbs in your rewritten sentences.

> **SAMPLE** Suddenly the ship rolled onto its side.
>
> **ANSWER** The ship <u>suddenly</u> rolled onto its side.

1. The agent patiently waited for the spy to appear.
2. Quickly the pirates joined the Halloween crowd.
3. We sometimes have apples for dessert.
4. The elderly woman walked briskly through the park.
5. Lately Dad has been doing most of the cleaning.

Adverbs Modifying Adjectives

Adverbs may also modify adjectives. An adverb that modifies an adjective usually comes just before the adjective that it modifies.

> Our dog is **quite** *deaf.* [*Quite* tells *to what degree* the dog is deaf.]
>
> Your ideas are **usually** *brilliant.* [*Usually* tells *how often* the ideas are brilliant.]

Exercise 4 Adverbs Modifying Adjectives On your paper, write the adverbs in the following sentences. Then write the adjective that the adverb modifies.

> **SAMPLE** Building the bridge will be extremely risky.
>
> **ANSWER** extremely—risky

1. That is a basically sound idea.
2. The lyrics were quite interesting.
3. Is he ashamed of his totally foolish behavior?
4. The storm is unusually fierce.
5. The bridge is made of exceptionally strong steel.
6. My cousin's job is sometimes hazardous.

7. Two extremely old owls blinked at us.
8. Very shrill laughter can be annoying.
9. The train is disgracefully late.
10. We saw a rather short movie.

Adverbs Modifying Adverbs

Sometimes adverbs modify other adverbs. Such adverbs usually come just before the adverbs that they modify, and they usually tell to what degree or extent.

We were laughing **quite** *loudly*. [*Loudly* is an adverb that modifies *were laughing*. *Quite* tells *to what extent* we were laughing loudly.]

The principal spoke **rather** *sharply*. [*Sharply* is an adverb that modifies *spoke*. *Rather* tells *to what extent* the principal spoke sharply.]

Exercise 5   Adverbs   *Step 1:* On your paper, write the adverbs in the following sentences. *Step 2:* Next to each adverb, write the word that the adverb modifies. *Step 3:* Write what part of speech the modified word is: *Verb, Adjective,* or *Adverb.*

SAMPLE   Chet did surprisingly well in his first try at gymnastics.

ANSWER   surprisingly—well, Adverb; well—did, Verb

1. Since childhood Chet has been extremely agile.
2. First he tried a handstand on the parallel bars.
3. As he carefully mounted the bars, he felt rather nervous.
4. However, he gripped the bars very tightly.
5. He finally swung his legs over his head until they were perfectly straight.
6. He held this position for almost ten seconds.
7. Chet decided that he would next try the rings.

8. He grasped the rings and lifted himself slowly from the ground.
9. Following the coach's directions, he then did a very nimble dismount.
10. Chet went to the tumbling pad, where he successfully executed a series of rather neat flips and somersaults.

Exercise 6 Adverbs in Sentences *Step 1:* On your paper, write the following sentences. In place of each blank, write an adverb that fits the meaning of the sentence. Do not use the same adverb more than twice. *Step 2:* Underline the adverb that you add to the sentence.

> SAMPLE   The driver sat __?__ in the seat.
> ANSWER   The driver sat <u>comfortably</u> in the seat.

1. The crew __?__ changed the tires.
2. The driver __?__ adjusted his helmet.
3. The crew __?__ poured fifty gallons of fuel into the tank.
4. They worked __?__ to get the driver back into the race.
5. In a few seconds, the crew __?__ told the driver to go.
6. He waited __?__ for an opening and then moved __?__ carefully onto the track.
7. The other cars were setting a(n) __?__ fast pace.
8. He pressed __?__ on the accelerator.
9. The engine responded __?__, and in seconds the driver was moving with the other cars.
10. The crew had done a(n) __?__ skillful job of getting him back into the race.

Adjective or Adverb?

It is sometimes difficult to decide whether a word is an adjective or an adverb. A large number of adverbs end in *-ly,* but so do some adjectives.

> ADVERB   The guide *yelled* **loudly.**
> ADJECTIVE   The *bear* seemed **friendly.**

Sometimes the same word may be used as either an adjective or an adverb.

ADVERB   Everyone *worked* **hard.**

ADJECTIVE   This is **hard** *work.*

To decide whether a modifier is an adjective or an adverb, figure out what part of speech the modified word is. If the modified word is a noun or a pronoun, the modifier is an adjective. If the modified word is a verb, an adjective, or an adverb, the modifier is an adverb.

You can also tell whether a modifier is an adjective or an adverb by deciding which question the modifier answers.

ADJECTIVE	ADVERB
1. Which?	1. How or in what manner?
2. What kind?	2. When?
3. How many?	3. Where?
	4. How often?
	5. To what extent or degree?

ADJECTIVE   Jan is an **early** *riser.* [**Think:** *Early* tells *what kind* of riser. *Early* modifies *riser,* which is a noun. *Early* is therefore an adjective.]

ADVERB   Jan *left* **early.** [**Think:** *Early* tells *when* Jan left. *Early* modifies *left,* which is a verb. *Early* is therefore an adverb.]

Exercise 7   Adjective or Adverb?   *Step 1:* On your paper, write the words that are in italic type in the following sentences. *Step 2:* Label each word *Adjective* or *Adverb. Step 3:* Write the word that is modified and tell what part of speech it is.

SAMPLE   That was a *long* game.

ANSWER   long—Adjective, game—Noun

1. The *kindly* manager gave us another key.
2. She spoke to us *kindly.*
3. Jets travel *fast!*
4. That plane is exceptionally *fast.*
5. We had a very *close* call.
6. We came *close* to missing our bus.
7. The path to success is seldom *straight.*
8. Their latest recording went *straight* to the top of the charts.
9. The mail came *late.*
10. The mail is *late.*

Assignment Adverbs in Writing   Write ten sentences. In each one, use one of the ten adverbs in the following list. Underline the adverb, and draw an arrow from it to the word that it modifies. Remember that an adverb may modify a verb, an adjective, or an adverb.

1. happily
2. ridiculously
3. early
4. yesterday
5. there
6. forward
7. frequently
8. sometimes
9. scarcely
10. too

Unit Practice

Practice 1

A. Adjectives *(pages 29–37)*   On your paper, list the adjectives in the following sentences. Next to each adjective, write the question that it answers: *Which?, What kind?,* or *How many?* Do not include articles.

1. The country fair features more than eighty exhibits.
2. In March the wet weather continued until the new grass appeared.
3. Joyce asked, "Are those green sweaters on sale?"
4. The cat, bedraggled and hungry, sat on the back step.
5. The plaster cast for your broken arm will set completely in several minutes.

B. Adjectives *(pages 29–37)*   On your paper, write the adjectives in the following sentences. Next to each adjective, write the noun or pronoun that it modifies. Do not include articles.

6. Andrea proofread her history assignment before handing it in.
7. Within a small area, Matt found many kinds of wild flowers.
8. Joyce's mother has gone shopping for new shoes.
9. Arthur said emphatically, "I want this one, not that one."
10. Our construction company has a contract to work on the Acme factory.

C. Adverbs *(pages 38–45)*   On your paper, list the adverbs in the following sentences. Next to each adverb, identify which of five questions is answered by the adverb: *How?, When?, Where?, How often?,* or *To what extent or degree?*

11. The stallion stamped and whinnied threateningly.
12. Hand in your book reports now.
13. Tomorrow the temperature will rise slightly.
14. Usually everything runs smoothly if everyone pays attention.
15. The paddle slipped overboard, and the canoe began to drift.

D. Adverbs *(pages 38–45)* On your paper, list the adverbs in the following sentences. Next to each adverb, write the word that it modifies. Then label the modified word *Verb, Adjective,* or *Adverb.*

16. The sudden shower completely soaked us.
17. The hot-air balloon rose silently.
18. Everyone who went cycling had an absolutely wonderful time.
19. Sam got up very slowly after he had been tackled.
20. Adam was quite pleased that he had finished the project.

Practice 2

On your paper, write the modifiers that are in italic type in the following paragraph. Next to each modifier, write the label *Adjective* or *Adverb.* Then write the word or words modified by each modifier.

(1) *Most* people have heard of the (2) *mighty* hero Hercules and (3) *his* twelve labors, but (4) *few* people know about the king whom he had to serve. The king was a small and (5) *cowardly* man. He was (6) *intensely* (7) *jealous* of Hercules. Boldly and (8) *quite* (9) *loudly,* he would send Hercules to perform (10) *many* (11) *dangerous* tasks, but the king would (12) *often* hide in (13) *quivering* terror when Hercules returned with his prize. (14) *Once,* the servants found the king, (15) *trembling* and (16) *whimpering,* in an (17) *empty* water urn. (18) *Eventually,* the king acknowledged that Hercules had completed the labors, and he (19) *reluctantly* allowed Hercules to leave (20) *his* kingdom.

Unit Tests

Test 1

A. Adjectives *(pages 29–37)* On your paper, list the adjectives in the following sentences. Next to each adjective, write the question that it answers: *Which?, What kind?,* or *How many?* Do not include articles.

1. The dashboard clock is broken.
2. May I have your answers?
3. Students have a choice of several daily activities at the summer camp.
4. The car, dusty and dilapidated, crept along the narrow road.
5. Are you laughing at those old photographs?

B. Adjectives *(pages 29–37)* On your paper, write the adjectives in the following sentences. Next to each adjective, write the noun or pronoun that it modifies. Do not include articles.

6. Put those buckets into the broom closet.
7. What did you think of Lydia's collection of various fossils?
8. Is the Mexican embassy sponsoring this tour?
9. There are several dangerous curves along the road that passes the Fletcher house.
10. What time is best for our next meeting?

C. Adverbs *(pages 38–45)* On your paper, list the adverbs in the following sentences. Next to each adverb, identify which of five questions is answered by the adverb: *How?, When?, Where?, How often?,* or *To what extent or degree?*

11. As he ran quickly, he suddenly stumbled.
12. Weather forecasters frequently make mistakes.
13. If you will wait here, Ms. Storm will see you shortly.
14. The extremely fierce storm damaged the town extensively.
15. The load shifted slightly, and the truck lurched dangerously.

D. Adverbs *(pages 38–45)* On your paper, list the adverbs in the following sentences. Next to each adverb, write the word that it modifies. Then label the modified word *Verb, Adjective,* or *Adverb.*

16. Hal pulled the rope hard and fastened it securely.
17. Very quickly the gentle rain became a storm.
18. We could barely hear the dinner bell.
19. Hannah, who is twelve years old, plays chess remarkably well.
20. The stone was an exceptionally large emerald.

Test 2

On your paper, write the modifiers that are in italic type in the following paragraph. Next to each modifier, write the label *Adjective* or *Adverb.* Then write the word or words modified by each modifier.

It was (1) *Sam's* turn at home plate. He stepped into the (2) *batter's* box. It was the eighth inning of a game that (3) *heavy* rains had delayed, and most (4) *players'* uniforms were the (5) *same* (6) *brown* color as the infield. Sam stood (7) *patiently* while the pitcher threw the pitch (8) *outside.* The (9) *next* pitch came (10) *inside,* and as Sam (11) *instinctively* twisted to avoid it, he slipped. (12) *Dirty* and (13) *embarrassed,* he rose from the mud. As he (14) *carelessly* wiped the mud from his hands, he decided to hit the (15) *next* pitch. When the bat made contact with the ball, he (16) *immediately* knew that it was a solid hit. It sailed over the (17) *outstretched* glove of the shortstop and dropped (18) *several* yards in front of the (19) *charging* outfielder. Muddy and (20) *proud,* Sam ended up on second base.

Unit 3

Prepositions, Conjunctions, and Interjections

Unit Preview

Suppose that a sports announcer suddenly lost control over the words that connect words and groups of words in a sentence. The announcer knew when connections were needed but could not think of the right words. The opener of a baseball telecast might sound like this:

(1) Welcome *by* Yankee Stadium, ladies *nor* gentlemen, *in* the game *against* the Royals *or* the Yankees. (2) It's time *until* the game to begin. (3) The umpires are meeting *under* home plate *against* the two managers. (4) The Yankees are about to run *over* the field. (5) We'll be back right *before* this word *to* our sponsor.

For Analysis   On your paper, answer the questions about the preceding telecast.

1. What word should the announcer have used instead of *by* in Sentence 1? What words should have been used instead of *nor, in, against,* and *or?*
2. Look at the words in italics in the rest of the passage. Rewrite the passage, replacing each word in italics with a word that makes more sense.

In the telecast the announcer misuses prepositions and conjunctions. Prepositions describe the relationships between people, places, or things. For example, leaves grow *on* branches, not *above* them. By using the wrong prepositions, the announcer causes confusion on the part of the reader.

Conjunctions join words or groups of words and express a relationship among the words that they have joined. For example, if you are going out with a group of friends, you say, "My friends *and* I are going out." It would be misleading to say, "My friends *or* I am going out." The telecaster used the wrong conjunctions, making the passage even more confusing.

To communicate well, you must understand prepositions and conjunctions. This unit introduces prepositions, conjunctions, and another part of speech, interjections.

3.1 Prepositions

A **preposition** is a word that expresses a relationship between a noun or a pronoun and another word in the sentence.

> The lake is **behind** the *cottage.* [The preposition, *behind,* shows where the lake is in relation to the cottage.]
>
> We swam **after** *lunch.* [The preposition, *after,* shows a time relationship between lunch and when we swam.]
>
> The lake was **like** a *mirror.* [The preposition, *like,* shows the similarity between a mirror and the lake.]

The prepositions in italic type in the following list are used frequently in speaking and writing.

about twenty minutes	*among* the chefs
above the tower	*around* the earth
across the bridge	*at* midnight
after the dance	*before* the exam
against all odds	*behind* the tiny door
along the ridge	*below* the street

beneath the tree
beside the bench
besides hard work
between you and me
beyond the trees
by seven o'clock
despite the loss
down the well
during the struggle
except my sister
for the school
from Officer Suarez
in his eyes
inside the refrigerator
into the frying pan
like a huge weight
near the rapids
of grapefruit slices
off the highway

on the huge egg
onto the trampoline
out the door
outside my house
over the lifeboat
past the last station
since the game
through the hedges
till tomorrow
to us
toward the end
under the new mayor
underneath the ledge
until the third quarter
up the chimney
upon her head
with the flamingos
within our class
without a sound

Some prepositions, called **compound prepositions,** are made up of more than one word. The compound prepositions are in italic type in the following list.

according to the paper
aside from your objections
as of yesterday
as well as his wallet
because of the rain
by means of a telephone
in addition to eggs
in front of the house

in place of sugar
in regard to a question
instead of my sister
in spite of everything
on account of the storm
on top of the mountain
out of the sky
prior to your call

Exercise 1 Prepositions On your paper, write the prepositions in the following sentences.

SAMPLE   Angela stood in front of the class.
ANSWER   in front of

1. She talked to us about artificial bait.
2. Angela had all kinds of knowledge.
3. She spoke well because of her interest in the subject.
4. She also has a great deal of information about bait.
5. During her talk she told us several interesting facts.
6. She also showed us pictures of plugs and flies.
7. Plugs move on top of the water.
8. They are pulled below the surface when a fish pulls on the line.
9. Streamer flies look like small fish.
10. They also sink beneath the surface.
11. You may choose between plugs and flies.
12. According to the experts, flies are preferable to worms if you want to catch certain kinds of fish.
13. However, for catching many fish, worms are effective.
14. Everyone except Paul learned a great deal from Angela's talk.
15. Perhaps she will speak to us again.

Exercise 2 Prepositions in Sentences On your paper, write the following sentences. In place of each blank, write a preposition that fits the meaning of the sentence. You may use the lists on pages 51–52. Underline the prepositions in your rewritten sentences.

> **SAMPLE** The swimmer dived __?__ the water.
>
> **ANSWER** The swimmer dived <u>into</u> the water.

1. School will be closed __?__ Friday.
2. __?__ the snow, the game has been postponed.
3. I am writing __?__ your letter __?__ December 1.
4. Our cat sleeps __?__ the TV set.
5. __?__ the heavy traffic, we arrived __?__ time __?__ dinner.
6. The ball sailed __?__ the fence __?__ a home run.
7. We had finished the dishes __?__ five o'clock.
8. The Hawks didn't score __?__ the seventh inning.

9. Sometime __?__ the night, it began to sleet.
10. I woke up __?__ a nightmare.
11. The clouds looked __?__ huge balls __?__ cotton.
12. I put the letter __?__ the mailbox __?__ the corner __?__ State Street.
13. I can't finish this project __?__ glue.
14. __?__ the latest weather forecast, it will rain all day.
15. We will meet you __?__ two o'clock __?__ the theater.

Prepositional Phrases

A preposition is usually followed by a noun or a pronoun, which is called the **object of the preposition.** The preposition together with the object and its modifiers is called a **prepositional phrase** (*Unit 4*).

                                prep.   object
Twenty dolphins performed **like playful acrobats.** [The prepositional phrase includes the preposition, *like,* the modifier, *playful,* and the object of the preposition, *acrobats.*]

A prepositional phrase may contain more than one object, as in the following example.

           prep.   obj.   obj.
I vacuumed **under the bed and the dressers.**

Exercise 3 Prepositional Phrases
On your paper, write the prepositional phrases in the following sentences. Underline the prepositions once and the objects or compound objects twice.

    SAMPLE   We were excited about the trip that our class was planning for the end of school.

    ANSWER   about the <u>trip</u>; for the <u>end</u>; of <u>school</u>

1. We had worked hard for months.
2. By spring vacation we had already held four auctions and five food sales.

3. The Junior High Players donated the proceeds from their play.
4. Everyone worked under great pressure.
5. Despite our efforts we had not reached our goal.
6. We still needed a large amount of money.
7. Without another auction or food sale, we could not raise that money.
8. We still had some hope for success.
9. There was enormous energy and determination among the class members.
10. Through the whole campaign, our advisers had been reminding us of our goal.
11. Because of their encouragement, we washed cars, walked dogs, and did yard work.
12. During the last two weeks, we raised a thousand dollars.

Preposition or Adverb?

Many of the words in the first list of prepositions (*page 51*) may be used either as prepositions or as adverbs. If the word has an object, it is a preposition. If the word does not have an object, it is usually an adverb.

PREPOSITION   We waited **inside the house.**

ADVERB   We waited **inside.**

Exercise 4   Preposition or Adverb?   On your paper, write the words in italic type in the following sentences. Next to each word, write the label *Preposition* or *Adverb*. If the word is a preposition, write the object of the preposition.

SAMPLE   We swam *near* the cruiser.

ANSWER   near—preposition, cruiser

1. The boy turned *around* and stared at us.
2. He ran quickly *around* the corner.
3. We climbed *up* the mountain.

4. We climbed *up* until we reached an overhang.
5. Take your hat *off.*
6. The hat fell *off* the shelf.
7. The tree toppled *over* with a crash.
8. We hung some holly branches *over* the door.
9. Come *in,* please.
10. During winter we get tired of staying *in* the house.
11. Marvin just walked *past.*
12. Marvin walked *past* the school.
13. Sheila fell *down* this morning.
14. Sheila fell *down* the stairs.

Assignment Prepositions and Adverbs On your paper, write two sentences for each word in the following list. In the first sentence, use the word as a preposition. In the second sentence, use the word as an adverb. Label your sentences *Preposition* or *Adverb.*

1. before
2. below
3. behind
4. past
5. down
6. under

Prepositional Phrases in Stories

Writers often use different kinds of prepositional phrases in different kinds of writing. Prepositional phrases often help to describe the setting and the action, as in the following passage from a mystery story.

> The detective moved carefully *toward the china cabinet.* She heard a screeching sound *outside the dining-room window*. She opened the window wide and poked her head *into the blackness.*

Too late! She felt something *like rough sandpaper* rasp *along her cheek.* She drew back *into the room.*

Step 1: Find two paragraphs in a mystery story in which the writer uses prepositional phrases. Write the prepositional phrases on your paper. *Step 2:* Write a paragraph of your own in which you use prepositional phrases to help show the action in a scene. Underline your prepositional phrases.

3.2   Conjunctions

A **conjunction** is a word that connects individual words or groups of words. A **coordinating conjunction** joins words or groups of words of equal rank. The coordinating conjunctions are in the following list:

and   but   for   nor   or   yet

Conjunctions Connecting Individual Words

Conjunctions may connect individual nouns, pronouns, verbs, adjectives, adverbs, or prepositions.

Sally **and** *Harriet* went to the ball game. [The conjunction, *and,* connects the nouns *Sally* and *Harriet.*]

He **or** *I* will go to the fair with Joe. [The conjunction, *or,* connects the pronouns, *He* and *I.*]

My pig is *fat* **but** *beautiful.* [The conjunction, *but,* connects the adjectives *fat* and *beautiful.*]

They played *swiftly* **yet** *carefully.* [The conjunction, *yet,* connects the adverbs, *swiftly* and *carefully.*]

Exercise 1   Coordinating Conjunctions   The following sentences contain words connected by coordinating conjunctions. On your paper, write the conjunctions and the words that they connect. Underline the conjunctions.

> SAMPLE   Holly, our cat, likes yarn and paper.
>
> ANSWER   yarn <u>and</u> paper

1. Holly is polite yet pushy.
2. When we're not looking, she tries to get into the sewing box or the wastebasket.
3. He uses every trick to keep Holly out of the wastebasket.
4. He tries putting the kitchen wastebasket in the pantry or the laundry room.
5. She reaches the wastebasket one way or another.
6. Last night she pushed and shoved her way into the pantry, where she spilled the wastebasket.
7. In the morning Andy was angry and upset.
8. He shouted and threatened.
9. I don't think Holly listened or cared.
10. Andy and I can never outsmart her.

Conjunctions Connecting Groups of Words

Conjunctions may connect groups of words such as verb phrases (*page 19*), prepositional phrases (*Unit 4*), and sentences.

> We found eggs *near the barn* **and** *in the coop.* [The conjunction, *and,* connects two prepositional phrases, *near the barn* and *in the coop.*]
> We *walked slowly* **and** *looked carefully.* [The conjunction, *and,* connects two verbs and their modifiers, *walked slowly* and *looked carefully.*]

Coordinating conjunctions may also connect two or more sentences (*Unit 5*).

You can hunt for eggs, **or** you can help in the field. [The conjunction, *or,* connects two sentences, *You can hunt for eggs* and *You can help in the field.*]

Exercise 2 Coordinating Conjunctions The following sentences contain words or groups of words that are connected by coordinating conjunctions. On your paper, write the conjunctions and the words or groups of words that they connect. Underline the conjunctions.

SAMPLE Headlines are written not by reporters but by copywriters.

ANSWER by reporters <u>but</u> by copywriters

1. Many men and women are employed by newspapers.
2. A top-flight editor or reporter has a great deal of responsibility.
3. Reporters may report their stories by telephone, or they may write them in the office.
4. A reporter's work is varied and interesting.
5. A reporter may cover a fire and a city council meeting on the same day.
6. Stories can be found anywhere and everywhere.
7. An ability to find news is important, but the ability to write well is even more important.
8. An editor in chief directs the writers and reporters.
9. Some reporters work on the scene and by telephone.
10. Other reporters do not write stories but instead gather facts.
11. Stringers do not work full time but turn in a story periodically.
12. Reporters may have a regular beat or may be on assignment.
13. Some newspapers assign reporters to foreign capitals and to other major cities.
14. Most newspapers have reporters on the scene in the state capital and in Washington.
15. Investigative reporters do research and expose corruption.

Assignment   Using Coordinating Conjunctions   On your paper, connect each of the following words or word groups with a coordinating conjunction. Use each connected pair in an original sentence.

1. job, sport
2. mysteries, romances
3. in the brambles, near the stone wall
4. ripped, tore

5. sweet, bitter
6. slowly, happily
7. carrots, lettuce
8. after school, on the weekend

3.3   Interjections

An **interjection** is an exclamatory word that usually expresses a strong emotion. An interjection can stand by itself, or it may be followed by a related sentence. An interjection that expresses strong feeling is followed by an exclamation point.

Good grief!
Wow! Look at that huge wave!

An interjection that shows mild feeling is followed by a comma. The word after the comma begins with a lower-case letter unless it is a word that is always capitalized.

Well, that's over.
My, I'm tired. [The pronoun *I* is always capitalized.]

You use interjections often in speech, but you should use them only occasionally in writing. Interjections are most useful for writing dialogue that sounds natural. Here is a list of common interjections:

aha	great	oh	tsk tsk
alas	help	oops	well
good grief	hey	ouch	whew
goodness	hurray	psst	wow

Exercise Interjections On your paper, write the following sentences, using an appropriate interjection from the preceding list of interjections. In the completed sentences, underline the interjections.

SAMPLE   __?__! We made it to the top.

ANSWER   Whew! We made it to the top.

1. __?__! We made another first down.
2. __?__! That's my bike.
3. __?__, we're on our way again.
4. __?__! My bike still works.
5. __?__, why can't we go too?
6. __?__! She just scored her third goal!
7. __?__! We won the game!
8. __?__, here's our train at last.
9. __?__! Veronica certainly knows her math.
10. __?__! How tall you have grown.

Using Interjections

Where would you expect to find these interjections?

Zap!   Bang!   Wow!   Pow!

Cartoonists often use interjections to give life and meaning to the action in their comic strips. Make a survey of the comic strips that appear in your local newspaper. On your paper, list the interjections used by the cartoonists and describe an action dramatized by each interjection. For example, the interjection *Crash!* in a cartoon might dramatize a drawing of something falling to the ground.

Below the list, write dialogue for a comic strip that you create. The characters and situation should be your own. In the dialogue be sure to use a generous supply of interjections. If you wish, you may draw the art to accompany the dialogue.

Unit Practice

Practice 1

A. Prepositions *(pages 51–57)* On your paper, list the prepositions in each of the following sentences.

1. In spite of the gloomy weather, the Andersons planned a picnic lunch at the campsite near their cabin.
2. Gerard skated down the wide street onto the gravel path.
3. According to the rules, Nan must not touch the chalk line with her foot.
4. The old bridge above the rapids creaked all night.
5. Leaflets were distributed among the volunteers by Ms. Foster.

B. Prepositions *(pages 51–57)* On your paper, write the following sentences, replacing each blank with a preposition. Circle the prepositions and underline the objects or the compound objects of the preposition.

6. What do you need to know __?__ the science fair entries?
7. Since their meal, the bears __?__ the zoo have been asleep.
8. Josh will paint the outside __?__ the barn.
9. The team had a celebration immediately __?__ the victory.
10. Choose a coat that hangs __?__ a rack __?__ the far wall.

C. Conjunctions *(pages 57–60)* On your paper, list the conjunctions in each of the following sentences.

11. There is a full moon tonight, but it is still difficult to see.
12. This fabulous new material is sturdy yet flexible.
13. Sheep and goats are raised on this farm.
14. Billy did not see the ballet, nor did he go to the movies.
15. I arrived early, for I wanted a good seat.

D. Conjunctions *(pages 57–60)* On your paper, write the following sentences and replace each blank with a conjunction. Circle the conjunction and underline the words or groups of words that the conjunction connects.

(Continue on the next page.)

16. Many feel that Margie __?__ Lynn will be the new president of our club.
17. We cannot go sailing __?__ there is not enough wind.
18. Red, white, __?__ blue are the colors of the American flag.
19. She is ill __?__ is resting comfortably.
20. That book is not in the bookstore, __?__ it is in the library.

E. Interjections *(pages 60–61)* On your paper, list the interjections in each of the following sentences.

21. Oh, the tea kettle is boiling.
22. Look out! The goat has gotten loose from its rope.
23. Kerry became ill, alas, just before the school trip.
24. Well, this has certainly been a surprising development.
25. I will soon be finished with my chores. Hooray!

Practice 2

On your paper, list the words in italic type in the following passage. Label each word *Preposition, Conjunction,* or *Interjection.*

Have you ever bumped your elbow   (1) *into* a chair (2) *or* some other solid object   (3) *and* felt a painful (4) *yet* ticklish sensation? People often do this   (5) *and* exclaim,   (6) *"Ouch!* I hit my funny bone!" Actually, what they hurt is not a bone   (7) *but* a sensitive place   (8) *at* the joint   (9) *of* the elbow.   (10) *In* this area, a nerve called the ulnar nerve lies   (11) *between* the skin   (12) *and* the bone. This nerve is practically unprotected because it is (13) *near* the surface of the skin.   (14) *Because of* this, the nerve is easily stimulated   (15) *by* even a slight blow. This stimulation produces pain   (16) *and* a tingling sensation in the ring finger and the little finger.   (17) *Of course,* there is usually no need   (18) *for* concern, for it takes a severe blow to cause damage. The next time you bump your elbow (19) *and* feel a funny sensation, you can say,   (20) *"Hey!* I just stimulated my ulnar nerve!"

Unit Tests

Test 1

A. Prepositions *(pages 51–57)* On your paper, list the prepositions in each of the following sentences.

1. Our team fell behind during the relay race at Jefferson Park.
2. Their voices will be projected by a microphone.
3. You will find the hidden key behind the cupboard door and underneath a blue plate.
4. I made a wreath with dried twigs and straw flowers according to the instructions.
5. At a square dance, a caller is the person who yells directions to the dancers.

B. Prepositions *(pages 51–57)* On your paper, write the following sentences, replacing each blank with a preposition. Circle the prepositions and underline the objects or the compound objects of the preposition.

6. Michelle was outside delivering newspapers __?__ the neighbors __?__ seven o'clock this morning.
7. Will you take this volleyball net __?__ the garage and store it carefully __?__ the shelf?
8. Jamal trimmed the bushes __?__ the porch and clipped the grass __?__ the apple tree.
9. We lived __?__ Milwaukee __?__ our move here two years ago.
10. That scary movie will be playing __?__ another week __?__ its popularity.

C. Conjunctions *(pages 57–60)* On your paper, list the conjunctions in each of the following sentences.

11. Today I will buy a bicycle bell, a safety helmet, and a new pair of sneakers.
12. Are you still tired, or do you want to play kickball?
13. Devon's broken arm is healed, but it is still slightly sore.

(Continue on the next page.)

14. Lemons are picked only when they are green and have reached a certain size.
15. My new winter jacket is warm yet lightweight.

D. Conjunctions *(pages 57–60)* On your paper, write the following sentences and replace each blank with a conjunction. Circle the conjunction and underline the word or groups of words that the conjunction connects.

16. You __?__ I have been classmates for ten years!
17. Wendy will be delayed, __?__ her train left Chicago several hours late.
18. Despite the many tales about them, wolves are not evil, __?__ they do not attack humans.
19. Those construction workers built the foundation quickly __?__ skillfully.
20. He __?__ his sister may win the state championship.

E. Interjections *(pages 60–61)* On your paper, list the interjections in each of the following sentences.

21. Great! Ursula will be the new treasurer.
22. Hmm, none of the race cars beat the world record.
23. Whew! Running a mile when you're out of shape is really hard work.
24. What! Did you hear the amazing news?
25. Say, if Chuck can help with the decorations, we can get the refreshments ready.

Test 2

On your paper, list the words in italic type in the following passage. Label each word *Preposition, Conjunction,* or *Interjection.*

To learn about the beginnings   (1) *of* the American circus, visit Somers, New York, a small town fifty miles north of New York City. (2) *In* the early 1800s, Hachaliah Bailey, one of the citizens of Somers, bought an elephant named Old Bet. (3) *Well,* curious residents were fearful (4) *yet* fascinated when they saw this creature (5) *for* the very first time. (6) *Because of* the interest in this elephant, Bailey began traveling (7) *throughout* New England, (8) *and* he charged a fee (9) *for* a look (10) *at* Old Bet. Local residents soon imported tigers, lions, and monkeys to exhibit (11) *in addition to* the elephant. People who bought stock in circus companies prospered, (12) *for* the traveling menageries were successful. (13) *Because of* Bailey's enthusiasm, nearly all the other citizens housed animals in their barns (14) *during* the winter and taught tricks to the animals. (15) *After* the start of the menagerie business, Bailey built the Elephant Hotel (16) *in* Somers, where there is a small circus museum. Bailey erected a monument to Old Bet when, (17) *alas,* she died. A wooden elephant, painted gold, stands (18) *on top of* a pedestal (19) *in front of* the hotel (20) *as* a reminder of the town's rich circus history.

Unit 4

Prepositional Phrases

Unit Preview

Good writers are as specific as they can be in describing characters, settings, and actions. They try to create a picture for the reader. The prepositional phrase is an important tool in making your writing specific.

For Analysis Read Paragraph A and Paragraph B. On your paper, answer the questions that follow the two paragraphs.

PARAGRAPH A
First, hold the balloon. Hold the nozzle. Next, grasp the nozzle. Use your lips. Then take a deep breath and fill the balloon. Use air. Finally, tie a secure knot. Tie the nozzle.

PARAGRAPH B
First, hold the balloon by the nozzle. Next, grasp the nozzle with your lips. Then take a deep breath and fill the balloon with air. Finally, tie a secure knot in the nozzle.

1. To blow up the balloon, how do you hold it?
2. What do you use to grasp the nozzle of the balloon?
3. With what do you fill the balloon?
4. Where do you tie a knot?
5. Which paragraph provides a clearer explanation of how to blow up a balloon? What makes the paragraph clearer?

Paragraph B has prepositional phrases that tie together several of the descriptive details. For instance, the first sentence of Paragraph B tells you to hold the balloon *by the nozzle. By the nozzle* is a prepositional phrase that tells how you should hold the balloon. Such prepositional phrases make Paragraph B clearer than Paragraph A. In this unit you will learn about the structure and the purpose of prepositional phrases.

4.1 Prepositional Phrases

A **phrase** is a group of related words used as a single part of speech. In this unit you will explore prepositional phrases used as adjectives and as adverbs.

A **prepositional phrase** consists of a preposition, its object or objects, and any modifiers of the object (*page 54*). The phrase expresses a relationship between the object and another word in the sentence. The relationship might have to do with location. By using a prepositional phrase, you tell your listener or reader *where* someone or something is.

prep.   obj.

Two sheep were **under the tree.**

In the preceding sentence, the prepositional phrase explains where the sheep were in relation to the tree; they were *under the tree. Under the tree* is a prepositional phrase that adds an important descriptive detail to the sentence.

Many prepositional phrases explain relationships of time. They tell *when* something happened.

prep.   obj.

We went to a restaurant **after the game.** [The prepositional phrase explains when we went to the restaurant.]

A prepositional phrase may have more than one object, as in the following example.

prep. obj.   obj.

They grazed contentedly **on weeds and grass.** [The prepositional phrase includes the preposition, *on*, and the objects, *weeds* and *grass.*]

Prepositional phrases are like adjectives and adverbs, for they add details that make sentences more informative and complete. To recognize and to use prepositional phrases, you should be able to identify prepositions. A list of the most frequently used prepositions appears on pages 51–52.

Exercise 1   Prepositional Phrases   On your paper, write the prepositional phrases in the following sentences. Underline the preposition once and the object(s) of the preposition twice.

> SAMPLE   Frequent changes in the weather are hard on all kinds of roads.
>
> ANSWER   in the weather; on all kinds; of roads

1. In the hot weather, the pavement in a road expands.
2. Because of this expansion, cracks may appear in the asphalt or concrete.
3. The pavement may even buckle during extremely hot weather.
4. On an expressway, a buckle of several inches may appear.
5. As a result, the traffic on the expressway must be directed around the buckle.
6. Road crews work fast to make the pavement smooth again and to open the expressway for traffic.
7. As summer changes into winter, roads face other kinds of wear.
8. During extremely cold weather, the pavement freezes and becomes brittle.
9. Cracks appear in the pavement as traffic moves over the brittle surface.
10. Snow adds to these problems, for as heavy plows keep the surface clean, they cause more wear and tear on the highway.
11. In January or February, potholes start appearing in heavily traveled roads.
12. Road crews fill the potholes with asphalt, but the filling makes the road passable only until summer.

13. With the arrival of warm weather, the crews rebuild sections of the road that have potholes.
14. If a road has many of these potholes, it may be completely rebuilt by construction crews.
15. The maintenance of roads is an enormous task, for every new road will have to be resurfaced in ten or fifteen years.

Exercise 2   Prepositional Phrases in a Paragraph

The sentences in the following paragraph have been numbered. On your paper, write the numbers 1 to 10. *Step 1:* Next to each number, write the prepositional phrase or phrases in the sentence. *Step 2:* Underline the preposition once and the object(s) of the preposition twice.

> SAMPLE   By early morning huge drifts of powdery snow had made the roads impassable.
>
> ANSWER   By early morning; of powdery snow

(1) Imagine a night in late winter just before daybreak.   (2) In front of our car, the snow falls heavily. (3) The snowbanks along the narrow, winding road are like the walls of a canyon.   (4) The car radio crackles with a call from the highway patrol.   (5) During the past ten hours, a foot of new snow has fallen.   (6) Because of the high winds, all cars have been ordered off the roads. (7) We peer through the clouded windshield in search of shelter.   (8) In the distance, a light flickers for a moment and goes out.   (9) Chunks of snow and ice fall from the snowbanks onto the road.   (10) We are alone on top of a mountain in the middle of a raging storm.

4.2   Prepositional Phrases Used as Adjectives

A prepositional phrase is used as an adjective when it modifies a noun or a pronoun. Such phrases are sometimes called **adjective phrases.** Adjective phrases answer the same questions answered by adjectives: *Which? What kind? How many?*

ADJECTIVE

My **European** *cousins* raise rabbits. [*Which* cousins?
My European cousins. The adjective, *European,*
modifies the noun *cousins.*]

PREPOSITIONAL PHRASE

My *cousins* **in Europe** raise rabbits. [*Which* cousins?
Cousins in Europe. The prepositional phrase, *in
Europe,* modifies the noun *cousins.*]

Adjectives usually come before the noun or pronoun
that they modify. However, adjective phrases usually follow
the words that they modify.

ADJECTIVES

Some rabbits have a **furry, brown** *coat.* [The adjectives
furry and *brown* come before *coat,* the noun that they
modify.]

PREPOSITIONAL PHRASE

Some rabbits have a *coat* **of brown fur.** [The prepositional phrase, *of brown fur,* comes after *coat,* the noun
that it modifies.]

A prepositional phrase sometimes modifies a noun or a
pronoun that is the object of another prepositional phrase.

┌─prep. phrase─┐
What are *some* of the *differences* between rabbits and hares?
                                 └──────prep. phrase──────┘

Exercise 1   Adjective Phrases   *Step 1:* On your paper,
write the prepositional phrases used as adjectives in the following sentences. *Step 2:* Write the noun or the pronoun that
each prepositional phrase modifies. *Step 3:* Write whether
each phrase tells *Which? What kind?* or *How many?*

SAMPLE   The discovery of twenty-two ferrets gave
              scientists hope for the survival of the species.
ANSWER   of twenty-two ferrets—discovery—Which?
              for survival—hope—What kind?
              of the species—survival—Which?

1. An adult panda with a hearty appetite can eat forty pounds of bamboo a day.
2. The world of the seal is extremely cold.
3. The giraffe at the zoo eats leaves from a nearby tree.
4. Have you ever gone to a zoo in which the animals are not kept behind bars?
5. Saving the whale has become one of the priorities of the environmental movement.
6. An oil spill can threaten the lives of many birds.
7. Several nests of grass and seaweed lined the shore.
8. Rocky islands along the coast are a nesting place for terns.
9. Scientists hung a collar with a tiny radio around the neck of the bear.
10. Layers of fat keep polar bears warm.
11. The hind legs of a frog make it an accomplished jumper on land and an expert swimmer in the water.
12. The narwhal is one of the toothed whales.
13. The porcupine has been called a pig with needles.
14. The anteater has a small mouth with a wormlike tongue.
15. The leader of a herd of elephants is usually a wise female.

Exercise 2   Adjective Phrases   On your paper, number from 1 to 10. Next to each number, write the prepositional phrase or phrases in the sentence. Write the noun or the pronoun that each prepositional phrase modifies.

SAMPLE   The exhibits at the outdoor art gallery on the
              Emeryville mud flats frequently change.
ANSWER   at the outdoor art gallery—exhibits
              on the Emeryville mud flats—gallery

(1) Artists in the San Francisco area have built whimsical sculptures.   (2) Their sculptures adorn a strip of mud flats between San Francisco Bay and a freeway.   (3) The result is an outdoor gallery of pop art.   (4) Some of the pieces are skillfully done.   (5) A driftwood tyrannosaur dominates one end of the display.   (6) A roadrunner with hubcap eyes is a popular attraction.   (7) A sculpture of King Tut recently appeared.   (8) Strips of rubber from tires form his beard.   (9) Two anonymous figures with plastic-foam heads sit nearby.   (10) Motorists from the freeway provide an appreciative audience.

Assignment   Using Prepositional Phrases   Write sentences for each of the ten prepositional phrases that follow. Use the phrases as adjectives. Underline the prepositional phrases once and the words that they modify twice.

1. for the party
2. behind the kettle
3. over the fence
4. from Mr. Korobkin
5. outside the forest

6. at the boat
7. onto the stage
8. under the porch
9. on the left
10. by the railroad

4.3   Prepositional Phrases Used as Adverbs

A prepositional phrase is used as an adverb when it modifies a verb, an adjective, or another adverb. Such phrases are sometimes called **adverb phrases.** Adverb phrases answer the same questions that adverbs do: *How? When? Where? How often?* or *To what extent?*

ADVERB

The beaver *built* its lodge **there.** [*Where* did the beaver build its lodge? There. The adverb, *there,* modifies the verb, *built.*]

PREPOSITIONAL PHRASE

The beaver *built* its lodge *on that pond*. [*Where* did the beaver build its lodge? On that pond. The prepositional phrase, *on that pond,* modifies the verb, *built.*]

Most prepositional phrases used as adverbs modify verbs or verb phrases. Some, however, modify adjectives or adverbs.

MODIFIES ADJECTIVE

Beavers are *busy* *beyond belief*. [The prepositional phrase, *beyond belief,* tells to what extent the beavers are busy. It therefore modifies the adjective, *busy.*]

MODIFIES ADVERB

They work *early* *in the morning* and *late* *at night*. [The prepositional phrase *in the morning* modifies the adverb *early.* The prepositional phrase *at night* modifies the adverb *late.*]

Like adjective phrases, adverb phrases often appear after the words that they modify.

The female hornbill *is sealed* *for weeks* *inside a tree trunk*.

However, adverb phrases may appear in other positions in a sentence.

For weeks the female hornbill *is sealed* *inside a tree trunk*.

Exercise 1 Adverb Phrases   *Step 1:* On your paper, write the prepositional phrases used as adverbs in the following sentences. *Step 2:* Write the word that each prepositional phrase modifies. *Step 3:* Write whether each adverb phrase tells *How? When? Where? How often?* or *To what extent?*

SAMPLE   A tiny mouse scurried across the field.

ANSWER   across the field—scurried—Where?

1. The harvest mouse lives in fields.
2. The female builds her nest off the ground.
3. Sometimes she builds it high in the grain stalks.
4. The female weaves the nest with shredded grass.
5. She shapes the nest like a grapefruit.
6. Several litters are raised in a year.
7. Newborn harvest mice do not grow hair for fifteen days.
8. The female always stays alert for signs of danger.
9. She usually stands on top of the nest.
10. The young eventually push their way out of the nest.
11. Deer mice are found in Colombia and North America.
12. Deer mice frequently dig tunnels in which they build nests.
13. They rebuild their nests frequently during a year's time.
14. When a nest becomes soiled on the inside, the deer mice will quickly build another.
15. Approximately five or six young are born at a time.

Exercise 2 Prepositional Phrases in a Passage

On your paper, number from 1 to 15. *Step 1:* Next to each number, write the prepositional phrase or phrases in the sentence. *Step 2:* Label each prepositional phrase *Adjective phrase* or *Adverb phrase. Step 3:* Write the word that each phrase modifies.

SAMPLE	A beaver keeps its lodge in good repair by constant work.
ANSWER	in good repair—Adverb phrase—keeps by constant work—Adverb phrase—keeps

(1) Because of their dams, beavers have been called the engineers of the animal world.   (2) All the beavers in a colony work together on the dam.   (3) Most of the work is done late at night.   (4) The dam is made out of sticks, stones, and mud.   (5) Beavers gnaw the wood for the dam with their front teeth and float it to the dam.   (6) They hold mud for the dam against their chests with their fore-

feet.   (7) Water collects behind the dam and forms a deep pond.   (8) Beavers cannot protect themselves from other animals.   (9) For this reason, they build their lodge in the pond behind the dam.   (10) The only entrances to the lodge are located under the water.   (11) The position of the tunnels and the thickness of the walls keep all harmful animals except the most expert underwater swimmers away from the lodge.   (12) On a dry platform inside the lodge, the beavers sleep and bear their young.   (13) Here they are safe from beasts of prey.   (14) An air hole at the top of the lodge is cleverly hidden by a mass of sticks.   (15) Beavers store their food in a room below the living quarters.

Assignment Using Prepositional Phrases   Write sentences for each of the six prepositional phrases below. Use some of the phrases as adjectives and some as adverbs. Underline the prepositional phrases once.

1. through the darkness
2. beyond time
3. among the horses

4. of the friends
5. without any help
6. underneath the rug

Prepositional Phrases in Descriptions

Copy a short description written by one of your favorite authors. Underline the prepositional phrases in the passage. Above each adjective phrase, write *Adjective,* and above each adverb phrase, write *Adverb.*

Then write a short description of a person, a place, or a thing. Use both adjective phrases (*Which? What kind? How many?*) and adverb phrases (*How? When? Where? How often? To what extent?*) Underline the prepositional phrases.

Unit Practice

Practice 1

A. Adjective Phrases *(pages 71–74)* On your paper, list the prepositional phrases used as adjectives in the following sentences. Next to each phrase, write the noun or the pronoun that it modifies.

1. The man in the wheelchair who is wearing a shirt with blue stripes is the principal of our school.
2. When you stand by this large tree, can you see the cabin across the field?
3. The telephone on the desk in the corner is white.
4. My cousin from Florida admired the paintings on the walls of the hallway.
5. A battle between the teams will take place after next week.

B. Adjective Phrases *(pages 71–74)* On your paper, write the following sentences. Replace each blank with an appropriate preposition to form an adjective phrase.

6. Becky saw many clowns __?__ colorful suits during her visit __?__ the circus.
7. The national flag __?__ Japan has a large red circle that is in the center __?__ a white background.
8. Next month our committee will have a meeting __?__ several teachers who teach __?__ local area high schools.
9. This year's campaign __?__ student council president was a close race __?__ Frank and Mary Ellen.
10. All of the club members __?__ Julie wanted to have the picnic in the least crowded section __?__ the state park.

C. Adverb Phrases *(pages 74–77)* On your paper, list the prepositional phrases used as adverbs in the following sentences. Next to each phrase, write the word or words that it modifies.

11. Monica sat beside Richard and listened with interest as the guest speaker lectured.
12. The speaker talked about his adventures so enthusiastically that his face was red with excitement.
13. He spoke of safaris, canoe trips, and deep-sea fishing for nearly two hours.
14. The students gathered after the lecture and talked briefly to the speaker.
15. Monica smiled during the ride home and thought about the future, when she would have similar experiences.

D. Adverb Phrases *(pages 74–77)* On your paper, write the following sentences. Replace each blank with an appropriate preposition to form an adverb phrase.

16. Michael walked __?__ Gwendolyn and Samuel as their hiking group climbed __?__ the steep hill.
17. Jerry ran swiftly __?__ the house and arrived promptly __?__ five o'clock.
18. These plants grow rapidly until their flowers bloom and fall __?__ the stems.
19. The mouse quickly scurried __?__ the road and disappeared __?__ a sound.
20. We knew __?__ the surprise but did not tell Thelma.

Practice 2

On your paper, list the prepositional phrases that are in italic type in the following passage. Label each prepositional phrase *Adjective phrase* or *Adverb phrase,* and write the word or words that it modifies.

(Continue on the next page.)

A guide dog is a dog that is especially trained to guide a blind person safely   (1) *through the streets.* The breeds best suited for the work   (2) *of a guide dog* are German shepherds, Labrador retrievers, golden retrievers, and boxers. A guide dog is trained   (3) *for a period*   (4) *of several months* before it is ready to work with a blind person. The owner and the dog then train together   (5) *for four weeks* so that they can adjust   (6) *to each other.* Dog and owner work together through the use   (7) *of the dog's harness.* The blind owner also communicates   (8) *to the dog* by using verbal commands. Most guide dogs work   (9) *until the age* of ten or twelve and provide their owners with eight to ten years   (10) *of service.*

Unit Tests

Test 1

A. Adjective Phrases *(pages 71–74)* On your paper, list the prepositional phrases used as adjectives in the following sentences. Next to each phrase, write the noun or the pronoun that it modifies.

1. That woman by the car with the black roof is a friend of my mother.
2. Did you see the goats in the pasture near the barn?
3. Phil remembered that his class for third period would see a film about first-aid techniques.
4. That new book by my favorite author will be the subject of a lecture.
5. Your composition about the mystery stories in your anthology should be done tomorrow.

B. Adjective Phrases *(pages 71–74)* On your paper, write the following sentences. Replace each blank with an appropriate preposition to form an adjective phrase.

6. I received a good mark __?__ my exam __?__ mathematics class.
7. Everyone __?__ Louisa agreed that the presentation __?__ the training __?__ athletes should be given again.
8. Barry's fear __?__ heights is the result __?__ a fall several years ago.
9. We asked the tall student __?__ the hall to reach a book __?__ the top shelf for us.
10. The sweater __?__ that large box __?__ Uncle Mark arrived two days after my birthday.

C. Adverb Phrases *(pages 74–77)* On your paper, list the prepositional phrases used as adverbs in the following

(Continue on the next page.)

sentences. Next to each phrase, write the word or words that it modifies.

11. We jogged around the track until we had run for two miles.
12. You must not dive into the pool until tomorrow because it will soon be cleaned by the sanitation staff.
13. The Robinsons jumped quickly into the car and drove toward town.
14. Everyone huddled under one umbrella and walked slowly down the street.
15. Thomas was reading despite the late hour; he enjoyed the book, which moved at a fast pace.

D. Adverb Phrases *(pages 74–77)* On your paper, write the following sentences. Replace each blank with an appropriate preposition to form an adverb phrase.

16. After the crossing guard gave a stop signal _?_ the traffic, we all walked _?_ the street.
17. My dog bounded quickly _?_ the yard and leaped _?_ a high snowdrift.
18. Cherelle's hands grew numb _?_ cold as she watched the game _?_ the bleachers.
19. The church bells chimed loudly _?_ several minutes this morning while I walked _?_ work.
20. His cold has become much better than it was yesterday, for he has stayed _?_ bed to rest.

Test 2

On your paper, list the prepositional phrases that are in italic type in the following passage. Label each prepositional phrase *Adjective phrase* or *Adverb phrase,* and write the word or words that it modifies.

The llama is a member   (1) *of the camel family* and
lives   (2) *in South America.* This unusual-looking animal
has a long neck and looks   (3) *like a camel,* but it is
smaller and has no hump. A llama's body is approximately
five feet long and has a coat   (4) *of thick, long hair.* Male
llamas over the age   (5) *of three years* are used   (6) *as
pack animals.* The Indians   (7) *of the South American
Andes* use llamas   (8) *in other ways* as well. The Indians
eat the meat   (9) *of the young animals.* They also use the
hide to make sandals and the long hair to make clothing
(10) *for the cold weather.*

Sentence Structure

Unit Preview

Suppose that a friend said to you, "found I locker in my glove our." Would you know what your friend meant? Would someone passing by understand what was being said? The words *found, I, locker, in, my, glove,* and *our* are meaningful words in English. Your friend, however, did not put them together in an order that communicates meaning.

In English the sentence is the basic unit of communication. Most sentences are made up of two main parts: (1) a subject, which tells the person, place, thing, or idea that the sentence is about and (2) a predicate, which tells something about the subject. In most but not all sentences, the subject comes first and is followed by the predicate. This order serves as the basis of communication.

For Analysis Look again at the sentence in quotation marks in the first paragraph above. On your paper, write the sentence so that the words are in meaningful order. Then answer the questions that follow.

1. What meaning does your sentence communicate?
2. In what other way could you rewrite your sentence so that it makes sense?
3. How does grouping words into subjects and predicates make what you and other people say easier to understand?

You have been speaking in sentences since you were very young. For several years you have been writing sentences in stories and reports. In this unit you will learn about the structure of the sentence so that you can speak and write sentences that communicate your ideas more clearly.

5.1   Sentence Purpose

A **sentence** is a group of words that has at least one complete subject (*page 95*) and one complete predicate (*page 96*) and that expresses a complete thought. A group of words is not a sentence if it makes sense only when used with another group of words.

NOT A SENTENCE   The car in the parking lot [What about the car in the parking lot?]

SENTENCE   The car in the parking lot had a flat tire.

There are four kinds of sentences, classified according to purpose: (1) sentences that make statements, (2) sentences that ask questions, (3) sentences that give commands, and (4) sentences that express strong or sudden feelings.

A **declarative sentence** makes a statement. It always ends with a period.

The fields grew yellow in the summer heat.
The day after tomorrow is a holiday.

An **interrogative sentence** asks a question. It ends with a question mark.

How are you feeling?
Did you see that girl run?

An **imperative sentence** gives a command or makes a request. If the command or request is mild, the sentence ends with a period. If the command or request is strong, the sentence ends with an exclamation point.

> Scrape the carrots and cut up some celery.
> Get out of the way!

An **exclamatory sentence** expresses strong or sudden feeling. Exclamatory sentences often begin with the modifiers *what* or *how*. An exclamatory sentence always ends with an exclamation point.

> What a hard question you've asked!
> How difficult it is!
> That's enough arguing!

Exercise   Sentence Purpose   Write the following sentences on your paper. Put the correct punctuation mark at the end of each sentence. Use an exclamation point only for strong commands. Label each sentence *Declarative, Interrogative, Imperative,* or *Exclamatory.*

> SAMPLE   Grab the rope
>
> ANSWER   Grab the rope!—Imperative

1. Please be quiet
2. My sister has a new tape recorder
3. What a clear sound those speakers have
4. Turn down that music this instant
5. Where are my shoelaces
6. The blackout lasted for four hours
7. Walk around the fallen tree
8. Don't move
9. Was the food in your refrigerator spoiled
10. Some birds can sing two hundred different melodies
11. Watch to see how I bait the hook
12. Did Curt and Angela really bake that casserole

13. Pay attention
14. Where did you learn those rope tricks
15. I'm saving for a trip to the Baseball Hall of Fame in Cooperstown, New York

Assignment Writing On your paper, write four sentences about each of the following topics. For each topic, the first sentence should be declarative; the second should be interrogative; the third should be imperative; and the fourth should be exclamatory.

1. A vehicle
2. A friend
3. An animal

5.2 Simple Subjects and Simple Predicates

Every sentence must have a subject and a predicate. The **subject** of a sentence tells the person, place, thing, or idea that the sentence is about. The **predicate** of a sentence tells something about the subject.

5.2a Simple Subjects

The **simple subject** is the noun or pronoun that tells whom or what the sentence is about. The simple subject does not include modifiers.

The entire brass **section** of the junior-high band has the flu. [The simple subject is the noun *section*. *The, entire,* and *brass* are modifiers of *section,* as is the prepositional phrase, *of the junior-high band.*]

Usually the simple subject is a single word. Sometimes, however, the simple subject consists of more than one word, as in the following examples.

NAME OF A PERSON   **Alphonse Mirando** can beat his grand-father at the game of bocci.

NAME OF A PLACE   **Boise, Idaho,** welcomes you.

TITLE   ***To Kill a Mockingbird*** is my favorite book.

COMPOUND WORDS   **No one** guessed your identity.

The simple subject of an imperative sentence is always *you. You* is usually understood rather than stated.

Feed the dog. [**Think:**   *You* feed the dog.]

The complete subject (*page 95*) consists of the simple subject and all modifiers of that subject. In this book the term *subject* used by itself refers to the simple subject.

Exercise 1   Simple Subjects   On your paper, write the simple subject of the following sentences. If the subject *you* is understood, write *you* in parentheses and underline it.

SAMPLE   Stay indoors during a severe storm.

ANSWER   (You)

1. The thunderstorms last night caused severe damage.
2. Hail accompanied the thunderstorms.
3. A major challenge to meteorologists is the prediction of life-threatening storms.
4. Congress appropriated funds for thunderstorm research in 1945.
5. Dr. Horace Beyers headed the project.
6. His team of pilots flew airplanes at high altitudes during raging storms.
7. Surprisingly enough, no one was hurt.

8. The worst part of a storm lasts only twenty or thirty minutes.
9. Always seek shelter during a thunderstorm.
10. Lightning presents the greatest danger during a thunderstorm.
11. Avoid high ground and open areas during a storm.
12. *Understanding Weather* is an excellent book about changes in the atmosphere.
13. Harry Milgram is the author.
14. He answers questions clearly and thoroughly.
15. The best way to protect yourself against storms is to understand them.

Exercise 2   Writing Subjects   On your paper, write the following sentences. Write a suitable subject in place of each blank. In each completed sentence, underline the simple subject.

> SAMPLE   _?_ sprinted toward the refreshment stand.
>
> ANSWER   The hungry <u>campers</u> sprinted toward the refreshment stand.

1. Over and over, _?_ counted her money.
2. _?_ will hike to the park after lunch on Thursday.
3. Did _?_ frighten you very much?
4. Over the hills crept _?_.
5. _?_ scampered up the tree.
6. _?_ is one of the ten best movies of the year.
7. _?_ bounced us around.
8. Did _?_ really win a prize?
9. _?_ is a well-known cartoon character.
10. Before the game _?_ performed on the field.

5.2b   Simple Predicates

The **simple predicate** is the verb or verb phrase that describes the action or states the condition of the subject.

The simple predicate does not include modifiers or words that complete the meaning of the verb.

> My sister **is** a private in the Army. [The linking verb, *is,* is the simple predicate. *Private* completes the meaning of the verb. The prepositional phrase, *in the Army,* is a modifier.]
>
> My family **will spend** the summer on Uncle Pete's farm. [The verb phrase, *will spend,* is the simple predicate. *Summer* completes the meaning of the verb. The prepositional phrase, *on Uncle Pete's farm,* is a modifier.]

The complete predicate (*page 96*) consists of the simple predicate and all the words that modify it or complete its meaning. In this book the term *predicate* used by itself refers to the simple predicate.

Exercise 3   Subjects and Predicates   Write the following sentences on your paper. Underline each simple subject once and each simple predicate twice. If the subject is the understood *you,* write *you* in parentheses and underline it.

> SAMPLE   Most people have heard of Benjamin Franklin.
>
> ANSWER   Most people have heard of Benjamin Franklin.

1. Franklin was good at many things.
2. He once flew a kite during an electrical storm.
3. His experiment proved the electrical nature of lightning.
4. Franklin applied his knowledge to the invention of the lightning rod.
5. Perhaps you have seen the line across the lens of a pair of bifocal eyeglasses.
6. Franklin made the first pair of bifocals.
7. His inventions won recognition from famous scientists.
8. Franklin was very bright as a child.
9. He was reading many advanced books of the time by the age of ten.
10. He had learned the printing trade before his twelfth birthday.

11. *Poor Richard's Almanack* was first published by Benjamin Franklin in 1773.
12. He issued the almanac annually for twenty-five years.
13. Many proverbs appeared in *Poor Richard's Almanack*.
14. The used key is always bright.
15. Lost time is never found again.
16. Little strokes fell great oaks.
17. The cat in gloves catches no mice.
18. Eat to live!
19. Necessity never made a good bargain.
20. A word to the wise is sufficient.

Assignment Subjects and Predicates In a magazine find a paragraph about a topic that interests you. Cut out the paragraph and tape it to a sheet of notebook paper. Underline each simple subject once and each simple predicate twice.

5.3 Compound Subjects and Compound Predicates

5.3a Compound Subjects

A **compound subject** consists of two or more simple subjects that have the same predicate. Coordinating conjunctions such as *and* and *or* frequently connect the subjects. In this book the term *compound subject* refers to a compound *simple* subject.

> **Marcia** and **Maggie** *cleared* the vacant lot. [*Marcia* and *Maggie* form the compound subject. They have the same predicate, *cleared*.]
> Low **clouds** and a **bank** of thick fog *covered* the harbor. [*Clouds* and *bank* form the compound subject. They have the same predicate, *covered*.]

Exercise 1   Compound Subjects   On your paper, write the subjects of the following sentences. Most of the sentences have compound subjects, but three sentences have single subjects.

SAMPLE   The blue rocks and the grey surf disappear into the night.

ANSWER   rocks, surf

1. Fog and mist reduce visibility in the night air.
2. The light and the foghorn warn passing ships about the coast.
3. A small house and a shed stand by the lighthouse.
4. A lighthouse keeper or an assistant keeps the light glowing.
5. Radar on board ships has made the lighthouse less important now than fifty years ago.
6. Fishing boats and pleasure craft still look for the light in a stormy sea.
7. A drizzle can make the lighthouse almost invisible.
8. Our trawler rocks in the waves like a toy.
9. The glow of the light and the sound of the foghorn warn boats away from the rocks.
10. The waves and the wind accompany us to port.

5.3b   Compound Predicates

A **compound predicate** consists of two or more verbs or verb phrases that have the same subject. The coordinating conjunctions *and, or,* and *but* are frequently used to connect the verbs or verb phrases in a compound predicate. In this book the term *compound predicate* refers to a compound *simple* predicate.

Fernando **delivers** papers and **baby-sits.** [*Delivers* and *baby-sits* form the compound simple predicate.]
He **has run** all the way to the station but **has missed** the train. [*Has run* and *has missed* form the compound simple predicate. Both verb phrases have the same subject, *He.*]

A sentence may have both a compound subject and a compound predicate.

Jody and **Allison kicked** and **dribbled** the soccer ball. [The compound predicate, *kicked* and *dribbled,* describes the action of the compound subject, *Jody* and *Allison.*]

Exercise 2   Subjects and Predicates On your paper, write the following sentences. Underline the simple subjects once and the simple predicates twice. Some of the subjects and predicates are compound.

SAMPLE The captain and the crew greeted us and introduced themselves.

ANSWER The <u>captain</u> and the <u>crew</u> <u>greeted</u> us and <u>introduced</u> themselves.

1. My mother and father flew to New York but have returned by train.
2. Paul diced the vegetables for the stew but forgot the potatoes.
3. Aunt Bea and Uncle Matt met their family at La Guardia Airport and drove them to Manhattan.
4. My grandmother and grandfather have always enjoyed musicals.
5. The foursome and their friends from Nigeria saw two Broadway plays and listened to jazz in Greenwich Village.
6. The seventh-graders and their teachers saw a group of mimes.
7. The old dog hobbled toward the visitor and licked his hand.
8. A man and a woman leaped onto the stage and did spectacular acrobatic feats.
9. Karen has opened her math book and will start her homework.
10. My friend and I stayed until the end of the play and then left for home.
11. Tyrone and I followed some friends but stayed hidden from view.
12. Every worker in the crew scraped paint or polished brass.

13. Tina and Ron walked along and did not notice the rain.
14. Several teachers and students shook their heads and laughed during the funny movie.
15. The mischievous children have opened the box and have scattered the contents all over the floor.

Exercise 3   Writing Subjects and Predicates   On your paper, write the following sentences. In place of each blank, write an appropriate compound subject or compound predicate. Provide a conjunction where one is needed. In the completed sentences, underline each compound simple subject once and each compound simple predicate twice.

> **SAMPLE**   __?__ of the traffic grew louder.
>
> **ANSWER**   The <u>rumble</u> and <u>roar</u> of the traffic grew louder.

1. After the picnic __?__ cleaned up the litter.
2. __?__ sent the princess on a secret mission.
3. The pitcher __?__ the mound and __?__ for the dugout.
4. __?__ look exactly alike to me.
5. We __?__ our blanket and __?__ our picnic lunch.
6. __?__ drove us indoors.
7. The lifeguard __?__ at the swimmers.
8. The hikers __?__ for several hours.
9. __?__ will meet you at the bus stop.
10. The people in the audience __?__.

Assignment   Writing Subjects and Predicates   On your paper, use each of the following groups of words in a sentence that has a compound subject, a compound predicate, or both a compound subject and a compound predicate. Add modifiers and other words to make your sentences interesting.

1. Wilbur Wright, Orville Wright, became, famous
2. chemicals, polluted, rivers, killed, fish

3. Tim, Jane, cooked, dinner, cleaned, kitchen
4. shoes, socks, were piled
5. costumes, dances, seemed, authentic

5.4 Complete Subjects and Complete Predicates

5.4a Complete Subjects

The **complete subject** of a sentence consists of the simple subject along with modifiers and other words that identify the simple subject.

┌───────── complete subject ───────┐
A young *guide* in a ski cap conducted the tour. [The noun *guide* is the simple subject. *A, young,* and *in a ski cap* modify *guide.*]

┌────── complete subject ────────┐
The *guide,* a college student, knew all about erosion. [*A college student* identifies *guide,* which is the simple subject.]

┌──────── complete subject ─────────┐
Many natural *bridges* and *arches* have resisted erosion. [The complete subject includes a compound simple subject, *bridges* and *arches.*]

In this book the term *subject* refers to the simple subject, not the complete subject.

Exercise 1 Complete Subjects On your paper, write the complete subject of each of the following sentences. Underline each simple subject.

SAMPLE   Most parts of the earth have witnessed some form of volcanic activity.

ANSWER   Most <u>parts</u> of the earth

95

1. Bubbling hot-water geysers are much less dangerous than volcanoes.
2. Such phenomena are often found in regions of dying volcanic activity.
3. The most spectacular geysers are found in Yellowstone National Park, in Iceland, and in New Zealand.
4. The world's most famous geyser, Old Faithful, erupts every hour.
5. The Geysir, a hot spring in Iceland, once erupted three times a day.
6. Several weeks now elapse between eruptions.
7. The English word for geysers was taken from the Icelandic *Geysir.*
8. The water in some hot springs contains minerals.
9. Grotesque pools of plopping mud develop around some hot springs.
10. A famous spring in New Zealand is surrounded by terraces of pink and white rocks.

5.4b   Complete Predicates

The **complete predicate** consists of the simple predicate along with modifiers and words that complete the meaning of the verb.

┌── complete predicate ──┐
A storm *washed* a whale ashore. [The simple predicate is the verb, *washed*. The noun *whale* completes the meaning of *washed*. The adverb, *ashore,* modifies *washed*.]

┌─────── complete predicate ───────┐
Uncle Stan *has landed* a muskie and *will want* someone to take a picture of it. [Included in the complete predicate is the compound simple predicate: *has landed* and *will want.*]

In this book the term *predicate* refers to the simple predicate, not the complete predicate.

Exercise 2   Subjects and Predicates   *Step 1:* On your paper, write the following sentences. Underline each complete subject once and each complete predicate twice. *Step 2:* Write *subj.* above each simple subject and *pred.* above each simple predicate.

SAMPLE The waves rose and fell twelve feet above our heads.

ANSWER The <u>waves</u> <u>rose and fell</u> twelve feet above our heads.

       _{subj.} _{pred.} _{pred.}

1. A rooster crowed far off to the north.
2. The road swerved sharply to the right and became a dirt path.
3. The group hiked past a farm and over the top of a hill.
4. Everyone stopped and looked westward at the view.
5. A family of deer stood at attention in an open field.
6. All snakes shed their skins several times a year.
7. The president rapped the gavel and called the noisy meeting to order.
8. The chalkboard in the classroom was covered with the names of the major bones in the human body.
9. The *Flying Spirit,* a seventeen-foot sailboat, capsized suddenly in the middle of the lake.
10. Many birds throughout the world migrate and return each year to the same place.
11. Fossils are the remains of animals and plants.
12. Foxhounds and pointers are probably descendants of the same ancestors.
13. The principal listened to their excuse and accepted it with a smile.
14. Fireplaces and chimneys should be cleaned every year and checked carefully for cracks.
15. The Nile River spills over its banks and deposits fertile silt on the fields along its course.

5.4c   Placement of Subjects and Predicates

Subjects and predicates may be placed in many different positions in sentences. The placement of the subject and predicate often depends on the purpose of the sentence.

Declarative Sentences. In a declarative sentence, the complete subject usually comes before the complete predicate. In the examples that follow, the complete subject is underlined once, and the complete predicate is underlined twice.

> The sea lions rested on the rocks. [The complete subject comes before the complete predicate.]

However, in some declarative sentences, the complete predicate comes before the complete subject.

> Above the roar of the waves came the grunts of the sea lions.
> There is the biologist's boat.
> Here are the binoculars.

In other declarative sentences, the complete subject appears between two parts of the complete predicate.

> Slowly and carefully, the small boat found its way through the jagged rocks. [The adverbs, *slowly* and *carefully,* modify the simple predicate, *found,* and are therefore part of the complete predicate.]

Interrogative Sentences. In an interrogative sentence, the complete subject usually appears between two parts of the complete predicate.

> What is she doing?
> Is she tagging those sea lions?

To find the subject and the predicate of a question, turn the question into a statement.

QUESTION Will she need help with the tagging?

STATEMENT She <u>will need help with the tagging.</u>

Imperative Sentences. In an imperative sentence the subject *you* is usually understood but not stated. Therefore, the entire sentence is the complete predicate.

<u>Feed the cat at noon.</u> [**Think:** *You* feed the cat at noon.]

Exclamatory Sentences. In many exclamatory sentences, the complete subject often comes before the complete predicate.

I <u>did it!</u>

Sometimes, however, the complete subject appears between two parts of the complete predicate.

<u>What a hard worker</u> Maria <u>is!</u>

Exercise 3 Subjects and Predicates *Step 1:* On your paper, copy the following sentences. *Step 2:* Draw one line under each complete subject and two lines under each complete predicate. *Step 3:* Write *subj.* above each simple subject and *pred.* above each simple predicate.

SAMPLE What a wild and colorful hat you are wearing!

　　　　　　　　　　　　　　　　　　　　　　subj.　　　pred.
ANSWER <u>What a wild and colorful hat</u> you are wearing!

1. Are you studying for the math quiz?
2. How red your face is!
3. In the summer, wildflowers grow in the grass.
4. Open the window wide.
5. Caroline walked slowly through the supermarket.
6. Play soccer for fifteen more minutes.

7. Will you wrap this package for me?
8. What a tennis match Lloyd and Austin played!
9. From a tree hung the rope for an an old swing.
10. Clean up after the rehearsal.
11. There are several insect eggs on that leaf.
12. How sleepy they were after the climb!
13. Have you set your alarm for five o'clock?
14. What an awful mess the tornado left!
15. On the topmost branch of the tallest tree, a thrush sang to the world.
16. Commit this to memory at once.
17. After breakfast my cousin drove us to the store in her new van.
18. How strong that wrestler must be!
19. Tycho Brahe, the Danish astronomer, produced the first accurate picture of the solar system.
20. Protect the ball in your arms like this.

Varying Sentences

Write a paragraph about one of the following topics. Your paragraphs should consist of from four to six sentences. In some of the sentences, the subject should not come first.

1. something you saw on the way to school
2. a summary of a scene in a favorite television show
3. the antics of a pet

5.5 Complements

A **complement** is a word or a group of words that completes the meaning of the predicate. Complements are always part of the complete predicate.

That jump set a new record. [Set *what?* Set a *record.* The noun *record* is a complement.]

The sky became dark. [Became *what?* Became *dark.* The adjective *dark* is a complement.]

The meaning of the sentences about the jump and the sky would be incomplete without complements.

The jump set

The sky became

In this unit you will study two kinds of complements: direct objects and subject complements.

5.5a Direct Objects

A **direct object** is a noun or a pronoun that follows an action verb and answers the question "What?" or "Whom?" A direct object receives the action of the verb. The modifiers of a direct object and the words that identify it do not form part of the direct object.

The elephant *munched* some **peanuts.** [**Think:** munched *what?* Munched *peanuts. Peanuts* is the direct object.]

Have you *met* my **uncle,** the zoo keeper? [**Think:** met *whom?* Met *uncle.* The noun *uncle* is the direct object.]

Everyone *envies* **him.** [**Think:** envies *whom?* Envies *him.* The pronoun *him* is the direct object.]

Do not confuse the object of a preposition with a direct object.

We went *to* the zoo. [*Zoo* is the object of the preposition *to*. The verb, *went*, does not have a direct object.]

Like subjects and predicates, direct objects may be compound. A **compound direct object** consists of two or more direct objects that complete the same verb.

I own a **fish** and a **parakeet**.

Exercise 1   Direct Objects   On your paper, write the simple predicate and the direct object of each sentence. For the three sentences without direct objects, write *None*.

SAMPLE   The team captains shook hands before the game.

ANSWER   shook—hands

1. The referee blew his whistle.
2. The cheerleaders encouraged the players.
3. Our team was trailing by one point.
4. Suddenly Sue had the ball.
5. She passed it to Pam.
6. The crowd cheered wildly.
7. The ball went through the hoop.
8. The other team congratulated the winners.
9. Her teammates carried Pam off the court.
10. The coach congratulated the team for not giving up when they were behind.

Exercise 2   Direct Objects   On your paper, write the simple predicate and the direct object or compound direct object in each of the following sentences.

SAMPLE   I am lending my raincoat and umbrella to Ms. Palmer.

ANSWER   am lending—raincoat, umbrella

1. We saw a movie and a cartoon.
2. Mother put the key into the lock for the front door.
3. My parents met Diane and Tom at the bus station.
4. Grandfather picked fresh lettuce from the garden as a supper-time treat.
5. We watched the game last night.
6. The exhibit will include sculpture and paintings.
7. On our field trip, we spotted a thrush and a wren.
8. Every Saturday my friend sweeps the front steps and the path for her elderly neighbor.
9. The American Society for the Prevention of Cruelty to Animals protects a variety of animals.
10. Throw out the papers and the garbage.

5.5b   Subject Complements

A **subject complement** is a word that comes after a linking verb (*page 17*) and either describes the subject or identifies it. Subject complements often follow forms of the verb *be*. Other commonly used linking verbs that take subject complements are listed below:

appear	look	sound
become	remain	stay
feel	seem	taste
grow	smell	

There are two kinds of subject complements: predicate nominatives and predicate adjectives.

Predicate Nominatives

A **predicate nominative** is a noun or a pronoun that follows a linking verb and identifies the subject of the sentence. The root of the word *nominative* is *nominate,* which means "to name." You might say that the predicate nominative renames the subject.

> P.N.
> *Cassandra* is a **biologist**. [The predicate nominative, *biologist*, follows the linking verb, *is*, and renames *Cassandra*.]
>
> P.N.
> The *garden* became a **showplace**. [The predicate nominative, *showplace*, follows the linking verb, *became*, and renames the subject, *garden*.]

A sentence may have a compound predicate nominative, which consists of two or more nouns or pronouns that identify the same subject.

> P.N.   P.N.
> The *winners* are **Tony** and **Janet**. [The compound predicate nominatives, *Tony* and *Janet*, follow the linking verb, *are*, and rename the subject, *winners*.]

Exercise 3   Predicate Nominatives   On your paper, write the predicate nominatives in the following sentences. Some sentences have compound predicate nominatives.

> **SAMPLE**   My favorite poets are Eve Merriam and Robert Frost.
>
> **ANSWER**   Eve Merriam, Robert Frost

1. Martina is a skilled gymnast.
2. Our dog suddenly became a hero.
3. The best players on the team are Lou and Sam.
4. My uncle is now a sergeant.
5. That bird will become a friendly pet.
6. Our dentist has become a specialist in gum disease.
7. We will remain his patients for a while.
8. Two famous inventors are Thomas Edison and Alexander Graham Bell.

CURRICULUM RESOURCES CENTER
R. I. COLLEGE · MANN HALL
600 MT. PLEASANT AVE.
PROVIDENCE, R.I. 02908

5.5b

Predicate Adjectives

9. Your sister will be an excellent leader.

10. Dr. Mary Walker eventually became an army surgeon.

Predicate Adjectives

A **predicate adjective** is an adjective that follows a linking verb and modifies the subject of the sentence.

Your *jokes* are **funny**. [The predicate adjective, *funny*, follows the linking verb, *are*, and modifies the subject, *jokes*.]

Sometimes your *voice* sounds **shaky**. [The predicate adjective, *shaky*, follows the linking verb, *sounds*, and modifies the subject, *voice*.]

A sentence may have a compound predicate adjective. A **compound predicate adjective** consists of two or more predicate adjectives that describe the same subject.

The last *joke* was **funny** but **familiar**.

Exercise 4 Predicate Adjectives

On your paper, write the predicate adjectives in the following sentences. Some sentences have compound predicate adjectives.

SAMPLE   The air smelled fresh.
ANSWER   fresh

1. Everyone remained calm after the accident.
2. The case against the smuggler seemed airtight.
3. The house appeared gloomy in the fading light.
4. Mavis seemed happy and relieved after the exam.
5. The yellowed paper looks old and interesting.
6. Aunt Martha's face was turning red with anger.
7. His answers were clear but incomplete.

8. The whooping crane is becoming extinct.
9. This chicken tastes delicious.
10. My uncle is feeling better today.

Exercise 5 **Complements** On your paper, write the complements in the following sentences. Label each complement Direct object, Predicate nominative, or Predicate adjective.

> **SAMPLE** Saturn is the most spectacular planet in our solar system.
>
> **ANSWER** planet—Predicate nominative

1. Sunspots cover huge areas of the planet Saturn.
2. Saturn's rings are bands around the planet's equator.
3. Some stars look brighter than others.
4. The two nearest planets to Earth are Mars and Venus.
5. The surface of Venus appears dry and dusty.
6. Mercury is barely visible at night.
7. From Earth, the sight of Venus is impressive.
8. From the nearest star, the entire solar system is a tiny speck.
9. The brightest star in our sky is Sirius.
10. Astronomers have been studying the stars and the constellations for centuries.

5.6 Simple and Compound Sentences

A **simple sentence** is a sentence that has only one complete subject and one complete predicate. The complete subject may contain a single simple subject or a compound simple subject. The complete predicate may contain a single simple predicate or a compound simple predicate. A simple sentence may contain any number of modifiers and prepositional phrases.

In the examples that follow, the complete subject is underlined once; the complete predicate is underlined twice.

The simple subjects (*subj.*) and the simple predicates (*pred.*) are labeled.

subj.   pred.
A huge breaker smashed broadside into the trawler.

subj.   subj.   pred.
The captain and the mate scrambled frantically toward the wheelhouse. [compound simple subject]

subj.   pred.   pred.
The trawler rolled sideways but did not sink. [compound simple predicate]

A **compound sentence** is a sentence that contains two or more simple sentences that are joined by a coordinating conjunction: *and, but, for, nor, or,* or *yet* (*page 57*). A comma is usually used before the conjunction that joins two sentences.

┌────── simple sentence ──────┐   ┌────── simple sentence ──────
A pilot sighted the trawler, **and** soon two motorboats were churning toward the capsized vessel.

You can also join the simple sentences in a compound sentence with a semicolon.

┌──────────── simple sentence ────────────┐ ┌─simple sentence──
Two members of the crew were rescued; the captain stayed aboard until the last moment.

Exercise 1   Simple and Compound Sentences   Copy the following sentences on your paper. Underline each complete subject once and each complete predicate twice. After each sentence write the label *Simple* or *Compound*.

SAMPLE   Some books inform and others entertain.

ANSWER   Some books inform and others entertain. — Compound

1. Barricades blocked the intersection, and a helicopter hovered overhead.
2. The streets in the area were cordoned off.
3. She beat me twice in exhibitions, but I always beat her in tournaments.
4. I tried hard, but nothing went right.
5. Queens and other females can live for many years, but smaller ants may live for only a few weeks.
6. The scientist peered through the microscope and reached for a tweezerlike instrument.
7. Sue walked through the woods and found an interesting fossil.
8. Some insect eggs are brightly colored; others are wrinkled and brown.
9. Am I confused, or are there two meanings for *peculiar?*
10. The jet touched down smoothly and taxied to the terminal.

Exercise 2   Compound Sentences   On your paper, use the conjunction in parentheses to combine each of the following pairs of simple sentences into a compound sentence. Remember to use a comma before the conjunction.

SAMPLE   We fished for hours. No one caught anything. (but)

ANSWER   We fished for hours, but no one caught anything.

1. Mario made lasagna. Betty made sukiyaki. (and)
2. The bake sale was a social success. The profits were small. (but)
3. Dad will drive us to O'Hare Airport. We may take the airport limousine. (or)
4. I flicked on the television. No picture appeared. (but)
5. The wind blew sleet in my face. My nose froze. (and)

Combining Sentences

When you first began school, much of what you read and wrote consisted of simple sentences:

Jan has a pet. I have a pet. We wash our pet. We walk our pet.

Now, however, you probably find this kind of writing childish and dull. To be interesting, a piece of writing should contain a variety of simple sentences and compound sentences. It should also contain a good mix of single subjects and predicates and compound subjects and predicates. *Step 1:* In a book intended for use in the early grades, find a passage made up entirely of simple sentences. Copy the passage on a sheet of paper. *Step 2:* On the same sheet of paper, rewrite the passage. Use compound subjects and predicates to combine some of the ideas in the original paragraph. Use compound sentences to combine other ideas. Use commas or semicolons to punctuate your compound sentences (*pages 212, 214*).

5.7   Writing Complete Sentences

A **complete sentence** is a group of words that has at least one subject and one predicate and that expresses a complete thought. You should use complete sentences in your writing. Many people make two common errors in writing sentences: they use sentence fragments and run-on sentences. Neither sentence fragments nor run-on sentences are acceptable. In this section, you will learn how to recognize these common sentence errors and how to correct them.

5.7a   Avoiding Sentence Fragments

A **sentence fragment** is a group of words that does not express a complete thought. Some sentence fragments lack a complete subject. Others lack a complete predicate. Some lack both a complete subject and a complete predicate.

FRAGMENT	Trotted to its mother. [The complete subject is missing. Who or what trotted to its mother?]
COMPLETE SENTENCE	The colt **trotted to its mother.**
FRAGMENT	A new colt. [The complete predicate is missing. What about the new colt?]
COMPLETE SENTENCE	**A new colt** can create a lot of excitement on a horse farm.
FRAGMENT	Under a street light. [Both a complete subject and a complete predicate are missing. A prepositional phrase cannot stand alone as a complete sentence.]
COMPLETE SENTENCE	The couple and their dog stood **under a street light.**
FRAGMENT	A very close game.
COMPLETE SENTENCE	The Sugar Bowl was **a very close game.** [The fragment has been corrected by adding both a complete subject and a complete predicate.]

Exercise 1   Sentence or Fragment?   On your paper, label each of the following word groups *Sentence* or *Fragment*.

SAMPLE	In the back yard.
ANSWER	Fragment

1. Dirt all over the floor.
2. Several people came up and spoke to us.
3. Came through the window with a loud crash.
4. A very entertaining show.
5. Gold braid on their uniforms.
6. Down one block and up the next.
7. Put on a sweater and go to the store.
8. Vetoed the spending bill.
9. Once he gets on base, Henderson is a threat to steal.
10. At the top of the charts.

Exercise 2 Complete Sentences   On your paper, correct the fragments in Exercise 1 by adding the words needed to make complete sentences. If you need help, refer to the examples on page 110.

5.7b   Avoiding Run-on Sentences

A **run-on sentence** consists of two or more complete sentences incorrectly written as if they were one sentence. In some run-on sentences, the sentences are separated only by a comma. In other run-on sentences, the sentences are not separated at all.

RUN-ON

> The fox sniffed at the cage, the rabbits perked up their ears. [A comma alone should not be used between two simple sentences.]

COMPOUND SENTENCE

> The fox sniffed at the cage, and the rabbits perked up their ears. [A comma and the conjunction *and* join the two simple sentences to form a compound sentence.]

RUN-ON
> The party was over then we cleaned up. [Two sentences should not be joined without punctuation.]

COMPOUND SENTENCE
> The party was over; then we cleaned up. [A semicolon separates the two sentences.]

SEPARATE SENTENCES
> The party was over. Then we cleaned up. [The run-on sentence has been made into two separate sentences.]

Exercise 3   Run-on Sentences   The following run-on sentences can be corrected in several ways. On your paper, write a correct sentence for each run-on. If you need help, refer to the examples on this page.

> SAMPLE   Our club had a yard sale it was very successful.
>
> ANSWER   Our club had a yard sale; it was very successful.

1. We swam out to the float then we sunbathed for a while.
2. Sue came over, we went for a long walk.
3. Our car broke down we waited an hour for the tow truck.
4. The weather seemed clear suddenly a dark cloud appeared in the east.
5. Do you like mystery stories I especially enjoy Sherlock Holmes.
6. Be careful that step is broken.
7. Here comes the bride, isn't her dress beautiful?
8. The dentist x-rayed my jaw then he cleaned my teeth.
9. Everyone in my family likes green vegetables, we grow beans, peas, cabbage, and zucchini in our garden.
10. Smoke from the fire damaged the furniture, it still smells.

Assignment   Complete Sentences in a Paragraph
On your paper, rewrite the following paragraph, correcting

the fragments and the run-ons. Three of the sentences are correct.

> Waves work endlessly. Wear down rocks into pebbles and sand. Some of the sand is coarse some is fine. Coarse sand is like blotting paper, the waves sink directly into it. Piles up loosely and moves around constantly. Steep beaches are formed from coarse sand. Fine sand packs much tighter. The waves do not sink in, their movement leaves a smooth, gentle slope. A much better beach from fine sand.

5.8   Sentence Diagrams

A sentence consists of several different parts of speech that work together to form a complete thought. One way to show the relationship between the words in a sentence is to diagram the sentence.

A **sentence diagram** is a picture of the structure of a sentence. In this section you will study some simple rules for diagraming sentences. With the help of a ruler and a few lines, you can create pictures that show how the words in a sentence work together.

5.8a   Diagraming Subjects and Predicates

Begin a sentence diagram by drawing a horizontal line with a ruler. This line is called the base line. Then divide the base line with a vertical line called the bar. The bar should be the same length above and below the base line.

BASIC DIAGRAM DESIGN

Write the simple subject of a sentence on the base line to the left of the bar. Write the simple predicate on the base line to the right of the bar.

DECLARATIVE SENTENCE   Joan Clark won.

Joan Clark	won

Notice that punctuation marks are not included in a diagram. The first word in the sentence should always be capitalized in a diagram, even when it is not a proper noun.

INTERROGATIVE SENTENCE   Did she win?

she	Did win

Notice that the words in a verb phrase go together in a diagram even when the predicate comes before the subject in the sentence. Note also that *Did* is capitalized because it is the first word in the sentence.

When you diagram an imperative sentence, write the understood subject in the subject position in the diagram. Put the understood subject in parentheses.

IMPERATIVE SENTENCE   Play!

(you)	Play

Exercise 1   Diagraming Subjects and Predicates
On your paper, diagram the following sentences. Remember to use a ruler.

1. Dogs bark.
2. Cows were bellowing.
3. Do sheep bleat?
4. Geese are hissing.
5. Stop!

5.8b   Diagraming Modifiers and Phrases

Diagraming Modifiers

To diagram an adjective or an adverb, draw a slanted line from the base line below the word that the adjective or adverb modifies.

The young player won easily. [The adjectives, *The* and *young,* modify the subject, *player.* The adverb, *easily,* modifies the verb, *won.*]

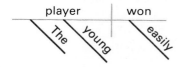

Some adverbs modify adjectives and other adverbs. Write this kind of adverb on an L-shaped line extending from the adjective or adverb that it modifies.

She plays very hard. [The adverb, *very,* modifies the adverb, *hard.*]

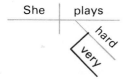

Exercise 2   Diagraming Adjectives and Adverbs

On your paper, diagram the following sentences. Remember to use a ruler. The sentences contain adjectives and adverbs.

1. A huge crowd gathered quickly.
2. Were any new stamps issued recently?
3. Some weeds grow very slowly.
4. That very rickety step will soon collapse.
5. The extremely hot weather finally ended.

Diagraming Prepositional Phrases

Prepositional phrases are often used as adjectives and adverbs in sentences (*page 70*). To diagram a prepositional phrase, draw a slanted line from the base line below the word that the phrase modifies. From the slanted line, draw a line parallel to the base line. Write the preposition on the slanted line. Write the object of the preposition on the line parallel to the base line. The words that modify the object of a preposition are written on slanted lines below the object.

The girl in the blue headband won at Wimbledon.

girl | won

The   in   headband   at Wimbledon

the   blue

Exercise 3 Diagraming Prepositional Phrases On

your paper, diagram the following sentences. Remember to use a ruler. The sentences contain adjectives, adverbs, and prepositional phrases.

SAMPLE   The very excited students at the special
assembly applauded with great enthusiasm.

ANSWER

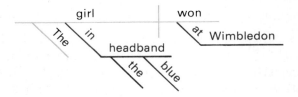

1. A visitor from Peru arrived quite unexpectedly at our house.
2. The loose shingles on the garage roof fell off during the severe storm.
3. Huge kettles of delicious vegetables were simmering gently on the stove.
4. A picture of our kittens will appear soon in the newspaper.
5. Everyone except my uncle returned to the campsite without difficulty.

5.8c Diagraming Complements

Diagraming Direct Objects

When a sentence has a direct object, extend the base line to the right of the predicate. Write the direct object on that extended base line. Separate the direct object from the predicate with a vertical line that extends above the base line but not below it. Place modifiers of the direct object on slanted lines below it.

Joan Clark won an extremely close game.

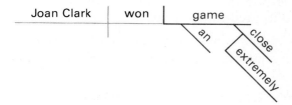

Diagraming Subject Complements

To diagram a predicate nominative or a predicate adjective, extend the base line to the right of the predicate. Write the predicate nominative or the predicate adjective on that extended base line. From the base line, draw a line that slants toward the subject and does not go below the base. Place any modifiers of the predicate nominative or predicate adjective on a slanted line below it.

PREDICATE NOMINATIVE   She is a fierce competitor.

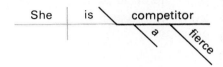

PREDICATE ADJECTIVE   She sometimes appears very tough.

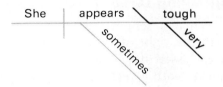

Exercise 4 Diagraming Complements   On your paper, diagram the following sentences. Remember to use a ruler. The sentences contain direct objects, predicate nominatives, and predicate adjectives.

SAMPLE   The woman on the motorbike is my homeroom teacher.

ANSWER

1. This stew tastes too salty.
2. Measure the door carefully with a ruler.

3. The lowly caterpillar became a beautiful butterfly with shining wings.
4. Our planet has the seven continents.
5. Earth is a watery planet.
6. Early beliefs about the universe were false.
7. Something made a very strange noise.
8. Are termites really ants?
9. The old house appeared vacant.
10. Is he your favorite singer?

5.8d   Diagraming Compound Elements

Compound elements are those elements that consist of two or more items. You diagram compound elements in much the same way that you diagram single elements in a sentence.

Compound Subjects and Compound Predicates

Write the parts of a compound subject or a compound predicate on parallel lines. Then connect the lines with a vertical line of dashes. On the line of dashes, write the conjunction that joins the compound elements. Connect the compound elements to the base of the diagram with a pair of solid diagonal lines.

COMPOUND SUBJECT   She and I played doubles.

If a compound element has a modifier or a complement, diagram the modifier or complement as you normally would.

COMPOUND PREDICATE   She and I played records and then went to the movies.

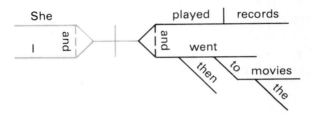

Compound Modifiers

When two or more modifiers are connected by a conjunction, write the modifiers on slanted lines below the word that they modify. Then draw a line of dashes between the slanted lines. Write the conjunction on the line of dashes.

The young but competitive gymnast performed gracefully and aggressively.

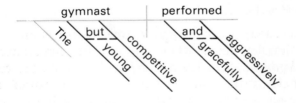

Compound Complements

Diagram a compound complement by writing the complements on parallel lines and connecting the lines with a line of dashes. Write the conjunction on the line of dashes. Connect the compound complement to the base of the diagram with a pair of diagonal lines.

COMPOUND DIRECT OBJECT

Do you favor Allen or Jeffers?

COMPOUND PREDICATE NOMINATIVE

My two favorites are Allen and Jeffers.

COMPOUND PREDICATE ADJECTIVE

They are powerful and skillful.

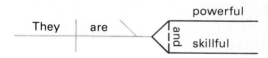

Exercise 5   Diagraming Compound Elements   On your paper, diagram the following sentences. Remember to use a ruler. The sentences contain compound subjects, compound predicates, compound complements, and compound modifiers. If you need help, refer to the models on pages 119–121.

1. Rain fell and froze during the night.
2. Several teachers and students attended the exhibit.
3. The veterans marched peacefully and silently.
4. The spectators cheered wildly and waved their hats.
5. My pet bird is talkative and friendly.

6. The favorites are you and I.
7. Pack the pots and pans in that carton.
8. Strawberries and peaches are my favorite fruits.
9. The small but hardy bushes survived the heavy snowfall.
10. Will the new governor and our mayor watch the fireworks?

5.8e   Diagraming Compound Sentences

Diagram each simple sentence in a compound sentence on a separate line. Then draw a line of dashes between the predicate of one clause and the predicate of the other. Put a step halfway down the line of dashes. On this step write the conjunction that connects the two clauses.

Allen won the first two sets, but Jeffers eventually won the match.

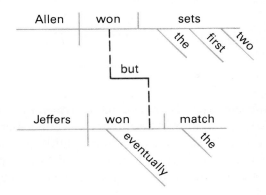

Exercise 6   Diagraming Compound Sentences   On your paper, diagram the following compound sentences.

1. A neighbor will collect our mail, or the post office can hold it.
2. Cartoonists are skillful artists, and most have taken several courses in art.

3. The Monarchs did not win the pennant, but they showed great improvement throughout the season.
4. Anita is the president of the computer club, and Greg is the vice-president.
5. We can go to the science museum, or we can play softball.

Assignment Writing and Diagraming Sentences
On your paper, write and diagram five sentences. Your sentences should include the following elements.

1. A subject modified by at least one adjective and a predicate modified by at least one adverb
2. An adjective modified by an adverb
3. A prepositional phrase
4. A compound subject and a compound predicate
5. A compound complement
6. A compound sentence

Unit Practice

Practice 1

A. Sentence Purpose *(pages 85–87)* On your paper, write whether each of the following sentences is declarative, interrogative, imperative, or exclamatory.

1. Don't talk with your mouth full.
2. Ralph won a blue ribbon at the county fair.
3. Can you see my house from here?
4. Sit still!
5. What a delicious casserole this is!

B. Subjects *(pages 87–98)* On your paper, write the complete subject of each of the following sentences. Underline the simple subject once.

6. Jerry, my oldest brother, is six feet tall.
7. Many friends and relatives stopped by our house last Sunday.
8. That lovely cabinet in the gift shop will make a great gift for my aunt.
9. The yellow house down the street belongs to the Marrone family.
10. Several photographs of Isabella and me are hanging on the wall.

C. Predicates *(pages 87–98)* On your paper, write the complete predicate of each of the following sentences. Underline the simple predicate twice.

11. Janet finished the letter and addressed the envelope.
12. No one who was going to the basketball game remembered to call Angela.
13. The tea kettle became hot and whistled loudly.
14. After the first ring, I answered the telephone.
15. Mrs. Kelley and her daughter love horseback riding.

D. Placement of Subjects and Predicates *(pages 98–100)* On your paper, copy the following sentences. Underline each complete subject once and each complete predicate twice. Write *Subj.* over each simple subject and *Pred.* over each simple predicate.

16. What a beautiful day this is!
17. From the black clouds came a sudden flash of lightning.
18. There are several errors in this paper.
19. Does he know the route to the beach?
20. Cross the street carefully.

E. Complements *(pages 101–106)* On your paper, write the complements in the following sentences. Label each complement *Direct object, Predicate nominative,* or *Predicate adjective.*

21. I will give the message to Pam.
22. This tree has grown big and strong.
23. Our choice for group leader is Kim.
24. The fruit bowl contained apples and oranges.
25. Harry sounded hoarse after his speech.

F. Simple and Compound Sentences *(pages 106–109)* On your paper, label each sentence *Simple* or *Compound.*

26. Mother's lovely canary sat in its cage and chirped.
27. Your broken typewriter will be fixed tomorrow.
28. We should be going home now, for it will be getting dark soon.
29. Alan and his friends built a treehouse and stayed in it for hours.
30. The students had all gone to lunch; the classroom was silent.

(Continue on the next page.)

G. Complete Sentences *(pages 109–113)* On your paper, write complete sentences by correcting each of the following run-on sentences and sentence fragments.

31. Flew across the yard and landed on a tree branch.
32. Jerry washed the dishes, Ellen scrubbed the floor.
33. Lisa told a funny story then everyone laughed.
34. A piece of paper blowing wildly in the breeze.
35. Mary's new hat.

H. Sentence Diagrams *(pages 113–123)* On your paper, diagram the following sentences. Remember to use a ruler.

36. Did you find the lost necklace?
37. Listen to that car without a muffler!
38. He and I are the organizers of this club.
39. Mr. Willis and Kevin went in the boat and caught fish.
40. The sharp steak knife should be handled gently and carefully.

Practice 2

On your paper, write the words and phrases that are in italics in the following passage. Label each one *Simple subject, Simple predicate, Compound subject, Compound predicate, Complete subject, Complete predicate, Direct object, Predicate nominative,* or *Predicate adjective.*

(1) *National Children's Book Week* is a (2) *week* set aside each November to stimulate the reading of good books by children. (3) *Franklin Mathiews,* an author, and *Frederic Melcher,* a publisher, (4) *developed* and *started* (5) *Book Week* in 1919. (6) *The Children's Book Council in New York City* is (7) *responsible* for planning and promoting the annual event. In addition, (8) *parents, teachers,* and *librarians* (9) *join* in the Book Week effort. Book Week (10) *has been celebrated in the past with book exhibits, television and radio programs, and story hours.*

Unit Tests

Test 1

A. Sentence Purpose *(pages 85–87)* On your paper, tell whether each of the following sentences is declarative, interrogative, imperative, or exclamatory.

1. Does Mandy's plane arrive at two o'clock?
2. Come over here right now!
3. Christopher Columbus was born in 1451.
4. Go down the hall and call Cindy.
5. How lovely that garden looks!

B. Subjects *(pages 87–98)* On your paper, write the complete subject of each of the following sentences. Underline the simple subject once.

6. A member of the other team congratulated us on our victory.
7. Several squirrels and chipmunks ate the walnuts that were on the ground.
8. Winifred, my second cousin, lives in the apartment building across the street.
9. The eagle and the albatross are birds with large wingspans.
10. Both Mary and Denise have finished their work.

C. Predicates *(pages 87–98)* On your paper, write the complete predicate of each of the following sentences. Underline the simple predicates twice.

11. Tom wrote his essay and typed it the next day.
12. Karl and my sister sang a duet in the variety show.
13. The kitten silently sat in the corner and licked its paw.
14. This weekend Effie decided to go rock climbing.
15. Seymour and his friends drove to the game.

D. Placement of Subjects and Predicates *(pages 98–100)* On your paper, copy the following sentences.

(Continue on the next page.)

Underline each complete subject once and each complete predicate twice. Write *Subj.* over each simple subject and *Pred.* over each simple predicate.

16. Here is the book that you wanted.
17. Quickly and expertly, Rhonda cast her fishing line into the water.
18. Are they coming to the party?
19. Remember to water the flowers while we are on vacation.
20. How wonderful that movie was!

E. Complements *(pages 101–106)* On your paper, write the complements in the following sentences. Label each complement *Direct object, Predicate nominative,* or *Predicate adjective.*

21. Have you seen our troop leader?
22. The rolls tasted warm and delicious.
23. Her cousins are Sylvia and Brian.
24. He sent a postcard to Emily from Idaho.
25. This leather feels dry and cracked.

F. Simple and Compound Sentences *(pages 106–109)* On your paper, write whether each sentence is simple or compound.

26. The corn and the tomatoes are ripe and ready to be picked.
27. Our car has finally been fixed; we will leave early tomorrow morning.
28. Brad hit a home run and the crowd cheered wildly.
29. The ice cube melted and made a small pool of water on the counter.
30. Mr. Preston likes spinach, but Christine prefers broccoli.

G. Complete Sentences *(pages 109–113)* On your paper, write complete sentences by correcting each of the following run-on sentences and sentence fragments.

31. Looking at the diner across the road.
32. Darlene wrote the story, Hank did the illustrations.
33. Jumped from a lily pad into the pond.
34. The spectacular rainbow.
35. Jan will be at the meeting Ted will also be there.

H. Sentence Diagrams *(pages 113–123)* On your paper, diagram the following sentences. Remember to use a ruler.

36. Those fantastic singers are members of the school choir.
37. He often seems rather quiet.
38. This is a wonderfully handy tool.
39. The boy in the playground is my nephew.
40. Joanne and he saw Michele and Pierre.

Test 2

On your paper, write the words and phrases that are in italics in the following passage. Label each one *Simple subject, Simple predicate, Compound subject, Compound predicate, Complete subject, Complete predicate, Direct object, Predicate nominative,* or *Predicate adjective.*

The homing (1) *pigeon* is a special (2) *breed* of pigeon used for racing and for carrying messages. These pigeons (3) *can be trained* to return home when released from a distant place. This homing ability (4) *has been increased by selective breeding.* (5) *The exact way in which pigeons find their way home across strange territory* is (6) *unknown.* Some (7) *think that the birds are guided by the position of the sun.* Some owners of homing pigeons even use their (8) *birds* for racing. Homing pigeons (9) *can travel* up to sixty miles per hour and *can cover* six hundred miles in one day. As one can see, the homing pigeon is remarkably (10) *hardy.*

UNIT 6

Usage

Unit Preview

What is wrong with the following quotations?

Imagine that the President says, ''One of the most important bills before the House are about farm prices.''

Imagine that a famous archeologist says, ''With the face of a horse, my assistant found the bones of a rare animal.''

Imagine that, in a commercial for a new automobile, a television announcer says, ''The bestest car is the Whiz.''

Imagine that the valedictorian at a high school graduation says, ''I wish to thank the faculty for learning me about life.''

The four quotations contain mistakes in usage. Each begins with the word *Imagine,* because the people speaking the made-up quotations are not likely to make such mistakes in usage. They already know something that you should know. If you make mistakes in what you say or write, your audience will have trouble understanding what you really mean. Even though they may understand you, they may not believe that what you say has any value.

Knowing the rules of usage and following them will give you confidence that what you are saying will be understood and believed. Knowing these rules can also help you to understand what you read and what others say to you.

For Analysis   Answer the following questions about the four quotations with the mistakes in usage.

1. How many bills is the President talking about?
2. Who has the face of a horse—the assistant or the rare animal?

3. If the Whiz is the "bestest" car, does that make it better than the *best* car?
4. Do teachers *learn* students, or do they *teach* them?
5. Why would a President, an archeologist, a television announcer, and a valedictorian be unlikely to make such mistakes?
6. On your paper, rewrite each quotation, correcting the mistakes in usage.

In this unit you will learn the rules of English usage. Remembering these rules will help you to express yourself clearly and correctly.

6.1 Correct Use of Verbs

The verbs that you use when you write or speak have different forms. These verb forms account for many common mistakes in usage. Using the correct form will make it easier for you to speak and write effectively.

6.1a Principal Parts of Verbs

Every verb has four basic forms called its **principal parts.** The principal parts are (1) the infinitive, (2) the present participle, (3) the past, and (4) the past participle. All other verb forms are made from the four principal parts.

Here are the principal parts of the verb *talk.*

INFINITIVE	PRESENT PARTICIPLE	PAST	PAST PARTICIPLE
talk	(is) talking	talked	(has) talked

The **infinitive** is the verb in its most basic form, the form given in the dictionary as the entry word.

The **present participle** consists of the infinitive plus *-ing*. A form of the auxiliary verb *be* (*page 20*) is used with the present participle.

Sometimes a spelling change occurs when -*ing* is added to the infinitive (*Unit 17*).

hope + -ing = hoping [Final *e* is dropped.]
shop + -ing = shopping [Final *p* is doubled.]

A verb is either a regular verb or an irregular verb, depending on how its past and its past participle are formed.

Regular Verbs

Verbs that form the past and the past participle by adding -*d* or -*ed* to the infinitive are called **regular verbs.** In a sentence a form of the auxiliary verb *have* is used with the past participle.

INFINITIVE			PAST	PAST PARTICIPLE
talk	+ -ed	=	talked	(has) talked
wade	+ -d	=	waded	(has) waded

Sometimes a spelling change occurs when -*ed* is added to the infinitive (*Unit 17*).

worry + -ed = worried [Final *y* is changed to *i*.]
permit + -ed = permitted [Final *t* is doubled.]

The following list shows the principal parts of three regular verbs. In this book the auxiliary verbs in parentheses are there to remind you to use a form of *be* with the present participle and a form of *have* with the past participle.

INFINITIVE	PRESENT PARTICIPLE	PAST	PAST PARTICIPLE
shop	(is) shopping	shopped	(has) shopped
repair	(is) repairing	repaired	(has) repaired
brush	(is) brushing	brushed	(has) brushed

The following sentences show the correct use of the principal parts of the regular verb *shop.*

inf.
We **shop** for food every Friday night.

pres.
aux.   part.
Dad **is shopping** for a new car.

past
We **shopped** at the mall last week.

past
aux.   part.
We **had** never **shopped** there before.

Exercise 1   Principal Parts   The following list includes the past form of ten regular verbs. On your paper, write the infinitive and the present participle of each verb.

SAMPLE   appealed

ANSWER   appeal, (is) appealing

1. puzzled
2. occurred
3. helped
4. defined
5. hurried
6. wrapped
7. studied
8. used
9. excused
10. buried

Exercise 2   Regular Verbs   On your paper, write the form of the verb given at the end of the sentence for each verb in parentheses.

SAMPLE   One muggy July day, we (*decide*) to take the train to the park.—Past

ANSWER   decided

1. A group had just (*finish*) a game of volleyball. —Past participle
2. We (*claim*) their court and (*start*) a game.—Past
3. After the third game, we (*rest*) in the shade of a big elm tree.—Past
4. The night before it had (*rain*).—Past participle

5. Huge puddles (*cover*) the ground.—Past

6. All of a sudden, a woman (*yell*) at her big, white sheep dog.—Past

7. The dog was (*race*) across the meadow toward the duck pond.—Present participle

8. She was (*call*) for it to stop.—Present participle

9. Just as she (*grab*) for the leash, the dog (*slip*) in the mud.—Past

10. It (*slither*) right into the pond but (*scramble*) out again.—Past

Irregular Verbs

Verbs that do not form the past and the past participle by adding -*d* or -*ed* to the infinitive are called **irregular verbs.** Here are the principal parts of the irregular verb *give.*

INFINITIVE	PRESENT PARTICIPLE	PAST	PAST PARTICIPLE
give	(is) giving	gave	(has) given

As with regular verbs, a form of the auxiliary verb *be* is used with the present participle, and a form of the auxiliary verb *have* is used with the past participle. The following sentences show the correct use of the principal parts of the irregular verb *give.*

inf.
Every week we **give** a report.

pres.
aux.   part.
We **are giving** one today.

past
Last week we **gave** a report on TV viewing.

past
aux.   part.
This is the first year that we **have given** weekly reports.

Because there are no rules for forming the past and the past participle of irregular verbs, you should memorize those principal parts that you do not already know. The principal parts of many common irregular verbs are listed below. Study the list and refer to it while doing the exercises that follow.

INFINITIVE	PRESENT PARTICIPLE	PAST	PAST PARTICIPLE
be	(is) being	was, were	(has) been
begin	(is) beginning	began	(has) begun
blow	(is) blowing	blew	(has) blown
break	(is) breaking	broke	(has) broken
bring	(is) bringing	brought	(has) brought
burst	(is) bursting	burst	(has) burst
catch	(is) catching	caught	(has) caught
choose	(is) choosing	chose	(has) chosen
come	(is) coming	came	(has) come
do	(is) doing	did	(has) done
drink	(is) drinking	drank	(has) drunk
drive	(is) driving	drove	(has) driven
eat	(is) eating	ate	(has) eaten
fall	(is) falling	fell	(has) fallen
fly	(is) flying	flew	(has) flown
freeze	(is) freezing	froze	(has) frozen
get	(is) getting	got	(has) gotten
give	(is) giving	gave	(has) given
go	(is) going	went	(has) gone
grow	(is) growing	grew	(has) grown
have	(is) having	had	(has) had
know	(is) knowing	knew	(has) known
lay	(is) laying	laid	(has) laid
lead	(is) leading	led	(has) led
leave	(is) leaving	left	(has) left
lie	(is) lying	lay	(has) lain
make	(is) making	made	(has) made
put	(is) putting	put	(has) put
ride	(is) riding	rode	(has) ridden
ring	(is) ringing	rang	(has) rung
rise	(is) rising	rose	(has) risen

run	(is) running	ran	(has) run
see	(is) seeing	saw	(has) seen
set	(is) setting	set	(has) set
shrink	(is) shrinking	shrank	(has) shrunk
sing	(is) singing	sang	(has) sung
sit	(is) sitting	sat	(has) sat
speak	(is) speaking	spoke	(has) spoken
spring	(is) springing	sprang	(has) sprung
steal	(is) stealing	stole	(has) stolen
strike	(is) striking	struck	(has) struck, (has) stricken
swim	(is) swimming	swam	(has) swum
take	(is) taking	took	(has) taken
teach	(is) teaching	taught	(has) taught
throw	(is) throwing	threw	(has) thrown
wear	(is) wearing	wore	(has) worn
write	(is) writing	wrote	(has) written

Exercise 3   Irregular Verbs   On your paper, write the past or the past participle of the verbs in parentheses in the following sentences. Tell which form you wrote. Remember that a form of the auxiliary verb *have* is used with the past participle.

SAMPLE   He (*lay*) the three spoons on the table.
ANSWER   laid—Past

1. Our school soccer team (*lead*) the league all season.
2. We (*begin*) the test at 2:30 P.M.
3. The campers have (*take*) down the tent poles.
4. They (*bring*) their lunch to the rehearsal.
5. I (*do*) my homework in record time.
6. Time had (*steal*) up on us.
7. I thought I (*know*) that formula.
8. My jogging shoes (*wear*) out along the outside of the heel.
9. The bubble had (*burst*) by the time we (*run*) into the lab.

10. Two hummingbirds (*fly*) into the tree.
11. It has (*be*) mild for days.
12. We have (*eat*) fresh vegetables all summer.
13. Soon the whole town had (*catch*) the spirit.
14. The coach has already (*choose*) the team.
15. That year winter had (*come*) unusually early.

Exercise 4 Irregular Verbs On your paper, answer each of the following questions by completing the statement with the past or past participle of the verb in italic type. Write the whole statement.

> **SAMPLE**   Did you *give* him the assignment?
> Yes, I __?__ it to him yesterday.
>
> **ANSWER**   Yes, I gave it to him yesterday.

1. Did you *write* to your grandfather?
   Yes, I have __?__ him a letter and a note.
2. Did the bell *ring*?
   Yes, it __?__ five minutes ago.
3. Did you *drink* the grapefruit juice?
   Yes, I have __?__ it all.
4. Did he *run* in the marathon?
   Yes, he __?__ the entire course.
5. Did she *break* her glasses again?
   Yes, she has __?__ them for the third time.
6. Did you *see* anything unusual?
   We __?__ nothing.
7. Did you *do* your best?
   I have always __?__ my best.
8. Did you *take* my pencil?
   No, someone else has __?__ it.
9. Did she *begin* her book report?
   No, she has just __?__ to read the book.

(Continue on the next page.)

10. Did the tomatoes *grow*?
    Yes, they __?__ several inches this past week.
11. Did you *lay* the book on the desk?
    Yes, I __?__ it next to the telephone.
12. Did they *swim* in the pool this afternoon?
    No, they __?__ early this morning.
13. Does everyone *know* Sheila?
    Yes, we have __?__ her for years.
14. Did you *take* your cousin to the movies?
    Yes, I __?__ him last evening.
15. Did he *fly* to Nevada for vacation?
    No, he __?__ to Colorado.

Assignment   Principal Parts of Irregular Verbs   On your paper, write five questions and answers similar to those in Exercise 4. Use irregular verbs from the list on pages 135–136. Do not complete the answers. Exchange papers with a classmate and answer each other's questions either orally or in writing.

6.1b   Verb Tense

A verb expresses time through tense. The **tense** of a verb makes clear whether something is happening now, has happened in the past, or will happen in the future.

Verbs in English have six tenses: (1) present, (2) past, (3) future, (4) present perfect, (5) past perfect, and (6) future perfect. You form the six tenses by using the principal parts of a verb and the auxiliary verbs *will* and *have*.

A **conjugation of a verb** lists all the forms of the six tenses of that verb. A conjugation also shows how the verb changes its form in the present tense when the subject is in the third-person singular.

Conjugation of the Verb *Play*

Principal Parts

Infinitive	Present Participle	Past	Past Participle
play	(is) playing	played	(has) played

Singular	Plural

Present Tense

I play	we play
you play	you play
he/she/it plays	they play

Past Tense

I played	we played
you played	you played
he/she/it played	they played

Future Tense

I will (shall) play	we will (shall) play
you will play	you will play
he/she/it will play	they will play

Present Perfect Tense

I have played	we have played
you have played	you have played
he/she/it has played	they have played

Past Perfect Tense

I had played	we had played
you had played	you had played
he/she/it had played	they had played

Future Perfect Tense

I will (shall) have played	we will (shall) have played
you will have played	you will have played
he/she/it will have played	they will have played

Present and Present
Perfect Tenses

Rule Use verbs in the present tense to show (1) an action that takes place in the present, (2) an action that is repeated regularly, and (3) a condition that is true at any time.

> The coach **wants** you. [The action takes place in the present.]
> We **practice** every Tuesday. [The action is repeated.]
> Our school **has** a large gymnasium. [The condition is true at any time.]

To show the present tense of regular and irregular verbs, use the infinitive form or add *-s* or *-es* to the infinitive form.

PRESENT   They **ride** their bikes everywhere. [infinitive]
She **rides** her bike to school. [infinitive plus *-s*]
He **polishes** his bike every week. [infinitive plus *-es*]

Rule Use verbs in the present perfect tense to describe an action that began sometime in the past and either is still going on or has just been completed.

> He **has** finally **begun** his homework. [The action is still going on.]
> Someone **has washed** the dishes. [The action has just been completed.]

To show the present perfect tense of a verb, use *has* or *have* as an auxiliary verb with the past participle.

                              past
                    aux.   part.
PRESENT PERFECT   Mom **has driven** three thousand miles this month.

                              past
                    aux.   part.
They **have replaced** the faulty muffler.

Past and Past Perfect Tenses

Rule Use the past tense to describe an action that was completed entirely in the past.

Last night Anita **removed** the broken glass from the window.

To show the past tense of a verb, use the past form of the verb. Regular verbs form the past by adding *-d* or *-ed* to the infinitive. Most irregular verbs have a special past form.

PAST   The teachers **offered** their help. [*Offered* is the past form of the regular verb *offer*.]

             The teachers **took** up a collection. [*Took* is the special past form of the irregular verb *take*.]

Rule Use the past perfect tense to describe an action that was completed (1) by a certain time in the past or (2) before some other action was completed.

They **had shingled** the dormer by the end of the day. [The action was finished by a certain time.]

past perfect   past
We **had boarded** up the windows before the storm **reached** us. [The action of boarding up the windows was completed before the arrival of the storm.]

To show the past perfect tense, use *had* as an auxiliary verb with the past participle.

                             past
                    aux. part.
PAST PERFECT   It **had rained** for three days before the river *overflowed*.

Future and Future Perfect Tenses

Rule Use the future tense to describe an action that will take place in the future.

The band **will travel** by train. [The action will take place in the future.]

To show the future tense, use the auxiliary verb *will* or *shall* with the infinitive form of the main verb.

FUTURE   They **will play** at each town along the railway line.
aux. inf.

aux.   inf.
We **shall meet** them at McReady's Junction.

Rule   Use the future perfect tense to describe an action that will end at a specific time in the future.

future perfect
They **will have played** in eight towns by next week. [The action will end at a specific time in the future.]

To form the future perfect tense, use the auxiliary verbs *will have* or *shall have* with the past participle.

aux.   aux.
FUTURE PERFECT   At the end of the trip, the band **will have**
past part.
experienced some memorable sights.

Exercise 5   Verb Tense   On your paper, write the verbs or verb phrases in the following sentences. Then tell whether the tense is *Present, Present perfect, Past, Past perfect, Future,* or *Future perfect.*

SAMPLE   They will have decided on a prize by tomorrow.

ANSWER   will have decided—Future perfect

1. They will skip lunch if necessary.
2. Barbara and Marvin have started a fan club.
3. By this time next week, you will have been at the beach for two days.
4. Greg takes down the flag before sundown.
5. By that time, the cement truck had lumbered to a halt.

6. They have passed the survival test.

7. Every year we vote for a new student council.

8. Tom and Rosalie will have designed the sets by then.

9. One of the tires exploded on the runway.

10. Several parents had already begun the search.

11. Everyone will enjoy the new rocking chair.

12. My watch stopped at four o'clock.

13. She had left the theater before the second act.

14. By next year, we will have finished building the house.

15. Jeremy has decided on a plan.

Assignment   Verb Tense   Choose three verbs from the list of irregular verbs on pages 135–136. Use each verb in three different sentences. In the first sentence, use the past tense. In the second sentence, use the present perfect tense. In the third sentence, use the past perfect tense.

SAMPLE   go

ANSWER   They went home.
                They have already gone home.
                They had gone home before the storm.

Writing About the Future and the Past

Step 1: Write a paragraph about a trip that you plan to take sometime in the future to a park, a museum, or another place in your community. Use verbs in the future tense to tell about the trip. *Step 2:* Imagine that you are writing a letter to someone after the trip is over. Rewrite the paragraph from Step 1, using the past, present perfect, and past perfect tenses. You may have to change other words in order to have your paragraph make sense.

6.2   Subject–Verb Agreement

A subject and a verb agree in number when they are both singular or both plural. In order to write effective sentences, you need to make sure that your subjects and verbs agree.

6.2a   Number

Number means singular (one) or plural (more than one). Most nouns and personal pronouns have different forms for the singular and the plural (*page 11*). Many auxiliary verbs and all verbs in the present tense have different forms for the singular and the plural.

Singular and Plural Nouns and Pronouns

If a noun or a personal pronoun refers to one person, place, thing, or idea, it is **singular** in number.

SINGULAR NOUNS   girl, street, mountain, book, thought

SINGULAR PRONOUNS   he, she, it

If a noun or a personal pronoun refers to more than one person, place, thing, or idea, it is **plural** in number.

PLURAL NOUNS   girls, streets, mountains, books, thoughts

PLURAL PRONOUNS   we, they

Exercise 1 **Singular and Plural** On your paper, write the following nouns and pronouns. Then label each word *Singular* or *Plural*.

SAMPLE whale

ANSWER whale—Singular

1. evening
2. he
3. pilots
4. trunk
5. oxen
6. cut
7. geese
8. she
9. dish
10. dictionary
11. they
12. watch
13. children
14. directors
15. branches
16. we
17. it
18. panes
19. club
20. mushroom

Singular and Plural Verbs

In the present tense, a verb has a singular and a plural form. Unlike nouns, the singular form of the verb ends in *s*.

SINGULAR PRESENT FORM
catches, sees, helps, runs, tackles

PLURAL PRESENT FORM
catch, see, help, run, tackle

Some auxiliary verbs also have singular and plural forms in the present tense. *Be* has singular and plural forms in the past tense as well as in the present tense.

AUXILIARY VERB	SINGULAR FORM(S)	PLURAL FORM(S)
be	is (present)	are (present)
	was (past)	were (past)
do	does	do
have	has	have

When *be, do,* and *have* are used as main verbs, they have the same singular and plural forms that they have as auxiliary verbs.

Exercise 2 Singular and Plural Verbs On your paper, write the following verbs. Label each verb *Singular* or *Plural*. If the verb is singular, write its plural form. If the verb is plural, write its singular form.

SAMPLE watches

ANSWER watches—Singular; watch

1. shines	6. trudge	11. argue	16. eat
2. dashes	7. hurts	12. make	17. flies
3. practice	8. honk	13. play	18. choose
4. decide	9. huddle	14. shout	19. pays
5. twists	10. breaks	15. rise	20. goes

Singular and Plural Subjects and Verbs

Rule A subject and its verb must agree in number.

Singular Subject. Use a singular verb with a singular subject.

> The *quarterback* **gives** the signals. [The singular noun *quarterback* and the singular verb *gives* agree in number.]

Plural Subject. Use a plural verb with a plural subject.

> The *coaches* **call** the plays. [The plural noun *coaches* and the plural verb *call* agree in number.]

Verb Phrases. In a verb phrase, use an auxiliary verb that agrees in number with the subject.

SINGULAR
> aux.
> The *quarterback* **was discussing** the play with the coaches.

> aux.
> *He* **has gone** back onto the field.

PLURAL
> aux.
> The *coaches* **were discussing** the play with the quarterback.

> aux.
> *They* **have returned** to the sideline.

The Pronouns *I* and *You*. The pronoun *I* is used with *am* and *was* and with the plural form of other verbs. The pronoun *you* is always used with the plural form.

I **am going**.	*You* **are going**.
I **was going**.	*You* **were going**.
I **go** there every week.	*You* **seem** unhappy.

Exercise 3   Subject-Verb Agreement   On your paper, write the verb or verb phrase that agrees in number with the subject of each of the following sentences. Then write whether the verb form is singular or plural.

> **SAMPLE**   Mario (has asked, have asked) for a raise.
>
> **ANSWER**   has asked—Singular

1. The houses (looks, look) empty.
2. Geraniums (blooms, bloom) all summer.
3. The clowns (has put, have put) on their make-up.
4. My cousins (is taking, are taking) the children to the zoo.
5. The turtles (has dug, have dug) big holes in the sand.
6. This paint (dries, dry) quickly.
7. Anne (paints, paint) houses in the summer.
8. They (mows, mow) lawns too.
9. You (is attracting, are attracting) too much attention.
10. She (has written, have written) a poem.
11. The sailboat (tugs, tug) at its line.
12. They (has gone, have gone) to the football game.
13. A screen (divides, divide) the room.
14. On Saturday the custodians (waxes, wax) the floors.
15. I (has seen, have seen) that movie three times.
16. Your questions (puzzles, puzzle) me.
17. My uncle (is bringing, are bringing) his fishing rod.
18. The players (has tried, have tried) their best.
19. The referee (waves, wave) the flag.
20. I (am going, is going) to Dallas next weekend.

6.2b   Locating the Subject

When the subject comes immediately before the verb, it is usually easy to choose a verb form that agrees with the subject in number. In some sentences, however, a phrase comes between the subject and the verb. In other sentences the subject comes after the verb. To choose the correct verb form, you must first locate the subject.

Prepositional Phrases Between the Subject and the Verb

A prepositional phrase that modifies the subject usually comes between the subject and the predicate.

prep. phrase
The *whiteness* of the cliffs **was** blinding. [The singular noun *whiteness* is the subject. The plural noun *cliffs* is the object of the preposition. The verb *was* agrees with the subject of the sentence, not with the object of the preposition.]

Now study these examples carefully:

SINGULAR   The *pile* of books **was** on the table. [**Think:** The pile was on the table.]

PLURAL   The *books* on the table **belong** to me. [**Think:** The books belong to me.]

Exercise 4   Interrupting Prepositional Phrases
Step 1: On your paper, write the subject of each of the following sentences. *Step 2:* Write the verb or verb phrase that agrees in number with each subject. *Step 3:* Label each verb *Singular* or *Plural*.

SAMPLE   The cheers of the crowd (makes, make) me play harder.

ANSWER   cheers—make; Plural

1. The bowls on the table (is, are) antiques.
2. The students in that school (wears, wear) brown uniforms.
3. The players on the team (stands, stand) silently before the game.
4. The owner of the cats (was, were) frantic.
5. The paint on the clapboards (was peeling, were peeling).
6. The cars along the pier (is, are) brand new.
7. A mile of choppy waves (lies, lie) ahead.
8. A song with eight lively verses (begins, begin) the show.
9. The hands on my watch (goes, go) backward.
10. The flowers near the barn (makes, make) me sneeze.
11. Several gallons of water (fills, fill) that tub.
12. The shelves against the wall (is, are) dusty.
13. These vegetables from the garden (tastes, taste) delicious.
14. The students from that school (has joined, have joined) our club.
15. The folder between those books (contains, contain) the information you need.

Subject After the Verb

In questions and in sentences beginning with *Here* or *There,* the subject comes after the verb. Saying the sentence to yourself in subject-verb order can help you to find the subject and make the verb agree with it.

Where **are** *they* going? [**Think:** They are going where.]
Have the *books* arrived? [**Think:** The books have arrived.]
Here **are** my *boots.* [**Think:** My boots are here.]

In other sentences in which the subject comes after the verb, find the subject. Then decide whether the subject is singular or plural and make the verb agree with it in number.

On the kitchen table **were** the *remains* of a hurried lunch.
[**Think:** The remains were on the kitchen table.]

149

Exercise 5   Subject After the Verb   *Step 1:* On your paper, write the subject of each of the following sentences. *Step 2:* Label each subject *Singular* or *Plural*. *Step 3:* Write the verb form that agrees in number with the subject.

SAMPLE   Here (is, are) the stories you asked for.

ANSWER   stories—Plural; are

1. In the clear night sky (was, were) the trails of a hundred meteors.
2. There (was, were) fourteen boulders in the rock slide.
3. Here (is, are) the extra parts for the engine.
4. Across the field (was, were) two old farm buildings.
5. There (was, were) soldiers on the bridge.
6. (Has, Have) the boys decorated the gym yet?
7. (Is, Are) there four stamps in that set?
8. Behind the cabin (was, were) a gravestone covered with moss.
9. There (was, were) several reasons for the accident.
10. Here (is, are) the gas for the lawn mowers.

6.2c   Determining the Number of the Subject

Certain kinds of subjects require special attention in order to make subjects and verbs agree in number.

Compound Subjects

A **compound subject** is made up of two or more subjects connected by a coordinating conjunction (*page 59*). Both subjects have the same verb. The conjunctions *and, or,* and *nor* are frequently used to join compound subjects.

Rule Use a plural verb with most compound subjects connected by *and.*

PLURAL   *Melanie and Sam* **have** more than one hundred customers on their paper route.

My younger *brother and sister* **are visiting** our grandparents.

Rule Use a singular verb with a compound subject that refers to one person or thing or to something that is generally considered as a unit.

SINGULAR   My *classmate and* closest *friend* **is** Jean Jackson. [One person is both classmate and friend.]

Bacon and eggs **is** the best buy on the menu. [one dish]

The *long and* the *short* of it **is** that our team lost. [one condition]

Rule Use a singular verb with a compound subject made up of singular nouns or pronouns connected by *or* or *nor*. Use a plural verb with a compound subject made up of plural nouns or pronouns connected by *or* or *nor*.

SINGULAR   His *curve or* his *slider* **is going** to make the difference.

Either the *guard or* the *detective* **was** the first one on the scene.

PLURAL   No artificial *colorings or preservatives* **are** used in this beverage.

Neither *pens nor pencils* **are** needed for the test.

Rule When *or* or *nor* connects a compound subject made up of a singular subject and a plural subject, use a verb form that agrees in number with the subject that is closer to the verb in the sentence.

Either the *children or* their *mother* **has taken** the boat out. [The singular noun *mother* is closer to the verb.]

Neither the *truck nor* the *vans* **are** here yet. [The plural noun *vans* is closer to the verb.]

Although correct, these sentences sound awkward. Whenever possible, you should rewrite such sentences to eliminate the awkwardness.

> Either the children have taken the boat out, or their mother has.
>
> The truck is not here yet, nor are the vans.

Exercise 6 Agreement with Compound Subjects

On your paper, write the compound subject of each of the following sentences. Include the conjunction. Then write the verb or verb phrase that agrees in number with the compound subject.

> **SAMPLE** Clancy or Paula (is, are) the best rider.
>
> **ANSWER** Clancy or Paula—is

1. Desmond and Maria (is, are) designing the sets for the play.
2. Gary or Susan usually (gets, get) the highest grade on spelling tests.
3. Musicians or jugglers (has, have) always performed in this square.
4. Neither the players nor the fans (seem, seems) happy with the decision.
5. A raccoon or a squirrel (visits, visit) our garden every night.
6. Normal wear and tear on this truck (costs, cost) around two thousand dollars a year.
7. You or your friends (is, are) mistaken.
8. My best friend and severest critic (is, are) my aunt.
9. Either the calendar or our watches (is, are) off by a hundred years.
10. Either Donna or John (knows, know) the way to the station.

Indefinite Pronouns as Subjects

Rule Use a singular verb with a singular indefinite pronoun. Use a plural verb with a plural indefinite pronoun.

Indefinite pronouns (*page 13*) are pronouns that refer to people or things in general. Some indefinite pronouns are always singular and therefore always take singular verbs. The following are examples of singular indefinite pronouns:

anybody	everybody	nobody	somebody
anyone	everyone	no one	someone
anything	everything	nothing	something
each	much	one	
either	neither	other	

SINGULAR   *Everybody* **was** there.

Nothing **tastes** quite like a mango.

Some indefinite pronouns are always plural and therefore always take plural verbs. The most common plural indefinite pronouns are *several, both, few,* and *many.*

PLURAL   *Many* of the clowns **have** sad lives.

Several **are staying** behind.

The following indefinite pronouns can be either singular or plural, depending on how they are used in a sentence.

all	enough	most	plenty
any	more	none	some

The preceding indefinite pronouns are singular when they refer to one person or thing or to a portion of something.

SINGULAR   *Most* of the salad **is** gone. [*Most* refers to a portion of the salad.]

Some of the report **was** interesting. [*Some* refers to a part of the report.]

The indefinite pronouns on the preceding list are plural when they refer to a number of individual persons, places, or things. Sometimes an indefinite pronoun refers to a word that is not in the sentence but is understood.

> PLURAL   *Most* of my friends **are** on the team. [*Most* refers to several friends.]
>
> *More* **were moving** west every year. [*More* refers to *people,* which is understood.]

Exercise 7   Agreement with Indefinite Pronouns

Step 1: On your paper, write the subject of each of the following sentences. *Step 2:* Label each indefinite pronoun *Singular* or *Plural*. *Step 3:* Write the form of the verb or auxiliary verb that agrees in number with the indefinite pronoun.

> SAMPLE   All of the buses (is, are) running despite the snow.
>
> ANSWER   All—Plural; are

1. None of the team (wants, want) to guard Matthews.
2. Several (has, have) arrived but not mine.
3. Most of the bowlers (has, have) already practiced.
4. Everything (go, goes) wrong on a rainy day.
5. Somebody (has, have) claimed it already.
6. Plenty of tomatoes (is, are) needed for a tasty sauce.
7. Few of those scaly creatures (have, has) been seen before.
8. Some of those records (does, do) not sound right.
9. Everybody (was, were) crying at the end of the movie.
10. Neither of those cats (remembers, remember) me.

Collective Nouns as Subjects

A collective noun is a noun that names a group of people or objects. *Team, class, band,* and *club* are collective nouns. These nouns look singular, but they may take a singular or a plural verb, depending on how they are used in a sentence.

Rule If a collective noun refers to a group as a single unit, use a singular verb. If a collective noun refers to the individual members or parts of a group, use a plural verb.

SINGULAR   The class **is going** to San Francisco. [The class is going as a single unit.]

PLURAL   The class **have** all **agreed** to visit Alcatraz. [The class members have agreed as individuals.]

SINGULAR   The crowd **is** restless tonight. [The crowd is a unit.]

PLURAL   The crowd **are heading** for their seats. [The people in the crowd are acting as individuals.]

Nouns Ending in *s* as Subjects

Most nouns that end in *s* are plural. However, some nouns that end in *s* are plural in form but singular in meaning because they refer to a single thing. Examples of such nouns are *news, mumps, mathematics,* and *economics.* Such nouns take a singular verb.

SINGULAR   *Mumps* **is** a very painful disease.
                  Today's *news* from the hospital **sounds** good.
                  Economics **has** always **been** a mystery to me.

Other nouns ending in *s* take a plural verb, even though they refer to one thing or one pair. Examples are *scissors, trousers, pants, glasses, spectacles, clothes,* and *thanks.*

PLURAL   His *pants* **are** too short.
              These *scissors* **cut** anything.
              My *glasses* **were broken** in the fall.

Exercise 8 Subject-Verb Agreement On your paper, write the verb that agrees in number with the subject of each of the following sentences.

SAMPLE   The scissors (is, are) in the sewing basket.

ANSWER   are

1. My pliers (has been, have been) lost for weeks.
2. The news from the mine (was, were) good.
3. The team (is, are) headed west for the championships.
4. Economics (is, are) of special concern to the energy industry.
5. The crowd (was, were) waving their programs.
6. Mathematics (is, are) a tool of science.
7. The committee (has, have) gone their separate ways.
8. These tweed trousers (has been, have been) shortened.
9. The herd (was, were) scattering in every direction.
10. The physics of flight (was, were) known to Leonardo da Vinci several centuries ago.

Titles as Subjects

The title of a book, story, play, movie, television program, musical composition, or magazine refers to an individual work. A title is therefore singular, even though it may include plural words.

Rule   Use a singular verb with a subject that is a title.

Plants and Animals **includes** photographs of wildlife.
Wheels is my favorite magazine.
"The Survivors" **was written** by Elsie Singmaster.

Words of Amount and Time as Subjects

Rule   Use a singular verb with words and phrases that express a fraction, a measurement, an amount of money, a distance, or specific intervals of time when they refer to a single unit.

SINGULAR   *Two meters* **is** all the lead that she had.
Seventy-two hours **was** all the time left.
Two hundred dollars **is** enough to buy a computer.

Rule Use a plural verb when an interval of time or an amount of money is considered as a number of separate units.

PLURAL *Six weeks* **have gone** by almost unnoticed.

Three quarters **are needed** for the washing machine.

Exercise 9 Titles, Amounts, and Time On your paper, write the form of the verb that agrees in number with the subject.

SAMPLE The last ten miles of the race (was, were) slow and painful.

ANSWER were

1. Twenty dollars (is, are) all that I have.
2. *Sports Extra* (was, were) canceled this season.
3. (Is, Are) "Birches" by Robert Frost a children's poem?
4. *Seven Brides for Seven Brothers* (features, feature) some athletic dance routines.
5. Twenty-five minutes (means, mean) the difference between being on time and being late.
6. Two thirds of the money (has, have) been recovered.
7. Four gallons (is, are) all it will hold.
8. "After Twenty Years" (is, are) my favorite O. Henry story.
9. *Horses and Hazards* (tells, tell) about courage and danger.
10. Two hours sometimes (seems, seem) like two years.

Assignment Subject-Verb Agreement Write ten sentences in which you use the following words or groups of words as subjects. Use *has* or *have, is* or *are, was* or *were, seems* or *seem* in your sentences as verbs or as auxiliary verbs.

SAMPLE her father or her mother

ANSWER Her father or her mother has promised her a new watch.

1. she
2. they
3. Huck or Tom
4. the books on the shelf
5. a box of crackers

6. the students or their teacher
7. some of his stories
8. some of the story
9. everyone
10. most of my relatives

Subject-Verb Agreement

Suppose that you have written a story about an unusual person. A friend has offered to illustrate it by drawing the main character. You need to tell your friend how the character should look in the drawing. In a paragraph describe the physical appearance of the person in your story. Some of your sentences should have phrases that separate the subject from the verb, such as *the color of her eyes*. Other sentences should have compound subjects, such as *his beard and his hair*. Be sure that the subjects and verbs agree in number.

6.3   Correct Use of Pronouns

Because pronouns have different forms to show person, number, gender, and case, it is important to learn the correct use of each form.

6.3a   Pronoun Antecedents

The **antecedent** of a pronoun is the word that the pronoun refers to or replaces in a sentence. A pronoun must agree with its antecedent in number, gender, and person (*pages 10–11*).

antec.

Tim made **his** first soup in cooking class. [The pronoun *his* refers to the antecedent *Tim.*]

antec.

To surprise **his** mother, **he** added some of **her** favorite flavorings to the soup. [The pronouns *his* and *he* replace the antecedent *Tim.* The pronoun *her* refers to the antecedent *mother.*]

Agreement in Number

Rule Use a singular pronoun to refer to a singular antecedent. Use a plural pronoun to refer to a plural antecedent.

Here is a list of singular and plural pronouns:

SINGULAR	PLURAL
I, me, my, mine	we, us, our, ours
you, your, yours	you, your, yours
he, him, his	they, them, their, theirs
she, her, hers	
it, its	

SINGULAR   After *Alfred* finished the song, **he** smiled at **his** mother.

antec.

PLURAL   The *girls* put **their** soccer ball away.

antec.

Rule Use a plural pronoun to refer to two or more singular antecedents joined by *and*.

plural

Elias and Virginia are going to bring **their** sisters along.

Rule   Use a singular pronoun to refer to two or more singular antecedents joined by *or* or *nor*.

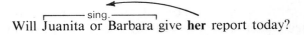

Will Juanita or Barbara give **her** report today?

Indefinite Pronouns as Antecedents.   The indefinite pronouns listed here are usually singular in meaning. When they are antecedents, use singular pronouns to refer to them.

anybody	everybody	nobody	somebody
anyone	everyone	no one	someone
anything	everything	nothing	something
each	much	one	
either	neither	other	

SINGULAR   *Anyone* can forget **his** shoulder pads.

Everything was on **its** correct shelf.

Some indefinite pronouns are plural in meaning, such as *several, many, both,* and *few.* When they are antecedents, use plural pronouns to refer to them.

PLURAL   *Several* have already paid for **their** yearbooks.

Some indefinite pronouns can be either singular or plural in meaning. Use singular or plural pronouns to refer to these indefinite pronouns, depending on the meaning of the sentence.

all	enough	most	plenty
any	more	none	some

SINGULAR   **Most** of the comedian's *routine* had lost **its** freshness. [The indefinite pronoun *Most* refers to the singular noun *routine.* The pronoun *its* refers to the singular antecedent *Most.*]

PLURAL   **Most** of the jokes had lost **their** freshness. [The indefinite pronoun *Most* refers to the plural noun *jokes.* The pronoun *their* refers to the plural antecedent *Most.*]

Collective Nouns as Antecedents. When an antecedent is a collective noun, the pronouns that refer to it should agree in number with the collective noun (*page 6*).

SINGULAR   The *committee* is giving **its** report now. [The committee is acting as a single unit.]

PLURAL   The *committee* are still arguing about **their** report. [The committee members are acting as individuals.]

Exercise 1   Agreement in Number   *Step 1:* On your paper, write the antecedent of the pronouns in parentheses. *Step 2:* Label each antecedent *Singular* or *Plural. Step 3:* Write the pronoun that agrees in number with the antecedent.

SAMPLE   Theodore and Abe used (their, his) new gloves at practice.

ANSWER   Theodore and Abe—Plural; their

1. Mrs. Jenkins or my mother will lend us (her, their) tape recorder.
2. The band will give (its, their) first concert next week.
3. Most of the trees had gypsy moths in (its, their) branches.
4. Alice and Barbara demonstrated (her, their) new calculators.
5. Tom or Pietro has asked for (his, their) money back.
6. All of the jury members studied (his, their) notes carefully.
7. Neither of my sisters remembered (her, their) camera.
8. Either will gladly give a couple of hours of (her, their) time.
9. I have several plants, and I water (it, them) every week.
10. Some of the students have not claimed (his, their) bus passes.

Agreement in Gender

Rule Use a pronoun that agrees with its antecedent in gender.

The **gender** of a noun or pronoun can be either masculine, feminine, or neuter (*page 11*). When the gender of an antecedent is masculine, use *he, him,* or *his* to refer to the antecedent. When the gender of an antecedent is feminine, use *she, her,* or *hers* to refer to the antecedent. When the gender of an antecedent is neuter, use *it* or *its* to refer to the antecedent.

MASCULINE   *Jeff* vacuumed **his** room and cleaned the kitchen.

FEMININE   *Mrs. Clinton* likes **her** new lawn mower.

NEUTER   The *storm* had spent **its** fury.

Sometimes it is not clear whether the antecedent is masculine or feminine. You can often use *his or her* to show that the antecedent could be either gender.

Everyone in the audience showed **his or her** approval.

Using *his or her* to refer to the same antecedent sometimes sounds awkward. It is usually better to rephrase the sentence so that both the antecedent and the pronoun are plural.

AWKWARD   A *surgeon* always scrubs **his or her** hands before surgery.

BETTER   *Surgeons* always scrub **their** hands before surgery.

Exercise 2   Agreement in Gender   On your paper, complete each of the following sentences with a pronoun that agrees in gender with its antecedent. Draw an arrow from each pronoun to its antecedent.

SAMPLE   Somebody left __?__ gym shirt in the locker room.

ANSWER   Somebody left his or her gym shirt in the locker room.

1. Susan brought __?__ new fishing rod on the trip to Ontario.
2. Everybody brought __?__ books to the assembly.
3. Ms. Carver showed us __?__ vacation slides.
4. My uncle flies __?__ own airplane.
5. The car lost one of __?__ hubcaps.
6. Someone put __?__ lunch in my locker by mistake.
7. A police officer always does __?__ best to prevent crime.
8. Bill has promised to play __?__ ukelele.
9. Will the owner please move __?__ car?
10. The colt lay next to __?__ mother.

Agreement in Person

Rule   Use a pronoun that agrees in person with its antecedent.

Pronouns are in either the first person, the second person, or the third person (*page 10*). First-person pronouns refer to the speaker or speakers. Second-person pronouns refer to the person or persons being spoken to. Third-person pronouns refer to person(s) or thing(s) being spoken about.

FIRST PERSON   I may baby-sit for **my** aunt.

SECOND PERSON   Will **you** lend me **your** pencil?

THIRD PERSON   **He** left **his** sweat shirt in the park.

Do not use *you* or *your* when the first person is clearly needed.

I like working after school because I meet such interesting people. [not *you meet*]

The indefinite pronoun *one* is in the third person. When *one* is an antecedent, use a third-person singular pronoun to refer to it.

One can always spend more of **his or her** free time reading. [not *your free time*]

Exercise 3   Pronoun Agreement   On your paper, complete each of the following sentences with a pronoun that agrees in person with its antecedent. Tell whether you used a first-person, second-person, or third-person pronoun. In your sentences, be sure that the pronouns also agree in number and gender with their antecedents.

SAMPLE   I repaired __?__ bicycle with spare parts.

ANSWER   I repaired my bicycle with spare parts.—First person

1. John and I will take __?__ bikes on the trip.
2. Did Beatrice remember to bring __?__ records?
3. Sam and Diane wasted __?__ time at the auction.
4. I take __?__ sister to the park every Saturday.
5. I like dancing because __?__ can exercise while having fun.
6. One can only do __?__ best.
7. The Venezianos left __?__ daughter with a baby sitter.
8. Many of you have not finished __?__ assignments.
9. The runners took __?__ marks.
10. Brady and Anita lent __?__ speakers to the dance committee.
11. The last time Brad wore his earphones, __?__ almost forgot where he was going.
12. Someone left __?__ bicycle in the driveway.
13. One should do __?__ work first.
14. Not everyone is as prompt at doing __?__ reports as you are.
15. The sunbeam never found __?__ way to the forest floor.

6.3b   Pronoun Case

Personal pronouns have three different forms, or **cases,** to show how they are used in a sentence.

NOMINATIVE CASE   I am a movie buff. [The pronoun *I* is the subject.]

OBJECTIVE CASE   Old movies interest **me**. [The pronoun *me* is the direct object.]

POSSESSIVE CASE   **My** hobby is watching old movies. [The possessive pronoun *My* shows ownership.]

Here are the forms for the three pronoun cases:

NOMINATIVE   I, you, he, she, it, we, they

OBJECTIVE   me, you, him, her, it, us, them

POSSESSIVE   my, mine, your, yours, his, her, hers, its, our, ours, their, theirs

Notice that the pronouns *you* and *it* are the same in the nominative and objective cases.

Pronouns in the Nominative Case

Rule   When a pronoun is a subject or a predicate nominative, use the nominative case.

SUBJECT
   They cleaned out the vacant lot.
   Has **she** planted a garden yet?

PREDICATE NOMINATIVE
   I was sure that the goalie was **she**.
   The flute player is **he**.

In informal usage, such as in a conversation among friends, people often say "It is me" instead of "It is I." In formal usage—that is, in most serious conversations and in writing—you should use the correct form, "It is I."

Pronouns in the Objective Case

Rule   When a pronoun is a direct object or an object of a preposition, use the objective case.

DIRECT OBJECT
>   The manager paid **us** for delivering groceries.
>   Did Elvin ask **them** for help with the posters?

OBJECT OF A PREPOSITION
>   This talk is just between you and **me**.
>   Behind **them** loomed a shadow.

Pronouns in Compound Constructions

Pronouns are sometimes used in a compound subject, in a compound direct object, or in a compound object of a preposition. A pronoun joined to a noun or another pronoun by *and, or,* or *nor* may pose a problem in pronoun usage. To decide which case to use, say the sentence to yourself without the noun or other pronoun and the conjunction.

>   Jan and **I** found a puppy in the park. [**Think:** **I** found]
>   The puppy followed Jan and **me** home. [**Think:** followed **me**]
>   It will make a fine pet for you and **me**. [**Think:** for **me**]

Exercise 4 Nominative or Objective Case?   On your paper, write the pronoun that is correct in each of the following sentences.

>   **SAMPLE**   Sid and (I, me) grew up together in Portland.
>   **ANSWER**   I

1. Mrs. Griffith and (I, me) will greet the new students.
2. The soloists will be Jenny and (he, him).
3. Between you and (I, me), I think that this dessert is too sweet.
4. May I speak to you and (she, her)?
5. Those exercises are too easy for Mother and (I, me).
6. Laurie and (I, me) have been friends since kindergarten.

7. Are you and (they, them) joining us?
8. The bridesmaids are my sister and (I, me).
9. It most definitely was not (I, me)!
10. Should Anita and (I, me) meet you at five o'clock?

Assignment Compound Constructions Use each of the following compound constructions correctly in an original sentence.

> **SAMPLE**   you and I
> **ANSWER**   The winner will be you and I.

1. you and me
2. she and I
3. Natalie and him
4. her mother and she
5. she and you
6. my friend and I

Pronouns in the Possessive Case

Possessive pronouns show to whom or to what something belongs.

Rule Use these possessive pronouns to replace or refer to nouns that show ownership: *mine, yours, his, hers, its, ours,* and *theirs*.

The possessive pronouns listed in the rule can replace nouns as subjects, predicate nominatives, and objects.

> SUBJECT   **Hers** is the striped goalie stick.
>
> PREDICATE NOMINATIVE   The maple desk is now **ours**.
>
> DIRECT OBJECT   I don't want your books; I want **theirs**.
>
> OBJECT OF A PREPOSITION   Mr. Righetti was happy with all the tryouts except **mine**.

Note: A possessive pronoun is written without an apostrophe (*page 219*).

Rule   Use these possessive pronouns to modify nouns: *my, your, his, her, its, our,* and *their.**

> **Your** new *position* has not been decided.
> **Their** *goal* was too ambitious.
> The tree has lost **its** *branches.*

Exercise 5   Possessive Pronouns   On your paper, complete each sentence with a possessive pronoun. Tell whether each pronoun that you write is used as a subject, a predicate nominative, a direct object, or an object of a preposition.

SAMPLE	The victory is finally __?__.
ANSWER	The victory is finally ours.—Predicate nominative

1. __?__ is the pink limousine with the running board.
2. Being a star has always been __?__ dream.
3. This table is ours; that one is __?__.
4. Your report is too short; __?__ is too long.
5. My books are under __?__.
6. __?__ may not be the best painting in the show, but it's the best I can do.
7. Those muddy sneakers must be __?__.
8. Your turn is after __?__.
9. She gave __?__ seat to an older woman.
10. __?__ is the best voice I have ever heard.

Who and *Whom*

When *who* and *whom* introduce questions, they serve as **interrogative pronouns.** *Who* is in the nominative case. *Whom* is in the objective case.

---

* The words *my, your, his, her, its, our,* and *their* are sometimes called pronominal adjectives.

Rule If an interrogative pronoun is a subject or a predicate nominative, use *who*. If it is an object, use *whom*.

It is sometimes difficult to tell whether the interrogative pronoun in a question is a subject or an object. For example:

(Who *or* Whom) did you ask for help?

To decide whether to use *Who* or *Whom,* rearrange the question into a declarative sentence.

You did ask whom for help. [The interrogative pronoun *whom* is the object of *did ask.* **Whom** did you ask for help?]

Now study these sentences carefully:

SUBJECT
Who washed the most cars? [*Who* is clearly the subject.]

PREDICATE NOMINATIVE
Who can that be? [**Think:** That can be **who.** *Who* is the predicate nominative after the linking verb *can be.*]

DIRECT OBJECT
Whom did you see at the car wash? [**Think:** You did see **whom.** *Whom* is the direct object.]

OBJECT OF A PREPOSITION
To **whom** does this sponge belong? [**Think:** The sponge does belong to **whom.** *Whom* is the object of the preposition *To.*]

In informal usage, such as in everyday conversations, people often use *who* to ask a question, without considering whether it is a subject or an object. In formal usage, such as in a serious conversation or in writing, you should follow the rules for using *who* and *whom.*

INFORMAL Who did you ask to the party?

FORMAL Whom did they appoint as ambassador?

Exercise 6 *Who* or *Whom*? On your paper, write *who* or *whom* to complete each of the following sentences correctly. Consider all the sentences to be formal.

SAMPLE   __?__ will you be taking to Camp David, Mr. President?

ANSWER   Whom

1. __?__ discovered the vaccine for polio?
2. To __?__ should the refund be sent?
3. __?__ will the general take on the tour of the Pentagon?
4. __?__ is selling tickets for the awards dinner?
5. __?__ has the mayor invited to the reception?
6. __?__ can it be at this time of night?
7. With __?__ are you going?
8. __?__ did you choose as a partner?
9. __?__ is coming to the concert?
10. For __?__ are you knitting that scarf?

Exercise 7 **Pronoun Case** On your paper, write the pronoun that is correct in each of the following sentences.

SAMPLE   You or (I, me) can help with the dishes.

ANSWER   I

1. (Who, Whom) can you ask for information about pollution?
2. Is this letter for Dad or (I, me)?
3. The winner is either Les or (he, him).
4. Dad asked Tom and (I, me) for our complete attention.
5. Save a place for Sheila and (I, me).
6. Are you and (she, her) helping or not?
7. After (who, whom) did Lincoln become President?
8. Carl and (she, her) won the blue ribbon for training the best dog in the show.
9. The Morrisons, Gladys, and (I, me) drove to the beach.
10. Let's keep this between you and (I, me); we'll never make it to the finals.

6.4 Correct Use of Modifiers

Misuse of adjectives and adverbs can make your sentences hard to understand. In this section, you will practice avoiding some common errors in the use of modifiers.

6.4a Comparison of Adjectives

Most adjectives have three degrees of comparison: the positive, the comparative, and the superlative.

In the **positive degree,** an adjective assigns a quality to a person, a place, a thing, or an idea. No comparison is made.

POSITIVE   The pond is **clear.**

John is **smart.**

In the **comparative degree,** an adjective compares one person, thing, place, or idea with another one.

COMPARATIVE   The pond is **clearer** than the lake.

John is **smarter** than I am.

In the **superlative degree,** an adjective compares one person, thing, place, or idea with at least two others.

SUPERLATIVE   That pond is the **clearest** pond in the state.

John is the **smartest** student in the class.

One-Syllable Adjectives.   If an adjective has only one syllable, add *-er* to form the comparative and *-est* to form the superlative. In some cases you must drop a final *e* or double a final consonant before adding the suffix (*Unit 17*).

fine, finer, finest

thin, thinner, thinnest

Two-Syllable Adjectives. For most two-syllable adjectives, add *-er* to form the comparative and *-est* to form the superlative. In some cases, you must change a final *y* to *i* before adding the suffix.

> mellow, mellower, mellowest
> lazy, lazier, laziest

If a two-syllable adjective is difficult to pronounce when *-er* and *-est* are added, you form the comparative and the superlative by using *more* and *most* instead.

> brittle, more brittle, most brittle
> cautious, more cautious, most cautious

Adjectives of Three or More Syllables. If an adjective has three or more syllables, always form the comparative and superlative degrees by using *more* and *most* before the positive form.

> energetic, more energetic, most energetic
> glorious, more glorious, most glorious

Comparisons Using *Less* and *Least*. For comparisons showing less of a quality, form the comparative and superlative degrees by using *less* and *least* before the positive form.

> angry, less angry, least angry
> lucky, less lucky, least lucky

Irregular Comparisons. Some adjectives do not form comparisons according to the preceding rules. The best way to learn the correct forms of irregular comparisons is to memorize them.

> good, better, best   bad, worse, worst
> many, more, most   ill, worse, worst
> much, more, most   far, farther, farthest
> little, less, least   far, further, furthest

Exercise 1 Comparative and Superlative Forms
On your paper, write the comparative and superlative forms
of each of the following adjectives.

  SAMPLE   extraordinary
  ANSWER   more extraordinary, most extraordinary

1. nice   6. fuzzy
2. ugly   7. loose
3. tall   8. dull
4. helpful   9. peculiar
5. strange   10. unusual

Exercise 2 Degrees of Comparison   On your paper,
list each adjective in the following sentences and write its degree of comparison.

  SAMPLE   Jones is faster at the hurdles than Lombard is.
  ANSWER   faster—Comparative

1. Alice was always the calmest of the Stevenson children.
2. You are the least athletic person I know.
3. The sky suddenly became dark.
4. This lettuce tastes more bitter than last year's.
5. These dance routines are the hardest I've ever done.
6. That kitten is friskier than this one.
7. My mother is shorter than I am.
8. The oldest parrot in the pet shop is thirty.
9. I am becoming less nervous about the contest.
10. My younger brother plays the bassoon.

Exercise 3 Irregular Comparisons   On your paper,
write the specified form of the adjective in parentheses.

  SAMPLE   I feel (*good*—comparative) than I did
           yesterday.
  ANSWER   better

173

1. Jed eats (*many*—comparative) vegetables than he used to.
2. Please, let's have (*little*—comparative) noise.
3. This is the (*bad*—superlative) cold I've ever had.
4. The (*good*—superlative) time to go to the park is in the late afternoon.
5. I feel (*ill*—comparative) now than I did this morning.
6. How can you have read (*many*—comparative) pages than I have?
7. Edmonton is the (*far*—superlative) away from home I've ever been.
8. This is the (*little*—superlative) homework we've had in a long time.
9. He feels (*bad*—comparative) about this than we do.
10. Because I'm the oldest, I have the (*many*—superlative) chores.

Exercise 4   Comparisons with Adjectives   On your paper, write each sentence, using the specified form of the adjective in parentheses.

> **SAMPLE**   Our class has had the (*few*—superlative) absences this week.
>
> Our class has had the fewest absences this week.

1. The (*near*—superlative) factory is only about a mile from here.
2. She is very (*active*—positive) in the local dental association.
3. He is the (*thin*—superlative) boy I have ever seen.
4. I'm sure this is a (*good*—positive) way to study for the test tomorrow.
5. Is algebra (*difficult*—comparative) than geometry?
6. That is the (*good*—superlative) salad I've ever tasted.
7. Today we played the (*tough*—superlative) game of the season.
8. You need a (*good*—comparative) lock on that door.
9. Here is the (*sharp*—superlative) pencil I have.

10. This is the (*expensive*—comparative) of the two jackets that I want to buy.

6.4b   Comparison of Adverbs

You can use adverbs to compare two or more actions. Like adjectives, adverbs have three degrees of comparison.

POSITIVE   Tom walks **fast.**

COMPARATIVE   Ed walks **faster** than Tom.

SUPERLATIVE   Joe walks the **fastest** of all the hikers.

The comparative degree of an adverb is used when comparing the actions of two persons or things. The superlative degree is used when comparing the actions of one person or thing with the actions of more than one other person or thing.

Like adjectives, most one-syllable adverbs form the comparative and the superlative by adding -*er* and -*est* to the positive form.

    fast, faster, fastest   hard, harder, hardest

Adverbs that end in -*ly* form the comparative and superlative by using *more* and *most* or *less* and *least* before the positive form.

    gently, more gently, most gently
    brightly, less brightly, least brightly

Like adjectives, some adverbs have irregular comparisons. Memorize these forms:

    well, better, best   little, less, least
    badly, worse, worst   much, more, most
    far, farther, farthest
    far, further, furthest

Exercise 5 Comparative and Superlative Forms
On your paper, write the comparative and superlative forms
of each of the following adverbs.

SAMPLE   much

ANSWER   more, most

1. slowly   3. poorly   5. well   7. fast
2. far   4. low   6. quickly   8. diligently

Exercise 6 Comparisons with Adverbs   On your
paper, write the correct form of the adverb given in parentheses for each sentence.

SAMPLE   They arrived (*early*) than you.

ANSWER   earlier

1. This car runs (*smoothly*) than that one.
2. Of the three brothers, Bill works the (*hard*).
3. The sun shone (*brightly*) yesterday than today.
4. Nell sings (*good*) than I.
5. Sarah dances the (*gracefully*) of all the students.
6. Some people study (*efficiently*) than others.
7. They came (*late*) than we expected.
8. She spoke (*intelligent*) than you.
9. Can't you skate (*faster*) than that?
10. Our dog barks (*loudly*) than yours.

Assignment Making Comparisons   Make a comparison by using each of the following groups of words in a sentence. Use precise adjectives and adverbs and correct
comparative and superlative forms.

SAMPLE   chess, checkers

ANSWER   Chess is more challenging than checkers.

1. movies, television
2. city, suburbs
3. oranges, grapefruit, lemons
4. police officers, firefighters

6.4c   Using Comparisons Correctly

Rule Avoid double comparisons.

Use either the suffixes *-er* and *-est* or the words *more* and *most* to form the comparative and the superlative degrees of adjectives and adverbs. Do not use *-er* or *-est* when you use *more* or *most*.

INCORRECT   The fruit was the **most bitterest** I've ever tasted.

CORRECT   The fruit was the **bitterest** I've ever tasted.
The fruit was the **most bitter** I've ever tasted.

Exercise 7   Correct Use of Comparisons   On your paper, rewrite the following sentences to make the comparisons correct. Errors include incorrect use of the comparative and superlative degrees, incorrect forms, and double comparisons.

SAMPLE   I ran more faster than Ruth Swartz.
ANSWER   I ran faster than Ruth Swartz.

1. I feel more better after drinking the broth.
2. She is the curiousest person I have ever known.
3. That is the most fattest dog on the block.
4. My cold is worser than yours.
5. Which is most valuable, pewter or brass?
6. Dale is the most strongest player on the team.
7. Nothing is worser than losing a shoe.
8. They are becoming more friendlier.
9. Who is taller—you, Lucy, or Lynn?
10. Our cat is more smarter than yours.

6.4d   Placement of Modifiers

Rule   Place a modifier as close as possible to the word that it modifies.

A misplaced modifier can make your sentence unintentionally funny and may make the meaning unclear.

MISPLACED ADJECTIVE
Blue and gentle, the swimmer looked at the ocean.
[What is blue and gentle—the swimmer or the ocean?]

CLEAR
The swimmer looked at the **blue and gentle** ocean.
[The adjectives *blue* and *gentle* clearly modify *ocean.*]

MISPLACED PREPOSITIONAL PHRASE
With the face of a rainbow trout, the scientist studied the rare lizard. [Who has the face of a trout—the lizard or the scientist?]

CLEAR
The scientist studied the rare lizard **with the face of a rainbow trout.** [The prepositional phrase clearly modifies *lizard.*]

To correct a sentence with a misplaced modifier, you must first find the word being modified. Then place the modifying word or phrase as close as possible to the word that it modifies. Be sure not to change the intended meaning of your sentence.

In the following example, a misplaced adverb makes the meaning of the sentence unclear. Notice that the two rewritten sentences have different meanings.

MISPLACED ADVERB
My adviser told me **often** to study. [Did the adviser say "study often," or did the adviser give the advice often?]

CLEAR
>   My adviser **often** told me to study. [I was told often.]
>   My adviser told me to study **often**. [I should study often.]

Exercise 8 Misplaced Modifiers   On your paper, rewrite the following sentences so that the misplaced modifiers are placed correctly. If necessary, rewrite a sentence in two ways to show two different meanings.

>   SAMPLE   Cold and windy, the geologists pushed on through the Yukon's weather.

>   ANSWER   The geologists pushed on through the Yukon's cold and windy weather.

1. My fencing teacher told me frequently to shift my weight from one foot to the other.
2. What do you think of the President as a student?
3. We walked after the fine dinner to the reservoir and back.
4. Thomas received a cat from his sister that loved to eat fish.
5. We were asked on the next day to see the principal.
6. Buy enough wool to finish your sweater before starting.
7. Fran watched the gulls swoop over the beach in a floppy hat.
8. Everyone praised the singer's performance after the concert.
9. He stumbled almost at the water's edge.
10. My grandmother's doctor told her often to eat.

6.5   Usage Notes

The following pages contain an alphabetical list of words and phrases that often present usage problems. Each entry describes the correct formal usage, and most entries include examples. Cross-references help you to locate related information. Refer to these usage notes when you are in doubt about which form to use.

a, an   Use the article *a* before words beginning with a consonant sound. Use the article *an* before words beginning with a vowel sound. The article that you use depends on the beginning *sound* of the word, not on the first *letter.*

> a hotel   a ewe   a unanimous decision
> an hour   an end   an upper tooth

a while, awhile   *Awhile* is an adverb. *While* is a noun and can be used as the object of a preposition. Do not use *for* or *in* before the adverb *awhile.*

> I will be ready in **a while.** [not *in awhile*]
> We'd like to stop here **awhile.** [adverb]

accept, except   *Accept* is a verb meaning "to agree" or "to receive." *Except* is a preposition meaning "leaving out" or "but."

> She will **accept** the advice with good spirit.
> Everyone is here **except** Marilyn Davis.

ain't   Do not use *ain't.*

all ready, already   *All ready* means "entirely ready" or "prepared." *Already* means "previously."

> They were **all ready** for the debate.
> The auditorium was **already** half filled when we arrived.

all right, alright   *All right* means "satisfactory," "unhurt," "correct," or "yes, very well." *Alright* is not a word. Do not use it.

> Everything seems to be **all right** in spite of the four-hour blackout.
> **All right,** who wants to give the first answer?

almost, most   The adverb *almost* means "nearly." The adjective *most* is the superlative of *many.*

> They attended **almost** every game. [*not* most]
> **Most** people with new jobs are very cautious at first.

among, between   Use *among* when you are discussing three or more persons or things. Use *between* when you are discussing two persons or things.

> She divided the fish **among** the four cats. [*not between*]
> She divided the fish **between** the two cats.

any more, anymore   The phrase *any more* describes quantity. The adverb *anymore* means "at present" or "from now on."

> I don't have **any more** time.
> They do not live in Clinton **anymore.**

beside, besides   *Beside* means "next to." *Besides* means "in addition to."

> They camped **beside** the river.
> **Besides** a bicycle, I own two pairs of roller skates.

between, among   See *among, between.*

between you and me   Do not use the nominative case *I* as the object of the preposition *between.*

> prep.   obj.
> Between you and **me,** I think they're not coming.

bring, take   Use *bring* when you mean "to carry to." Use *take* when you mean "to carry away."

> **Bring** your homework to class.
> **Take** your books home over the weekend.

bust, busted   Do not substitute these words for forms of the verbs *break* and *burst.*

> My bicycle is **broken** again. [not *busted*]
> Don't **burst** those balloons. [not *bust*]

can, may   *Can* means "be able to." *May* means "have permission to." Do not confuse the two.

> I **can** play the clarinet.
> **May** I play for you? [not *Can*]

can't hardly, can't scarcely   *Hardly* and *scarcely* are negative words. Do not form double negatives by using *hardly* and *scarcely* with other negative words, such as *can't.* (See also *double negative.*)

> I **can hardly** wait until the weekend. [not *can't hardly*]
> We **can scarcely** see the crack in the wall. [not *can't scarcely*]

could of, might of, should of, would of   Do not use these phrases for *could have, might have, should have,* and *would have.*

different from, different than   Do not use *different than.* One thing differs *from* another.

> Their defense is **different from** ours. [not *than*]

double negative   A double negative is the use of two negative words when only one is called for. Do not use *not* or *n't* with words such as *no, none, never,* or *nothing.* (See also *can't hardly, can't scarcely.*)

> I have **no** clean shirts.
> I **don't** have **any** clean shirts.
> The plumber found **nothing** wrong with the pump.
> The plumber did**n't** find **anything** wrong with the pump.

double subject A double subject is the incorrect use of a noun and a pronoun together as a single subject. Use one or the other, but not both.

INCORRECT My sister she is in the Air Force.

CORRECT My sister is in the Air Force.

CORRECT She is in the Air Force.

every day, everyday *Every day* (separate words) means "each day." Do not confuse it with *everyday,* an adjective meaning "ordinary."

> **Every day** we get closer to our goal.
> The store carries **everyday** objects like pots and pans.

every one, everyone *Every one* refers to each individual in a group. It is usually followed by *of. Everyone* is an indefinite pronoun meaning "everybody" or "every person."

> **Every one** of these magazines is torn.
> **Everyone** had a good time at the play.

fewer, less Use *fewer* to refer to things that you can count. Use *less* to refer to quantities that you cannot count. Also use *less* to refer to amounts of time, money, or distance when the amount is a single quantity.

> **Fewer** cars were on the road.
> Studying spelling should take **less** time now.
> I have **less** than five dollars to my name.

good, well Always use *good* as an adjective. Use *well* as an adverb to mean "ably" or "capably" or as an adjective to mean "satisfactory" or "in good health."

> She is a **good** athlete. [adjective]
> She always performs **well**. [adverb meaning "ably"]
> She feels **well**. [adjective meaning "in good health"]

got, have   *Got* is the past tense of the verb *get*. It means "obtained." Avoid using *got* with *have* or in place of *have*.

> I **got** some paperbacks at the library. [obtained]
> I **have** a cold. [not *have got* or *got*]

in, into   Use *in* to mean "within" or "inside." Use *into* to suggest movement toward the inside from the outside.

> Robert was **in** the living room.
> Robert tiptoed **into** the kitchen. [not *in*]

its, it's   *Its* is a possessive pronoun. *It's* is the contraction for "it is." Do not confuse the two.

> The puppy was chasing **its** tail. [possessive pronoun]
> **It's** never going to work. [contraction]

kind of, sort of   Do not use these phrases to mean "somewhat" or "rather."

> The team was feeling **rather** let down after the season. [not *kind of*]

lay, lie   *Lay* is a verb meaning "to put or place something somewhere." It always takes a direct object. *Lie* is a verb meaning "to rest" or "to recline." It does not take a direct object. See page 135 for the principal parts of these irregular verbs.

> We always **lay** our jackets on the ground. [*Jackets* is the direct object of *lay*.]
> They **were laying** about three hundred bricks a day. [*Bricks* is the direct object of *were laying*.]
> James **laid** his calculator on the bench. [*Calculator* is the direct object of *laid*.]
> Where **could** I **have laid** my notebook? [*Notebook* is the direct object of *could have laid*.]

The verbs in the following sentences are all forms of the verb *lie*. They do not have direct objects.

Before supper I always **lie** down for a nap.
Broken glass **was lying** on the porch.
During half time, I **lay** on the bench.
Those orders **have lain** on the general's desk for days.

learn, teach *Learn* means "to gain knowledge." *Teach* means "to give knowledge." Do not use *learn* when you mean "to give knowledge."

I **am learning** to paint with oils.
Mr. DeVose **is teaching** me how to paint. [not *is learning*]

leave, let *Leave* means "to go away from" or "to abandon." *Let* means "to allow."

We will **leave** the school at exactly 3:00 P.M.
The planes **left** on schedule.
My aunt **let** us stay up late. [not *left*]
Let us begin. [not *Leave*]

less, fewer See *fewer, less.*

lie, lay See *lay, lie.*

loose, lose *Loose* is an adjective meaning "not tight," "not bound," or "free." *Lose* is a verb that means "to fail to find," "to misplace," or "not to win."

Is this coat too **loose** on me?
I **lose** my pencils all the time.

many, much Use the adjective *many* to describe things that you count (*toys, persons*). Use the adjective *much* to describe things that you cannot count (*water, justice*). When used as indefinite pronouns, *much* is singular and *many* is plural.

>Not **much** fruit is left, but we have **many** vegetables.
>*Much* of her wealth **has** been given away. [singular]
>*Many* **are** hoping for donations. [plural]

may, can   See *can, may.*

may be, maybe   In the verb phrase *may be, may* is an auxiliary. The adverb *maybe* means "perhaps."

>Herbert **may be** absent today.
>**Maybe** he is visiting his grandfather.

might of   See *could of, might of, should of, would of.*

most, almost   See *almost, most.*

much, many   See *many, much.*

nohow, noway   *Nohow* and *noway* are not standard English. Do not use them. You can, however, use *no way* correctly as two words.

INCORRECT   **Noway** can I solve that problem.

CORRECT   There is **no way** to solve that problem.

off, off of   After *off,* the word *of* is not necessary. Do not use *off* in place of *from.*

>The napkin fell **off** the tray. [not *off of*]
>Victor got that record **from** his brother. [not *off*]

passed, past   *Passed* is the past tense of the verb *pass. Past* can be a noun, an adjective, an adverb, or a preposition depending on its use in a sentence.

I **passed** the test on chemical elements. [verb]
In the **past**, people worked very hard. [noun]
This **past** fall, I stopped watching football. [adjective]
The car sped **past**. [adverb]
Turn left just **past** the bakery. [preposition]

raise, rise   *Raise* is a verb that means "to lift something" or "to make something go upward." *Raise* always takes a direct object. *Rise* is a verb that means "to move upward." It does not take a direct object. *Raise* is a regular verb. See page 135 for the principal parts of the irregular verb *rise*.

> They **raised** the barn roof in a day. [*Roof* is the direct object of *raised*.]
> When the judge entered, everyone **rose**. [*Rose* has no direct object.]

real, really   *Real* is an adjective; *really* is an adverb.

> Is that **real** silk? It is **really** smooth. [not *real*]

said, says   *Said* is the past tense of the verb *say*. *Says* is the third person singular of the present tense. Do not substitute *says* for *said*.

> Dad turned and **said,** "Here are the keys." [not *says*]

set, sit   *Set* is a verb meaning "to place." It always takes a direct object. *Sit* is a verb meaning "to rest in an upright position." It does not take a direct object.

> I **set** the book down. [*Book* is the direct object of *set*.]
> Please **sit** down. [no direct object]

should of   See *could of, might of, should of, would of.*

slow, slowly   *Slow* is an adjective. *Slowly* is an adverb. You may use *slow* as an adverb in informal speech,

187

especially in commands or for emphasis. In writing, however, use *slowly* when an adverb is needed.

> Drive **slow**. [adverb, informal]
> The train moved **slowly** into the station. [adverb]

sort of, kind of See *kind of, sort of.*

supposed to, used to Remember to spell *supposed* and *used* with a final *d*. Both are past forms and must end with a -*d*.

> I was **supposed** to go to the park today. [not *suppose*]
> I am **used** to this glove. [not *use*]

take, bring See *bring, take.*

teach, learn See *learn, teach.*

than, then Use *than* in comparisons. Use *then* as an adverb to show a sequence of events.

> This winter is going to be colder **than** last winter.
> First, we jogged a mile; **then** we walked a mile.

their, there, they're *Their* is the possessive form of the pronoun *they*. *There* points out a place or introduces a sentence. *They're* is the contraction of *they* and *are*.

> **Their** new car got caught in the flood.
> The noise came from over **there**.
> **There** are three things that we might do.
> **They're** already at the station.

this here, that there Simply say *this* or *that*. *Here* or *there* is unnecessary.

> **This** store sells the freshest eggs. [not *this here store*]
> **That** photo makes him look like a movie star. [not *that there photo*]

used to, supposed to   See *supposed to, used to.*

well, good   See *good, well.*

who's, whose   *Who's* is the contraction of *who is* or of *who has. Whose* is the possessive form of *who.* Do not confuse the two.

> **Who's** at the door? [contraction]
> **Whose** book is this? [possessive]

would of   See *could of, might of, should of, could of.*

Unit Practice

Practice 1

A. Correct Use of Verbs *(pages 131–144)* On your paper, rewrite the following sentences, correcting all errors in the use of verbs.

1. Last summer I swum almost a mile without stopping.
2. I hope we completed this project by next Tuesday.
3. Hurry! Janice be leaving right now!
4. All night the puppy has laid on our bed.
5. The fox stealed away into the night.
6. Every spring we have went on a week's vacation.
7. Mother catched the cat in her knitting bag.
8. All the puddles had froze overnight.
9. Sheila started to run before the starting gun has been fired.
10. By the end of the week, we will have saw every vacant apartment in the city!

B. Subject-Verb Agreement *(pages 144–158)* On your paper, write the verb form that correctly completes each of the following sentences.

11. The roses (is, are) wilting.
12. A mass of mud and twigs (hangs, hang) from the branch.
13. Here in my pocket (is, are) my missing gloves.
14. Bill and Mario (enjoys, enjoy) the cooking class.
15. Neither the horses nor the cattle (seems, seem) well.
16. Several of the tickets (remains, remain) to be sold.
17. The group (has, have) all contributed three hours of work to this project.
18. Gymnastics (is, are) my favorite sport.
19. Three fourths of the papers (shows, show) good effort.
20. (Has, Have) the construction been completed?

C. Correct Use of Pronouns *(pages 158–170)* On your paper, write a pronoun that is correct in each sentence. Be sure that the pronoun you use makes sense and that it agrees with the antecedent, if there is one.

21. Several still owe the teacher __?__ book reports.
22. Forward the mail to __?__ promptly so that she can answer it without delay.
23. The last ones to finish were Jasper and __?__.
24. __?__ did you ask about the deadline?
25. Stanley and Janice opened __?__ desks.
26. Elaine brought one of __?__ drawings.
27. Did somebody drop __?__ book?
28. I think __?__ project will win first place.
29. My cousins and __?__ enjoy family parties.
30. Carl was overjoyed that the trophy was finally __?__.

D. Correct Use of Modifiers *(pages 171–179)* On your paper, rewrite the following sentences, correcting all errors in the use of modifiers.

31. Foggy and wet, they sailed the small boat into the night.
32. She was the tallest of the twins.
33. The tribe lived in the most primitivest of conditions for generations.
34. Does Dominic feel iller than he did yesterday?
35. Jacqueline finished this revision most quickly than the other.
36. My memory is poorer.
37. This sweater is more softer than that one.
38. What is the most far you have ever hiked?
39. For years I told him about the dream I have had.
40. What is the wonderfulest surprise you have ever had?

(Continue on the next page.)

Practice 2

On your paper, rewrite the following passage, correcting all errors in the use of verbs, pronouns, and modifiers.

From the time I was four years old in the Appalachian Mountains, we spent ours summers in a small log cabin. There were a living room with a small kitchen attached to one side. Above the living room was one large room using for sleeping. Wrapping around the front, one side of the cabin had a large porch. Large enough to seat three children, hanging on the side porch was a swing. The only running water we been having was the stream at the bottom of the hill in front of the cabin. The summers I been spending in that cabin are the most happiest and the vividest childhood memories I have.

Unit Tests

Test 1

A. Correct Use of Verbs *(pages 131–144)* On your paper, rewrite the following sentences, correcting all errors in the use of verbs.

1. The heat breaked the vase.
2. By tomorrow I corrected my mistake.
3. At this time the meeting continued.
4. A pipe in the basement has broke.
5. By six o'clock they had ate supper.
6. Each morning the alarm rung at seven-thirty.
7. The mayor spoke to the reporters briefly.
8. Ben had maked the bed.
9. Mom came home before we have washed the dishes.
10. By July the temperature will have rose to one hundred degrees.

B. Subject-Verb Agreement *(pages 144–158)* On your paper, write the verb form that correctly completes each sentence.

11. The books (was, were) lying on the floor.
12. The beat of the drums (makes, make) me want to march.
13. There (sits, sit) the glass for the window.
14. Joyce and Seth (shares, share) the paper route.
15. The nurses or the doctor (answers, answer) the phone.
16. Neither (wants, want) the assignment.
17. The band (schedules, schedule) performances on Saturdays.
18. The scissors (was, were) dull.
19. Ten minutes (has, have) gone by already.
20. (Is, Are) the reporter or the editor taking credit for the story?

(Continue on the next page.)

C. Correct Use of Pronouns *(pages 158–170)* On your paper, write the pronoun that correctly completes each sentence. Be sure that the pronoun you use makes sense and that it agrees with the antecedent, if there is one.

21. Most of the class cleaned out __?__ lockers.
22. Give it to __?__ so that I can examine it.
23. We were told to report to __?__.
24. Between you and __?__, I think we should have enough money.
25. Will Hank and Michelle bring __?__ records?
26. Dominick forgot the last few lines of __?__ speech.
27. Everything has to be put back in __?__ place.
28. I have to do __?__ chores before I can go outside.
29. My brother and __?__ are planning a party for our parents.
30. Since you forgot your anthology, I'll lend you __?__.

D. Correct Use of Modifiers *(pages 171–179)* On your paper, rewrite the following sentences, correcting all errors in the use of modifiers.

31. In the store window, the cat eyed the fish on display.
32. That is the handsomest of the two dogs.
33. I buy more fewer records than my friends do.
34. This is the goodest I've ever done on a test.
35. I think about my old neighborhood more oftener than I really want to.
36. This winter was colder.
37. My package is more prettier than yours.
38. This is the littlest snow that has ever fallen in February.
39. Often she told me that she was there.
40. Which plan do you think is the sensiblest?

Test 2

On your paper, rewrite the following passage, correcting all errors in the use of verbs, pronouns, and modifiers.

Jean Laffite was a Frenchman whom became a smuggler and a pirate along the coast of New Orleans in the early 1800s. He and his brother raid Spanish and neutral ships in the Gulf of Mexico with a fleet of ships at his command. In 1814 when the British were at war with the United States, them wanted him to help they attack New Orleans. However, he choosed to inform the United States of the British plans and offer their services to fight against England. Laffite fighted under General Andrew Jackson in the Battle of New Orleans. Although he received a pardon from President Madison, Laffite return to a life of piracy.

Unit 7

Mechanics

Unit Preview

Suppose that capital letters and punctuation marks did not exist. Imagine how difficult it would be to read this sign in the school cafeteria:

saladplate95centsspecialhotlun
ch100125withvegetablessoup50ce
ntsfruit30cents

Now imagine that one of your friends handed you this flyer for a dance in the school gymnasium:

dancetothemusicofalexan
draalmedaandassociatesfro
m70010001314yrolds10012yrolds75cents

These examples should help you understand why you must follow certain rules of capitalization and punctuation when you put your thoughts on paper. Without the rules of mechanics, writing can be very difficult to read.

For Analysis Answer the following questions about the cafeteria sign and the flyer.

1. Why are both passages difficult to read?
2. Rewrite one of the passages, inserting spaces where needed and correcting as many of the mistakes in mechanics as you can. Why is the rewritten passage easier to read?
3. Why is knowing the rules of mechanics important?

When you capitalize the first word of a sentence, your readers do not have to think about when a new thought begins. When you put a period or another mark at the end of a sentence, your readers know when a thought ends. Within a sentence, commas show pauses and mark important divisions between the parts of a sentence. Each punctuation mark makes your writing clearer to your readers. To write clearly, therefore, you must be able to use the rules of mechanics with ease. This unit will help you to learn and to practice those rules.

7.1 Capitalization

Capital letters are used for two main purposes in English: to show the beginning of a sentence and to show that a noun is a proper noun (*pages 4–5*).

7.1a Capitalization in Sentences

Rule Capitalize the first word of a sentence.

It was a day of nearly perfect weather.

Rule Capitalize the first word of a direct quotation that is a complete sentence. A **direct quotation** contains the exact words that a person has said, written, or thought.

Al said, "**Let's** go to the beach."
Mary thought, "**What** a beautiful day!"

Interrupted Quotation. When a quoted sentence is interrupted by an expression like *she said* or *they mumbled,* begin the second part of the quotation with a lower-case letter.

"Turn on the radio," said Lena, "**and** listen for the weather report."

New Sentence in a Quotation. If the second part of the quotation is a new sentence, put a period after the interrupting expression. Then begin the second part of the quotation with a capital letter.

"I think it may rain," someone said. "**Those** clouds certainly look threatening."

Rule   Capitalize the first word of each line in most poems even when the line is not a complete sentence.

The sea was wet as wet could be;
The sands were dry as dry.
You could not see a cloud, because
No cloud was in the sky.
                              Lewis Carroll, "The Walrus and the Carpenter"

Note: Some poets do not capitalize the first word of each line. If you copy a poem, be sure to follow the capitalization used by the poet.

Exercise 1   Capitalization in Sentences   On your paper, write the following sentences and lines of poetry. Use capital letters where they are needed. If no added capitalization is needed, write *None* on your paper.

SAMPLE   "it's too bad," said Tom, "that you don't enjoy escape stories."

ANSWER   "It's too bad," said Tom, "that you don't enjoy escape stories."

1. tomorrow is a holiday.
2. the trainer said, "that's a frisky pony."
3. What a great idea!
4. who has seen the wind?
   neither I nor you;
   but when the leaves hang trembling,
   the wind is passing through.
                              Christina Rossetti, "Who Has Seen the Wind?"

5. "hurry up," said Tom, "or we'll miss the cartoon."
6. the shopper asked, "are these local peaches?"
7. my friend wrote, "please visit me next weekend."
8. "that's all right," said my parents. "we know how you feel."
9. Kara thought, "how exciting space travel must be!"
10. It has been said that no one is perfect.

7.1b   Proper Nouns

Rule Capitalize the names of people and the initials that go with their names.

>   my sister **Jean**   **Cecilia S. Ramor**
>   **Herbert L. Cooper**   **Alice Toomey**

Family-Relationship Words. Capitalize words that show family relationships when they are part of a person's name or when they take the place of a person's name.

>   Today **Aunt Mary** leaves for Rome.
>   Is **Grandmother** going with her?

Do not capitalize family-relationship words when they are used as common nouns or when they are preceded by a possessive noun or a possessive pronoun.

>   I have six **aunts** and eight **uncles**.
>   My **grandmother** likes to travel.

Personal and Official Titles. Capitalize a personal or an official title or its abbreviation when it is used in direct address (*page 213*) or when it comes before a person's name.

>   DIRECT ADDRESS   Will you attend the meeting, **Mayor?**
>
>   BEFORE NAME   Yesterday **Mayor** Green attended several meetings.

>   **Mr.** Elliott   **Senator** Munson
>   **Congresswoman** Jeanette Rankin   **Dr.** Raja

Do not capitalize a preposition, a conjunction, or an article that is part of a title unless it begins a sentence.

the Reverend Mr. King   **Secretary of Labor** Perkins

Do not capitalize a title that follows a person's name unless it is the title of a head of a national government.

TITLE BEFORE NAME	TITLE FOLLOWING NAME
Senator Jonathan Smith	Jonathan Smith, **senator**
Coach Alicia Stagg	Alicia Stagg, **coach**
President John Adams	John Adams, **President**
Chancellor Helmut Kohl	Helmut Kohl, **Chancellor**

Do not capitalize a title that is a substitute for a person's name unless it is the title of a head of a national government.

The **governor** has an appointment with the **President.**

Capitalize the names and abbreviations of academic degrees or honors that follow a person's name. Capitalize the abbreviations *Sr.* and *Jr.*

David Burke, **Doctor of Divinity**   Alfred Svenson, **Jr.**
Rosanna Lum, **M.D.**   Theodore Brink, **Sr.**

Gods of Mythology. Capitalize the names of the gods of mythology. Do not capitalize the word *god* when it refers to the gods of mythology.

The Roman **god Jupiter** was originally the **god** of the sky.

Rule   Capitalize the names of particular places.

Place names include the names of countries, states, cities, mountains, streets, oceans, lakes, rivers, and so forth.

Nigeria	Rocky Mountains	Lake Erie
Alabama	Pacific Avenue	the Lee River
Salt Lake City	Pacific Ocean	North Road

Compass Points. Capitalize compass points that refer to specific geographic areas or that form part of a place name. Do not capitalize a compass point that merely shows direction or a general region.

> We moved to the **South** last winter. [**Think:** The *South* is a specific geographic area of the United States.]

BUT   We now live in **south** Florida.

> Have you ever visited **North** Dakota? [**Think:** *North Dakota* is the name of a state.]

BUT   I haven't been farther **north** than Nebraska.

Heavenly Bodies. Capitalize the names of planets, stars, and constellations. Do not capitalize *sun* and *moon*.

Orion	the Milky Way
Neptune	the North Star

Capitalize *Earth* when you mean this planet and only when the word does not have *the* before it.

The space shuttle will make three orbits before returning to **Earth.**

The satellite circled **the earth** every two hours.

Rule Capitalize words that name peoples, races, tribes, nationalities, and languages.

Danish	Chinese	Iranian	Zambian
Peruvian	Aztec	Mohawk	German

Rule Capitalize the names of days, months, holidays, special days, and special events. Do not capitalize the name of a season unless it is part of a proper noun.

Friday	Fall Festival	Yom Kippur
April	Arbor Day	spring

Rule   Capitalize the names of historical events, historical periods, awards, and documents.

the Civil War	the Nobel Prize
the Middle Ages	the Emancipation Proclamation

Rule   Capitalize the first and last words and all other important words in titles of books, movies, songs, works of art, and so forth. (See also pages 217, 225.)

BOOK	*To Kill a Mockingbird*
MOVIE	*A Night at the Opera*
SONG	"Now We'll Make the Rafters Ring"
PAINTING	*Mother and Child*

Conjunctions, Articles, and Prepositions in Titles. Capitalize a conjunction, an article, or a preposition only when it is the first or last word in a title. Capitalize any preposition that has five or more letters.

"**If** You but Knew"
"**A** Life in the Day of a Writer"
"Search **Through** the Streets of the City"

Rule   Capitalize the name of a school subject when it is a language or when it is followed by a course number.

Latin	history
Algebra II	home economics
Hebrew	History I
algebra	Economics 36

Rule   Capitalize the names of structures (buildings, bridges, monuments) and the names of organizations and their members (religions, businesses, government bodies, clubs, schools). In such names, do not capitalize the articles *a* and *the*.

the Sears Tower	the Aspen Pharmacy
the Golden Gate Bridge	the Senate
the Statue of Liberty	Yale University
Judaism	a Buddhist

Capitalize a word such as *college, university, high school, club, society,* or *store* only when it is part of a proper noun.

Seton Hall **University**	BUT	a small **university**
the Ogden Nash **Club**	BUT	a poetry **club**

Rule Capitalize trade names. Do not capitalize a common noun that follows a trade name.

Shinebrite car wax   **True-Sound** records

Rule Capitalize the names of ships, trains, rockets, planes, and spacecraft. (See also page 225.)

Atlas I	U.S.S. *Missouri*	the *Kitty Hawk*
the *Meteor*	the *Orient Express*	the *Enterprise*

Exercise 2 Capitalization of Proper Nouns On your paper, write each of the following phrases, using capital letters where necessary.

SAMPLE   the east coast of maine

ANSWER   the east coast of Maine

1. herbert c. hoover
2. uncle sam
3. my mother
4. governor grasso
5. the reverend flynn
6. elizabeth II, queen of england
7. the god mercury
8. easygrow plant food
9. indian ocean
10. luke seldon, d.d.s.
11. the southwest
12. the sun and the moon
13. northwest of spokane
14. dad's home computer
15. the nile river
16. saturn's rings
17. mount rushmore
18. lake oswego
19. elkhart, indiana
20. sycamore lane

Exercise 3 Capitalization of Proper Nouns On your paper, write each of the following words and phrases, using capital letters where necessary. Titles of books, songs, and so forth are underlined (italicized) or are enclosed in quotation marks. Include the underlining and the quotation marks in your answers.

SAMPLE   *a stranger on the ball club*
ANSWER   A Stranger on the Ball Club

1. cleer toothpaste
2. the orinox corporation
3. the kenyans
4. the *silver meteor*
5. the boston tea party
6. the planet pluto
7. the emmy awards
8. geometry II
9. central park
10. speedo sneakers
11. *gone with the wind*
12. wednesday night
13. the atomic energy commission
14. "fire and ice"
15. the university of hawaii
16. americans
17. the immigration act
18. a unitarian
19. flag day
20. history

7.1c   Other Uses of Capitalization

Rule   Capitalize the pronoun *I*.

Am **I** late?
You and **I** have been locked out.

Rule   Capitalize the letters in the abbreviations *A.D., B.C., A.M.,* and *P.M.* Capitalize the letters in the Postal Service state abbreviations.

anno Domini	**A.D.**	Alabama	**AL**
before Christ	**B.C.**	Missouri	**MO**
ante meridiem	**A.M.**	Ohio	**OH**
post meridiem	**P.M.**	Texas	**TX**

Note: Use the abbreviations *A.D., B.C., A.M.,* and *P.M.* with dates or times. *A.D.* precedes the date. *B.C.* follows the date.

I'll meet you at 11:00 A.M. [not *in the A.M.*]
from 44 B.C. to A.D. 33 [not *33 A.D.*]

Note: Use Postal Service state abbreviations only with ZIP codes in addresses.

Chelsea, **AL** 35043	Blue Rock, **OH** 43720
Independence, **MO** 64052	Gonzales, **TX** 78629

Exercise 4 Other Uses of Capitalization   On your paper, write each sentence, using capital letters where needed.

> SAMPLE   The game began at 3:04 p.m.
>
> ANSWER   The game began at 3:04 P.M.

1. After dinner, i did my homework, watched the news at 10:00 p.m., and was in bed by 11:00 p.m.
2. Attila the Hun invaded Gaul in a.d. 451.
3. Add the following line to my address: Richmond, va 23235.
4. This vase dates back to 200 b.c.
5. Sometimes i'm out of the house before 7:00 a.m.

Exercise 5 Capitalization   Write each sentence, using capital letters where needed.

> SAMPLE   he read *the red badge of courage* last year.
>
> ANSWER   He read <u>The Red Badge of Courage</u> last year.

1. the scientist galileo was the first to discover that the planet jupiter has several moons.
2. in 1941 congress passed a law saying that thanksgiving would be the fourth thursday in november.
3. vigdis finnbogadottir, president of iceland, is referred to as "president vigdis," as is the custom in her country.
4. after breakfast mother said, "stop at the supreme market on junction boulevard and buy some rediquick oatmeal and a box of sweetsun raisins."
5. the united nations was organized shortly after world war II.
6. my sister often studies her goverment I text until 11:00 p.m.
7. my father wrote on the letter "sara p. feldman, governor."

8. the moon shone over the amazon river, and venus sparkled brightly in the east.

9. the *washington post* reported that over the weekend the president would be at camp david.

10. last friday we saw *my fair lady,* the musical adaptation of george bernard shaw's *pygmalion.*

11. the strait of gibraltar is the gateway from the atlantic ocean to the mediterranean sea and separates europe from africa.

12. john marshall raised the prestige of the supreme court and molded the constitution into a living document.

13. we traveled north until we reached mount emmons, which is east of salt lake city.

14. the band at eisenhower park played "columbia, the gem of the ocean" and "the battle hymn of the republic."

15. according to *the age of fable,* apollo was the god of music, poetry, and medicine.

16. chill december brings the sleet,
    blazing fire, and christmas treat.

    sara coleridge, "the months"

17. valentina tereshkovna orbited the earth forty-eight times in *vostok VI.*

18. emerson blackhorse mitchel, a navajo, attended the institute of american indian arts and is the author of the poem "the path i must follow."

19. "look at the sky at 9:00 p.m.," wrote dad. "that's the best time to view the milky way."

20. yesterday, in a letter, i reminded my grandfather of our ZIP code: loveland, co 80537.

Assignment **Capitalization**   Many advertising copywriters do not use the rules of capitalization correctly. Look through several magazines and newspapers to find advertisements that break these rules. Cut out ten examples of broken rules and tape each one on a separate sheet of paper. Rewrite each advertisement, correcting the capitalization errors that the copywriter has made.

Using Capital Letters

Write a brief history of your family. Include the full names of all family members known to you (parents, brothers, sisters, grandparents, aunts, uncles, and so forth). Tell where and when the oldest and youngest members of your family were born. Identify those members of your family who have any of the titles discussed on pages 199–200. If any of your family members took part in a historical event or witnessed one, tell about that too.

Make your history specific and interesting to other members of the family. When you have finished writing, check your work carefully for correct capitalization.

7.2 Punctuation

Punctuation marks tell your readers when to stop and when to slow down. They also give other signals about your writing. In this section, you will explore the uses of punctuation marks.

7.2a The Period

Rule Use a period at the end of every declarative sentence (*page 85*).

The basketball team players run three miles every day.

The test began with an essay question.

Rule   Use a period at the end of a sentence that asks a polite question or gives a mild command.

> Will you please sweep the stairs.
> Throw the ball over here.

Rule   Use a period after an initial that is part of a person's name or title.

> **J. S.** Bach   Marva T. Peterson, **M.D.**

Rule   Use a period after most standard abbreviations. Do not use a period after abbreviations for the units of measurement and time. You should, however, use a period after *in.* to show that you are writing the abbreviation of *inch,* not the word *in.*

USE PERIODS

Dr.	doctor	**A.D.**	anno Domini
Sr.	senior	**Nov.**	November
A.M.	ante meridiem	**Tues.**	Tuesday

DO NOT USE PERIODS

h	hour	lb	pound
g	gram	kg	kilogram

Abbreviations for Companies and Organizations. Do not use periods when the abbreviation for the name of a company or an organization is all in capital letters.

> **CBC**   Canadian Broadcasting Company
> **NFC**   National Football Conference

Postal Service Abbreviations. Do not use periods with Postal Service abbreviations for states followed by the ZIP code. Use periods, however, with more traditional state abbreviations without the ZIP code.

> Duluth, **MN** 55803
> BUT   We are moving to Duluth, **Minn.,** next month.

Note: Avoid using abbreviations in your written work.

7.2b   The Question Mark

Rule   Use a question mark at the end of an interrogative sentence (*page 85*).

How do we get to the bridge?
Are we laughing at the same thing?

7.2c   The Exclamation Point

Rule   Use an exclamation point at the end of an exclamatory sentence (*page 85*).

What a clever dog he is!
I scored the winning goal!

Rule   Use an exclamation point after a forceful command.

Stop talking at once!
Get me to the airport right away!

Rule   Use an exclamation point after a strong interjection (*page 60*) or other exclamatory expression.

Bravo! You scored the winning point.
Good for you!

Exercise 1   End Punctuation and Abbreviations

The following sentences are written without periods, question marks, and exclamation points. On your paper, write the sentences correctly, using appropriate punctuation.

SAMPLE   Was Cicero born in 106 BC
ANSWER   Was Cicero born in 106 B.C.?

1. Select a career that you care about
2. Wow The runner just stole home plate
3. Maya Angelou went to school in Stamps, Arkansas

4. What a touching poem
5. The baby weighed 6 lb 4 oz at birth
6. Rev Mr. SJ Alonso, Jr, will award the diplomas
7. When are you leaving for California
8. Hang up this minute
9. The FBI is a division of the Department of Justice
10. Will you help me, please
11. I need to know the ZIP code for this address in Baltimore, Md
12. I rewrote the address as Baltimore, MD 21216

Exercise 2 Abbreviations   On your paper, write the correct abbreviation for each of the following words or phrases. If necessary, use your dictionary.

> **SAMPLE**   Captain
> **ANSWER**   Capt.

1. Senior
2. Doctor
3. gram
4. post meridiem
5. Professor
6. second

7. anno Domini
8. February
9. Federal Trade Commission
10. Avenue
11. American Federation of Labor
12. National Broadcasting Company

7.2d The Comma

Commas in a Series

Rule   Use commas to separate three or more items in a series. Put a comma after each item except the last.

> We saw **rubies, sapphires,** and **diamonds** at the museum.
> **Adventures, comedies,** and **mysteries** are popular kinds of books.

Do not use commas if all the items in a series are joined by conjunctions.

They traveled by camel **and** bus **and** truck.

Do not use commas to separate pairs of nouns that are thought of as a single unit.

— unit —
We had vegetable soup, **macaroni and cheese,** and fruit salad for lunch. [**Think:** *Macaroni and cheese* is thought of as a single unit.]

Prepositional Phrases. Use commas to separate three or more prepositional phrases in a series.

We searched near the thicket, under the tent, and along the stream.

Commas After Introductory Expressions

Rule Use a comma to show a pause after certain words or phrases at the beginning of a sentence.

Prepositional Phrases. Use a comma after a prepositional phrase of four or more words at the beginning of a sentence.

At the town's only hardware store, a crowd gathers every Saturday morning.
In case of fire, dial 911.

Yes, No, and Interjections. Use a comma to separate *yes, no,* and interjections, such as *oh* and *well,* from the rest of the sentence.

Yes, you did a good job.
Well, I can't really guess what my present is.

Confusing Sentence Parts. Use a comma to separate sentence parts that might be confusing if read together.

Two minutes before, the game had begun.

Exercise 3   Commas   On your paper, write the following sentences, using commas where necessary. If no commas are needed, write *None* on your paper.

> **SAMPLE**   Near the end of our trip we stayed at a motel with a heated swimming pool.
>
> **ANSWER**   Near the end of our trip, we stayed at a motel with a heated swimming pool.

1. The ship carried a cargo of teas spices and silk.
2. Well why didn't someone call me?
3. Soon after the rain stopped.
4. Of all outdoor activities we enjoy hiking the most.
5. Last night we watched a program about the Swiss Alps.
6. That horse looks old weak and sick.
7. Yes I'm going to the swim meet.
8. The performer sang of love of sadness and of pain.
9. Orpheus was handsome and brave and talented.
10. Far below the pilot could see a small village.
11. We hiked across the bridge along the riverbank and through the woods.
12. For breakfast we cooked potatoes bacon and eggs and griddle cakes.

Commas to Separate Sentence Parts

Rule   Use a comma before a coordinating conjunction that joins the simple sentences in a compound sentence.

> The underbrush was parched, **and** smoke rose from numerous fires.

Rule Use commas to set off certain words or phrases within a sentence.

Direct Address. Use a comma or a pair of commas to separate words of direct address from the rest of the sentence. The words of **direct address** name the person or persons spoken to.

Listen carefully, **everybody.**

I wish, **Emma,** that you would write more legibly.

Abbreviated Title or Degree. Use a comma or a pair of commas to set off an abbreviated title or a degree following a name.

We attended a lecture by John Osborne, **Ph.D.**

Al Steegstra, **Jr.,** seems to have grown another inch every time we see him.

Dates or Addresses. Use commas before and after the year when it is used with the month and the day. Use commas before and after the name of a state, province, or country, when it is used with the name of a city.

My cousin was born on **October 24, 1960,** on the way to the hospital.

Paris, France, is my grandmother's home.

Do not use a comma when only the month and the year are given. Do not use a comma between the state and the ZIP code.

We visited my uncle in Anchorage in **July 1982.**

Wales, WI 53183

Rule Use a comma after the salutation and the closing of a friendly letter.

Dear Aunt Maria,   Sincerely yours,

Exercise 4   Commas   On your paper, write the following sentences, using commas where necessary. If no commas are needed, write *None* on your paper.

SAMPLE   Lucy B. Hobbs D.D.S. graduated from the Ohio College of Dental Surgery in June 1886.

ANSWER   Lucy B. Hobbs, D.D.S., graduated from the Ohio College of Dental Surgery in June 1886.

1. A full moon peeked over the hills and coyotes howled in the distance.
2. Alan Ryall Ph.D. runs a network of seismographs throughout the West.
3. I started school in September 1973.
4. I wrote the following address on the package: 168 West Boston Road Hinckley OH 44233.
5. President Lincoln delivered the Gettysburg Address on November 19 1863 in Gettysburg Pennsylvania at the dedication of a national cemetery.
6. The letter was dated December 11 1909 and was in very poor condition.
7. Dear Jan
   My new address is 37 Bristol Place Bay Head NJ 08742. Don't forget! You promised to write first.
                                        Your friend
                                        Ann
8. John please rake the leaves.
9. Several dolphins were submerged in the pool but only the tops of their heads were visible.
10. My cousin's book was published on January 14 1983 in Denver Colorado by the Wildlife Press.

7.2e   The Semicolon

Rule   Use a semicolon in a compound sentence to separate two or more simple sentences that are not joined by a coordinating conjunction.

We watched the door; no one came in.
My tooth hurts; I must have a cavity.

BUT   I called the dentist, but he is on vacation.

Exercise 5 **Semicolons** In some of the following sentences, commas have been incorrectly used in place of semicolons. On your paper, write the sentences, substituting semicolons where necessary. If a sentence is already correct, write *Correct* on your paper.

SAMPLE   No one had come to meet me, I was alone in the big city.

ANSWER   No one had come to meet me; I was alone in the big city.

1. The small car came to a sudden stop, three people and a Great Dane climbed out.
2. The dock had disappeared under the water, only its piles were visible in the choppy bay.
3. The water is warm, and the fish are sluggish.
4. The bus stopped, everyone moved toward the front exit.
5. The contest ends on Monday, the winners will be announced before Friday.

7.2f   The Colon

Rule Use a colon to introduce a list of items. The statement before the list will often contain a demonstrative word (*these* or *those*) or an expression such as *the following* or *as follows*.

The **following** members will go on the trip to Chicago: **Becky Smith, Jay Rogers, Ben Murphy, and Barbara Chan.**
You will need **these** materials for the experiment: **two small beakers, one flask, and three test tubes.**

Rule   Use a colon to separate the hour and minutes in an expression of time and to separate the chapter and verse in a Biblical reference.

> At **12:37** P.M., my stomach began to growl.
> We read Psalms **131:2**.

Rule   Use a colon after the salutation of a business letter.

> Dear Mrs. Wirtz: Dear Sir or Madam:

Exercise 6   Colons   Some of the following sentences need colons. On your paper, write each sentence, using colons where necessary. If a sentence does not need a colon, write *None* on your paper.

> SAMPLE   The following family members missed our
>   reunion my grandparents, two uncles, and six
>   cousins.
>
> ANSWER   The following family members missed our
>   reunion: my grandparents, two uncles, and six
>   cousins.

1. These flowers were part of the bridal bouquet orchids, roses, and stephanotis.
2. Dear Madam
3. Does the chartered bus leave at exactly 6 30 A.M.?
4. Our literature course this year includes the following authors Poe, Whittier, and Longfellow.
5. He read Revelation 10 8-11.
6. The following people made decorations Roy, Jeanne, and Phil.

7.2g   Quotation Marks

Rule   Use quotation marks to show that you are quoting someone directly (*pages 197–198*). Put quotation marks at both the beginning and the end of the quotation.

"**I'm almost finished now,**"Jeff said.

"**After practice,**" said Jeff, "**let's go for a hike.**"

"**Think about it,**" he said. "**The foliage is too good to miss.**"

Do not use quotation marks with an indirect quotation. An **indirect quotation** is a retelling in the writer's words of what someone else has said, written, or thought.

INDIRECT QUOTATION   Judith said that she was ready to go.

DIRECT QUOTATION   Judith said, "**I'm ready to go.**"

Rule Each time the speaker changes, begin a new paragraph and use a separate set of quotation marks.

"**I think I hear something,**" said Paul, looking nervously around the room.

"**There you go again,**" said Beatrice with a laugh. "**Don't you ever give your imagination a rest?**"

Rule Use quotation marks to set off titles of short works such as stories, poems, songs, articles in newspapers and magazines, and the chapters or units in a book.

SHORT STORY   Have you read O. Henry's "**The Third Ingredient**"?

SHORT POEM   A popular Frost poem is "**The Road Not Taken.**"

MAGAZINE ARTICLE   I usually read "**Science People**" in *Discover* magazine.

UNIT IN BOOK   You are now studying "**Mechanics,**" the seventh unit in this book.

Other Punctuation with Quotation Marks. The following rules will help you decide where to put other punctuation marks when you write a passage that includes quotation marks.

Rule Use a comma or commas to separate an explanatory phrase, such as *he said* or *Kim concluded,* from the quotation itself. Place the commas outside the opening quotation marks but inside the closing quotation marks.

> Nell asked, "May I go with you?" [The comma is outside the opening quotation marks.]
>
> "We'll pick you up at noon," Ron replied. [The comma is inside the closing quotation marks.]

Rule Place a period inside the closing quotation marks.

> A fascinating mystery story is Poe's "The Purloined Letter."

Rule Place a question mark or an exclamation point inside the quotation marks when it is part of the quotation. Place a question mark or an exclamation point outside the quotation marks when it is part of the entire sentence. If both the quotation and the sentence require a question mark or an exclamation point, put the punctuation mark inside the quotation marks.

INSIDE THE QUOTATION MARKS

> Someone asked, "Where are you going?" [The question mark is part of the direct quotation.]
>
> I just read Bliss Carman's "What Is It to Remember?" [The question mark is part of the title.]
>
> Who asked, "When is the test?" [Both the direct quotation and the sentence require a question mark.]

OUTSIDE THE QUOTATION MARKS

> Have you read "The Purloined Letter"? [The question mark is part of the entire sentence.]
>
> Did you say, "Come here"? [The question mark is part of the entire sentence.]

Exercise 7   Quotation Marks Some of the following sentences need quotation marks. On your paper, write each sentence, using quotation marks where they are needed and punctuating each direct quotation correctly. Make a new paragraph if necessary. If a sentence does not need quotation marks, write *None* on your paper.

SAMPLE	To belittle, said Grandpa, is to be little.
ANSWER	"To belittle," said Grandpa, "is to be little."

1. I like the poem Sea Fever by John Masefield.
2. Father, you can't go on, said Dick. I've got to go on, said Mr. Park. The mail must go through.
3. Did someone say, I move we adjourn?
4. Mrs. Cohen asked, Do you know how to apply mouth-to-mouth resuscitation?
5. Did Bret Harte or O. Henry write The Outcasts of Poker Flat?
6. Grandmother, begged Elsie, please tell us about your interview with President Wilson.
7. Mr. Selby warned us that it would rain.
8. On the bus ride we sang The Bear Went over the Mountain, A Hole in the Bucket, and You Are My Sunshine.
9. Dad asked what I wanted for my birthday dinner.
10. The police officer asked, What's the rush?

7.2h   The Apostrophe

Rule   Use an apostrophe to show possession.

Singular Nouns. Use an apostrophe and an *s* (*'s*) to form the possessive of singular nouns, including those ending in *s, x,* or *z.*

the terrier that belongs to Sue	Sue's terrier
the buzz of the bee	the bee's buzz
the roar of the lynx	the lynx's roar

Plural Nouns. Use an apostrophe and an *s* (*'s*) to form the possessive of a plural noun that does not end in *s.*

the ties belonging to the men	the men's ties
the yokes on the oxen	the oxen's yokes

Plural Nouns Ending in s. Use an apostrophe alone to form the possessive of a plural noun that ends in *s.*

the books belonging to the boys   the boys' books
the barking of the dogs   the dogs' barking
the bikes belonging to the Wus   the Wus' bikes

Possessive Pronouns. Do not add an apostrophe to a possessive pronoun: *yours, ours, his, hers, its, theirs.* These words already show possession.

The dog drank **its** water.
Sometimes I'm glad that old car is still **ours.**

Rule   Use an apostrophe to replace letters or numbers that have been omitted to form a contraction.

it is   **it's**   you would   **you'd**
should not   **shouldn't**   1983   **'83**

Rule   Use an apostrophe and an *s* (*'s*) to form the plural of letters, numbers, signs, symbols, and words referred to as such. Underline (italicize) the letters, numbers, signs, symbols, and words, but do not underline (italicize) the *'s.*

Did you forget to cross your *t*'s?,
All the *30*'s and *70*'s line up on the other side of the gym.
Every time I think of working, I think of *$*'s.
I wish I didn't use so many *uh*'s when I speak.

Exercise 8   Apostrophes   In the following sentences, plurals, possessives, and contractions have been written incorrectly. On your paper, write the sentences, using the correct forms.

SAMPLE   Your *a*s look just like *o*s.
ANSWER   Your a̲'s look just like o̲'s.

1. They used rows of *x*s as a border on the poster for the sale.
2. Isnt that your moms car?

3. The Jeffersons cat caught it's tail in the garage door.

4. Heres my book; wheres yours?

5. Orpheus' music was so lovely that the gods permitted him to enter Hades.

6. It took us four hours to paint the Davises fence.

7. Is that Tillies glove or your's?

8. Theres enough food to satisfy even Tims hearty appetite.

9. This year Im making my little sisters birthday present.

10. Dont you agree that Mark Twains stories are usually funny?

Exercise 9 Possessives On your paper, write the possessive of each of the following words. Then use each possessive in a sentence.

SAMPLE	fox
ANSWER	fox's—The fox's cunning often keeps it out of tight spots.

1. men
2. firefighter
3. Dickens
4. Thomas
5. rats

6. sisters
7. Japan
8. Max
9. Dr. Sidney Katz
10. the Smiths

Exercise 10 Contractions On your paper, use the contraction of each of the following pairs of words in a sentence.

SAMPLE	will not
ANSWER	won't—I won't watch any more television on school nights.

1. can not
2. does not
3. it is
4. could not
5. are not

6. do not
7. is not
8. I will
9. we are
10. they are

7.2i   The Hyphen

Rule Use a hyphen to show the division of a word at the end of a line. Always divide a word between its syllables.

Carl says that he dreams of horses whenever he hears a whinnying sound. (not *whe-never*)
Tomorrow we have tests in math, in history, and in science. (not *hi-story*)

Do not divide a word so that one letter stands by itself. Do not divide a one-syllable word.

INCORRECT	a-bout	th-rough
CORRECT	about	through

Prefixes and Suffixes. Divide a word with a prefix after the prefix. Divide a word with a suffix before the suffix.

AFTER PREFIX	BEFORE SUFFIX
un-natural [unnatural]	laugh-ing [laughing]
pre-view [preview]	lov-able [lovable]

Compound Words. Divide a compound word (*page 5*) that is written as one word between the words that form the compound. Divide a hyphenated compound word at the hyphen.

BETWEEN WORDS	AT HYPHEN	
school-	sister- *or*	sister-in-
child	in-law	law

Rule Use a hyphen after the prefixes *all-, ex-,* and *self-.* Use a hyphen to separate any prefix from a word that begins with a capital letter.

all-state	**non**-Taiwanese	BUT	**non**violent
ex-major leaguer	**inter**-American	BUT	**inter**act
self-discipline	**post**-Revolution	BUT	**post**war

Rule Use a hyphen to separate compound numbers from *twenty-one* through *ninety-nine*.

	fifty-six	seventy-three
BUT	one thousand	three hundred

Exercise 11 Hyphens On your paper, write each of the following words. Use hyphens to show the correct way or ways that each word may be divided at the end of a line. If necessary, use your dictionary.

SAMPLE   policy

ANSWER   pol-icy or poli-cy

1. evening
2. science
3. saxophone
4. ex-president
5. funny
6. mechanic
7. invent
8. all-state
9. foot-pound
10. vitamin

Exercise 12 Hyphens On your paper, write the following sentences, using hyphens where needed. If no hyphens are needed, write *None* on your paper.

SAMPLE   I expect to be practicing law when I'm twenty four.

ANSWER   I expect to be practicing law when I'm twenty-four.

1. "Is self improvement really for me?" asked Jane as she did her forty third pushup.
2. The ex governor's remarks were anti English and pro French.
3. That shop is nonunion.
4. He is a student of post Revolutionary politics.
5. My grandmother will celebrate her ninety fifth birthday on the twenty second of next month.

7.2j   The Dash

Rule   Use a dash to show a sudden change in thought or in speech or to indicate an interruption. If the sentence continues, use a second dash to mark the end of the interruption.

> "I wish—**oh, how I wish**—for a new bike!"
> "Hello, hello, is this the **resi**—" Then the phone went dead.

Note: Avoid overusing dashes in your written work.

Exercise 13   Dashes   On your paper, write the following sentences, using dashes where needed.

> SAMPLE   The best fruit for the money I'm serious is the tomato.
>
> ANSWER   The best fruit for the money—I'm serious—is the tomato.

1. "What do you think no, no, not you about the election?" asked Ned.
2. "There was a loud noise, then a smell like" gasped Sue as she grabbed her throat and began to cough.
3. What was it I stopped to think that had me so worried?
4. Ogden Nash you must have heard of him was a funny poet.
5. We're supposed to use black ink whoops, I don't have any.

Punctuation in Dialogue

When you write a narrative that has dialogue, you must be especially careful to punctuate correctly. Punctuation tells the reader when one person has stopped talking and when another person has started talking. It also separates the dialogue from the descriptive and explanatory parts of a story.

Think of an episode from history that you would have liked to observe. Do some reading about that episode. Then imagine that you had been there, and write an eyewitness account of the episode. In your account be sure to use dialogue. After you have written the account, check closely to make sure that you have used correct punctuation.

7.3 Italics

Italic type (*slanted letters such as these*) is used for a variety of reasons. When you are writing or typing something that should be in italic type, use underlining to represent the italics.

Rule Italicize (underline) the titles of books, lengthy poems, newspapers, television series, paintings, ships, and so forth. Do not capitalize or italicize (underline) articles (*a, an, the*) at the beginning of a title unless they are part of the title.

> *The Pigman*   *60 Minutes*
> the *Dallas Times Herald*   Picasso's *Guernica*

> I like to read *Mystery* magazine after midnight when there is a full moon.
> My mother sailed to England on the *Queen Elizabeth II*.

Rule Italicize (underline) letters, numbers, symbols, and words when you are referring to them as such.

> I didn't learn to spell *alphabet* until several years after I had learned the alphabet.
> That's *Mudd* with two *d*'s.
> People often confuse *can* with *may*.

Exercise Italics In the following sentences, words that should be underlined to indicate italic type are not. On your paper, write each sentence correctly, underlining all the words that should be in italic type.

> **SAMPLE** We saw the play The Merchant of Venice last week.
>
> **ANSWER** We saw the play <u>The Merchant of Venice</u> last week.

1. From Mary O'Hara's novels, Marion chose Green Grass of Wyoming.
2. The reporter on Face the Nation asked questions about the budget.
3. When Newsweek arrives, I always skim the sports section first.
4. We always read the movie reviews in the Chicago Tribune.
5. Clutz's painting Joggers captures the energy of an urban street.
6. Is between a preposition?
7. Leonard often forgets to cross his t's and dot his i's.
8. I misspelled parallel.
9. I loved the ending of The Cheese Stands Alone, a novel by Marjorie Prince.
10. When I was younger, I used to make every s and every 2 backwards.

Assignment   Titles   Make a "Favorite Titles" poster. On a large sheet of paper, print the titles of your favorite book, long poem, television show, painting, newspaper, magazine, and play. Use capital letters correctly (*page 202*) and underline the titles to indicate italic type. Illustrate all or some of the titles with pictures from old magazines.

7.4   Using Numbers in Writing

Rule   Spell out numbers of *one hundred* or less and all numbers that are rounded to hundreds.

> My grandfather, who is **ninety-one** years old, sailed to the United States in 1906.

Almost **four hundred** people showed up for the game.

BUT   About **450** people showed up.

Rule Use numerals for numbers greater than *one hundred* that are not rounded numbers.

After the game, **65,013** people spent three hours getting out of the traffic jam that they created.

BUT   Only **eleven hundred** people went to the rock concert.

Rule If a number appears at the beginning of a sentence, spell out the number or rewrite the sentence.

INCORRECT   **117** citizens attended the meeting.

CORRECT   **One hundred seventeen** citizens attended the meeting.

CORRECT   There were **117** citizens at the meeting.

Note: The word *and* is unnecessary in writing out numbers except those between *one hundred* and *one hundred and ten, two hundred* and *two hundred and ten,* and so forth.

One hundred seventeen citizens

BUT   **One hundred and seven** citizens

Rule Use words to express the time unless you are writing the exact time with the abbreviation A.M. or P.M..

The surprise party is at **five o'clock.**

We are leaving here at **quarter past four.**

BUT   The party is at **4:30** P.M.

Rule Use numerals to express dates, street numbers, room numbers, apartment numbers, telephone numbers, page numbers, and percentages. Spell out the word *percent*.

February 29, 1960	Apartment 4	page 79
112 Pulaski Street	555-4896	75 percent

Rule Use numerals without the endings *-st, -nd, -rd, -d,* and *-th* to name the day of the month.

INCORRECT June **6th,** 1944   April **1st**

CORRECT June **6,** 1944   April **1** or **first** of April

Exercise Numbers in Writing On your paper, write the following sentences, using the correct forms for numbers in writing. If no corrections are needed, write *None* on your paper.

SAMPLE 2550 fans cheered the team to victory.

ANSWER A crowd of 2550 fans cheered the team to victory.

1. On August 17th I will be 13.
2. We are traveling twenty-two hundred miles to see my sister graduate on June 3.
3. We received a rent increase of seventeen percent.
4. You will find some excellent illustrations of frog muscles on pages 23 and 29.
5. The noise from Apartment Three can be deafening.
6. The President will speak at three fifteen P.M.
7. He will arrive at the hotel around three o'clock.
8. The fishing boat unloaded nine hundred forty-seven pounds of salmon.
9. If I had 10 dollars for every time I've forgotten my key, I would have 1000 dollars by now.
10. We live at 2527 East Fairway in Apartment 6E.

7.5 Proofreading Symbols

Proofreading symbols are often used to identify and correct errors in composition. Use them when you proofread and revise your writing.

∧	insert something	on her way the market
#	space	was the first person to
¶	begin new paragraph	of one another. There is a time
∿	transpose letter or words	our goal clearly is
ℓ	delete	studied the ~~the~~ history of
◯	close up letters	do g
....	let it stand (under something crossed out)	He was ~~obviously~~ unaware of the time.
≡	capitalize	an ancient persian carpet
/	make lower case	She wrote to her Mother.

7.6 Manuscript Form

Unless your teacher gives you other instructions, use the
following guidelines when you prepare a manuscript.

Suggestions for Handwritten Manuscripts

Paper. Write compositions on standard paper (8½ by 10
inches or 8½ by 11 inches). Write on one side only.

Ink. Use black or blue ink.

Margins.   Leave margins of 1½ inches at the left side and 1 inch at the right side. The left margin must be even.

Title.   Write the title of the composition in the center of the top line. Skip at least one line between the title and the first paragraph. Do not put quotation marks around the title.

Indentation.   Indent the first line of every paragraph about 1 inch.

Suggestions for Typewritten Manuscripts

Paper.   Use standard white typewriter paper (8½ by 11 inches). Double space and use only one side of the paper.

Ribbon.   Use a black ribbon.

Margins.   Leave margins of 1½ inches at the left side and 1 inch at the right side. The left margin must be even. The right margin should be as even as possible. On all pages except the page with the title on it, place the first line at least 1 inch below the top of the page. Leave a margin of 1 inch at the bottom of every page.

Title.   Center the title at least 2 inches from the top of the page. Do not put quotation marks around the title. Begin the first paragraph four lines below the title.

Indentation.   Indent the first line of every paragraph five spaces.

Labeling and Numbering Pages

Write your name, the subject, and the date (in that order) in the upper-right corner of the first page. On every page except the first page, put the page number in the upper-right corner. Use Arabic numerals.

If your paper consists of more than one page, attach the pages at the upper-left corner with a staple or a paper clip.

Unit Practice

Practice 1

A. Capitalization *(pages 197–207)* On your paper, write each of the following sentences, correcting all errors in capitalization.

1. "be sure to drive carefully," eric said. "the roads may be slippery from the snow."
2. when sylvia and uncle ron arrive on friday, we will have a celebration.
3. mr. donovan met congresswoman alice murphy last week.
4. they are learning about danish customs in geography class.
5. the class learned a great deal about the planet saturn at the freeport planetarium.
6. "don't forget," sheila added, "to get some gloweez light bulbs at the store."
7. has monica read *the old man and the sea* yet?

B. Punctuation *(pages 207–225)* On your paper, write each of the following sentences, correcting all errors in punctuation.

8. Ask Dr Marvin S Robertson to step into the office
9. On February 23 1980 my niece was born in Duluth Minnesota
10. Did you get tickets for the NHL game
11. Henry needs the following items a pair of scissors some paper clips and a stapler Sue said
12. The winning entry in the students writing contest is Marks short story its entitled The Path to the North
13. Marie bought bread salt and pepper and milk at the store.
14. As the time drew near everyone stood up

C. Italics *(pages 225–226)* On your paper, copy each of the following sentences. Underline the words that should be italicized.

(Continue on the next page.)

15. I spelled the word referred incorrectly on my paper.
16. The British steamship Queen Mary crossed the Atlantic in August 1938.
17. Mario forgot that address contains two d's.
18. Science Today is an immensely popular television series.
19. Do you have a + key on your typewriter?

D. Using Numbers in Writing *(pages 226–228)* On your paper, copy each of the following sentences, using the number form that correctly completes each sentence.

20. More than (80 percent, eighty percent) of the club members went on the trip.
21. On October (27th, 27), we will gather at (296, two hundred ninety-six) Harris Road at (ten forty-five, 10:45) A.M.
22. (725, Seven hundred twenty-five) gift certificates will be given away on April (29th, 29).
23. Look on page (eighty-three, 83) of your directory for a list of about (350, three hundred fifty) area codes.
24. Justine wrote Room (fifty-six, 56) on the envelope and left it with the desk clerk.

Practice 2

Rewrite the following passage. Make all necessary corrections in capitalization, punctuation, italicizing (underlining), and the use of numbers.

> a banyan is an unusual tree that grows in india it gets its name from the hindu word banian meaning trader the tree grows in a rather peculiar way it has a big central trunk and many smaller trunks scattered around it the smaller trunks grow down from the branches and take root as soon as they touch the soil a single banyan can resemble a small forest the largest known banyan is located on the island of sri lanka this massive tree has about three hundred large trunks and over 3000 small ones

Unit Tests

Test 1

A. Capitalization *(pages 197–207)*   On your paper, write each sentence correctly. Use appropriate capitalization.

1. on wednesday afternoon, stacey and i purchased several rolls of snapquick film at roland's department store.
2. "this afternoon," steve said, "we will be going to see aunt grace and mr. swenson."
3. the test in history II was on the industrial revolution and the reign of king frederick II of prussia.
4. the famous leaning tower of pisa is located in northwestern italy.
5. venus and mars are the two planets that are closest to the earth.
6. the first few lines of hodgson's poem read:
     time, you old gypsy man,
     will you not stay,
     put up your caravan
     just for one day?
7. my brother met me at school at 2:30 p.m.
8. the envelope was addressed to danvers, ma 01923.
9. tony entitled his painting *a look across the sea.*
10. the movie *gone with the wind* is playing at the franklin theater tomorrow at 7:00 p.m.

B. Punctuation *(pages 207–225)*   On your paper, write each sentence correctly. Use appropriate punctuation.

11. Has your clubs ex president her name is Teri introduced herself to you yet
12. On January 3 1959 Alaska gained its statehood there were then forty nine states in the Union
13. I am glad that you had a good time Janet said Do you plan to go again next year

(Continue on the next page.)

14. Well during most of the afternoon we read and did our homework

15. Has he ever read Paul Darcy Boless short story entitled Night of Vengeance

16. Yes Monica Richard Johnson Jr came to visit in August . 1982

17. Hey Come over here this instant

18. Its hard for me to get my dog to enjoy wearing its collar twenty four hours a day

19. At 230 PM the following people will replace the first group of volunteers Brian Ferris Jeanette Corey and Donna Baxter said Jennifer.

20. Will you please wait for Dr Murphy Mrs Caulkin and Mr Wilson after you return from the NFL game this afternoon

C. Italics *(pages 225–226)*   On your paper, copy each of the following sentences. Underline the words that should be italicized.

21. Don't forget to pick up a copy of the Times this afternoon.

22. Andrew Wyeth's technique is very impressive in the painting entitled Teel's Island.

23. Make sure to write clearly so that your a's don't look like o's.

24. Lucy mistakenly spelled disappoint with two s's.

25. Sharon's favorite novel is Thomas Hardy's Jude the Obscure.

D. Using Numbers in Writing *(pages 226–228)*   On your paper, copy each of the following sentences, choosing the number form that correctly completes each sentence.

26. On June (17 and 18, seventeenth and eighteenth), (nineteen twenty-eight, 1928), Amelia Earhart flew across the Atlantic Ocean at the age of (29, twenty-nine).

27. About (two thousand five hundred, 2500) people purchased advance tickets for the show to be held on May (5th, 5).

28. (One hundred and two, 102) strays are housed in the animal shelter at (69, sixty-nine) Meadow Drive.
29. Melinda's train will leave at (3:27, three twenty-seven) P.M. on May (twenty-first, 21).
30. The birthday party is at (four, 4:00) o'clock.

Test 2

Rewrite the following passage. Make the necessary corrections in capitalization, punctuation, italics (underlining), and the use of numbers.

a soapbox derby is a coasting race in which small motorless cars compete the word soapbox is used because at one time many of the cars were built from wooden soapboxes persons from 10 to 15 years old are allowed to enter every contestant must build his or her own car the size weight and cost of the vehicles are governed by specific rules the winners of local races qualify for the national soapbox derby held every august in akron ohio this derby features contestants from the united states canada and several other countries

Part Two

Composition

When you write sentences and paragraphs, your goal is to express your ideas in a clear and interesting way. To write well, you can use a series of steps to develop, to organize, and to present your ideas. In Part Two, you will learn and follow those steps. As you practice your writing, the process will become easy and enjoyable.

Units 8 through 11 present the basic process of writing in three steps: prewriting, writing, and revising. Units 12 through 14 explain how you can apply those steps to three important purposes for writing: explaining, describing, and narrating. Units 15 and 16 examine two forms of writing that you will use often: reports and letters.

UNIT 8

Prewriting

Unit Preview

Good writing starts long before you put the first sentence on paper. Writing is a three-step process, which includes prewriting, writing, and revising.

Prewriting, the first step, is the thinking, planning, and preparation that you do before you write. Prewriting gives you the opportunity to collect your thoughts on paper in the form of notes. From these notes, you can choose the most interesting ideas for your writing.

The prewriting notes that follow were written as the writer thought about visitors to her home town.

Places to visit when tourists come to Washington, D.C.:

MUSEUMS	BUILDINGS AND MONUMENTS
Air and Space	Capitol
National Archives	White House
National Gallery of Art	FBI Building
Natural History	Printing and Engraving
History and Technology	Lincoln Memorial
	Washington Monument

When is the best time of year to visit? —Spring or fall, when the weather isn't too hot and humid or too cold.

How can you plan ahead? —Contact office of your senator or representative for information and passes to congressional sessions, hearings, special tours.

For Analysis   On your paper, answer the following questions about the prewriting notes.

1. What are the two methods that the writer used to collect ideas for her subject?
   a. Listed places to visit in Washington, D.C.
   b. Wrote information about Washington, D.C., in a paragraph
   c. Asked and then answered questions about Washington, D.C.
2. Which of the following possible topics do the notes suggest?
   a. Planning a tour of Washington, D.C.
   b. Transportation in Washington, D.C.
   c. Historic monuments in Washington, D.C.
3. What questions would you ask if you wanted to learn more about Washington, D.C.?

The answers to these questions suggest what happens in prewriting. In this unit you will learn that many of the ideas you already have can serve as topics for writing. You will also learn how to gather your ideas and how to focus them for a specific assignment. You will discover that thoughtful prewriting will make the writing process itself easier and more effective.

8.1 Finding Ideas for Writing

How many times have you stared at a blank sheet of paper and asked yourself, "What will I write about?" Even experienced writers admit that the most difficult part of the writing process is getting started. Fortunately, there are several things that you can do to make getting started easier. First, you can set up a writer's notebook. Then, in your notebook, you can keep an inventory of your interests and make a list of your experiences. When you need a topic, you can look through your notebook to find ideas on a variety of subjects.

8.1a   Keeping a Writer's Notebook

You can make a writer's notebook out of any folder or binder that will hold your notes, clippings, and sheets of blank paper. On the blank paper, you can record interesting ideas whenever they occur to you.

Use the following strategies to keep your notebook filled with current ideas and experiences.

Strategies

1. *Take notes on anything you see, hear, think, or do that you want to remember.* You need not record your ideas in complete sentences. For example:

   Watched chicks hatching
   First baby-sitting job
   What makes leaves change color?

2. *Record interesting things that you hear people say and your reactions to their comments.* For example:

   Aunt Roberta said, "Don't count your chickens before they hatch." What does that mean? Don't get your hopes up? Don't count on anything until it happens?

3. *Include articles, advertisements, and pictures.* Read newspapers and magazines regularly, and clip and save those items that interest you. For example, you might include an article about an escaped alligator, a news photo that shows the damage done to a lake by water pollution, or a comic strip that humorously points out what true friendship is.

Exercise 1   Prewriting: Writer's Notebook   Look through recent newspapers and magazines and clip examples of at least three of the following items that could be used to suggest an idea for a writing assignment. Put the clippings in your writer's notebook.

1. A cartoon or a comic strip that makes an interesting point
2. An advertisement about which you have an opinion
3. A newspaper photograph that captures an important idea
4. An illustration that you like
5. An article that captures your interest

8.1b Taking an Interest Inventory

Another way to gather ideas for your writer's notebook is to take an interest inventory. An **interest inventory** is a list of those subjects that you are interested in now and those subjects that you would like to know more about.

Part of an interest inventory might look like this:

WHAT I KNOW ABOUT	MY HOBBIES
coins	collecting coins
different kinds of clay	making pottery
ten-speed bicycles	reading

WHAT I WANT TO KNOW ABOUT	MY ARTISTIC SKILLS
making papier mâché masks	making pencil sketches
soccer	writing haiku
the Northern Lights	making pottery

Keep a special section in your writer's notebook for your inventory so that you can add to it as new interests occur to you.

Exercise 2 Prewriting: Interest Inventory Make an interest inventory in your writer's notebook. Use the following questions to get started. For each question that you use, make a heading and list your answers under it.

1. What subjects do I know about?
2. What are my hobbies?
3. What are my favorite sports?
4. What do I enjoy most about school?
5. What kinds of artistic skills do I have?
6. What interests me about my family members?
7. What clubs or organizations do I belong to?
8. What kinds of books do I like to read?
9. What would I like to learn more about?
10. What skills would I like to learn?

Exercise 3   Prewriting: Interest Inventory   In your writer's notebook, list three of the following subjects. Next to each subject that you list, write two related items that you would like to know more about.

SAMPLE   Sea animals

ANSWER   Sea animals: dolphins, sea urchins

1. Aircraft	6. Farm animals	11. Music
2. Artists	7. First aid	12. Oceans
3. Birds	8. Inventions	13. Outer space
4. Computers	9. Islands	14. Presidents
5. Explorers	10. Medicine	15. Weather

8.1c   Drawing Upon Your Experiences

Another valuable source of ideas is your participation in events and activities. You may be surprised to discover how much you have learned from your own experiences. Suppose, for example, that you went on a nature walk as part of a school activity. You could draw upon that single experience to write about some of the following subjects:

The importance of cooperation (planning the trip, being on time, and so forth)

The kinds of trees growing where you live
Marking a trail
How to prevent poison ivy

Record your experiences in your writer's notebook.

Exercise 4   Prewriting: Experiences   In your writer's notebook, complete the following sentences with examples from your own experiences.

SAMPLE   My earliest childhood memory is __?__.

ANSWER   My earliest childhood memory is of my father
              reading me my favorite bedtime story—*Lyle,
              Lyle, Crocodile.*

1. I laughed so hard when __?__.
2. I learned about sharing when __?__.
3. The one decision that I will never forget is __?__.
4. I learned that first impressions may be misleading when __?__.
5. I was pleased to be able to __?__.
6. The most exciting event that I have ever witnessed was __?__.
7. An important tradition in our family is __?__.
8. One New Year's resolution that I did not keep was __?__.
9. The best Saturday that I have ever had was spent __?__.
10. I learned about patience when __?__.

Exercise 5   Prewriting: Experiences   In your writer's notebook, make a list of specific examples of three of the following experiences.

SAMPLE   Family occasions

ANSWER   At Thanksgiving one year, there were twenty-
              five people at our table.

              For my tenth birthday party, my mother hired
              a pony for the day.

1. Learning to do something new
2. Unusual happenings
3. Learning to get along with people
4. Caring for pets
5. Vacation adventures

Assignment 1   Prewriting   Select one of the clippings that you put in your writer's notebook for Exercise 1 on page 240 or a clipping that you have read recently. Read the clipping carefully. In your writer's notebook, make comments on your reactions to the clipping.

Assignment 2   Prewriting   Keep your writer's notebook up to date for three days. At the end of each day, record under the date at least three ideas and one experience that especially interested you. Include comments on what you did, heard, and observed.

Continuing Assignment   Prewriting   From your notebook, select three ideas about which you would like to write. Choose one subject from your interest inventory, a second subject from your list of experiences, and a third subject from the other information in your notebook. Write each subject on a separate sheet of paper. Save your papers.

Assignment Checklist

Check your assignments for the following points:

✔ 1. Did you write your thoughts about the items in your writer's notebook?

✔ 2. In the Continuing Assignment, did you choose from your writer's notebook three ideas that you would like to write about?

8.2 Gathering and Developing Ideas

Your writer's notebook, which includes your interest inventory and your list of experiences, should provide a rich source of ideas for writing. Each idea that you have written down is a subject that you can develop in writing.

When you select an idea from your writer's notebook, you can develop it by making lists of information related to it and by asking and answering questions about it.

8.2a Making Lists

Begin developing your subject by listing all the ideas that come to mind when you think of that subject. Your goal is to let your ideas flow freely and to get them down on paper. Think for several minutes with a pencil in your hand. List any idea that comes to you. At this point do not reject any ideas. Write them in whatever order they occur to you. You can organize them later.

Suppose that you plan to write about your favorite pastime. In your writer's notebook, you find windsurfing listed in your interest inventory as one of the things that you enjoy doing. Your list on windsurfing might look like this:

The thrill of skimming the water
Takes practice to ride the sailboard.
A combination of sailing and surfing
First surfboard outfitted with sail in 1966.
To steer, tip and turn the movable mast and sail.
If you fall, let go of boom, and board will stop.
Always wear a life vest.
13-year-old windsurfing champion

Exercise 1   Prewriting: Making Lists   Choose three of the following subjects. On your paper, list at least six ideas that come to mind for each subject.

SAMPLE   Birds as pets
ANSWER   Clean cage regularly.
            Need affection.
            Kinds: large, small, talking, singing
            Like to be talked to.
            Keep in room with people.
            Easily frightened.

1. Amusement parks
2. Baby-sitting
3. Basketball
4. Building models
5. Cycling

6. The moon
7. Movies
8. Puppets
9. Tropical fish
10. Swimming

8.2b   Asking Questions

When you need information, you usually ask questions: "Why has the schedule been changed?" "What will I need for the camping trip?" In the same way, asking and answering questions about a subject will help you to gather information about it.

With your list of ideas in front of you, start asking questions that begin with *Who, What, When, Where, Why,* and *How.* If you do not have ready answers for some of your questions, ask someone who might know, or find answers in a book, a magazine, or another reference. The answers to your questions will give you information that you need in order to write about your subject.

Here are questions and answers related to windsurfing.

1. *Who* can windsurf? —Anyone who can swim and who is near a lake or a beach where sailboards are rented
2. *What* is windsurfing? —A combination of surfing and sailing on a surfboard with a movable sail attached to it

3. *When* did windsurfing begin? —In 1966 when two people disagreed about which was better fun, surfing or sailing
4. *Where* can windsurfing be done? —On a lake, a wide river, along the ocean shore
5. *Why* do people enjoy windsurfing? —Can be done well with only a little practice; is somewhat easier than surfing and far less expensive than sailing
6. *How* does one control a sailboard? —By standing on the board and tipping and turning the mast and sail with the boom and by moving to the other side of the sail to change course

You are now ready to probe the subject even further by asking follow-up questions. Not all of the following questions apply to every subject, but you can use those that do.

1. What are the special characteristics of the subject?
2. What are examples of the subject?
3. What terms need to be explained?
4. What processes (how to do something) need to be explained?
5. Can the subject be compared with something else?
6. Can any contrasts (advantages and disadvantages, safety and danger, and so on) be developed for the subject?
7. What are my experiences with the subject?

The following notes are the result of asking further questions about windsurfing.

Terms to be explained: Boom, sailboard, mast

Processes to be explained: How to control the sailboard and how to change course

Comparison: Surfing and sailing

My experiences: Renting a sailboard and falling off several times before mastering the boom

Exercise 2   Prewriting: Asking Questions   Choose one of the following subjects and write it on your paper.

Then write related questions that ask *who, what, when, where, why,* and *how.* Answer the questions.

1. Baseball	5. Gymnastics	8. Soccer
2. Bicycle safety	6. Pottery	9. Training animals
3. Folklore	7. Scouting	10. Woodworking
4. 4-H clubs		

Exercise 3   Prewriting: Asking Questions   On your paper, write questions and answers to at least two of the follow-up questions on page 247 for the subject that you chose in Exercise 2.

Assignment   Prewriting   Choose a subject from your writer's notebook. Develop it by making lists and by asking and answering questions.

Continuing Assignment   By making lists and by asking questions, develop each of the subjects that you selected for the Continuing Assignment on page 244. Save your papers.

Assignment Checklist

Check your assignments for the following point:

 ✔ Did you list all the ideas and information about the subject that came to mind while you were making lists and asking questions?

8.3   Focusing Your Ideas

At this point you have developed a stack of prewriting notes. Now you need to make your notes useful for specific writing assignments. To do so, you must focus all the ideas that you have collected by stating a purpose, identifying your audience, and choosing a suitable topic.

8.3a   Identifying Your Purpose and Audience

Whenever you write, you should keep in mind your purpose and your audience. Your **purpose** is what you plan to accomplish with your writing. Your **audience** is the reader or group of readers for whom your writing is intended. How you treat your subject will depend on what your purpose is and who your audience is.

Purpose

Common purposes for writing are to inform or explain, to entertain, to describe, to narrate (tell a story), or to express an opinion. You might actually have more than one purpose in anything that you write. The details that you include and the ideas that you emphasize depend upon your purpose(s).

For example, suppose that you want to write about a rafting trip that you took with your scout troop. If your purpose is to entertain your audience with humorous tales of your misadventures, you would include such details as these:

1. How I lost the paddle before we were out ten minutes
2. How I paddled through a stretch of water—backwards
3. How I arrived at the end of the trip, covered with dabs of calamine lotion on each of my forty mosquito bites

On the other hand, if your purpose is to inform your readers about rafting safety, the details that you use would be quite different:

1. Travel only with an experienced guide.
2. Use reliable equipment.
3. Always wear a helmet, life jacket.
4. Never go rafting alone or when the river is too high.
5. Plan carefully: equipment, provisions, transportation back to the starting point

Audience

In preparing a writing assignment, consider your classmates and other people whom you know as part of your audience. Keep in mind how much or how little they know about your subject. If they are familiar with the subject, give them new information. If they are unfamiliar with the subject, give them basic information that they can understand.

An audience of experienced rafters, for instance, would already know the safety facts listed in the examples about rafting. They would be more interested in reading about new techniques in rafting or about a successful trip on a river that had never before been used for rafting. However, the details on safety might be of special interest to those planning to try this sport for the first time.

Exercise 1 Prewriting: Purpose On your paper, list the following topics. For each topic, write the most appropriate purpose or purposes from the following. Be prepared to explain your answers.

To inform or explain To tell a story
To describe To express an opinion

SAMPLE Planning a personal exercise program
ANSWER To inform
To express an opinion

1. How it feels to run twenty-six miles in a marathon
2. What I think about video games
3. How to get a fishing license
4. How my summer vacation fell apart
5. Four ways to improve softball pitching
6. My trip to San Antonio
7. What I think about an expressway in my neighborhood
8. The countryside in autumn

9. What I like about canoeing
10. Rules for playing table tennis

Exercise 2   Prewriting: Audience   On your paper, list the numbered topics. From the following list, write the audience or audiences who you think would be most interested in each topic. Be prepared to explain your answers.

Teachers and students	Someone interested in geology
Parents	An environmentalist
A stamp collector	An amateur photographer
A sports fan	A member of the community

SAMPLE   How pesticides pollute our local streams

ANSWER   Someone interested in the environment

1. Designing a stamp for the United States Postal Service
2. Your need for sneakers or another article of clothing
3. How thoughtless fans disrupt ballgames
4. Planning a school activity calendar
5. How to be a successful class president
6. Local traffic problems and what to do about them
7. A recent geologic discovery
8. How to display photographs
9. The effects of polluted lakes and streams
10. Fads in teen-age television viewing

8.3b   Choosing a Topic

With your prewriting notes at hand and with ideas about your purpose and audience in mind, you are now ready to choose a topic. A **topic** is a specific aspect of your subject. In choosing a topic, you limit your subject and what you will say about it. For example, "Baseball fans" is too general to be a topic. However, the notes that you have taken on the subject might suggest the following topic for an audience of sports fans: "How thoughtless baseball fans can disrupt a game."

The following steps will help you to determine a topic.

Procedure

1. *Review your prewriting notes on the general subject.* Write down ideas for topics that appear in your notes or are suggested by them. You may find a topic in a note or on a list or in your answer to a question about the general subject.

2. *Look in your notes for other information that fits your topic ideas.* You may find details in the form of examples, descriptions, reasons, and so forth.

3. *Check your topics against your intended purpose and audience* to make certain that the topics are appropriate for both.

4. *Choose the topic that interests you the most and that suits your assignment.*

5. *Write a phrase that clearly identifies what your topic is and what you will say about it.*

6. *Ask and answer questions about your limited topic.* By asking and answering these questions, perhaps for the second time, you will have the information that you need to plan your writing.

Now that you know how to get started on your writing, you will find it much easier to approach any writing task. Each composition unit in this book will give you further practice in prewriting for particular kinds of writing.

Exercise 3   Prewriting: Focusing Ideas   Each of the following items includes a subject, a purpose, and an audience, followed by three topics. On your paper, write the topic that is most appropriate for the purpose and audience.

SAMPLE To describe weather to someone who has never experienced below-freezing temperatures.
a. What snow is like
b. What a tornado looks like
c. What a monsoon is like

ANSWER What snow is like

1. To explain soccer to classmates who have played it for three years.
   a. The basic rules of soccer
   b. How to improve your passing accuracy
   c. Why I enjoy playing soccer

2. To express an opinion about first aid to members of the school committee.
   a. Why first aid should be a required subject
   b. How knowing first aid saved my life
   c. How to apply direct pressure on a wound

3. To explain basic cooking to someone who does not know how to cook.
   a. How to hard-boil an egg
   b. How to prepare a three-course meal for six
   c. How to make French pastry

4. To tell a story about a vacation to adults.
   a. Why I enjoyed being a teen-age camp counselor
   b. How I took a vacation right in my own community
   c. How to apply for a passport

Exercise 4 Prewriting: Focusing Ideas Read the following prewriting notes on the subject of meteorites. On your paper, answer Questions 1–4.

Few meteorites ever discovered
Fall in ocean, remote places
Break into small pieces
Stony meteorites; iron meteorites
Largest known iron (60 tons) still buried in South Africa
Meteor showers; how to view meteor showers
Meteor Crater, Arizona
Source of knowledge about planets, stars
Best examples in Antarctica
Shooting stars
Who studies meteorites? —Geologists
What is the difference between a meteorite, a meteoroid, and a meteor? —Meteorite, a meteoroid that falls to the earth; meteoroid, rock particles that fall through space; meteor, light caused by heat of falling meteoroid.
Where do most meteorites fall? —In the ocean and hard-to-reach places
Why does Antarctica have the best examples of meteorites? —Frozen in ice; easy to examine; unchanged by weather and pollution
How do meteorites form craters? —Explode on impact

1. What are two possible limited topics for the general subject "Meteorites"?
2. List the details that you would use if you were writing about "How meteorites help us to learn about space."
3. What would be an appropriate purpose for the topic "How meteorites help us to learn about space"?
4. Who would be a likely audience for the topic "How meteorites help us to learn about space"?

Assignment 1   Prewriting   *Step 1:* From your writer's notebook, select a subject that you would like to develop. *Step 2:* Develop the subject by making a list of related ideas and by asking questions about it. *Step 3:* From your notes, identify two possible purposes and audiences for that subject.

Assignment 2 Prewriting *Step 1:* Use the prewriting notes that you developed in Assignment 1. On your paper, write two different limited topics: one for the first purpose and audience and one for the second purpose and audience. *Step 2:* Under each topic, write the notes that relate to that topic. Some details will apply to both topics; some will apply to only one.

Continuing Assignment Prewriting In the Continuing Assignment on page 248, you developed three different subjects. For each of those subjects, write a purpose, an audience, and a specific writing topic. Then, list the prewriting notes that you would use to write about each topic.

Assignment Checklist

Check your assignments for the following points:

   ✔ 1. Did you identify two possible purposes and audiences for your subject?

   ✔ 2. Did you write a specific topic to fit each purpose and audience?

   ✔ 3. In the Continuing Assignment, did you select the prewriting notes related to your topics?

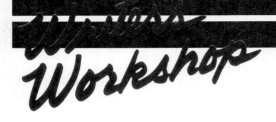

Life Story: Preparing Questions for an Interview

Situation: You are a reporter for your local newspaper. For the Founder's Day issue of the newspaper, you are going to interview the oldest person in your community, a man who was born ninety-five years ago. You are curious about what life was like in your community in earlier times. Before the interview, you will develop questions to ask during your visit. You already have some notes from which you can build your questions. Keep in mind the following information as you plan the interview.

Writer: you as newspaper reporter
Audience: readers of local paper
Topic: questions to ask during an interview
Purpose: to plan interview questions

Directions: To prepare your questions, follow these steps.

Step 1.   On a separate sheet of paper, make a chart like the one on the facing page. Leave space between each item.

Step 2.   As you read each subject, form two questions about it. Begin your questions with the words suggested. For an example, see the first item on the chart.

Step 3.   In a sentence, state the purpose of the interview. What do you, the reporter, want to find out from this man?

Subjects	Questions
Memories	What is your strongest memory of your childhood here? What was the most exciting thing that happened in this community?
School	Where ...? What ...?
Recreation	What ...? How ...?
Special events	What ...? Where ...?
Transportation	How ...? What ...?
Famous people	Who ...? When ...?
The community, then and now	What ...? How ...?

Unit Assignments

Assignment 1 You have been given the subject of weather forecasting for a writing assignment. Write at least five ideas or facts related to weather forecasting, two personal experiences involving weather forecasts, and three examples of the uses of weather forecasting.

Assignment 2 Imagine that you are to write a special guest column in your local newspaper in which you interview a notable person in your community. Choose the person whom you will interview. On your paper, write ten questions that you think your readers would like to have you ask.

Assignment 3 Choose a personal experience that you recorded in your writer's notebook. Focus on three possible writing topics suggested by that experience. State a purpose and an audience for each topic.

Assignment 4 You have been given a writing assignment with "expressing an opinion" as its purpose. *Step 1:* Look in your writer's notebook for a suitable subject. *Step 2:* Develop the subject by listing ideas and asking questions. *Step 3:* Focus your ideas in two specific topics, each for a different audience. Write the topics and the audiences on your paper.

Assignment 5 From your writer's notebook, choose a subject that could be the topic for a narrative about an experience that you have had. On your paper, make two lists of details about the experience. In one list include the details that you would write about for an audience of very young children. In the second list, include the details that you would write about for an audience of parents and teachers.

Unit Tests

Test 1

A. Number your paper from 1 to 5. Next to each number, write *True* if the sentence is true or *False* if it is false.

1. Your writer's notebook can provide ideas when you need to choose a subject for a writing assignment.
2. In your writer's notebook, you can record things that you have learned from your experiences. *
3. You must use complete sentences in your writer's notebook.
4. When you list ideas to develop a subject, list them in whatever order they come to your mind.
5. If you do not know the answer to a question that you ask about a subject, you should make a guess about what is the right answer.

B. Number your paper from 6 to 10. Next to each number, write the letter of the term that correctly completes the sentence. You will use all but one of the terms.

a. question   d. interest inventory
b. purpose   e. audience
c. topic   f. prewriting

6. __?__ is the thinking, planning, and preparation that you do before you write.
7. A(n) __?__ is a list of subjects that you are interested in now and subjects that you would like to know more about.
8. A(n) __?__ is a specific aspect of a general subject.
9. Your __?__ is what you hope to accomplish with your writing.
10. Your __?__ is the reader or the group of readers for whom your writing is intended.

Test 2

Choose one of the Unit Assignments or one that your teacher suggests. Complete the assignment as directed and hand it in to your teacher.

Unit 9

Writing Sentences

Unit Preview

As you read the following sentences, try to picture what they tell you.

A cat slept.
A man sat on the bus.
The woman wrote a letter.

The sentences are grammatically correct, but they are uninteresting, and they do not give you much information.

Here is how one writer expressed the same ideas:

1. A tiger-striped cat dozed in the morning sun.
2. A distracted businessman stared out the window of the bus.
3. The elderly woman bent over her kitchen table and wrote with careful strokes on a scrap of air-mail stationery.

In Sentence 1 the writer uses the adjective *tiger-striped* to create a picture of the cat. The writer also uses a specific verb, *dozed*, and a prepositional phrase, *in the morning sun*, to add interest to the sentence. In Sentences 2 and 3, the writer includes details that you can visualize. In contrast with the first set of sentences, these sentences are interesting and informative.

For Analysis On your paper, answer these questions about Sentences 2 and 3.

1. In Sentence 2, how does the noun *businessman* help create a more vivid picture than the noun *man*?

2. In Sentence 2, which words create a picture of the businessman?
3. In Sentence 2, how do the prepositional phrases add to the picture being created?
4. Which words and phrases make Sentence 3 vivid and interesting?

In this unit you will learn to express your ideas in several different ways to make your sentences clear, informative, and interesting. You will also learn to make your sentences fit your audience and your purpose.

9.1 Expressing Your Ideas in Sentences

Sentences, as you know, express complete thoughts. They all make a statement (a predicate) about someone or something (a subject). In Unit 5, "Sentence Structure," you studied subjects and predicates. Now you will study several ways to use subjects and predicates in writing your sentences.

Before you write sentences, you probably already have some ideas or some prewriting notes on a topic. Now you need to express your ideas as subjects and predicates. Suppose that you have ideas about ice-skating. There are many ways that you can express those ideas in sentences. If you want to focus on ice-skating, then make *ice-skating* the subject of your sentence. What you say about ice-skating will be your predicate.

SUBJECT (WHAT)   Ice-skating

PREDICATES   requires good balance
                  is a necessary skill for hockey

You may change your focus but still express ideas about ice-skating. If you and your friends like to ice-skate, you may focus on yourselves in your subject and present the idea of skating in your predicate.

SUBJECT (WHO)   My friends and I

PREDICATES   are learning to ice-skate
                skate at the rink every weekend
                cleared our pond for skating

The following strategies will help you to write clear and informative sentences.

Strategies

1. *Focus your idea for the sentence.* Decide what the subject will be. If your focus is rainy days, for example, make *rainy days* your subject. If you focus on a specific aspect of rainy days, make it the subject.

   SUBJECTS   Rainy days
              Watching the rain
              My wet shoes

2. *Write a predicate* in which you make a statement about the subject. You may put your ideas about the topic in the predicate of your sentence.

   Rainy days *make traveling difficult.*
   Watching the rain *lulls me.*
   My wet shoes *left mud on the kitchen floor.*

3. *Choose the words that best express your ideas.* Use concrete nouns and vivid verbs that make your subject and your predicate specific.

   TOPIC   Rainy days

   CONCRETE NOUNS AND VIVID VERBS
              Thunderstorms rumbled most of the day.
              A *downpour drenched* us as we ran home.
              Big *raindrops pelted* our faces.

Exercise 1   Writing: Subjects and Predicates   On your paper, write two sentences for each of the following predicates. Use a different person, place, thing, or idea for each subject.

SAMPLE   _?_ depends on your cooperation.

ANSWER   The success of the show depends on your cooperation.

Mrs. Trujillo depends on your cooperation.

1. _?_ caused a traffic jam on the highway.
2. _?_ is an easy way to get to school.
3. _?_ should get involved in sports.
4. _?_ can be an enormous help when you are in a hurry.
5. _?_ enjoyed the basketball game.
6. _?_ floated down the river on the current.
7. _?_ presented me with a problem.
8. _?_ takes a lot of time.
9. There, right in front of my eyes, was _?_.
10. Here are _?_.

Exercise 2   Writing: Subjects and Predicates   On your paper, write two sentences for each subject below.

SAMPLE   Riding a bicycle _?_.

ANSWER   Riding a bicycle is a good form of exercise.

Riding a bicycle at night can be dangerous.

1. Vacations _?_.
2. My dentist _?_.
3. The corner store _?_.
4. Not enough sleep _?_.
5. Flickering lights _?_.
6. The television programs _?_.
7. The ringing telephone _?_.
8. Visiting my relatives _?_.
9. Today's high temperature _?_.
10. An embarrassing moment _?_.

Exercise 3   Prewriting: Specific Words   On your paper, copy the sentence that is more specific from each pair.

Underline the words that make the sentences specific.

SAMPLE   a. A person looked out the window.
b. A child gazed out the window.

ANSWER   A <u>child gazed</u> out the window.

1. a. The man slumped over his desk.
   b. The man sat at his desk.

2. a. Tulips, daffodils, and lilacs are three flowers that bloom in April and May.
   b. Many flowers bloom in the spring.

3. a. I heard a car go down the street.
   b. I heard a jalopy sputter down the street.

4. a. A scream terrified the visitors.
   b. A noise surprised the visitors.

5. a. You can work at the hospital.
   b. Teen-agers can volunteer at the hospital.

6. a. The town in the valley is quiet.
   b. The town nestled in the valley is peaceful.

7. a. Miniature schnauzers come from Germany.
   b. Miniature schnauzers were used by German farmers as rat catchers.

8. a. A quarry is a large pit from which stone is dug.
   b. A quarry is a large hole.

9. a. Because spiders have a two-part body and eight legs, they are not classified as insects.
   b. Spiders are not insects.

10. a. Dogs have many uses.
    b. Dobermans can be used for protection.

Exercise 4   Writing: Subjects and Predicates   On your paper, write two sentences for each of the following topics. In one sentence, use the topic as the subject of your sentence. In the other sentence, use the topic in the predicate.

SAMPLE   Talking on the telephone

ANSWER   Talking on the telephone is easier than writing a letter. [subject]

Sarah enjoys talking on the telephone. [predicate]

1. The entire family
2. A deserted house
3. Skateboarding
4. Collecting rocks
5. Washing a car
6. Our cafeteria
7. A hushed audience
8. Cooking over a campfire
9. Tropical fish
10. The Wild West

Assignment Writing On your paper, write two sentences about each of the following topics. Carefully focus what you want to say about each topic. Use specific and vivid words. In some sentences use the topic in the predicate of your sentence.

1. Breakfast
2. Flooding
3. Baby-sitting
4. Sports equipment
5. Traffic
6. Typewriters
7. Video games
8. Modern buildings
9. Puppet shows
10. A rainbow

Assignment Checklist

Check your assignment for the following points:

  ✔ 1. Did you focus on a specific and clear subject for each sentence?

  ✔ 2. Did you make a statement about the subject in the predicate of each sentence?

  ✔ 3. Did you use the topic in some predicates?

  ✔ 4. Did you use concrete and vivid words?

9.2   Expanding Sentences with Modifiers

To make your sentences more informative and more interesting, add details in the form of modifiers. By answering questions about parts of the sentence, modifiers help you to express your idea clearly. Modifiers can be single words, such as adjectives or adverbs, or groups of words, such as prepositional phrases. The following examples show how you can use modifiers to expand sentences. The examples expand the sentence *Our team won the game.*

WHICH ONE?

Our *basketball* team won the game.

Our team won the *last* game *of the season.*

HOW?

Our team won the game *by one point.*

Our team *easily* won the game.

WHEN?

Our team won the game *in overtime.*

Our team won the game *on Friday night.*

WHERE?

Our team won the game *on the opposing team's court.*

Each of the preceding sentences has a different emphasis, depending on what details have been added. You can also use modifiers to answer such questions as *what kind?* and *how many? (page 29)* or *to what degree or extent? (page 38).* Of course, you can add more than one modifier to a sentence.

Exercise 1   Writing: Modifiers   On your paper, expand each of the following sentences by adding a modifier that answers the question in parentheses. The modifiers may be single words or phrases.

> **SAMPLE** __?__, Jeannie and Andrew walked home. (When?)
>
> **ANSWER** After the movie, Jeannie and Andrew walked home.

1. The baby cried __?__. (How?)
2. __?__, the bulldozer moved across the vacant lot. (How?)
3. The officer directed traffic __?__. (Where?)
4. Traveling by air has become commonplace __?__. (When?)
5. Luke stopped short __?__. (Where?)
6. The __?__ dog barked __?__. (What kind? How?)
7. Dinah planted __?__ petunias __?__. (How many? Where?)
8. Mr. Roberts was the __?__ person to speak at the __?__ hearing. (Which one? What kind?)
9. Birds build nests __?__ and __?__. (Where? How?)
10. I __?__ come home hungry __?__. (When? When?)

Exercise 2 Writing: Modifiers On your paper, write the following sentences, adding at least two modifiers. The modifiers may be single words or groups of words.

> **SAMPLE** A handbag was found.
>
> **ANSWER** A handbag full of dollar bills was found under a seat on the bus.

1. The audience applauded.
2. The smell of paint filled the house.
3. A cheer rose from the crowd.
4. The sky looked threatening.
5. Derek ran the race.
6. A skier raced down the mountain.
7. The children were delighted to see a puppy appear.

8. As the day wore on, the carpenter completed the fence.
9. The driver brought the car to a stop.
10. Martha invited us to come to her house.

Assignment 1   Writing   Choose two of the following groups of details. Focus on a subject for each group. Then write a sentence that includes all the information listed for that group.

1. brisk wind
   snow
   people at bus stop
   boots, coats, gloves, hats
2. soldiers at attention
   three perfect lines
   brass buttons
   uniforms neatly pressed
3. dark green car
   four doors
   dents in several places
   flat tire
4. white sand
   sunburned swimmers
   humid breeze
   cool water

Assignment 2   Writing   *Step 1:* Choose five of the following topics. For each topic, write a clear and informative sentence in which you include two or more modifiers. *Step 2:* Write a second sentence for each, using different modifiers.

1. How it feels to be cold
2. How it feels to be on vacation
3. How it feels to be tired
4. How it feels to be young
5. How it feels to be among strangers
6. How it feels to be surprised
7. How it feels to be on an adventure
8. How it feels to be in a dark place
9. How it feels to be bored
10. How it feels to be happy

Assignment Checklist

Check your assignments for the following points:

   ✔ 1. Did you focus the ideas for subjects and predicates in your sentences?

   ✔ 2. Did you add modifiers that make your sentences informative and interesting?

9.3   Suiting Sentences to Audience and Purpose

Because you can write so many sentences about any topic, you must decide which sentences are best suited for a particular situation. By keeping your audience (*page 249*) and your purpose (*page 249*) in mind, you can more easily focus your subject, write a predicate for it, and supply appropriate modifiers.

Suppose, for example, that your purpose is to explain to a first-grader what a terrapin is. You might write the following sentence:

> A terrapin is a special kind of turtle.

If your audience were made up of teen-agers or adults, your explanation would include different words and a few details:

> Certain freshwater or tidewater turtles, especially the
> diamondback, are called terrapins and may be found in
> the United States on the Gulf and Atlantic coasts.

Write your sentences, using words and details that are appropriate for your audience. To make them appropriate, consider the age, the interests, and the level of knowledge of your audience.

Similarly, consider the purpose for your sentences. Are you trying to explain an idea, to describe something that you saw, or to tell a story? Notice how each of the following sentences accomplishes a purpose.

Purpose: To inform or explain
The two most important elements for healthy houseplants are light and water.

Purpose: To describe
On the log where I sat, there was a clump of red-fringed lichen.

Purpose: To entertain
My garden attracted every bug within a two-mile radius.

Purpose: To narrate (tell a story)
Far from our destination when night came, we decided to make camp in unfamiliar territory.

Purpose: To express an opinion
No one should pass up an opportunity to learn something.

Exercise 1   Prewriting: Audience and Purpose   On your paper, list the audience and purpose given for each of the following pairs of sentences. Then write the sentence that best suits both audience and purpose.

SAMPLE   *Audience:* a child   *Purpose:* to explain
a. A skyscraper is a very tall building that seems to touch the sky.
b. Tall buildings, called skyscrapers, were built in the nineteenth century after the invention of the elevator.

ANSWER   *Audience:* a child   *Purpose:* to explain
A skyscraper is a very tall building that seems to touch the sky.

1. *Audience:* potential employer   *Purpose:* to explain
   a. I would really like this job.
   b. I am qualified for the position of stock clerk because I am reliable, careful, and organized.

2. *Audience:* a good friend   *Purpose:* to entertain
   a. During the summer recess, I became acquainted with several individuals from Japan.
   b. At camp this summer, I met two teen-agers from Japan who taught me how to fold paper into different shapes.

3. *Audience:* teachers, classmates   *Purpose:* to describe
   a. A spider is a creepy-crawly bug.
   b. A spider is an eight-legged arthropod.

4. *Audience:* people who enjoy snowmobiling
   Purpose: to express an opinion
   a. Snowmobiles are fun to ride, but they can be dangerous and even destructive.
   b. Snowmobiles have ski-like runners and continuous-track treads.

Exercise 2   Writing: Audience and Purpose   Choose five of the following items. On your paper, write a sentence about the topic for the audience and purpose given.

SAMPLE	*Audience:* Adults
	Topic: Causes of hay fever
	Purpose: To inform
ANSWER	In many parts of North America, ragweed pollen causes hay fever in late August and early September.

1. *Audience:* Someone who has always lived in Alaska
   Topic: A desert
   Purpose: To describe

2. *Audience:* Your family
   Topic: Something that happened on your way to school
   Purpose: To narrate

3. *Audience:* Children in kindergarten
   Topic: An unusual animal
   Purpose: To entertain

4. *Audience:* A friend
   Topic: A certain kind of clothing
   Purpose: To express an opinion

5. *Audience:* Your friends
   Topic: An experience that you have had
   Purpose: To entertain

6. *Audience:* Your neighbor
   Topic: Caring for your dog while you are away
   Purpose: To inform

7. *Audience:* A family member who missed the first scene
   Topic: A television show
   Purpose: To narrate

8. *Audience:* Your principal
   Topic: A school policy
   Purpose: To express your opinion

9. *Audience:* A person who repairs electrical appliances
   Topic: What is wrong with your radio
   Purpose: To explain

10. *Audience:* The mayor of your community
    Topic: A problem in your community
    Purpose: To describe

Assignment 1 Writing Choose a topic about which you would like to write, and then choose two of the following combinations of audience and purpose. Write a sentence about your topic for each combination that you chose.

1. *Audience:* preschoolers   *Purpose:* to explain
2. *Audience:* your classmates *Purpose:* to describe
3. *Audience:* adults   *Purpose:* to express an opinion

Assignment 2 Writing Write one clear, informative sentence about yourself for each of the following audiences.

1. Someone who might employ you part-time
2. A pen pal whom you have not met
3. A guidance counselor in your school

Assignment Checklist

Check your assignments for the following points:

✔ 1. Did you focus your subjects and predicates clearly?
✔ 2. Did you use concrete and vivid words?
✔ 3. Did you use appropriate details for your audience and purpose?

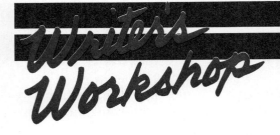

T.V. Scribe: Program Listings

Situation: You are a staff writer for *T.V. Scribe,* a weekly program guide. You write program listings that describe the shows and stimulate interest in them. As you work on the program guide, keep in mind the following information.

Writer:　　you as staff writer for *T.V. Scribe*
Audience:　readers of *T.V. Scribe*
Topic:　　highlights from a day's program listings
Purpose:　to describe each show in one sentence

Directions: To write your sentences, follow these steps.

　　Step 1. Read the Information Sheet that gives the shows to be listed.
　　Step 2. To construct a sentence for each listing, answer these questions:

　　　　　　Who or what is the main character? (subject of your sentence)

　　　　　　What happens to the character(s)? (predicate of your sentence)

　　　　　　What additional details from the Information Sheet will add interest to your sentence?

　　　　For example, by answering these questions, you might write the listing for the program *The More the Merrier* like this:

　　　　　　The Thomases arrive at Elk Lake to find a skunk in their cabin.

　　Step 3. Be sure that each sentence is complete.

Information Sheet for Program Listings

<u>Cooking</u> <u>with</u> <u>Louise</u>--Instruction   Ch. 4, 10:00 A.M.
    Character: Louise Avery
    Setting: Blue Ribbon Institute
    Plot: bakes vegetable casserole; gives recipe tips

<u>Search</u> <u>for</u> <u>the</u> <u>Hidden</u> <u>City</u>--Movie   Ch. 30, 4:00 P.M.
    Characters: members of a scientific expedition
    Setting: jungles of Peru
    Plot: have series of adventures; discover lost
          city

<u>Oh,</u> <u>Brother</u>--Comedy   Ch. 7, 7:30 P.M.
    Characters: Tim and Tom Tate, identical twins
    Setting: Carver High
    Plot: first day of school, twins cause confusion

<u>Run,</u> <u>Annie,</u> <u>Run</u>--Drama   Ch. 4, 8:00 P.M.
    Character: Ann Salazar
    Setting: Chicago, Illinois
    Plot: high-school track star, afraid of failing,
          conquers fear; goes on to compete in
          Olympics

<u>The</u> <u>More</u> <u>the</u> <u>Merrier</u>--Comedy   Ch. 6, 8:30 P.M.
    Characters: Thomas family--Mom, Dad, Billy, Chip
    Setting: a cabin at Elk Lake
    Plot: family arrives; finds skunk in cabin

<u>In</u> <u>Our</u> <u>Time</u>--Drama   Ch. 13, 8:00 P.M.
    Characters: two pioneer families, the Brents and
             the Harmons
    Setting: California during the Gold Rush
    Plot: families move west by covered wagon; settle
          in California

<u>Over</u> <u>the</u> <u>Rainbow</u>--Documentary   Ch. 5, 9:00 P.M.
    Characters: Orville and Wilbur Wright
    Setting: Kitty Hawk, North Carolina, 1903
    Plot: brothers build airplane, attempt first
          flight

275

Unit Assignments

Assignment 1   Your class is preparing a class book in which each person will be remembered with a single statement. Write one sentence that captures what you would like your classmates to remember about you.

Assignment 2   Write two related sentences telling how you helped a friend or how a friend helped you.

Assignment 3   Write three related sentences in which you inform a friend about something that you have recently learned.

Assignment 4   Write three related sentences narrating something that you did today. Make yourself the subject of only the first sentence. Change the focus for the other two sentences in the group.

Assignment 5   Choose one of the following topics. Write three sentences about that topic that are clear, interesting, and informative.

   1. Pets   2. Music   3. Pastimes

Assignment 6   Choose a topic that interests you. On your paper, list four ideas about the topic that you have chosen. Then write one sentence about each idea. Your sentences should be clear, interesting, and informative.

Assignment 7   Choose a topic that interests you. Write two sets of three sentences each. The first set of sentences should explain the topic to a group of adults. The second set of sentences should explain the same topic to a group of young children.

Unit Tests

Test 1

A. Number your paper from 1 to 4. Next to each number, write the letter of the word that correctly completes the sentence. You will use all but one of the words.

a. modifier
d. subject
b. paragraph
e. predicate
c. audience

1. To focus an idea in a sentence, you decide first what the __?__ will be.
2. You can expand a sentence by adding a(n) __?__.
3. In the __?__ you make a statement about the subject.
4. Plan and write your sentences, using words and details that are appropriate for your __?__.

B. Read the following sentences. Then number your paper from 5 to 7. Next to each number, write the letter of the item that correctly answers the question about the sentences.

SENTENCE 1   I was surprised to hear an oven talk to me in a low, dull voice.

SENTENCE 2   A special oven that is operated by the sound of a voice can help a blind person in the kitchen.

5. Which sentence tells how the oven sounds?
   a. Sentence 1   b. Sentence 2
6. Which sentence makes a statement about the use of the oven?
   a. Sentence 1   b. Sentence 2
7. Which sentence better presents the special type of oven to first-grade students?
   a. Sentence 1   b. Sentence 2

Test 2

Choose one of the Unit Assignments. Write the assignment as directed and hand it in to your teacher.

Unit 10

Writing Paragraphs

Unit Preview

As you read the following paragraph, notice how each sentence contributes to the main idea. The sentences have been numbered to help you locate the details referred to in the left margin.

(1) Main idea: remarkable woodpecker

(2) Extremely strong bill

(3) (4) Drilling speed

(5) (6) Great endurance

(7) Unmatched speed and intensity

(1) The woodpecker is a remarkable bird. (2) Its extremely strong bill enables it to drill through the bark of a tree for insect food or to hollow out a tree for a nest. (3) The woodpecker can drill with tremendous speed. (4) In a single second, it can drum its head against a tree more than twenty times. (5) The woodpecker also has great endurance. (6) It can continue its rapid drumming for almost an hour. (7) If any other bird tried to peck wood with the speed and intensity of the woodpecker, it would probably die of exhaustion within minutes.

The main idea of a well-developed paragraph is expressed in a sentence that is usually placed at the beginning. The main idea is then developed sentence by sentence, detail by detail. In some paragraphs, a sentence at the end states a conclusion or summarizes the other sentences.

Notice that the first line of the paragraph is indented, or set in. A paragraph indentation is a signal to your readers that all the sentences that follow will be about the same idea.

For Analysis On your paper, follow these instructions about the model paragraph.

1. Draw a box representing the paragraph. In the box draw a horizontal line showing where the first sentence begins and ends. On the line, state in your own words the main idea of the paragraph.
2. Draw horizontal lines inside the box showing the positions of Sentences 2–6. On the lines, briefly list the details about the main idea that these sentences provide.
3. Draw horizontal lines inside the box showing where Sentence 7 begins and ends. On the lines, express in your own words the conclusion that the writer made.

In this unit you will practice writing paragraphs. In the prewriting stage, you will find a topic narrow enough for a paragraph and will list details for that topic. Then you will write the sentences that make up a paragraph: a topic sentence, supporting sentences, and a concluding sentence.

10.1 What Is a Paragraph?

A **paragraph** is a series of sentences that develops a single idea or topic. You can write paragraphs for many purposes, such as explaining how to do something or telling a story. The sentences in a paragraph must, however, always relate to a single topic. A group of sentences about more than one topic is not a paragraph.

Most paragraphs are made up of a topic sentence, a series of supporting sentences, and a concluding sentence.

A **topic sentence** states the main idea of a paragraph. Whenever you write, your readers must know exactly what your topic is. In writing a paragraph, you state your topic in a single sentence. It is usually best to place the topic sentence at the beginning of a paragraph so that your readers will know right away what the paragraph is about.

Supporting sentences explain or develop what is stated in the topic sentence. You may need as few as three or as many as ten supporting sentences in a paragraph. In each supporting sentence, you give specific information or details related to the main idea.

A paragraph may also have a concluding sentence to bring it to a close. In a **concluding sentence,** you may summarize the supporting sentences or state a conclusion about the main idea.

Paragraph Unity.   A paragraph in which each supporting sentence contributes to the main idea is said to have **unity.** In the following paragraph, the topic sentence is in italic type. Notice how the supporting sentences develop the main idea by providing specific details.

Model

Topic sentence

Chief among the legendary figures of the American Wild West were the lawmen of the frontier towns. Federal Marshall Wyatt Earp

Supporting sentences

earned his reputation by bringing law and order first to Dodge City, Kansas, and later to Tombstone, Arizona. Earp is best remembered for the stand that he and his brothers made against the Clanton gang at the famous O.K. Corral. Another legendary lawman was Bat Masterson. Masterson served as sheriff of Ford County, Kansas, and assisted Wyatt Earp in ridding Dodge City and Tombstone of outlaws. Perhaps the most celebrated peace officer of the time was Wild Bill Hickok. Hickok's bravery and determination put an end to lawlessness in the rough Kansas cattle towns over which he

Concluding sentence

presided. These peace officers who tamed the wildness of the Old West have become legends.

The model paragraph begins with a clearly stated topic sentence. The supporting sentences include only those details that are related to the idea stated in the topic sentence. The model is an example of a unified paragraph.

As you read the following sentences, ask yourself if they are part of a unified paragraph.

> Chief among the legendary figures of the American Wild West were the lawmen of the frontier towns. One of the most famous of these figures was Wild Bill Hickok. Hickok was a fine marshall and a very good marksman. However, he was not as good a sharpshooter as Annie Oakley. Annie was only a teen-ager when Wild Bill Hickok died, but she went on to become one of America's greatest Wild West performers. Of course, the Wild West had its share of outlaws too. Who has not heard of Billy the Kid, Frank and Jesse James, or Butch Cassidy? In fact, not too long ago a movie was made called *Butch Cassidy and the Sundance Kid.*

This example has several topics, not just one. Like the model paragraph, it begins with a statement about the lawmen of the Wild West. However, it then goes on to mention three other topics: (1) the performer Annie Oakley, (2) outlaws of the Old West, and (3) the movie *Butch Cassidy and the Sundance Kid.* The reader cannot tell from one sentence to the next what the main idea is. The sentences are not part of a unified paragraph.

Exercise 1 Prewriting: Paragraph Unity On your paper, write the numbers of the groups of sentences that are examples of unified paragraphs.

1. Somewhere in the darkest corner of your closet, you may find something very useful: old shoes. They are exactly what you need for jobs that involve getting dirty. Such jobs include painting, raking, or cleaning. Old shoes also are just right for situations where you are bound to get wet, such as washing the car or watering the lawn. When you don't want cleanliness to interfere with having fun, old shoes are the

answer. A volleyball game on a dirt court or the exploration of a muddy field are typical examples of situations in which old shoes come to the rescue. Considering their usefulness, old shoes should be cherished, not tossed into the trash can.

2.   If you love animals, you should consider a career as a veterinarian. Pets can be both interesting and enjoyable. However, people who want pets must be willing to take care of them. There are more than a hundred million dogs and cats in this country. Unfortunately, many of them are strays. One of the main problems with stray animals is that they can injure themselves or contract diseases. Then they need the services of a veterinarian.

3.   Today's teen-agers have a great deal of responsibility. Many have their driver's licenses, and some even have their own cars. More fortunate teen-agers have adequate allowances, and many have steady part-time jobs. Even in school, teen-agers are given certain responsibilities. Many clubs handle large sums of money, and in some schools the Student Council is given a voice in planning extracurricular activities. It is little wonder that both the business and college communities are impressed by the responsibleness of young people.

Exercise 2   Prewriting: The Paragraph   On your paper, write the topic sentence of each unified paragraph that you identified in Exercise 1. Below the topic sentence, briefly list the details given in the supporting sentences. Finally, restate the concluding sentence in your own words.

Assignment   Prewriting   *Step 1:* On your paper, draw two paragraph boxes, as you did on page 279. *Step 2:* In each box write one of the sets of topic sentences and concluding sentences given below. Put each sentence where it belongs in each box. *Step 3:* Between each topic sentence and concluding sentence, list four details that you might include in the supporting sentences of a unified paragraph. Use details that clearly relate to the topic sentence.

1. *Topic sentence:* Different sports require different athletic skills.

Concluding sentence: That is why an athlete who excels in one sport may do poorly in another.

2. *Topic sentence:* The type of music that I enjoy depends on my mood.

Concluding sentence: Regardless of my mood, I can always find just the right music to fit it.

Assignment Checklist

Check your assignment for the following points:

✔ 1. Did you put the topic sentence at the beginning of the paragraph and the concluding sentence at the end?

✔ 2. Does each supporting detail clearly relate to the topic sentence?

10.2 Planning a Paragraph

10.2a Selecting and Limiting a Topic

In selecting a topic, keep in mind that you have only a few sentences to work with in a paragraph. If you choose a general topic, such as "Soccer" or "Historic monuments in the United States," you may find that you have too much to write about. On the other hand, if you choose a limited topic like "Scoring in soccer" or "Gettysburg," you will be able to cover your topic completely in a paragraph.

The following suggestions will help you to limit a general topic so that it is suitable for a paragraph.

Strategies

1. *Select an example of the general topic.*

   General topic: Great inventors
   Limited topic: Thomas Edison

2. *Substitute a shorter time period for a longer one.*

   General topic: Top songs of the decade
   Limited topic: Top songs of the current year

3. *Divide your subject into parts, and focus on one of the parts.*

> *General topic:* The human body
> *Limited topic:* How the heart works

4. *Limit your general topic to a specific condition, place, or purpose.*

> *General topic:* Bicycling
> *Limited topic:* Bicycling in traffic [condition]
> *General topic:* Active volcanoes
> *Limited topic:* Active volcanoes in Hawaii [place]
> *General topic:* Studying
> *Limited topic:* Studying for a test [purpose]

Exercise 1 Prewriting: Limited Topics Study the following lists of possible topics for paragraphs. On your paper, write the letter of the most limited topic in each list.

1. a. How to assemble a bicycle
   b. How to put on a bicycle chain
   c. How to maintain and repair a bicycle
2. a. World War I flying aces
   b. Famous airplane pilots
   c. Amelia Earhart, first woman to fly the Atlantic
3. a. The disappearance of the Mayans
   b. Lost civilizations
   c. Mysteries of the past
4. a. Battles of the American Revolution
   b. The Battle of Lexington
   c. What started the Battle of Lexington

Exercise 2 Prewriting: Limited Topics In each of the following lists of topics, the items become more limited as you move down the list. On your paper, write a topic that is even more limited than the last item on each list.

SAMPLE	Musical instruments
	Guitars
	Electric guitars
ANSWER	My brother's electric guitar

1. North America
   The United States
   Texas
2. Plants
   Vegetables
   Green vegetables
3. Queens
   English queens
   Queen Elizabeth II
4. Cooking
   Italian cooking
   Cooking pasta
5. Tools
   Power tools
   Power saws
6. Aches and pains
   Headaches
   Ways to cure a headache

Exercise 3   Prewriting: Limited Topics   The following topics are too general for paragraphs. Limit each topic, using the method described on the right. On your paper, write the limited topic.

SAMPLE	TOPIC	LIMIT TO
	Running	a special purpose
ANSWER	Running to stay in shape	

TOPIC	LIMIT TO
1. National holidays	one member of the group
2. Twentieth-century heroes	a shorter time period
3. My home	one part of the subject
4. Natural wonders	a special place
5. Buying clothes	a special purpose

10.2b Listing and Choosing Details

One way to limit your topic is to write it down and then list below it as many related details as you can. Some of these details may be ideas that you already have. Others may be ideas that you find in reference books. The following is an example of this kind of list.

Topic: Tidal waves

1. Begin far out at sea, usually as result of underwater earthquake or volcanic eruption.
2. Misnamed, because tides have nothing to do with tidal waves.
3. Called *tsunami* in Japan, from *tsu,* meaning "harbor," and *nami,* meaning "wave."
4. Waves only one or two feet tall in early stages because of great depth of the water.
5. Travel across ocean at speeds greater than four hundred miles per hour.
6. Speed decreases while height increases as waves approach coast; can exceed one hundred feet.
7. Scientists able to predict exact time that wave will strike coast following undersea earthquake.
8. Number of minutes taken by earthquake tremor to reach certain spot equals number of hours taken by tidal wave to reach same spot.
9. Shoreline water may recede before wave strikes; ocean floor visible.
10. Strikes coast with tremendous force, uprooting trees, knocking down buildings, and flooding land.

If you have done a good job of listing details, each detail will relate to the general topic. However, you will probably find that the details in your list relate to the topic in different ways. For example, in the list on tidal waves, Items 2 and 3 relate to the naming of tidal waves, while Items 7 and 8 indicate to the time that a tidal wave will reach shore. The remaining six details (Items 1, 4, 5, 6, 9, and 10) describe the journey made by a tidal wave. Because the last group is the largest, you will probably choose those details for your paragraph and set aside the other four details. In this way you can limit your topic from "Tidal waves" to "The journey made by a tidal wave."

Exercise 4 Prewriting: Choosing Details   Under the following topic is a list of details related to it. *Step 1:* Group the details according to how they relate to the topic. *Step 2:* On your paper, write the numbers of those details that form the largest group. *Step 3:* Write the limited topic of the largest group of details.

Topic: Being blind

1. Blind persons often able to get around without help of other people, using either long cane or a guide dog.
2. In United States, approximately one out of 650 persons is blind.
3. Thanks to Braille and "speaking" computers, blind person can read almost anything sighted person can.
4. Medical research has shown that blindness can often be avoided by treatment of eye inflammation in babies.
5. Blind person can learn to use either regular typewriter or Braille typewriter for writing.
6. Blind people able to perform most everyday tasks efficiently, because they develop powerful memories and sharp senses of hearing, smell, taste, and touch.
7. Naturally, people who lose their sight are afraid at first.
8. Blind persons can pursue many careers pursued by sighted persons; there are blind factory workers, teachers, business executives, and lawyers.

Assignment Prewriting   Write three of the following general topics on your paper. Think of two ways to limit each topic, and write the limited topics below the general topic.

SAMPLE	General topic: Hobbies
ANSWER	Hobbies
	Limited topics: Drawing cartoons
	Water-color painting

1. Comic strips	3. Outer space	5. Spiders
2. Horseback riding	4. After-school clubs	6. Dancing

Continuing Assignment Prewriting   *Step 1:* In a five-minute period, write down as many topics as you can. *Step 2:* From your list of topics, select the two that interest you most and write them each on a separate piece of paper. Under each topic list eight or more details that relate to the topic. Express each detail in just a few words. You may need to refer to an encyclopedia or another reference book to obtain information. *Step 3:* For each list decide which of the details are related closely enough to use in developing a paragraph. Put a checkmark beside those details that form the largest group. Then write a limited topic for the details that you checked. Save your paper. You will develop this assignment as you continue with the unit.

Assignment Checklist

Check your assignment for the following point:

> ✓ 1. Did you give two limited topics for each topic?

Check your Continuing Assignment for these points:

> ✓ 2. Did you list at least eight details for the two topics that you chose?
> ✓ 3. Did you place a checkmark next to those details in each list that are closely related in some way?
> ✓ 4. Did you write a limited topic for the largest group of related details?

10.3 Writing a Topic Sentence

Writing a good topic sentence helps both you and your readers. It helps you, the writer, to begin to put into words the main idea that you want to communicate in your paragraph. As you write your paragraph, the topic sentence helps you to keep to your main idea. A topic sentence helps your readers by telling them, in just one sentence, what the paragraph is about.

10.3a Writing Complete Sentences

When writing a topic sentence, keep in mind that you must write a complete sentence (*page 57*). Like any sentence, a topic sentence must have a subject and a predicate and must express a complete thought. Do not confuse a topic sentence with a topic or with a title.

TOPICS	How to earn pocket money
	Records or cassettes?
TITLES	How to Earn Pocket Money
	Records or Cassettes?
TOPIC SENTENCES	An ambitious student can earn pocket money in a number of ways.
	Which are better—records or cassettes?

Exercise 1 Prewriting: Complete Sentences On your paper, write the number of each of the following items that is expressed as a topic sentence. Next to each number, write the topic sentence and punctuate it correctly.

1. Why some birds fly south for the winter
2. During a fire, you should never panic
3. Where the flag of Mexico came from
4. Learning to style your hair
5. Is flying in an airplane safer than driving in a car
6. The night that my family and I saw a meteor shower
7. Collecting old baseball cards can be profitable
8. Construction work sometimes is exhausting
9. How to look up a difficult word in the dictionary
10. What it would be like to be a world-famous entertainer

Exercise 2 Writing: Complete Sentences On your paper, write as a complete sentence each item in Exercise 1 that is not a sentence.

10.3b Stating Your Topic

To be effective, a topic sentence must state the idea that unifies the other sentences in the paragraph. You might think of a topic sentence as a promise that you make to your readers. You promise that in your paragraph you will discuss the idea stated in your topic sentence. It is important, therefore, not to promise too much. For example, the topic sentence "The ocean liner *Titanic* sank because it had several flaws in its design" promises too much if your paragraph discusses only *one* flaw.

Just as your topic sentence should not promise too much, it should also not promise too little. For example, the topic sentence "Air pollution is a major problem in big cities" promises too little if the paragraph discusses not only air pollution but also water and noise pollution.

Before writing a topic sentence, it is helpful to review the details that you have chosen for your paragraph. Study the following limited topic and the list of details.

Limited topic: The number of stars in the universe

Enormous star systems in the universe known as galaxies.

Ten trillion stars in our own galaxy, the Milky Way.

Milky Way just one of many galaxies.

Telescope at Mount Palomar Observatory in California has photographed more than sixteen million galaxies.

Astronomers estimate that average galaxy contains one hundred billion stars.

Multiply one hundred billion by sixteen million, and you will get an idea of vast number of stars in universe.

Many more stars may exist beyond range of our telescopes.

Now consider the following statements as possible topic sentences for a paragraph written from these details.

A. The universe contains many more stars and planets than scientists originally thought.

B. One of the largest star systems in the universe is the Milky Way.
C. The universe contains an astonishing number of stars.

Statement A goes beyond the details on the list. It promises to discuss not just the number of stars in the universe but also the number of planets. Because the list does not include any details on planets, Statement A promises too much. It would not be a good choice for a topic sentence for the listed details.

Statement B ignores several details on the list. This statement promises to discuss only the stars of the Milky Way. Although the list does include details about stars in the Milky Way (Item 2), it also includes details about stars in other galaxies. Because Statement B promises too little, it would not be an effective topic sentence for the listed details.

Unlike Statements A and B, Statement C covers each detail on the list and does not call for details that are not on the list. Statement C expresses what the details have in common: they all relate to the astonishing number of stars in the universe. Statement C, then, would be an effective topic sentence for a paragraph based on the details listed.

Exercise 3 Prewriting: Topic Sentences Three possible topic sentences are given for each of the following lists of details. On your paper, write the topic sentence that would be most suitable for a paragraph written from the listed details.

1. According to Greek mythology, there originally were three Cyclopes: Arges, Brontes, and Steropes.

   Cyclopes—one-eyed giants who made thunderbolts for god Zeus.

   Descendents were savage race of monsters who lived in Sicily.

   Well-known legend involving a Cyclops told by Homer in ancient poem the *Odyssey.*

Homer described how Greek hero Odysseus escaped from cave of Cyclops Polyphemus by blinding him while he slept.

Possible topic sentences:

a. The ancient Greeks had many legends about giants and monsters.
b. An entertaining Greek legend is the story of how Odysseus escaped from the Cyclops Polyphemus.
c. Some of the most entertaining Greek legends were those involving the Cyclopes.

2. In Boston, law against taking bath without prescription from doctor.

If you live in Ashland, Wisconsin, you must return all marbles won in a match; playing for keeps is illegal.

Barber in Elkhart, Indiana, can get into trouble with law for threatening to cut off child's ears.

In Michigan, illegal to hitch crocodile to a fire hydrant, and in Nevada you may not drive camels down major highway.

Law forbids Californians to set mousetrap without first obtaining hunting license.

Possible topic sentences:

a. Some cities have old laws that no longer make sense.
b. In every city and state, there are old laws that do not make sense.
c. Some cities and states have old laws that no longer make sense.

Exercise 4   Writing: Topic Sentences   On your paper, write two possible topic sentences for each of the following topics. Begin both topic sentences with the same subject, but in each sentence make a different statement about the subject.

SAMPLE	Whales
ANSWER	Whales vary quite a bit in size.
	Whales need to be protected from hunters.

1. Halloween	3. Swimming lessons
2. Junkyards	4. Newspaper comic strips

Assignment Writing List four topics that you are interested in or familiar with. Write a topic sentence for a paragraph on each topic. Make sure that each topic sentence is a complete sentence and is limited enough to be developed in a paragraph.

Continuing Assignment Writing In the Continuing Assignment on page 288, you wrote limited topics for your lists of details. On your paper, write topic sentences for the two limited topics. Save your paper.

Assignment Checklist

Check your assignments for the following points:

✔ 1. Is each topic sentence a complete sentence?
✔ 2. Is each topic sentence limited enough to be developed in a paragraph?

Check your Continuing Assignment for this additional point:

✔ 3. Does each topic sentence state the limited topic of each group of details?

10.4 Developing a Paragraph

10.4a Writing Supporting Sentences

If you have planned your paragraph well, you will have a list of details to include in your supporting sentences. As you write your supporting sentences, keep the following guidelines in mind.

Strategies

1. *State the details in complete sentences (page 57).* When you list the details that you plan to use in a paragraph, you do not need to use complete sentences. Remember, however, that a paragraph is not a list of ideas. It is a series of complete sentences.

2. *Relate each sentence to the idea stated in the topic sentence.* Each supporting sentence must help to develop the main idea of the paragraph. If it does not, the paragraph will lack unity.

3. *Use topic reminders.* A topic reminder is a word or a phrase that reminds readers of the topic of the paragraph. Topic reminders include key words in the topic sentence and synonyms for those words.

The writer of the following paragraph uses each of these strategies. Notice that she has expressed all of the supporting details in complete sentences. Notice also how each supporting sentence contributes to the idea expressed in the topic sentence. The words in italic type are topic reminders. The sentences have been numbered to help you locate the details referred to in the left margin.

Model

Topic sentence
(1) Main idea: trees talk

Supporting details:
How often (2)
How loud (3)
When (4)

Sounds (5, 6, 7, 8, 9)

(1) Not everybody knows this, but trees do talk. (2) Some *trees talk* almost all the time, and others *talk* only once in a while. (3) Some are loud and clattery; others are quiet and whispery. (4) When the air is still, they hardly *say* anything at all, but when the wind blows hard, they *sigh* and *shout*. (5) Some *trees* even *sing*. (6) Listen to different *trees*. (7) *Pine trees* sound different from *poplars*. (8) *Oak trees* sound different from *willows*. (9) Dry *leaves*

Why people
never hear
trees (10)

Concluding
sentence (11)

make a crackling rustle in the fall, and empty *branches* blown by winter winds have a *sound* of their own. (10) Most people never hear *trees talk* because they don't take time to listen. (11) If you want to hear *trees talk,* or bees buzz, or any other special sound, all you have to do is listen.

Mollie Rights, *Beastly Neighbors*

Exercise 1 **Prewriting: Paragraph Unity** On your paper, write the topic sentence of the following paragraph. Under the topic sentence, write the numbers of the two sentences that do *not* relate directly to the topic sentence.

(1) The Los Angeles Dodgers received their nickname in the 1920s when the team was started in Brooklyn. (2) At that time the chief means of transportation in Brooklyn was the trolley system. (3) Today the subway and the bus have replaced the trolley car. (4) So frequently did the trolleys roll through Brooklyn that it was often a challenge to cross the street without being struck. (5) People from the neighboring borough of Manhattan used to say that one had to be a "dodger" of trolleys to survive in Brooklyn. (6) Thus, when the baseball team from the city of trolleys needed a name, "Dodgers" seemed a fitting choice. (7) The naming of the Pittsburgh Pirates, a major rival of the Dodgers, grew out of charges made by Philadelphia newspapers that the Pittsburgh team had stolen, or pirated, an outstanding player from the Philadelphia Athletics.

Exercise 2 **Prewriting: Topic Reminders** *Step 1:* Copy the topic sentences of the two paragraphs from Exercise 1 on your paper. Underline the most important words in each topic sentence. *Step 2:* List those words used in the related supporting sentences that help to remind readers of the topic. Give the number of the sentence in which each topic reminder appears.

Exercise 3 Writing: Supporting Sentences Use the following list of details to write supporting sentences for a paragraph. *Step 1:* On your paper, write the topic sentence provided. *Step 2:* Select the five details in the list that best support the topic sentence. Express each of these five details in a complete sentence. Include in your sentences words that will remind readers of the topic. *Step 3:* Underline each topic reminder.

Topic sentence: Reading enables you to have adventures that you would otherwise be unable to have.

Explore ocean floor with Jacques Cousteau.
Take balloon trip around the world in eighty days with Phileas Fogg.
Increase knowledge of events in far-off places.
Scale Mount Everest with Edmund Hillary.
Play a part in American Revolution with Johnny Tremain.
Get to know many interesting people.
Walk on moon with the *Apollo 11* astronauts.

10.4b Organizing Supporting Sentences

In a well-organized paragraph, each supporting detail is like a step leading to a destination. You should therefore arrange the details so that the reader never questions why one idea follows another or where the paragraph is headed. Arranging your supporting sentences in a sensible order and using transitional words and phrases can help you write a clear, orderly paragraph.

Orderly Arrangement of Details

Arrange your supporting details in an order that will be easy for your readers to follow. For example, if you are using physical details to describe someone or something, arrange the details in **spatial order.** You may organize the details from left to right, from top to bottom, or from near to far.

If, however, you are telling a story or explaining how to do something, the details will probably be a series of events or steps. Arrange those events or steps in **chronological order,** the order in which they happen. Start at the beginning and move, event by event or step by step, to the final event or step.

As you read the following paragraph, notice how the writer has arranged the details in chronological order.

Model

The Olympic games have a long history. According to tradition, they first took place at Olympia in ancient Greece. Every four years for more than a thousand years, the Greeks held these games in honor of the god Zeus. Then in A.D. 394, the games were abolished by Emperor Theodosius I of Rome. The Olympic games were re-established many centuries later in 1896. The first modern Olympic games were held, appropriately enough, in Athens, Greece. Every four years since then, except during World Wars I and II, the games have been held in various parts of the world.

The model paragraph begins at a time early in history and proceeds, event by event, to the present. The resulting paragraph is easy to follow.

Transitional Words and Phrases

The model paragraph about the Olympic games is not only arranged in time order, but it also includes signals that make the order clear to the reader. For example, the second sentence contains the word *first.* The fourth sentence begins with *Then.* The fifth sentence contains the word *later,* and the final sentence contains the words *since then.* Words like these are called **transitional words.** They provide a bridge from one event to another or from one step to another.

As you read the following paragraph, pay special attention to the transitional words and phrases in italic type.

Model

The planet Jupiter has several interesting features. *First of all,* it has thirteen or fourteen satellites, four of which are as large as our own moon. Jupiter is *also* the biggest and fastest-moving planet in the solar system. Its volume is thirteen hundred times greater than that of Earth, *yet* Jupiter requires fewer than ten hours to rotate. *Another* unusual feature of Jupiter is that it is the only planet known to radiate its own heat. One of Jupiter's most fascinating features, *however,* is its Great Red Spot. *For decades* scientists were puzzled by the tremendous size of the spot, by its changing shape and color, and by its habit of rotating more slowly than the rest of the planet. *Then,* in 1974, photographs taken during a space probe revealed that the Great Red Spot is, in fact, an enormous drifting storm.

The transitional words and phrases in the model paragraph make clear how each supporting detail about Jupiter relates to the other supporting details. These transitions enable the reader to move smoothly from one sentence to the next. The resulting paragraph is easy to follow.

Exercise 4   Prewriting: Organizing a Paragraph

Below the following topic sentence is a list of supporting sentences. On your paper, write the sentences in the order that would be easiest for readers to follow.

Topic sentence: The ride through the haunted house is one of the most popular attractions at the amusement park.

As you enter the house, you are ushered into a room that seems to expand, while a chilling voice warns you of the terrible frights ahead.

You leave the ride knowing that all of it has been faked, but marveling at the realism of the special effects.

From the expanding room, you walk along a dimly lighted hallway, complete with ghoulish pictures and a coffin that refuses to stay shut.

Out of the darkness appears one delightfully creepy scene after another: a banquet hall where spirits dine and dance, a huge room with strange objects floating in space, a grave-yard more alive than dead, and much more.

At the end of the hallway, you are seated in a car that whisks you away into darkness.

When your car finally comes to a halt, you discover that all along you have been riding with a mysterious companion.

Exercise 5 Prewriting: Transitional Words On your paper, list all of the transitional words and phrases used in the list of supporting sentences in Exercise 4.

Exercise 6 Prewriting: Organizing a Paragraph Use the following topic sentence, list of supporting sentences, and list of transitional words and phrases to write a well-organized paragraph. *Step 1:* Begin the paragraph with the topic sentence. *Step 2:* Write the supporting sentences in an order that will be easy for readers to follow. *Step 3:* Fill in the blank spaces in the supporting sentences by selecting the most suitable transitional word or phrase from the list.

Topic sentence: What makes a good cheerleader?

1. You __?__ must have a strong enough voice to be heard by people in the stands.
2. __?__, you should enjoy sports and sports fans.
3. __?__ to a strong voice, you should be able to perform routines on cue.
4. __?__, you should know something about the sport that you are cheering for.
5. __?__, you might lead the fans in the wrong cheer.
6. __?__, you should have an outgoing personality.
7. __?__, you wouldn't want to yell "We want a touchdown!" when the opposing team has the ball.

Transitional words and phrases

also	for example	most important	second
first	in addition	otherwise	

Assignment 1 Prewriting Choose one of the following topic sentences and write it on your paper. Below it, list at least five supporting details. Make sure that each detail develops the idea stated in the topic sentence.

1. The modern circus deserves its reputation as "the greatest show on earth."
2. Being a successful disc jockey takes great talent.
3. Rainy weather can be very miserable.
4. I had an interesting dream last night.

Assignment 2 Writing Write a paragraph using the topic sentence and the list of supporting details that you wrote for Assignment 1. Make certain that you express each supporting detail in a complete sentence. Arrange the details in an order that will be easy for readers to follow. Include at least three topic reminders and three transitional words or phrases in the paragraph, and underline them.

Continuing Assignment Writing In the Continuing Assignment on page 293, you wrote topic sentences for your two lists of details. Now arrange each list of details in the order that will be easiest for readers to follow. Then write the supporting details as complete sentences. Be sure to include topic reminders and transitional words in the supporting sentences. Save your paper.

Assignment Checklist

Check your assignments for the following points:

✔ 1. Do your supporting details develop the topic sentence?

✔ 2. Did you express your supporting details in complete sentences?

✔ 3. Did you arrange your supporting details in an order that the reader can easily follow?

✔ 4. Did you include topic reminders and transitional words or phrases in your supporting sentences?

10.5 Writing a Concluding Sentence

Once you have written a topic sentence and supporting sentences, you will sometimes want to end your paragraph with a concluding sentence. A **concluding sentence** repeats what you have said in the topic sentence or offers a final comment on the topic. By repeating the idea of the topic sentence, you remind the reader of the main idea of the paragraph. You should, of course, word the concluding sentence differently from the topic sentence.

In the following paragraph, the concluding sentence says the same thing as the topic sentence but in a different way.

Model

Topic sentence

I'll never forget the first baseball glove that I ever owned. I found it at the playground one day inside a trash can. Apparently, someone had thought that it was worthless and had dropped it there. The glove wasn't very big, and its shape left much to be desired. Although I constantly pounded it with my fist, the glove never formed a real pocket. During games the foam padding used to slip out of the fingers onto my wrist. I don't recall ever catching a line drive with that old glove, but I do know that I kept it long after I'd been given a new one. *That glove will always be part of my most treasured memories.*

Concluding sentence

Repeating the idea stated in your topic sentence is just one way to conclude a paragraph. You may also state a conclusion, express your own reaction, ask a question, recommend a course of action, and so on. You must, however, base your concluding sentence on what you have already said in the paragraph. You could use any one of the following concluding sentences for the paragraph on the baseball glove.

Often our first experiences are our most memorable ones.

The glove may have been a castoff, but it was *my* glove!

Who would have thought that the one possession that I would cherish the longest would be something that I found in a trash can!

Instead of repeating what has been said in the topic sentence, each of these concluding sentences makes a final statement about the topic.

Exercise 1   Prewriting: Concluding Sentences
Three possible concluding sentences are given after the following paragraph. On your paper, write the number of the most suitable concluding sentence for the paragraph.

Structurally, the human body is a masterpiece of design. The skeleton is made up of approximately two hundred bones that are joined in a way that provides flexibility as well as strength. This structure gives people their shapes, allows them to stand upright, and protects their internal organs. Over six hundred muscles cling to the skeleton. They function like cables, pulling bones back and forth and enabling parts of the body to move. The genius of the human structure is that it has a fixed shape but is still able to move in a smooth, coordinated manner.

1. We should take good care of our bodies.
2. All movements, from walking and jumping to eating and laughing, are possible because bones and muscles work together in harmony.
3. Not all creatures have both bones and muscles.

Exercise 2 Writing: Concluding Sentences On your paper, write two other concluding sentences that could be used for the paragraph in Exercise 1.

Assignment Writing Write a paragraph on a topic of your choice. Then write two possible concluding sentences after your paragraph. In the first, repeat the idea stated in the topic sentence, using different words. In the second, express your own reaction or ask a question related to the main idea of the paragraph.

Continuing Assignment Writing In the Continuing Assignments in this unit, you have developed two paragraphs. Now write a concluding sentence for each paragraph.

Assignment Checklist

Check your assignments for the following points:

  ✔ 1. Did you write a concluding sentence that repeats the idea stated in your topic sentence?

  ✔ 2. Did you write a concluding sentence that expresses a personal feeling or that asks a question?

Famous Faces: Writing a Paragraph

Situation: You are a writer for the Famous Faces trading card series. Your job is to write brief summaries of the lives of athletes so that each printed summary fits on a three-by-five-inch trading card. You are allowed between five and seven sentences per card. As you work, keep in mind the following information.

Writer: you as a writer of trading cards
Audience: card collectors (ten-to-twelve-year-old fans)
Topic: an athlete's life
Purpose: to inform in a paragraph

Directions: To write your paragraph, follow these steps.

Step 1.   Read the fact sheet about the two athletes.
Step 2.   Choose the athlete that you will write about. Organize the facts about that person in the following order:
        Type of skill
        Greatest accomplishment
        Development of career
        Ambition
        Advice to young athletes
Step 3.   Write the paragraph. In your topic sentence, identify the athlete, and mention what he or she is famous for. Include the remainder of the facts in your supporting sentences. You may include more than one fact in a sentence. Write no more than

(Continue on page 306.)

FACT SHEET

BETH KAPLAN

Speed skater

Won three gold medals at
the 1980 Lake Placid Winter
Olympics

First skated when three
years old

Discovered by skater Angela
Farmer when Beth was twelve

Began winning streak at
fifteen, bringing her six
international titles in
three years

Coached by Angela Farmer

Wants to set up a training
camp for young skaters

5'6" tall, weighs 125 lbs

Born in Madison, Wisconsin,
in 1965

Beth says, "You have to
have confidence in yourself
and believe in your
abilities, no matter what."

KIP JOHNSON

Skier

Won gold medal at the 1980
Lake Placid Winter
Olympics. Won medal for
giant slalom

Unmatched in his speed on
the turns

Has skied for eighteen
years, since age four

Born in Denver, Colorado

Discovered by downhill
racer John Kiley, who
became Kip's coach

Wants to ski the Matterhorn
someday

6'1" tall, weighs 165 lbs

Kip says, "Many times I
wanted to quit, but I kept
going, and that makes all
the difference between
failure and success."

seven sentences. Be sure that each sentence is complete.

Step 4. Put the following information at the top of the page on which you write your paragraph. Fill in the information from the fact sheet.

Name of Athlete

Height:
Weight:
Place of Birth:

Unit Assignments

Assignment 1   Select three of the following topics and limit them so that each topic is suitable for development in a paragraph.

1. Famous Americans
2. Sports
3. Books

4. Pets
5. Winter storms
6. Holiday preparations

Assignment 2   Select two of the topics that you limited for Assignment 1 and list details related directly to each topic. Use an encyclopedia or other source to find the details that you need.

Assignment 3   Carefully study the two sets of details that you listed for Assignment 2. First, write a topic sentence for a paragraph using each set of details. Then for each paragraph state the details in a series of sentences that support the topic sentence.

Assignment 4   Write a paragraph for each topic sentence and series of supporting sentences that you developed for Assignment 3. Arrange the supporting sentences in an order that will be easy to follow. Add transitional words and phrases, and provide topic reminders.

Assignment 5   Write a concluding sentence for each paragraph that you developed for Assignment 4. The concluding sentence for one paragraph should repeat the idea stated in the topic sentence. The concluding sentence for the other paragraph should express your own reaction to the topic.

Revising Your Assignments

For help in revising a paragraph, consult the Checklist for Revision on the last page of this book.

Unit Tests

Test 1

A. Number your paper from 1 to 5. Next to each number, write *True* if the sentence is true or *False* if it is false.

1. The topic sentence must follow the supporting details.
2. A concluding sentence summarizes the supporting sentences or states a conclusion about the main idea.
3. It is best to limit a general topic so that it is suitable for development in a paragraph.
4. A topic sentence is the same as a title.
5. You should arrange supporting details in an order that is easy for readers to follow.

B. Number your paper from 6 to 10. Next to each number, write the letter of the term that correctly completes the sentence. You will use all but one of the terms.

    a. supporting sentences   d. paragraph
    b. unity   e. concluding sentence
    c. transitional words   f. topic sentence

6. A(n) __?__ is a series of sentences that develops a single idea.
7. A(n) __?__ states the main idea of a paragraph.
8. __?__ explain or develop what is stated in the topic sentence.
9. A paragraph in which each supporting sentence contributes to the main idea has __?__.
10. __?__ are signals that help make clear the order in a paragraph.

C. Number your paper from 11 to 15. Read the following paragraph. Next to each number on your paper, write the letter of the item that correctly answers the question.

    (1) George Boyle was not very successful as one of the first pilots for the Air Mail Service of the United States Post Office.   (2) On May 15, 1918, he took off on a flight from Washington, D.C., to Philadelphia.   (3) Observers thought that he was going in the wrong direction.   (4) Soon, Boyle called the airport to confirm that he had gone south instead of north.   (5) On the next day, the officials gave Boyle

another chance. (6) They even sent another plane to accompany him for part of the way. (7) After the other plane left him, Boyle got lost and ran out of gas. (8) The officials sent him back to flight school. (9) It is amazing that the Air Mail Service ever succeeded when it started with a pilot like George Boyle.

11. Which one of the following is the limited topic?
    a. Planes
    b. Flying from Washington, D.C., to Philadelphia
    c. Boyle's problems as a pilot for the Post Office
    d. Boyle's first flights for the Post Office

12. Which one of the following is the topic sentence?
    a. Sentence 1   c. Sentence 8
    b. Sentence 2   d. Sentence 9

13. Which of the following is the order of the supporting details?
    a. Order in which the events happened
    b. Order from left to right
    c. Order from most to least interesting
    d. Order in which the writer thought of them

14. Which one of the following sentences begins with a transitional word?
    a. Sentence 1   c. Sentence 6
    b. Sentence 4   d. Sentence 9

15. Which one of the following does the writer do in the concluding sentence?
    a. Asks a question
    b. Expresses a personal feeling
    c. Recommends a course of action
    d. Summarizes the topic sentence

Test 2

Choose one of the Unit Assignments or a topic that your teacher suggests. Write the assignment as directed and hand it in to your teacher.

Revising

Unit Preview

After you finish the first draft of a paragraph or of a longer piece of writing, you can usually improve it by revising it. When you revise, you reorganize and rewrite your first draft. You may have to rearrange sentences, add or remove some sentences, combine short choppy sentences, and separate long sentences so that your readers will understand what you have written.

The following is the first draft of a paragraph. Next to it the writer has made some notes for revisions. Read the first draft and the notes. Then compare the draft with the revised version that follows it. In the revised draft, the sentences have been numbered to help you answer the questions for analysis.

FIRST DRAFT

Make topic sentence precise.	No one likes to kill whales, but the New England settlers had to. The settlers had depended on candles, rushes, and fireplaces as their main
Move phrase to beginning.	sources of illumination before the introduction of whale oil. In the early part of the seventeenth
Combine sentences.	century, the Dutch had extracted oil from whale blubber, they had used it successfully in lamps. By
Combine sentences.	1650, whaling had been established in the American colonies, The use of whale oil became
Add sentence	widespread in New England.

REVISED DRAFT

(1) The idea of killing whales bothers many of us, but whale oil once supplied a much-needed source of light for the New England settlers. (2) Before the introduction of whale oil,

the settlers had depended on candles, rushes, and fireplaces as their main sources of illumination. (3) In the early part of the seventeenth century, the Dutch extracted oil from whale blubber and used it successfully in lamps. (4) By 1650, whaling was well established in the American colonies, and the use of whale oil became widespread in New England. (5) We can appreciate the value of whale oil to the colonists, but we no longer need to kill whales for their oil.

For Analysis On your paper, answer the following questions about the revisions made by the writer.

1. How does revised Sentence 1 state the idea that unifies the other sentences in the paragraph?
2. In Sentences 3 and 4, how did the writer combine the two original sentences?
3. Why did the writer add Sentence 5—to sum up what has been said in the paragraph or to offer a final comment on the topic?

In answering these questions, you have seen how a writer revises a first draft. In this unit you will practice techniques for revising paragraphs and sentences.

11.1 Revising Paragraphs

A good paragraph should provide enough information to make your point. It should also be unified (*pages 280–281*) and well organized (*pages 296–297*).

11.1a Unity

To be clear, your paragraph must have unity (*pages 280–281*). A paragraph has unity when all of the supporting sentences are directly related to the idea stated in your topic sentence. Use the following strategies to revise for unity.

Strategies

1. *Check to be sure that your paragraph has a main idea that you have stated in a topic sentence.*

   NO MAIN IDEA

   > The building next door is brick. Our house is brick, too. Bricks are made of clay that has been baked. A brick building usually lasts longer than one built of wood.

   MAIN IDEA STATED IN TOPIC SENTENCE

   > Bricks have many advantages as a building material. They are suitable for constructing both small and large buildings. In addition, bricks usually require less maintenance than wood, and they tend to last longer. Although a brick building may be more expensive to construct than one made of wood, brick is more resistant to fire and other damage.

2. *Make sure that your topic sentence makes clear what the paragraph is about.* If your topic sentence is vague, rewrite it to make it more precise.

   VAGUE   My next-door neighbor is nice.

   PRECISE   My next-door neighbor is the kindest and the best-humored person that I know.

   Words such as *nice* and *good* can make the meaning of a sentence vague. If you explain what you mean by such words, you will make the sentence precise.

3. *Make sure that the remaining sentences support the topic sentence.* Take out any sentence that does not support or develop the idea stated in your topic sentence. Be sure that you have included enough supporting information to make your point.

Exercise 1   Revising: Unity   *Step 1:* On your paper, state the main idea of Paragraph 1 in a topic sentence that is precise. *Step 2:* Write the two sentences in Paragraph 2 that do not provide supporting details for the topic sentence.

1.   A wheelchair ramp now leads from the sidewalk to the lobby of the theater. There, an elevator serves all floors. All doors have been widened recently and handrails have been installed. In the auditorium itself, special listening devices are available for the hearing impaired, and the programs for the performances are available in Braille for blind patrons.

2.   In different parts of the world, different animals provide people with milk. In the United States and in most other English-speaking countries, the cow furnishes most of the milk. Milk is valuable in the diet of adults and is an almost complete food for infants. The desert tribes of Arabia get their milk from the camel. In Egypt milk is provided by the water buffalo, and in Lapland by the reindeer. Reindeer milk has about five times as much protein as cow's milk. The llama is a milk-producing animal in Peru. In Tibet people get their milk from the yak. In many countries, of course, the goat is an important supplier of milk. The cow is definitely not the only animal capable of providing this valuable food.

Exercise 2   Revising: The Paragraph   On your paper, revise the following paragraph. *Step 1:* Rewrite the topic sentence (in italic type) to make it precise. *Step 2:* Add two or more sentences that give additional information about (a) how door-to-door transportation can be arranged and (b) how help with heavy chores can be provided.

We should help our senior citizens. Older people can do their own shopping if they have door-to-door transportation. Having someone to help with heavy housecleaning chores is often necessary for an elderly person who lives alone. People in the neighborhood can make independent living easier and less lonely for their older neighbors by calling or visiting them regularly.

11.1b Organization

To be clear, your paragraph has to be well organized. Your readers must be able to see how the ideas in your paragraph relate to one another. Use the following strategies to revise for organization.

Strategies

1. *Make sure that you have introduced your topic before you begin to discuss it.* It is usually best to place your topic sentence at the beginning.

2. *Check to be sure that you have organized your supporting sentences in an order that makes sense to your readers.* If you are telling about events that take place over a period of time, arrange the details in chronological order—the order in which they happen (*page 297*). If you are describing something, arrange the details in spatial order—from top to bottom, from left to right, and so forth (*pages 296–297*).

3. *Use transitional words and phrases* to connect the ideas in your paragraph and to make your paragraph read smoothly (*pages 297–298*).

Exercise 3   Revising: Organization   On your paper, revise the following paragraphs to improve their organization. In Paragraph 1, identify the topic sentence and move it to the beginning. In Paragraph 2, arrange the supporting details in chronological order. In Paragraph 3, add transitional words and phrases to connect the ideas and to make the paragraph read smoothly.

1.   The young lion cubs are ready to play at dawn. While the lioness sleeps, they scramble all over the lion, pulling at his mane and chewing his tail. The lion takes it all patiently,

but occasionally he gives them a gentle cuff. Then the cubs back off for a brief period before resuming their tumbling, tussling antics. A typical early morning scene in the lion family follows a certain routine.

2.   We need to do several gardening chores before winter. Once the garden is mulched, we can carefully clean the tools and wheelbarrow. Finally, before it gets too cold, we can repair the tools and give the wheelbarrow a fresh coat of paint. Next, we will spread all of the raked-up leaves on the vegetable beds as mulch. First, I will take down and store the bean poles. Then you can help me rake the yard.

3.   The apple mystery has been solved at last. Anne collected a basket of crabapples from the orchard. We had a large bowl of apples in the kitchen. We put the basket on the back porch to keep the apples cool. Dave noticed that the apples were disappearing. Betsy saw half-eaten apples here and there along the top rail of the fence. The dog was very excited. We looked out the window and saw a squirrel grab an apple and run up onto the fence. It munched on the apple and left the rest of it on the fence.

Assignment Revising   The following paragraph is a first draft. To the left of the draft are notes for needed revisions. On your paper, write a revised draft, using the notes as a guide.

Make topic sentence precise.

Remove sentence.

Add transitional words throughout.

You can easily make a career montage. A montage is made from a variety of pictures or designs. It is different from a collage. Search through old magazines for pictures that relate in some way to the career that you are illustrating. Tear out each page that has a picture that you want. Cut out details from each picture. For example, if your montage is about a career as a police officer, you may want to cut part of a uniform from one picture and part of a patrol car from another. Arrange and

Put sentences in correct order.

Add concluding sentence.

rearrange your cutouts on a sheet of stiff paper until you have an arrangement that you like. Cut out background material too—a picture of a city street, for example. Glue the pieces carefully, making sure that you cover all of the paper backing.

Assignment Checklist

Check your assignment for the following points:

✔ 1. Did you begin the revised draft with a topic sentence that is more specific?

✔ 2. Did you relate all of the supporting sentences to the idea stated in the topic sentence?

✔ 3. Did you use transitional words and phrases?

✔ 4. Did you end with a concluding sentence?

11.2 Revising Sentences: Coordination

Once you are satisfied that your paragraph is unified and well organized, you can begin revising your sentences to make them clearer and to make them fit smoothly into the paragraph.

One way to improve your sentences is to combine related sentences by making compound subjects, compound predicates, and compound sentences. Combining related ideas into compound structures is called **coordination.** The structures that you combine must be of equal grammatical rank, for example, subjects, predicates, and sentences.

11.2a Compound Subjects

A compound subject (*page 91*) is made up of two or more simple subjects with the same predicate. When you combine subjects that have the same predicate, your revised sentences will convey your meaning more concisely and more smoothly. Use the coordinating conjunctions *and* and *or* to connect compound subjects. The following examples show how you can combine sentences by using compound subjects.

TWO SENTENCES
> Pompeii was buried during the eruption of Mount Vesuvius. Herculaneum was buried during the same eruption.

REVISED SENTENCE WITH COMPOUND SUBJECT
> **Pompeii** and **Herculaneum** were buried during the eruption of Mount Vesuvius.

TWO SENTENCES
> Berlin is cut off from the southern part of New Hampshire by the White Mountains. Gorham is cut off in the same way.

REVISED SENTENCE WITH COMPOUND SUBJECT
> **Berlin** and **Gorham** are cut off from the southern part of New Hampshire by the White Mountains.

TWO SENTENCES
> Flowers decorated some ancient Pueblo pots. Birds decorated other ancient Pueblo pots.

REVISED SENTENCE WITH COMPOUND SUBJECT
> **Flowers** or **birds** decorated ancient Pueblo pots.

Exercise 1   Revising: Compound Subjects   On your paper, revise each pair of sentences by writing one sentence with a compound subject. Underline the conjunction that you use to connect the subjects.

SAMPLE   Aluminum is an excellent conductor of heat.
Copper is also an excellent conductor of heat.

ANSWER   Aluminum <u>and</u> copper are excellent conductors of heat.

1. Begonias will bloom in a shady spot in the garden. Cyclamen will also bloom in the shade.
2. The Swiss Alps are excellent for hiking and skiing. The Italian Alps offer the same sports.
3. The subways were delayed by the terrible storm. The railroad was behind schedule too.
4. Leaves were swirling around the yard in the wind. Litter was also swirling around.
5. Winston Churchill buoyed the spirits of the people during World War II. Franklin Roosevelt did too.
6. My mother's parents came from Nova Scotia. My father's parents came from Nova Scotia too.
7. The shops have been decorated for the holiday. The town hall has also been decorated.
8. The stable needs painting. The wagon shed needs painting.
9. These crates would be useful for storing vegetables temporarily. These baskets would be useful instead of the crates.
10. Some of this hay would be a good mulch for the shrubs. These leaves would be a good mulch.

11.2b Compound Predicates

A compound predicate (*page 92*) is made up of two or more simple predicates with the same subject. When you combine sentences that have the same subject, your revised sentence will convey your meaning more concisely and smoothly. Use *and, but,* and *or* to connect compound predicates. The following examples show how you can combine sentences by using compound predicates.

TWO SENTENCES
>The Minoans built a great civilization on Crete. They vanished around 1100 B.C.

REVISED SENTENCE WITH COMPOUND PREDICATE
>The Minoans **built** a great civilization on Crete but **vanished** around 1100 B.C.

TWO SENTENCES
> The pilot checked the instruments. Then the pilot gave the signal for takeoff.

REVISED SENTENCE WITH COMPOUND PREDICATE
> The pilot **checked** the instruments and then **gave** the signal for takeoff.

TWO SENTENCES
> The valuable coins were stolen. Perhaps they were misplaced.

REVISED SENTENCE WITH COMPOUND PREDICATE
> The valuable coins **were stolen** or **have been lost.**

Exercise 2   Revising: Compound Predicates   On your paper, revise each pair of sentences by writing one sentence with a compound predicate. Underline the conjunction that you use to connect the predicates.

SAMPLE
> Joe noticed an unusual cloud formation. He stopped to look at it.

ANSWER
> Joe noticed an unusual cloud formation <u>and</u> stopped to look at it.

1. The tourists began their trip in Miami. The tourists then flew to Mexico City.
2. Electrical impulses stimulated the woman's paralyzed leg muscles. The impulses prompted her to walk.
3. Tonight the Wilbur Theatre will preview *Almost an Eagle.* The theatre will present *The Nutcracker* during the holidays.
4. In the movie, Barbarossa pretends to be dead. He escapes from his tormentors.
5. The Arabs built a platform covered with carpets and cushions. They called it a "suffah."
6. The Hebrews fashioned a long backless couch, or "sapāh." They usually put it along a wall.
7. Today's houses are built in a variety of styles. They are often mixtures of several styles.

8. For patients with slipped discs, doctors prescribe traction. They suggest surgery instead.
9. The weather will turn windy. It will also become much colder.
10. The fishing fleet returned to the harbor. The fleet anchored there until the storm ended.

11.2c Compound Sentences

By combining two or more simple sentences into a compound sentence (*page 107*), you can eliminate choppy sentences from your writing. However, the sentences that you combine must be related in meaning.

NOT RELATED   The ancient Egyptians traveled on ships with huge sails, but they wove nets out of reeds.

RELATED   The ancient Egyptians traveled on ships with huge sails, but the sails were used only on the Nile River.

You use the coordinating conjunctions *and, but,* and *or* to connect simple sentences. Each of these conjunctions expresses a different relationship between ideas. The conjunction *and* expresses addition. The conjunction *but* expresses a contrast. The conjunction *or* expresses a choice. The following examples show how you can join two related simple sentences in a compound sentence.

TWO SENTENCES
    The eagles' nest is a great heap of sticks. The eagles return to it every year.

COMPOUND SENTENCE
    The eagles' nest is a great heap of sticks, **and** the eagles return to it every year. [addition]

TWO SENTENCES
> The bald eagle is dark brown. Its tail feathers are white.

COMPOUND SENTENCE
> The bald eagle is dark brown, **but** its tail feathers are white. [contrast]

TWO SENTENCES
> To illustrate your report, you can photograph an eagle in the aviary at the zoo. You can also find a picture in the library.

COMPOUND SENTENCE
> To illustrate your report, you can photograph an eagle in the aviary at the zoo, **or** you can find a picture in the library. [choice]

Remember to use a comma before the coordinating conjunction in a compound sentence (*page 212*).

Exercise 3 Revising: Compound Sentences On your paper, revise each group of sentences by combining them into one compound sentence. Use the coordinating conjunction given in parentheses. Remember to use a comma before the conjunction.

SAMPLE   The Santa Fe Trail led from Missouri to New Mexico. The Old Spanish Trail led from there to California. (*and*)

ANSWER   The Santa Fe Trail led from Missouri to New Mexico, and the Old Spanish Trail led from there to California.

1. The Continental Congress approved a postal system for the United Colonies. The British inland service came to an end in 1775. (*and*)

2. The French settlers in Ohio disapproved of the Ohio Company's traders. They were even more concerned by the intrusion of the Pennsylvania traders. (*but*)

3. The Philadelphia-Lancaster Turnpike had proved a financial success. Many toll roads were soon built in New England. (*and*)

4. You can take the steamboat *New Orleans* between Louisville and New Orleans. You can go from Brownville to New Orleans on the *Enterprise*. (*or*)

5. Gold was discovered in Nevada in 1860. The gold rush did not begin until 1863. (*but*)

6. Columbus was marooned in Jamaica in 1503. He did not return to Spain until 1504. (*and*)

7. The ship *Mary Guildford* explored the North Atlantic. Her companion ship, *Samson*, foundered on the voyage from Plymouth, England. (*but*)

8. Sir Walter Raleigh sent a group of colonists to Virginia in 1585. The colony was abandoned in 1586. (*but*)

9. Thomas Jefferson was the first rector of the University of Virginia. He also designed its first buildings. (*and*)

10. Breckenridge's party encountered many difficulties. They would not turn back. (*but*)

Assignment Revising   On your paper, revise the following paragraph by coordinating some related sentences. Use compound subjects, compound predicates, and compound sentences.

> Summer can bring pleasure. It can also bring discomfort. During the summer, we do not attend school. We do not concern ourselves with homework. We have no lessons. Every day is a holiday. Families can take their picnic baskets to a nearby park. They can eat under the trees. Drivers can open the car windows. They can ride in air-conditioned comfort instead. Summer does have its discomforts, however. Humid days contribute to our discomfort. Hot nights are another source of discomfort. Thunderstorms roll in unexpectedly. They can ruin the best-laid plans. Children

must stay indoors because of long periods of rain. Adults must stay indoors too. Pain can result from careless overexposure to the sun. Sleepless nights result too. For the most part, however, the pleasures of summer far outweigh the discomforts.

Assignment Checklist

Check your assignment for the following points:

✔ 1. Did you combine sentences that have the same predicates by making compound subjects?
✔ 2. Did you combine sentences that have the same subject by making compound predicates?
✔ 3. Did you combine sentences that are related in meaning into compound sentences?
✔ 4. Did you use a comma before the coordinating conjunction in a compound sentence?

11.3 Revising Sentences: Prepositional Phrases

Sometimes you can combine sentences by using prepositional phrases (*page 69*). The prepositional phrase may already appear in one of the sentences that you are combining, or you may have to write an original prepositional phrase. The prepositional phrases are in italic type in the following examples.

TWO SENTENCES
    We found the key. It was *under the mat.*

REVISED SENTENCE WITH PREPOSITIONAL PHRASE
    We found the key *under the mat.* [The prepositional phrase is from the second sentence.]

TWO SENTENCES
>A car is parked outside. It has California license plates.

REVISED SENTENCE WITH PREPOSITIONAL PHRASE
>A car *with California license plates* is parked outside.
>[The second sentence has been rewritten as a prepositional phrase.]

THREE SENTENCES
>Martina rides her bike. She rides it *to school.* She rides it *on Tuesdays.*

REVISED SENTENCE WITH PREPOSITIONAL PHRASES
>*On Tuesdays* Martina rides her bike *to school.*

Exercise Revising: Prepositional Phrases On your paper, revise each group of sentences by writing a single smooth sentence that includes a prepositional phrase.

>SAMPLE   That cat is a Manx cat. It doesn't have a tail.
>
>ANSWER   That cat without a tail is a Manx cat.

1. Jane lives in that white house. It has bright yellow shutters.
2. Greg found some firewood. He found it near the shed.
3. They insulated the ice house. They used hay.
4. The donkey was domesticated five thousand years ago. The ancient Egyptians domesticated it.
5. Scorpions hide. They hide during the day. They hide in dark places.
6. A needle is a tool. It has a sharp point and an eye.
7. The planets in our solar system move. They move in orbits. They move around the sun.
8. Milk nourishes the body. Milk has essential minerals.
9. The mathematician Archimedes was also an inventor. He invented many scientific devices.
10. The workers built a dam. They built it across the valley.

Assignment Revising On your paper, revise the following paragraphs by using prepositional phrases to combine some of the sentences.

American families have a long tradition of space-saving dinner tables. The Pilgrims used tables. They used tables of planks. The planks were on trestles. These tables could easily be taken apart and set aside. This was done after the meal. Another space-saving table was the hutch table. It could be used as a chair. It could be used this way with the top tipped back. The hutch table also had a drawer or box. The drawer or box was for storage. The drawer or box was under the seat. Before long, two other space-saving tables came into use. One style was the gate-leg table. The gate-leg table had movable legs and drop leaves. The other style was the drop-leaf table. The drop-leaf table had supports. The supports were for the leaves. Both tables folded compactly and could be stored. They could be stored against the wall. Even today, space-conscious families dine at drop-leaf tables.

Assignment Checklist

Check your assignment for the following point:

✔ Did you use prepositional phrases correctly to combine sentences?

11.4 Revising Sentences: Conciseness

Conciseness means stating your ideas directly and briefly. Do not try to put too many ideas or too many words into your sentences. Revise your sentences for conciseness by removing any words that add nothing to your ideas.

11.4a Avoiding *and* and *so*

Do not join too many ideas in one sentence by over-using *and* and *so*. You can revise sentences with too many ideas by dividing them into two or more sentences. If appropriate, you can also form compound subjects or predicates.

WORDY   The refrigerator was broken, and so I called the repair service, and I called right away, and I was pleased by their prompt response.

CONCISE   The refrigerator was broken. I called the repair service right away and was pleased by their prompt response.

Exercise 1   Revising: Conciseness   On your paper, revise the following sentences by using two or more sentences to express the ideas more concisely. Form compound subjects or predicates if appropriate.

1. The Community Education Center catalogue lists many interesting courses, and Betsy gave me an application, and so I filled mine out immediately.
2. Jane Deccio is giving a pizza workshop, and Robert Martin is teaching a course on silk-screening, and so I will take both courses.
3. The classes begin at 6:30 P.M., and I took a bus to get there, and so I arrived early.
4. Ahmad enjoyed his class on photography, and so he signed up for camera maintenance too.
5. The most interesting course is a video workshop, and Vincent Wehrlin taught it last year, and Madge Borneo is teaching it this year.
6. Many people enjoy studying as a recreation, and our teacher has studied macramé for fun for years.
7. The cooking class was full, and so we went to a class on making seashell jewelry, and we liked it.
8. There are several teachers for the aerobic dance class, and we dance to popular music, and everyone enjoys it.
9. The Community Education Center does not give grades, and so many people can enjoy studying difficult subjects.
10. Last fall I took banjo lessons, and I studied oriental cooking this spring for variety, and next summer I plan to take a course in basic bookkeeping.

11.4b Avoiding Unnecessary Words

When you write sentences that contain unnecessary words, your reader may become confused. In the following examples, the writers have used excess words that do not clarify the sentence or that repeat an idea already expressed in the sentence. The revisions, on the other hand, are clear and concise.

UNNECESSARY WORDS

> After a long day, there is nothing better than a home-cooked meal prepared in your own kitchen. [The words *prepared in your own kitchen* do not add anything to the idea expressed in the sentence.]

REVISED FOR CONCISENESS

> After a long day, there is nothing better than a home-cooked meal.

UNNECESSARY WORDS

> In this book the author writes about her childhood on a ranch in Wyoming as a young girl. [*In this book* does not make the sentence clearer. *As a young girl* repeats the idea expressed by *her childhood*.]

REVISED FOR CONCISENESS

> The author writes about her childhood on a ranch in Wyoming.

Exercise 2 Revising: Conciseness   On your paper, revise the following sentences to make them concise.

1. Vacuum cleaners make cleaning easier by making the house easier to clean.
2. The latest fashions of today are quite extreme.
3. Harry Truman succeeded Roosevelt as the next President.
4. Francine likes pizza, and it is her favorite food.
5. We ate raw vegetables with our lunch, and they weren't even cooked.
6. Please be on time and don't be late.

7. The two Prieto twins have joined the bowling team.

8. The commentator on the evening news finished the nightly report with an account of the fatal death of a famous, well-known violinist.

9. The letters were far too numerous in number for personal replies.

10. The sky was gray in color, and throughout the whole day we expected rain.

Assignment   Revising   On your paper, revise the following paragraphs to make the writing more concise.

　　　Americans are beginning to realize how useful water buffaloes can be. Water buffaloes can work for at least twenty years, and so they never need a tune-up or an oil change, and they are very fuel efficient, and they live well on skimpy grasslands and never have to be filled up with gasoline. The meat of a water buffalo is delicious and its milk is considered better than cow's milk, and they can live in just about any climate and they resist many common diseases. Water buffaloes are now recognized for their usefulness and may soon be more common in the United States.

Assignment Checklist

Check your assignment for the following points:

　✔ 1. Did you rewrite sentences to avoid overuse of the conjunctions *and* and *so*?

　✔ 2. Did you eliminate unnecessary words?

11.5 Revising Sentences: Variety

　　　Too many sentences of the same kind can be distracting or monotonous to your readers. Use the following strategies to revise for variety in your sentences.

Strategies

1. *Vary the beginnings of your sentences.* Occasionally place adverbs, adjectives, or prepositional phrases before the subject.

   ADVERB
   > Cautiously, the cat stepped onto the porch.

   ADJECTIVE
   > Disappointed, the team left the field.

   PREPOSITIONAL PHRASE
   > In an instant, the dog ran out the open door.

   Be careful, however, to avoid a series of sentences with the same kind of beginning. Such a pattern can be as monotonous and distracting as beginning every sentence with the subject.

2. *Vary the length and the structure of your sentences.* Use a mixture of (a) short simple sentences, (b) longer sentences with compound subjects, compound predicates, or both, and (c) compound sentences.

   MONOTONOUS
   > The telephone rang. Tanya dashed across the room. Natalie dashed across the room. They bumped into each other. They hit their heads. Natalie rubbed her head. Tanya answered the phone.

   VARIED
   > The telephone rang. Tanya and Natalie dashed across the room. They bumped into each other and hit their heads. Natalie rubbed her head, and Tanya answered the phone.

Exercise 1   Revising: Variety   On your paper, revise each of the following sentences by putting part of the sentence before the subject.

SAMPLE   The photographer developed the negative with
            great care.

ANSWER   With great care, the photographer developed
            the negative.

1. The countdown was suddenly suspended.
2. The United States purchased Alaska through the efforts of
   Secretary Seward.
3. The hikers, tired and footsore, refused to turn back.
4. Dr. Johnson finished the novel *Rasselas* in a single week.
5. The sailor stealthily left the ship.
6. The guests played charades at the birthday party.
7. The squirrels, hungry and aggressive, ate all of the bird seed.
8. Flooding is a real danger because of the heavy spring rains.
9. Sunsets on the prairie are unusually colorful.
10. We received a telephone call during the night from my sister
    in Vancouver.

Exercise 2   Revising: Variety   On your paper, revise
the following paragraph by varying some sentence beginnings
and by using compound subjects, compound predicates, and
compound sentences.

> Marnie drove to Chicago. Rose went with her. Rose
> drove from New Orleans to Louisville. Marnie drove the
> rest of the way. They stayed with Marnie's aunt in Chicago.
> They visited Rose's great-grandfather. They went to the zoo
> one day. They visited several museums on the same day.
> Rose wants to take the turnpike on the return trip. Marnie
> prefers country roads. The turnpike is faster. It is less
> interesting. The turnpike will get them home by Thanksgiv-
> ing. The country roads will also get them home by Thanks-
> giving.

Assignment   Revising   On your paper, revise the following paragraph for sentence variety. Vary some sentence
beginnings and combine some sentences.

Guide dogs have been used by blind persons for many years. Hearing-dogs are being trained now. These dogs can wake their owners in the morning at the sound of the alarm. They can lead hearing-impaired parents to a crying child. They can alert hearing-impaired persons to other sounds. Hearing-dogs provide security. They also provide companionship.

Assignment Checklist

Check your assignment for the following points:

✔ 1. Did you move at least one prepositional phrase to the beginning of a sentence?
✔ 2. Did you use compound subjects and compound predicates to combine some sentences?
✔ 3. Did you combine some sentences so that the paragraph contains simple and compound sentences?

11.6 Completing Your Revision

Proofreading

The final step in revising is proofreading. **Proofreading** is the careful checking for errors in grammar, usage, spelling, capitalization, and punctuation. If you proofread your work carefully, you will do a better job of getting your ideas across to your readers.

When you proofread your written work, examine each word and sentence individually. In this way you can be sure of discovering any errors. Use the following guide for proofreading, and then make a finished copy of your work.

1. Are all of your sentences complete (*Unit 5*)?
2. Do all verbs agree with their subjects (*Unit 6*)?
3. Did you spell words correctly (*Unit 17*)?
4. Did you punctuate your sentences correctly (*Unit 7*)?
5. Did you use correct capitalization (*Unit 7*)?

An Example of Revising and Proofreading

The following is a first draft of a paragraph about Harriet Tubman. To the left of the draft are notes for revisions. Read the first draft and the notes. Then compare the first draft with the revised draft that follows it.

FIRST DRAFT

Correct spelling.

Combine
sentences.

Put phrase
at beginning.

Put adverb
at beginning.

Spell out.

Combine
sentences.

Harriet Tubman was an unusual women. In 1820 she was born a slave on a plantation in Maryland. She was named Araminta. Later she took her mother's name, Harriet. She worked hard as a maid, a field hand, a cook, and a woodcutter from early childhood. In 1844 she married John Tubman, a freedman. She heard rumors about being sold and fled to Philadelphia. She made her way to Baltimore later and led her sister to freedom in Canada. That journey was the first of 19 trips on the Underground Railroad to Canada. Harriet Tubman became the railroad's most famous "conductor." She was known as the Moses of her people.

REVISED DRAFT

Harriet Tubman was an unusual woman. In 1820 she was born a slave on a plantation in Maryland. She was named Araminta but later took her mother's name, Harriet. From early childhood, she worked hard as a maid, a field hand, a cook, and a woodcutter. In 1844 she married John Tubman, a freedman. She heard rumors about being sold and fled to Philadelphia. Later she made her way to Baltimore and led her sister to freedom in Canada. That journey was the first of nineteen trips on the Underground Railroad to Canada. Harriet Tubman became the railroad's most famous "conductor" and was known as the Moses of her people.

Exercise Revising: Proofreading   Proofread the following paragraph for errors in spelling, punctuation, and capitalization. Then, on your paper, rewrite the paragraph with the needed corrections.

> Charles William Beebe was an american naturalist who studied underwater life He built a marine labratory in the bermudas and studied see life there, In 1930, he explored the underwater world from a bathysphere a two-ton steal globe. Four years later he and Otis barton decended more than three thousand feet to observe life never seen befor. Beebe is best rememberd for this record-breaking dive.

Assignment Revising   On your paper, revise and proofread the following paragraph.

> Life forms exist in the dessert. They exist with very little water. The Kangaroo rat never takes a drink. It gets it's water from the juicey plants on which it feeds. The camel drinks large quantities of water. It stores the water. It stores it for later use. Camels store fat in their humps. Snakes hide from the sun. They hide during much of the day. They require very little water. Even desert plants can hibernate. They hibernate during dry seasons.

Assignment Checklist

Check your assignment for the following points:

✔ 1. Did you combine related sentences by using compound predicates and compound sentences?
✔ 2. Did you use prepositional phrases to combine some sentences?
✔ 3. Did you vary some sentence beginnings?
✔ 4. Did you omit the unrelated sentence?
✔ 5. Did you proofread to correct errors in grammar, usage, spelling, capitalization, and punctuation?

Feather Facts: Revising a Paragraph

Situation: You are writing the introduction to a catalogue of down-filled products. Your first paragraph will describe the insulating properties of the fine, soft feathers known as down. Your editor has suggested some ways you can revise the first draft. As you revise, keep in mind the following information.

Writer: you as catalogue writer
Audience: catalogue readers
Topic: feathers
Purpose: to revise a paragraph for clarity, conciseness, and variety

Directions: To revise the draft, follow these steps.

Step 1.   Read the rough draft on the facing page and the editor's notes about each numbered sentence.

Step 2.   To revise, work with each sentence or pair of sentences according to your editor's notes. You may have to omit words, combine sentences, or correct mistakes in grammar.

Step 3.   On a separate sheet of paper, write your final revised paragraph. Proofread for spelling, punctuation, and grammar.

(1) Birds are unique and distinctive. **(2)** It is a masterpiece of design, a single feather by itself. **(3)** Feathers are made of keratin. **(4)** It is the same material from which our own nails are formed. **(5)** The construction of a feather is much more complex than that of a fingernail. **(6)** Each feather have a central shaft that extends from the quill's holow tip. **(7)** Along either side of each shaft there are many narrow parallel barbs, and each has its own set of smaller barbs that end in tiny hooks, and so in down-like feathers, this overlapping helps the feathers trap air and provide insulation. **(8)** We have made use of these properties of the feather. **(9)** We have created garments that use down for warmth. **(10)** The only thing that keeps a person warm on the arctic ice cap is the feathery down of an arctic duck. **(11)** The word <u>down</u> refers to one or all of the soft fluffy feathers on a young bird or beneath the outer feathers of an adult bird.

Editor's notes for revising

Sentence 1: Remove sentence; it does not support topic.

Sentence 2: This is your topic sentence. Rewrite to omit unnecessary words <u>it</u> and <u>by itself</u>. After Sentence 2 insert Sentence 11, which defines <u>down</u>.

Sentences 3 and 4: For variety, omit the words <u>it is</u> and combine the two sentences into one.

Sentence 5: Add transitional word <u>However</u>.

Sentence 6: Check spelling and grammar.

Sentence 7: Make into two complete sentences by omitting <u>and so</u>. Adjust punctuation and capitalization.

Sentences 8 and 9: Combine to form one sentence with a compound predicate.

Sentence 10: For variety, use a transitional word (<u>Indeed</u>) and a prepositional phrase ("on . . . ") to begin the sentence.

Unit Assignments

Assignment 1   Select a paragraph that you have written for a previous assignment. Use the information in this unit to revise your first draft. Then proofread it and make your finished copy.

Assignment 2   Write a paragraph about something that you have done recently at home, in school, or elsewhere. Tell about the part of the activity that you especially remember. Revise and proofread your draft. Then make a finished copy.

Assignment 3   Write a paragraph about something that frightened you. Describe what happened and what you did. Revise and proofread your draft. Then make a finished copy.

Assignment 4   Write a paragraph using the following topic sentence and supporting details. Eliminate details that do not support the topic sentence. Then arrange the related details in an order that is easy to follow. Revise and proofread your first draft. Then make a finished copy.

> *Topic sentence:* Certain safety precautions should be observed when using a stepladder.
>
> *Details:* Fully open and lock folding braces in position.
>
> Inspect steps and legs of wooden ladders for splits, breaks.
>
> Never climb higher than second step from top.
>
> Use gloves for messy jobs.
>
> Make sure that all four feet of ladder are on firm, level surface.
>
> Place ladder near enough to work to avoid leaning over at dangerous angle.
>
> Glue rubber to feet of old wooden ladders to prevent slipping.
>
> Metal ladders are easier to handle.
>
> Keep both feet on step while working.
>
> Never use stepladder as a straight ladder.

Assignment 5   Write a paragraph about a sport that interests you. Tell about a sports event that you took part in or one that you watched. Write for an audience that knows little about the sport. Revise and proofread your draft. Then make a finished copy.

Assignment 6   Write a paragraph about a job that someone in your family has. Inform your classmates about the main duties of someone who has that job. Revise and proofread your draft. Then make a finished copy.

Revising Your Assignments

For help in revising your writing, consult the Checklist for Revision on the last page of this book.

Unit Tests

Test 1

A. Number your paper from 1 to 5. Next to each number, write *True* if the sentence is true or *False* if it is false.

1. The first thing to do when you revise a paragraph is to check it for spelling errors.
2. When you revise a paragraph, you should check to see that it has a main idea stated in a topic sentence.
3. When you revise, you can give your paragraph variety by adding one or more unrelated details.
4. When you coordinate sentences, you divide them.
5. You can use prepositional phrases to combine sentences.

B. Number your paper from 6 to 10. Next to each number, write the letter of the term that correctly completes the sentence. You will use all but one of the terms.

a. unity   d. compound predicate
b. variety   e. proofreading
c. compound subject f. revising

6. _?_ is the correcting of errors in grammar, usage, spelling, punctuation, and capitalization.
7. Using different beginnings gives _?_ to the sentences in a paragraph.
8. You can revise two sentences that have the same predicate by combining them into one sentence with a _?_.
9. You can revise two sentences that have the same subject by combining them into one sentence with a _?_.
10. A paragraph has _?_ when all of the supporting sentences relate directly to the idea stated in the topic sentence.

C. Number your paper from 11 to 15. Next to each number, write the letter of the item that correctly answers the question.

11. Which of the following is the most precise topic sentence for a paragraph?
    a. Bread is a good food.
    b. Bread is a nutritious food.
    c. Bread is a basic food needed for good health.
12. Which one of the following do you *not* do to revise for conciseness?
    a. Avoid using *and* and *so* to join many sentences.
    b. Eliminate unnecessary words.
    c. Add a topic sentence.
13. Which one of the following do you *not* do to revise your sentences for variety?
    a. Make every sentence the same length.
    b. Vary your sentence beginnings.
    c. Use a mixture of simple and compound sentences.
14. Which one of the following does *not* make your paragraph well organized?
    a. Tell your readers what you are talking about before you begin to discuss the topic.
    b. Use transitional words and phrases.
    c. Combine some sentences.
15. Which of the following steps do you do last when revising?
    a. Proofread for errors.
    b. Check for unity and order.
    c. Revise your sentences.

Test 2

Choose one of the Unit Assignments or a topic that your teacher suggests. Write and revise the assignment as directed and hand it in to your teacher.

Explaining

Unit Preview

The goal of a good explanation is to make yourself clear. If you want to show some friends how to prepare an omelet, you can always take them into the kitchen and show them what to do. Sometimes, however, it is necessary to explain in writing how to make an omelet, how to set up an aquarium, or how to get to the public library.

In an explanation your purpose is always to make the steps so clear that the reader can follow them without asking a single question. Keep the reader—your audience—in mind as you write. Put the steps in the order in which they must be followed, and include all the information that your reader will need.

The following paragraph is an explanation. It begins with a topic sentence—a sentence that tells what the paragraph is about.

Topic sentence ¬

Step 1 ⊢

Step 2 ⊢

Step 3 ⊢

Step 4 ⊢

Step 5 ⊢

Step 6 ⊢

> You can make a toy pinwheel for a child by using only a piece of stiff paper, an unsharpened pencil with an eraser, and a straight pin. First, cut a six-inch square from the paper and draw two diagonal lines joining its opposite corners. Next, draw a circle with a radius of one and a half inches around the center of the square, where the diagonal lines cross. Then cut along each line from the corner to the edge of the circle. Now gently bend every other corner a little past the center without creasing the paper, until the head of the pinwheel is complete. Next, carefully insert the pin through the four corners and the center. Finally, push the pin firmly into the side of the pencil eraser, leaving enough of the pin clear so that the pinwheel can spin freely.

For Analysis On your paper, answer the following questions about the explanation.

1. How do you know what the writer is explaining?
2. Into how many steps is the explanation divided?
3. Write the first word in each of the steps. How do these words help you to follow the steps?
4. If possible, carry out the directions. Are all the necessary steps included? Are the steps in the right order? Do the directions give any information that is not needed?
5. Are the directions clear and easy to follow?
6. In answering Questions 1–5, what did you discover about writing explanations?

In this unit you will learn how to write clear explanations. As you write your explanations, you will follow the three steps of the writing process: prewriting, writing, and revising.

12.1 Explaining How to Get to a Place

Which set of directions for getting from one place to another is more helpful?

PARAGRAPH 1

Here is the most direct way to get from the post office to the courthouse. First, drive east on Main Street to the third traffic light. Then turn right on Culver Street and drive six blocks to Moreno Avenue, one block beyond the fire station. The courthouse is a red brick building on the northwest corner of Culver and Moreno.

PARAGRAPH 2

Go along Main Street for a while and turn right. Drive along Culver Street for a few blocks. Keep watching the right side of the street. The courthouse should be on about the sixth corner.

The first set of directions tells where to turn, how many blocks to go, and what corner to look for. It is more exact than the second set, and is therefore more helpful. The guidelines that follow will help you to write directions that are clear and easy to follow.

Strategies

1. *Begin with a topic sentence.* In your first sentence, you should state what you are going to explain. For example, you might write, "Here is the most direct way to get from the post office to the courthouse." The topic sentence tells the reader immediately what the purpose of the paragraph is.

2. *Divide the explanation into steps and present them in chronological order.* On a sheet of scratch paper, list the steps in the order in which they should be followed. Use the list as you write the supporting sentences that tell the reader how to get from one place to another.

3. *Use transitional words to tie the steps together.* Transitional words, such as *first, then, next, now,* and *finally,* help the reader to follow the steps in order.

4. *Give accurate and complete information.* Write exact instructions, such as "Drive east on Lancaster Street to the third traffic light." Whenever possible, mention landmarks that will help your reader know where he or she is. For example, you might write, "Finally, turn left on Jerusalem Avenue, just beyond the high school." Mentioning the high school will alert the reader to the location of Jerusalem Avenue.

5. *Include only essential details.* Extra information makes directions hard to follow.

A model paragraph of directions appears in the letter below. The writer of the paragraph made this list as a guide.

Topic: Shortest route from parking lot to auditorium

1. Park in lot behind school.
2. Enter building through double doors at back.
3. Inside, go down hall until you reach library, on left.
4. Take stairway across from library and walk up one flight to auditorium lobby.

The middle paragraph in the following letter explains in complete sentences the steps on the list. The transitional words are printed here in italic type.

Model

March 12, 19—

Dear Uncle Jonathan,

I'm happy that you will be able to come to Tyler to see our class play on March 30. Since I will be backstage getting into my costume and make-up, I will be unable to say hello before the curtain goes up.

Topic sentence ⊣ This is the shortest route from the
Step 1 ⊣ parking lot to the auditorium. *First,* park in
Step 2 ⊣ the lot behind the school. *Then* enter the
building through the double doors at the back.
Step 3 ⊣ *Next,* go straight down the hall until you see
Step 4 ⊣ the library, which will be on your left. *Finally,*
take the stairway directly across from the library entrance and walk up one flight to the auditorium lobby.

I'll meet you at the trophy case in the lobby after the show. I hope that you enjoy it!

Love,

Joy

Exercise 1   Prewriting: Complete Directions   Some
of the steps in the following directions do not give enough
information. On your paper, write the numbers of the incomplete steps.

(1) This is the best route to follow when you drive
from St. Louis to Lake of the Ozarks.   (2) First, take
Interstate 44 southwest out of St. Louis for approximately
twenty-five miles to the junction with Route 50.   (3) Then
stay on Route 50 for a while until you get to Jefferson
City.   (4) Drive through Jefferson City.   (5) Next, at the
junction of Route 50 and Route 54, take Route 54 south.
(6) Finally, drive approximately fifty miles on Route 54,
which will take you directly into the Lake of the Ozarks area.

Exercise 2   Prewriting: Chronological Order   Choose
one topic from the following suggestions. On your paper, list
in order the steps that explain how to get from the first place
to the second place.

1. How to get from your home to the nearest fire station
2. How to get from your home to the nearest shopping center
3. How to get from your English classroom to the school
   cafeteria

Exercise 3   Prewriting: Transitional Words   Read
the following paragraph, which explains how to get from a
library to a ball field. On your paper, list the transitional
words in the paragraph.

This is the shortest way to get from the library to the
ball field. First, turn left on Roosevelt Avenue as you come
out the front door of the library. Then walk to the corner of
Third Street and cross to the west side. Next, turn left and
go south on Third Street until you come to a high fence.
Finally, walk along the fence until you see an opening. The
ball field will be in full view.

Exercise 4 Prewriting: Unnecessary Information
The following directions need to be revised by removing the
sentences that are not needed. On your paper, write the
numbers of the sentences that do not belong.

(1) It is easy to travel by bus from New York City to
my home in Elizabeth, New Jersey. (2) First, go to Ticket
Window 1 in the Port Authority Bus Terminal at 40th
Street and Eighth Avenue. (3) The bus terminal has been
renovated, and the tickets are now computerized. (4) Ask
for a ticket to Elizabeth on the Number 15 Somerset bus.
(5) Then take the escalator to the upper level and follow the
overhead signs to Platform 74. (6) Buses to many places in
New Jersey leave from this level. (7) Board a Number 15
Somerset bus. (8) When the bus goes along North Broad
Street in Elizabeth, be on the lookout for Shaw's Pharmacy,
on the right-hand side of the street. (9) Get off at Parker
Road, the first stop beyond the pharmacy. (10) Finally,
walk east along Parker Road until you come to Number 520,
the first green house on the block.

Assignment 1 Prewriting Make a list of four topics
for directions that explain how to get from one place to another in your community. For example, you might list how
to go from the post office to a bank or how to go from your
home to the city or town hall. Save your paper.

Assignment 2 Prewriting Choose one of the topics
from Assignment 1. List the steps in the directions in chronological order. Include only essential details, giving landmarks
when possible. Save your paper.

Assignment 3 Writing/Revising *Step 1:* Write a
topic sentence for the set of directions that you planned in
Assignment 2. *Step 2:* Using the chronological list of steps,
write the rest of the paragraph. *Step 3:* Revise the paragraph.
Use the Assignment Checklist that follows Assignment 4 as a
guide to revision.

Assignment 4   Prewriting/Writing/Revising   Plan and write one paragraph of a letter to a friend who will visit you. In the paragraph explain how to get from the nearest bus station (or train station or airport) to your home. Then revise the paragraph.

Assignment Checklist

Check your writing assignments for the following points:

- ✓ 1. Did you begin with a topic sentence?
- ✓ 2. Did you present the steps in chronological order?
- ✓ 3. Did you use transitional words to make clear the order of the steps?
- ✓ 4. Did you give accurate and complete information?
- ✓ 5. Did you mention landmarks when possible?
- ✓ 6. Did you give only essential information?
- ✓ 7. Did you proofread your paragraph for correct grammar, usage, spelling, and punctuation?

12.2 Explaining How to Make or Do Something

A second kind of explanation tells how to make or do something. When you write this sort of explanation, you should follow the guidelines that you use when you write directions for getting to a place. You need to follow two additional guidelines, however.

Strategies

1. *Limit your topic.* Choose a topic that you can explain completely in a single paragraph. It is usually difficult to explain more than six steps in one paragraph. By making a list of the steps beforehand, you will be able to tell whether your topic is limited

enough. If a topic is too broad, choose a limited part of the broader topic. The following examples show how to choose a smaller topic that is part of a larger one.

BROAD TOPIC
How to make pottery
LIMITED TOPIC
How to make a clay candle-holder
BROAD TOPIC
How to camp in the woods
LIMITED TOPIC
How to pitch a tent

2. *Mention any tools and supplies that are needed.* Give this information early in the paragraph so that your reader can have all the necessary equipment on hand. If any of the items are unusual, you should explain them.

The following paragraph explains the limited topic "How to make rubbings of historical markers." Notice that the materials are listed in the second step and that the writer briefly explains *newsprint*.

Model

Topic sentence ─| Making rubbings of interesting historical markers is an unusual hobby that is easy to

Step 1 ──────| learn. *First,* you must get permission to make a rubbing of the historical marker that you

Step 2 ──────| have chosen. *Then* collect your materials: inexpensive crayons, newsprint (inexpensive paper available in most stationery stores), tape,

Step 3 ──────| a nail brush, and a small paintbrush. *Now* brush the marker clean with the nail brush and

Step 4 ──────| remove the fine dirt with the paintbrush. *Next,* center the paper on the marker and tape it

Step 5 ——————| down securely. *Then* gently rub the nail brush
over the marker until the design and letters
Step 6 ——————| begin to show through the paper. *Finally,* rub
the crayon smoothly over the whole surface.
The design and letters will stand out clearly on
the newsprint.

The writer of the model paragraph followed the guidelines for writing explanations. The paragraph begins with a topic sentence, which introduces the subject and also arouses the reader's interest. The rest of the paragraph gives the essential steps in chronological order. Transitional words, which are printed here in italic type, make the order of the steps clear to the reader.

The explanation that you have just read tells how to make something. The following paragraph tells how to do something.

Model

Topic sentence —| Pitching a tent is not difficult if you
Step 1 ——————| follow these simple directions. *First,* find a
level spot with no tree branches directly
Step 2 ——————| overhead. *Then* carefully spread out the tent
and place stakes in the loops along the bottom
Step 3 ——————| edge of the tent. *Next,* drive the stakes into the
Step 4 ——————| ground. *Now* put the support poles inside the
tent, placing them at each end between the
Step 5 ——————| peak of the roof and the floor. *Then* drive two
stakes into the ground outside the tent. One
stake should be several feet from the front of
the tent, and the other stake should be several
Step 6 ——————| feet from the back of the tent. *Finally,* take the
guy lines attached to the ends of the tent top
and loop each one around the nearest stake,
adjusting the lines so that the top of the tent is
straight.

Notice that the writer has given all the essential information without adding anything that might confuse the reader. The writer has also put the steps in chronological order, as someone pitching a tent would follow them. Finally, the writer has provided transitional words, printed here in italic type, that make the steps easy to follow.

Exercise 1 Prewriting: Limiting Topics Each of the following topics is too broad to be explained completely in one paragraph. For each broad topic, write a limited topic that can be explained in a single paragraph.

> SAMPLE   How to take care of your bicycle
>
> ANSWER   How to repair a puncture in a bicycle tire

1. How to prepare nutritious meals
2. How to play basketball
3. How to make a costume
4. How to make wooden furniture
5. How to play a guitar

Exercise 2 Writing: Topic Sentences Each of the following topics is limited enough to be explained in one paragraph. Choose three of the topics. On your paper, write a topic sentence for each. If you are unfamiliar with a subject, look it up in an encyclopedia or another reference book.

> SAMPLE   How to repair a puncture in a bicycle tire
>
> ANSWER   Repairing a puncture is not difficult if you follow five simple steps.

1. How to dribble a soccer ball
2. How to make a clay pot
3. How to grow tomatoes on a sunny balcony or porch
4. How to pack for an overnight camping trip in cold weather
5. How to prepare an aquarium for tropical fish
6. How to make a garden salad

Exercise 3   Prewriting: Chronological Order   Read the following topic and the list of steps that explain it. The steps are not in the correct order. On your paper, write the numbers of the steps in the correct chronological order.

Topic: How to press flowers
  1. First, pick the flowers when they are in full bloom.
  2. Finally, put several heavy books on top of the newspapers for twenty-four to forty-eight hours, or until the flowers are completely pressed.
  3. When the flowers are dry, lay them flat between two layers of tissue, making sure that the head of each flower is positioned attractively.
  4. Next, strip the leaves from the stems, and tie the flowers in bunches.
  5. Then hang the bunches upside down to dry in a cool, dry, dark place for a week or two.
  6. Now put the flowers with the layered tissue between sheets of newspaper.

Assignment 1   Prewriting/Writing   Plan a paragraph that explains one of the following topics or a topic of your own choice. *Step 1:* List all the steps that explain the topic. *Step 2:* Arrange the steps in chronological order, crossing out any that are not really needed. *Step 3:* Write a topic sentence for your paragraph. Save your paper.

  1. How to change a bicycle tire
  2. How to do a cartwheel
  3. How to teach an animal to do a trick
  4. How to make a healthful breakfast cereal
  5. How to add a stamp to a stamp album

Assignment 2   Writing/Revising   Write the paragraph that you planned in Assignment 1. Then revise the paragraph, using as a guide the Assignment Checklist that follows Assignment 3.

Assignment 3 Prewriting / Writing / Revising *Step 1:* Select a topic from the following list or choose one of your own. *Step 2:* Follow the steps given in Assignment 1. *Step 3:* Write the paragraph and revise it.

1. How to plant a tree
2. How to choose athletic shoes that fit properly
3. How to build a simple window box
4. How to wash a dog
5. How to take a telephone message

Assignment Checklist

Check your writing assignments for the following points:

✔ 1. Did you limit your topic to one that can be fully explained in one paragraph?
✔ 2. Did you begin your paragraph with a topic sentence?
✔ 3. Did you mention any tools and supplies that are needed?
✔ 4. Did you put the steps in chronological order?
✔ 5. Did you use transitional words to make clear the order of the steps?
✔ 6. Did you include only essential information?
✔ 7. Did you proofread your paragraph for correct grammar, usage, spelling, and punctuation?

On the Trail of the Brontosaurus: Giving Directions

Situation: Recently you visited a natural history museum to see the new exhibit of dinosaurs. You were particularly interested in the brontosaurus. Several of your friends have asked you to write directions so that they can see the brontosaurus too. You have made some notes as preparation for writing the directions. You also have a floor plan of the museum that you brought home from your visit. As you plan and write your set of directions, you will keep in mind the following information.

Writer: you as a recent visitor to the museum
Audience: your friends
Topic: how to find the brontosaurus
Purpose: to give directions

Directions: To write your explanation, follow these steps.

Step 1. Study the floor plan and read over your notes, which are on the facing page.

Step 2. Write a topic sentence, in which you state what you are going to explain.

Step 3. Select only the essential information from your notes and explain the most direct route. Give the information in separate steps. Present them in chronological order, using such transitional words as *first, next, then,* and *finally.*

Step 4. Read over your directions, revising them as needed. Omit any sentences that are not necessary, and make sure that the directions are complete and accurate.

Floor Plan of Natural History Museum

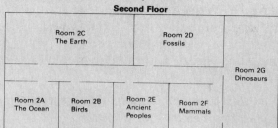

Second Floor

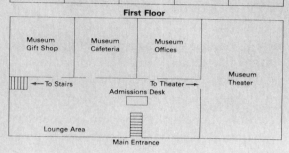

First Floor

Notes

— Take Museum Street bus to end of line.
— Go in front entrance of museum.
— Inside museum turn left at Admissions Desk.
— Follow arrows to stairs.
— Walk up stairs to second floor.
— Go straight down hallway.
— Go past rooms 2A, 2B, 2E on right.
— Go past rooms 2C, 2D on left.
— Room 2F, with mammals, at end of hall on right, just before Room 2G, with dinosaurs.
— You can turn right into Room 2F and then left into Room 2G.
— You can also reach Room 2G by turning left through last doorway at end of hall.
— Brontosaurus is in center of Room 2G.

Unit Assignments

Assignment 1 Write a paragraph that gives directions for getting from your home to one of the following places. Write the directions for a visiting relative. Make your directions clear by including street names, directions for turns, and landmarks.

1. How to get to the nearest playing field or sports center
2. How to get to the nearest movie theater
3. How to get to the nearest library

Assignment 2 Write a paragraph that gives directions for one of the following topics. Write the directions for a new classmate. Make the steps complete but include only essential details.

1. How to get from the school gymnasium to your locker
2. How to get from a social studies classroom to an art or music classroom
3. How to get from the front entrance of your school building to your homeroom

Assignment 3 Write a paragraph explaining one of the following topics to your classmates. Make your explanation complete and mention any needed supplies and tools.

1. How to prepare fruit for the freezer
2. How to organize a scrapbook or a photograph album
3. How to use a stencil

Assignment 4 Write a paragraph explaining one of the following topics. Use transitional words to make clear the order of the steps.

1. How to sand wood
2. How to make shelving from cardboard cartons
3. How to plant a row of tomatoes

Assignment 5   Write a paragraph explaining one of the following topics to an eight-year-old. Keep the age of your reader in mind as you write the directions.

1. How to cover a book
2. How to paint a face on a pumpkin
3. How to get a library card

Assignment 6   Write a paragraph explaining one of the following topics to your classmates. Be sure to present the steps in the correct order.

1. How to do a simple gymnastics routine
2. How to do a back dive
3. How to do a card trick

Assignment 7   Write a paragraph explaining one of the following topics to your classmates. Make your explanation as clear as you can.

1. How to introduce a classmate to an older person
2. How to write a social letter
3. How to write an invitation

Assignment 8   Write a paragraph explaining one of the following topics to a friend who has asked you for instructions. Be sure to mention the necessary ingredients or supplies and equipment.

1. How to make your favorite dish
2. How to make bookends
3. How to make a key chain.

Revising Your Assignments

For help in revising an explanation, consult the Checklist for Revision on the last page of this book.

Unit Tests

Test 1

A. Number your paper from 1 to 5. Next to each number, write *True* if the sentence is true or *False* if it is false.

1. Any topic is suitable for a paragraph in which you explain how to do or make something.
2. When you write directions, you use transitional words to make clear the order of the steps.
3. You include every possible detail and all the information that you can when you write directions.
4. Mentioning landmarks when you explain how to get to a place is helpful to your reader.
5. An explanation of how to do or make something often includes a list of the tools or supplies that will be needed.

B. Number your paper from 6 to 10. Next to each number, write the letter of the term that correctly completes the sentence. You will use all but one of the items.

    a. explanation   d. audience
    b. limited topic   e. transitional words
    c. topic sentence   f. chronological order

6. __?__, such as *first, next,* and *finally,* help to signal the beginnings of steps in an explanation.
7. In an explanation your purpose is to explain the steps so clearly that your __?__ can follow them easily.
8. A(n) __?__ tells what a paragraph is about.
9. You should use __?__ to present the steps of an explanation.
10. When you explain how to do or make something, you should choose a(n) __?__ that you can cover completely.

C. Read the following paragraph. Two of the sentences in it have been reversed. Number your paper from 11 to 15. Next to each number, write the letter of the item that correctly answers the question.

(1) Creating decorative Chinese lanterns that you can hang is simple to do. (2) You need brightly colored construction paper, tape, and scissors. (3) First, place the two short sides of a piece of construction paper together. (4) Then fold the paper. (5) Cut five or six slits through this folded edge to an inch from the opposite edge. (6) Chinese lanterns add to the festivities for the Chinese New Year. (7) Now unfold the paper and place the long edges together so that you form a cylinder. (8) Finally, place tape along the joined side of the lantern. (9) Now hang up your lantern. (10) To make a handle, cut a narrow strip from a fresh piece of paper and tape the ends of the strip to the opposite sides of the lantern top.

11. Which of the following is the topic sentence?
   a. Sentence 1   c. Sentence 3
   b. Sentence 2   d. Sentence 4

12. Which of the following are *not* in chronological order?
   a. Sentences 3 and 4   c. Sentences 7 and 8
   b. Sentences 4 and 5   d. Sentences 9 and 10

13. Which of the following contains a transitional word?
   a. Sentence 1   c. Sentence 3
   b. Sentence 2   d. Sentence 5

14. Which of the following gives unnecessary information?
   a. Sentence 8   c. Sentence 3
   b. Sentence 6   d. Sentence 5

15. Which of the following mentions supplies that you would need to make the lantern?
   a. Sentence 4   c. Sentence 2
   b. Sentence 3   d. Sentence 1

Test 2

Choose one of the Unit Assignments. Write the assignment as directed and hand it in to your teacher.

Unit 13

Describing

Unit Preview

A good description is the result of careful observation. Do you sometimes observe only the most obvious things about people: whether they are tall or short, young or old, dark or fair? Do you notice only things that you sense with your eyes, while overlooking sounds, textures, or smells? If you use all your senses—sight, hearing, touch, smell, and taste—you can describe a subject so clearly that it will seem to come alive for your reader.

The following description shows the results of careful observation. The writer uses details that appeal to several senses, making it possible for you to see, hear, feel, and smell the place being described as though you were there. Notice that the writer begins the paragraph with a sentence that identifies what will be described.

> I was crawling down the cold, damp corridor of the cave. The air was thick with a musty smell. As I crawled, I could feel the cold water oozing from the muddy ground and seeping through the knees of my jeans. From somewhere in the distance came the gurgling sound of an underground stream. The flashlight that I carried cut into the darkness with a wavering beam.

> *(Adapted)*
> *Jackie McCoy, Woodbridge Senior High School*
> *Woodbridge, Virginia*

For Analysis On your paper, answer the following questions about the description that you have just read.

1. What is the writer describing?
2. To what senses does the description appeal?
3. Which detail tells how the cave smelled? Which details tell what the writer felt, heard, and saw?
4. Find these words in the paragraph: *musty, oozing, seeping, gurgling,* and *wavering.* To which sense does each word appeal? What do these words contribute to the effect of the paragraph?

As you answered the questions, you saw how important it is to observe carefully with all your senses in order to write a good description. In this unit you will learn more about using your senses to write vivid descriptions. As you practice writing descriptions, you will follow the three steps in the writing process: prewriting, writing, and revising.

13.1 Using Your Senses

How good an observer are you? When you walk into a supermarket, for example, do you explore it with all your senses, not just your eyes? Do you *hear* the voices of other shoppers, the clang of shopping carts, the whir of cash registers? Do you *feel* the cooled air on your face, and do you discover the varying textures of boxes, bags, and other containers? Do you *smell* the mild fragrance of fruit and the harsher odor of disinfectant? Do you recall the sweet *taste* of strawberries and the crisp tang of raw carrots?

To write effective descriptions, you must first learn how to observe a person, a place, or a thing with all five senses. The details that you observe are **sensory details,** those details that appeal to your readers' senses.

In each of the following descriptions, the writer concentrates on one of the five senses. As you read each description, try to identify the sensory details.

Model: Details of Sight

On a high chair beside the chimney sat a little old gentleman. His face had a strong masculine cast. His mouth seemed greedy, brutal, and dangerous. The upper lip was full. The small eyes were almost comical in expression. Beautiful white hair hung round his head and fell into a single curl.

Robert Louis Stevenson,
"The Sire de Malétroit's Door"

Model: Details of Sound

The pearl divers came up one by one, expelling breath with piercing whistles, shriller than the cries of gulls.

Kim Yong Ik, "The Sea Girl"

Model: Details of Touch

It certainly was cold, he concluded as he rubbed his numb nose and cheekbones with his mittened hand. He was a warm-whiskered man, but the hair on his face did not protect the high cheekbones and the eager nose that thrust itself aggressively into the frosty air.

Jack London, "To Build a Fire"

Model: Details of Smell

As he came near the wall of the well, he gently kicked it and swung away. The wall was slimy and cold to the touch of his bare toes; the wall smelled of moss and frogs and salamanders.

Phillip Bonosky, "The Wishing Well"

Model: Details of Taste

We were to have a superb dinner consisting of pickled pork and a pair of crisp stuffed fowls. A succulent mince pie had been made yesterday morning, and the sweet pudding was already on the boil.

Charles Dickens, *Great Expectations*

The persons, places, and objects that you describe usually have qualities that appeal to more than one sense. Good descriptions, therefore, include a mixture of sensory details. In the following passage, the writer presents details that appeal to the reader's sense of sight. He then provides other details that appeal to the senses of hearing and touch.

Model: Mixed Sensory Details

Sight	I can remember the bare wooden stairway in my uncle's house, and the turn to the left above the landing, and the rafters and the slanting roof over my bed, and the squares of moonlight on the floor, and the white cold world of snow outside, seen through the
Sound	curtainless window. I can remember the howl-
Touch	ing of the wind and the quaking of the house
Touch	on stormy nights, and how snug and cozy one felt under the blankets. . . . I can remember how very dark that room was, in the dark of
Sound	the moon, and how packed it was with ghostly
Sound	stillness . . . and how dismal were the hoo-hoo-ing of the owl and the wailing of the wolf, sent mourning by on the night wind.

Samuel Clemens,
The Autobiography of Mark Twain

This passage shows how effective certain words are in appealing to the senses. For example, the words *bare* and *wooden* help you to "see" the staircase. The words *howling* and *quaking* help you to "hear" and "feel" the wind.

Exercise 1   Prewriting: Sensory Details   On your paper, write the sense or senses—sight, hearing, taste, touch, or smell—to which each of the following items appeals.

SAMPLE   A blue jay
ANSWER   Sight, hearing

1. A moving train
2. The ocean
3. A blizzard
4. A sunrise
5. A baseball game
6. A bakery
7. A leather jacket
8. A dish of baked apples
9. A pine tree
10. An old book

Exercise 2   Prewriting: Sensory Details   Divide your paper into five columns headed *Sight, Hearing, Taste, Touch,* and *Smell.* List under the appropriate headings at least ten details of your classroom that appeal to your senses. Try to notice details that you may not have noticed before.

Exercise 3   Prewriting: Textures   For each of the following items, list on your paper one or more sensory details that appeal to the sense of touch.

SAMPLE   Sandpaper
ANSWER   Gritty, coarse

1. A dog's coat
2. A concrete sidewalk
3. A sponge
4. An eggshell
5. Glue
6. A balloon

Exercise 4   Prewriting: Sounds   For each of the following items, list on your paper one or more sensory details that describe its sound.

SAMPLE   A brook
ANSWER   Gurgling, splashing

1. A thunderstorm
2. A baseball field
3. A busy street
4. A songbird
5. A drum
6. A helicopter

Assignment Prewriting   For one full week, list in your writer's notebook (*pages 239–240*) descriptive details of the persons, places, and things around you. Remember to observe with all your senses.

Assignment Checklist

Check your assignment for the following points:

✔ 1. Did you include in your notebook details from each of the five senses?

✔ 2. Did you include sensory details that give accurate impressions of the persons, places, and things that you observed?

13.2 Using Descriptive Words

Once you have chosen the sensory details for your description, the next step is to choose the words and phrases that will make the details clear and appealing to your reader. Using many words does not necessarily make a description good. Instead, you should use the single noun, verb, adjective, or adverb that expresses exactly what you mean.

You know that adjectives (*page 29*) and adverbs (*page 38*) describe persons, places, things, and actions. Other words also can be used to make your description clear and interesting. The following suggestions will help you to choose descriptive words.

Strategies

1. *Use specific nouns.* A specific noun is usually better than a general noun that is modified by several adjectives. "A tall building with concrete and steel supports" is wordy and unclear. The specific noun *skyscraper* says exactly what is meant.

2. *Use strong verbs.* Strong verbs capture the action and can make your descriptions vivid and clear. For example, *leap* is more vivid than *jump high; slouched* is more descriptive than *sat carelessly.*

3. *Use adjectives and adverbs carefully.* Add modifiers only after you have chosen specific nouns and strong verbs. Then, include only modifiers that give your readers new and necessary information.

The writer of the following paragraph uses descriptive words effectively.

Model

> Every night after I put up the canoes and set camp, I would find a suitable perch and wait eagerly for the magic to begin. In the distance, the sun would appear to be sinking into the glassy waters of the lake. Then, shades of violet, magenta, pink, and pearl would blend slowly into a shimmering band of color. Soon a loon would begin its lullaby, and then the moon would rise into the darkening sky. Every night this occurred, and each time it grew more magical.
>
> *Paula Bieneman, Fenton High School*
> *Bensenville, Illinois*

This passage shows that specific nouns and strong verbs can make a description clear and vivid. The nouns *perch* and *lullaby* and the verbs *blend* and *rise* present impressions simply and clearly. The adjectives and adverbs *eagerly, glassy,* and *magical* help to create a vivid impression.

Exercise 1   Prewriting: Specific Nouns   For each noun listed on the following page, write at least two nouns that are specific.

SAMPLE	Building
ANSWER	Courthouse, supermarket

1. Flower
2. Relative
3. Clothing
4. Sport
5. Insect

6. Animal
7. Tool
8. Tree
9. Worker
10. Vegetable

Exercise 2 Prewriting/Writing: Strong Verbs On your paper, write the stronger verb in each pair given below. Then use the stronger verb in a sentence.

SAMPLE	Walk, saunter
ANSWER	Saunter—The gardener sauntered down the path.

1. Try, struggle
2. Spring, run
3. Brush, touch
4. Hit, clobber
5. Whisper, speak

6. Fall, plummet
7. Hold, clutch
8. Splinter, break
9. Clean, scrub
10. Bellow, cry

Exercise 3 Revising: Nouns and Verbs On your paper, rewrite each of the following sentences. In Sentences 1–5, substitute more specific nouns for the nouns in italic type. In Sentences 6–10, substitute stronger verbs for the verbs in italic type.

1. An *animal* howled in the night.
2. A *vehicle* drove up in front of the store.
3. That *water* is polluted.
4. *People* build igloos for shelter.
5. A *bird* nested in the pine tree.
6. The cat *went* up the tree.
7. The batter *moved* to first base.
8. His heart *beat* rapidly.
9. A sudden noise *broke* the silence.
10. A snake *moved* across the clearing.

Exercise 4   Revising: Modifiers   On your paper, rewrite each sentence, adding adjectives and adverbs that make the sentence more descriptive.

> SAMPLE   The woman sipped her tea.
>
> ANSWER   The nervous woman impatiently sipped her tea.

1. The bus stopped.
2. A man walked across the road.
3. The moon rose in the sky.
4. The child cried.
5. The runner crossed the finish line.
6. The bird chirped.
7. The rain fell.
8. The crowd cheered.

Assignment   Writing   Choose three of the following topics. On your paper, write a sentence describing each topic. Use specific nouns and strong verbs, and add modifiers if they are needed to make your description more vivid.

> SAMPLE   The trees in autumn
>
> ANSWER   The maples formed bright patches of gold and scarlet.

1. A race car
2. An old barn
3. An abandoned house
4. A road at night

5. The skin of a snake
6. The water in a swimming pool
7. A doctor's waiting room
8. The sky after a storm

Assignment Checklist

Check your assignment for the following points:

✔ 1. Did you use specific nouns and strong verbs?
✔ 2. Did you use vivid modifiers?
✔ 3. Did you proofread your sentences for correct grammar, usage, spelling, and punctuation?

13.3 Describing Places and Persons

No two persons or places are the same. When you write a description of a person or a place, your purpose is to give your reader a clear and vivid impression of the particular person or location.

13.3a Describing a Place

A good description of a place will make your readers feel as though they are there. The following suggestions will help you to describe a place effectively.

Strategies

1. *Begin with a topic sentence.* Like any paragraph, a descriptive paragraph has a topic sentence in which you introduce your subject (*pages 290–291*).

2. *Select only the most vivid details*—those that made the greatest impression on you. The details that you choose should capture the uniqueness of the place.

3. *Arrange the details in an easy-to-follow order.* Usually, the best order is spatial order, the way in which you observed the place from left to right, from top to bottom, from front to back, or from outside to inside.

4. *Use words and phrases that emphasize the order in which the details are arranged.* Phrases such as *to the right, directly ahead,* or *in the middle* help to provide a clear picture of the place that you are describing.

5. *End your paragraph with a concluding sentence* in which you indicate that your description of the place is complete.

Notice how the writer of the following description begins with a topic sentence that introduces the place being described. As indicated to the left of the passage, the writer has organized the details about the room from right to left in the order that they were observed. Words and phrases that reveal the order of the details are in italic type.

Model

Topic sentence —	The reporter stood in one deserted dressing room. He turned slowly, making one
Right ———————	final inspection. A make-up table stood against the *right* wall. Its speckled mirror had several pictures and papers wedged between it and the frame. *In the corner* an old-fashioned coat rack stood, with a gray tweed coat hanging from it,
Back ———————	covering all but the carved legs. *About one fifth of the way down the back wall,* a bare window looked out on a dark alley. *Between* the window and *left corner* sat an old wooden desk
Left ———————	with a warped top. The *left wall* was taken up
Front ———————	by two sliding doors. The wall *where the door to the hall was located* was decorated with a painting of a barn. A shaded bulb hung from the ceiling, dimly illuminating the room.

(Adapted)
Tim Peterson, Marshfield High School
Marshfield, Massachusetts

Exercise 1   Prewriting: Order of Details   The following paragraph describes a room. On your paper, list the subject of the description and the words and phrases that signal the order in which the details are arranged.

Even before I reached the dining room, I knew that a wonderful Thanksgiving feast awaited us. The aroma of the browning turkey was so strong that I could almost taste it.

In the middle of the dining room, the table was draped in a starched linen cloth, so white that it sparkled. Rising from the center of the table were my great-grandmother's candlesticks, which stood like soldiers at attention, protecting the centerpiece of rust and gold chrysanthemums. Around the edge of the table, which was opened to twice its usual size, were twelve precisely set places: salad fork, fork, plate with napkin, knife, and spoon. All of my family had worked for hours to make our celebration special.

Exercise 2 Prewriting: Sensory Details On your paper, list three vivid sensory details about each of the following places.

SAMPLE   A library

ANSWER   Sight of faded book covers on shelves
            Quiet sound of pages being turned
            Smell of the glue used to repair book bindings

1. A beach at noon
2. A street fair
3. A field in the spring
4. A bus depot before a holiday
5. A mountain in the fall
6. A store during a sale

13.3b Describing a Person

The following suggestions will help you to write a vivid description of a person, a description that will make the person seem to come to life for your readers.

Strategies

1. *In your topic sentence, introduce the person whom you will describe.* In this sentence you may also mention the most striking characteristic or feature of that person.

2. *Include a variety of sensory details.* You must, of course, describe your subject's appearance. Also be

sure to include details to show the person's individuality, such as the sound of the person's voice or footsteps, the texture of the hair or skin, or the smell of perfume or shaving lotion.

3. *Include details that describe your subject's motions.* Tell how the person stands, sits, walks, moves his or her hands, and uses facial expressions. Use words that vividly capture these movements.

4. *Arrange the details in logical order.* You should group together and arrange the details so that you create a clear impression of the person. For example, if you are describing someone who is especially attractive, you might begin with a description of facial features.

5. *Use specific words.* For example, instead of describing hair color as blond, you might describe it as golden or platinum.

In the following description, the writer uses a topic sentence to introduce the person and to mention his most striking characteristic—his extreme age.

Model

He was the *oldest* man I had ever seen. He appeared to be made of *stone,* as though some sculptor had *carefully carved* out each *deep wrinkle.* He wore an *ancient hat* and a *worn coat.* Next to him lay an orange-colored cat. Both remained *perfectly still* by the fire. The man's face had the *sunburned, weathered* look of years of experience. The appearance of *peaceful old age* was marred by a *large scar* on his right *cheek* and a *patch over one eye.*

> *Heidi Parker, South Pasadena High School*
> *South Pasadena, California*

Notice that the writer uses descriptive words, which are printed in italic type, and carefully selected details to present a vivid picture of her subject.

Exercise 3 Prewriting: Sensory Details For each type of worker that is listed below, write a sensory detail or a detail of movement that helps to describe a particular person who has that position. Use specific words.

SAMPLE   A sports announcer

ANSWER   Talks quickly, running words together

1. A baseball player
2. A TV performer
3. A traffic officer
4. A politician
5. A singer
6. A salesperson

Exercise 4 Prewriting: Logical Order Read the following list of details that describe a weaver named Sheryl. On your paper, write the numbers of the details in an order that is logical. Group together details that are similar.

1. Iron-gray hair pulled back in a barrette
2. Calluses on index fingers and thumbs
3. Lean and five feet ten inches tall
4. Green eyes with flecks of gold
5. Sitting bent over her loom
6. Sixty-year-old woman
7. Olive complexion
8. Smiling to self as working
9. Long arms threading loom
10. Staring intently at work

Exercise 5 Writing: Describing a Person Using the list that you organized for Exercise 4, write a description of Sheryl. Be sure to introduce her in the topic sentence. Write clear and interesting sentences, changing the wording of the details as needed.

Assignment 1   Prewriting   *Step 1:* Choose a place that you know well and then imagine that you are there. On your paper, list all the sensory details that you can think of to make the place real for your readers. *Step 2:* Decide on a location from which to view the place—for example, from a doorway or from a park bench. *Step 3:* Arrange the details from Step 1 as you would observe them from the location that you have chosen. Save your list.

Assignment 2   Writing/Revising   Using the list of details from Assignment 1, write a paragraph that describes the place. Then, using the Assignment Checklist that follows, revise your paragraph and copy it on a clean sheet of paper.

Assignment 3   Prewriting   With permission from a relative or a friend, carefully observe that person. Make a list of sensory details using all of the appropriate senses. Include details that you might not have noticed before as well as appropriate details of movement. Select the best details and arrange them in a logical order.

Assignment 4   Writing/Revising   Using the details that you arranged for Assignment 3, write a paragraph that accurately describes the person whom you observed. Begin with a topic sentence that introduces your subject. Revise the paragraph and copy it on a clean sheet of paper.

Assignment 5 Prewriting/Writing/Revising Create an interesting person or place in your imagination. Make a list of all the sensory details that you can think of to create an effective description. Then choose the best details and arrange them in a logical order. Write a descriptive paragraph based on these details. Be sure to include a topic sentence. Finally, revise the paragraph and copy it on a clean sheet of paper.

Assignment Checklist

Check your writing assignments for the following points:

✔ 1. Did you begin with a topic sentence that introduces your subject?

✔ 2. Did you include vivid details from more than one sense?

✔ 3. Did you arrange the details in an easy-to-follow order?

✔ 4. Did you use words and phrases to make that order clear?

✔ 5. When you described a place, did you emphasize its one-of-a-kind quality?

✔ 6. When you described a person, did you emphasize the most striking characteristic or feature of that person?

✔ 7. Did you proofread your paragraph for correct grammar, usage, spelling, and punctuation?

A Fossil Find: Describing an Object

Situation: On a dig near the outskirts of town, you discovered a perfect fossil of a seed-fern leaf. The Science Club, to which you belong, has asked you to write a description of the fossil. The description will appear in the next issue of the club's bulletin. In preparation for writing the description, you took a photograph of the fossil and prepared a fact sheet about it. As you plan and write your description, you will keep in mind the following information.

Writer: you as a fossil collector
Audience: readers of the Science Club's bulletin
Topic: the fossil of a seed-fern leaf
Purpose: to describe the fossil

Directions: To write your description, follow these steps.

Step 1.   Study the photograph and the fact sheet, which appear on the facing page.

Step 2.   Write a topic sentence that identifies the fossil and tells where it was found.

Step 3.   Using complete sentences and specific words, describe the fossil. Present the details of shape, size, color, and texture in the order in which they appear on the fact sheet. If you noticed additional details when you studied the photograph, you may include them in your description. You should place them next to similar details.

Fact Sheet: Fossil of Seed-Fern Leaf

1. Treelike species from the late Carboniferous Period
2. Found in Anderson's Field, Sanford, Illinois, Sept. 12, 1983
3. <u>Shape</u>. Rock — oblong
4. <u>Size</u>. Rock — 9 ½ in. long, 3½ in. wide. Leaf imprint — 7½ in. long, 2 in wide
5. <u>Color</u>. Gray with brown specks
6. <u>Texture</u>. Rock — grainy with small pockets, or holes. Leaf imprint — one 7-in. groove and about 40 1-in. grooves on both sides of long groove. Each 1-in. groove is center line of imprint of small leaflet with curved tip.

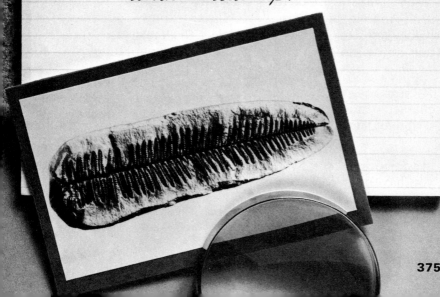

Unit Assignments

Assignment 1   Stand in the doorway of a room at home, at a school, or at some other place where you spend a lot of time. Imagine that you are seeing the room for the first time. Observe it carefully with all your senses and write a paragraph describing it.

Assignment 2   Choose an outdoor setting where something interesting has happened to you. It might be the soccer field where you scored your first goal, the campsite where you spent your first overnight trip, or the park where you heard your first outdoor concert. Recall as many sensory details as you can about the setting. Then select the most vivid details and write a paragraph that describes the setting as you remember it.

Assignment 3   Write a description of someone whom you know well. Mention a striking characteristic or feature. Include details from several senses in your description.

Assignment 4   For five days observe a television newscaster. Make a list of the details that contribute to this person's individuality: size, age, facial expressions, sound of voice, gestures, and so forth. Select the most interesting details and write a paragraph describing the newscaster.

Assignment 5   Write a paragraph describing a fictional character in a story that you have read. Use the author's descriptive details, but put them into your own words.

Assignment 6   Write a description of a place in which you have noticed loud noises or pleasant smells. In your description include details that will give your reader a clear impression of the noises or smells as well as the appearance of that place.

Assignment 7 Imagine a room in which you would like to spend a rainy afternoon. Then write a description of that room. Include vivid details in your description. Arrange the details in the order in which you would see them as you entered the room.

Assignment 8 Write a description of a person who works outdoors. For example, you could describe a construction worker, a farmer, or a forest ranger. In your description include details that describe the motions as well as the appearance of your subject.

Revising Your Assignments

For help in revising a description, consult the Checklist for Revision on the last page of this book.

Unit Tests

Test 1

A. Number your paper from 1 to 5. Read the following passage. Next to each number, write the letter of the item that correctly answers the question.

(1) When my brother and I came to the end of the raised wooden walkway through the fields, I was about to enter a bird blind for the first time. (2) A packed dirt floor sloped down from the edge of the walkway. (3) Two wooden walls separated us from the marsh in front of them, but we could see the marsh through horizontal slits in the walls. (4) On the other side of the walls, bright blue jays, spotted bitterns, and flashy red-winged blackbirds flitted from cattail to cattail. (5) The calls of the birds came from all around us. (6) The blue jays screamed. (7) The bitterns called *pump-er-lunk* over and over, and the blackbirds joined in with their shrill *konk-ker-ree*. (8) Fascinated by the scene before us, we stayed in the blind for more than an hour.

1. From which of these places do the people view the scene?
   a. A marsh   b. A woods   c. A bird blind   d. A field
2. Which sense(s) does the writer use for details in the passage?
   a. Sight   c. Sight and smell
   b. Hearing   d. Sight and hearing
3. In what order does the writer present the details of sight?
   a. Near to far   c. Left to right
   b. Top to bottom   d. Right to left
4. Which adjective in the passage describes the noise of the birds?
   a. Bright   b. Shrill   c. Flashy   d. Blue
5. In Sentence 4 what verb describes the motion of the birds?
   a. Side   b. Spotted   c. Flashy   d. Flitted

B. Number your paper from 6 to 10. Read the following passage. Next to each number, write the letter of the item that correctly completes the sentence. You will use all but three of the items.

(1) The agent was a red-faced man with patches of freckles on his face and hands. (2) He had thin sand-colored hair and eyebrows, and his eyes were so light blue they looked milky. (3) He wore a dark gray suit with a closely buttoned vest, a white shirt, and a blue necktie. (4) His face was fat; it bulged over his collar.

Hal Borland, *When the Legends Die*

a. touch   c. clothing   e. walk   g. was
b. eyes   d. bulged   f. topic   h. sight

6. The subject of the description is introduced in the __?__ sentence.
7. The passage describes not only the physical characteristics of the man but also his __?__.
8. "Patches of freckles on his face and hands" is a descriptive detail from the sense of __?__.
9. The adjective *milky* in Sentence 2 describes the man's __?__.
10. In Sentence 4 __?__ is a strong verb.

Test 2

Choose one of the Unit Assignments. Write the assignment as directed and hand it in to your teacher.

Unit 14

Narrating

Unit Preview

Narrating is telling a story about a true or an imaginary happening. A story can have one paragraph, or it can have many paragraphs.

The paragraph that follows shows that even a brief happening can be the topic of a complete story.

> My older brother, Jim, was determined to catch a frog. Feet positioned carefully on two branches, he slowly made his way out across the shallow pond. When a frog surfaced, Jim reached out for it with his net. The frog swam toward the middle of the pond. Jim inched out farther. The branches on which he stood touched the surface of the pond, sending ripples through the muddy water. Jim made a desperate attempt to reach the frog. Suddenly one branch gave way, and with a loud cry he fell into the pond. Seconds later, he stood up with the net in one hand and the frog in the other.

> *Peter Siekmeier, Ann Arbor Pioneer High School*
> *Ann Arbor, Michigan*

Like all narratives, this story answers the question "What happened?" It tells about the actions in chronological order, the order in which they happen. The story has a definite beginning and a definite ending. It also has a high point, where the suspense is greatest. Early in the story, the writer introduces you to the person, or character, who takes part in the actions. The writer also gives the setting of the story—the place where the actions occur.

For Analysis On your paper, answer the questions about the brief narrative that you have just read.

1. Who is the character in the narrative?
2. What is the setting of the story?
3. In which sentence does the writer tell about the action that is the high point of the story?
4. What happens at the end of the story? Is the ending a good one? Why or why not?

In this unit you will learn how to plan a narrative. You will also learn the skills that are important for writing a good story. As you plan and write your narratives, you will follow the three steps of the writing process: prewriting, writing, and revising.

14.1 Planning Your Narrative

An interesting story is the result of careful planning and good writing. After choosing a topic for your story, you should develop a plan that includes who the characters are, what the setting is, and what happens. Make notes as you plan your story.

Choosing a Topic

The first step in planning a narrative is to choose a suitable topic, or story idea. If you decide to narrate a story about something that happened to you (or to someone you know), you will write about actions that really happened and about the real people who participated in the actions.

You may decide to write a fictional narrative—that is, a narrative about an imagined event or a series of imagined events. For a fictional narrative, you will make up the characters and the details of what happens to them. However, a fictional narrative does not have to come solely from your imagination. It may come from one of your own experiences, which you can narrate as fiction by changing the details. The experiences of other people may also help you to choose a topic for a fictional narrative. For example, if you hear a news story about someone attempting to cross the ocean in a balloon, you may imagine what it would be like to have such an adventure.

Whether you are writing a true story or a fictional story, you must build it around a specific problem or situation. Otherwise, your narrative will wander aimlessly. For example, in the paragraph about Jim *(page 380),* the question is whether he will succeed in catching a frog. The paragraph ends with his success.

Listing the Characters

Once you have decided on a topic, make a list of the characters in your story. Include only those persons who are directly involved in what happens. If you write a true story about something that you have experienced, you will be one of the characters, along with the other persons who were part of what happened. If you write a fictional story, the characters will come from your imagination, but you may model them on people you know.

Deciding on the Setting

The **setting** is the time and place of the story. If the time of day, the season of the year, or the year itself is important to what happens in the story, remember to include that information as part of the setting. For example, in a story about someone who is marooned in a storm, it might be important to know that the story takes place before the invention of the telephone or the automobile.

Planning the Actions

Think carefully about how your story will answer the question "What happened?" In a one-paragraph story, you should plan to tell what happened by writing about a series of connected actions that occur within a few hours or on the same day. In a longer story, you should plan to place each group of related actions in a paragraph of its own.

Whether a story has one paragraph or many paragraphs, it must have a beginning, a middle, and an ending.

1. *The Beginning.* At the beginning of your story, introduce the characters and present the setting. Also present the situation or the problem that must be settled by the end of the story.
2. *The Middle.* In the middle of your story, narrate the actions up to and including the **high point,** the action that creates the most excitement or suspense.
3. *The Ending.* At the end bring the actions of the story to a conclusion. Settle the situation or the problem that you have presented.

In your prewriting notes, list the important actions that you plan to narrate in all three parts of your story. List the actions in **chronological order,** the order in which they happen.

The prewriting notes that follow show how one story was planned.

BEGINNING

Situation: How to earn money to buy a ten-speed bicycle
Characters: Myself, my sister, and my mother
Setting: Place—my hometown. Time—the summer I was eleven years old
Action: I try to think of a way to earn money.

MIDDLE

Actions: (1) I decide to custom-wash cars for five dollars each. (2) I write, copy, and deliver an advertisement. (3) My sister offers to help.

High point: I discover that I am fifty dollars short of my goal, with no more cars to wash.

ENDING

Actions: (l) My mother comes to the rescue. (2) I buy the bicycle.

Conclusion: I still wash cars but now am saving for a racing bike.

The prewriting notes for the beginning of the story list the situation, the characters, and the setting. They also list the action that the writer plans to narrate at the beginning. In the notes for the middle of the story, the writer lists the actions in chronological order and identifies the high point. The notes for the ending of the story list the actions that occur after the high point and show how the writer plans to bring the story to a conclusion.

Exercise 1   Prewriting: Story Situations   Each of the following paragraphs begins a story. On your paper, write a sentence in which you explain the situation or problem that must be settled before the end of each story.

1.   I have always had a fear of heights. Ever since I can remember, elevators, high balconies, ladders, and steep stairways have turned my hands to ice and my stomach into a tight knot. I have usually been able to control my fears or to avoid places that are too high. One day, however, I was faced with a real problem. The Service Club had voted to go on a one-day ski trip to Jagged Mountain. I had to go. I was, after all, the president of the club.

2.   The letter on the hall table was the first thing that I noticed when I came in from school on the Monday before

Thanksgiving. It was from my sister, who was away at college and was coming home for the first time since September. We are very close, and as I ripped open the envelope, I was already making plans for how we would spend the time together. Halfway through the first paragraph, I stopped reading. My sister was bringing home a friend. How would my sister and I have any time together?

Exercise 2 Prewriting: Chronological Order The actions in the following prewriting notes are not listed in chronological order. On your paper, write the actions (with their original numbers) in the correct order.

1. Everyone at camp told me that water-skiing was easy and that anyone could do it.
2. Everyone persuaded me to give it a try.
3. John started up the boat again.
4. I leaned too far forward, lost my balance, and for a moment flew along the surface of the water.
5. I came up out of the water, pulled by the line.
6. Finally, I remembered to let go of the line and hit the water—hard.
7. John dropped me off in the middle of the lake and handed me the skis.
8. I caught the line that he threw me and crouched in the water waiting.
9. I'll never let anyone talk me into anything again.
10. I said that I didn't think I could stay upright.
11. I put on a life vest and climbed into the boat.
12. Still wearing the life vest, I swam to shore.

Exercise 3 Prewriting: Parts of a Story Divide your paper into three columns labeled *Beginning, Middle,* and *Ending.* Using the chronological list in your answer to Exercise 2, write each action in the column in which it belongs. You may list the actions in the shortened form of notes.

Assignment 1   Prewriting   On your paper, list five situations or events in your life that would be suitable topics for a narrative. It may help you to think of story ideas if you ask yourself the following questions.

1. What is one of the most exciting or interesting things that has ever happened to me?
2. What did I do during the summer that might be of interest to my reader (for example, winning or losing a swimming meet or spending time with a student from another country)?
3. What do I remember about my first day at a new school or about my first time away from home?
4. What is the hardest thing that I have ever done?
5. What is the funniest thing that has ever happened to me?

Assignment 2   Prewriting   Choose two of the topics that you listed for Assignment 1. For each topic prepare prewriting notes like those on pages 383–384. In your notes be sure to include answers to these questions:

1. What is the situation or problem that must be settled before the end of the story?
2. Who are the people involved in the story?
3. What is the setting of the story?
4. In chronological order, what are the actions of the story?
5. What is the high point of the story?

Assignment 3   Prewriting   On your paper, list three story ideas for a narrative about an imagined event or a series of imagined events. You may base your topic on an experience of your own or on something that you have heard or read about. The incomplete topics that follow may help you to think of a topic of your own.

1. A trip to __?__
2. A visitor from __?__
3. The day __?__ disappeared
4. My first day as __?__
5. My surprise when __?__

CURRICULUM RESOURCES CENTER
R. I. COLLEGE - MANN HALL
600 MT. PLEASANT AVE.
PROVIDENCE, R.I. 02908

14.2

Writing a Narrative

Assignment 4 Prewriting Prepare prewriting notes for one of the story ideas that you listed in Assignment 3. Divide your notes into *Beginning, Middle,* and *Ending.*

Continuing Assignment Prewriting *Step 1:* Choose one of the topics for which you prepared prewriting notes in Assignment 2 or Assignment 4. Since you will be asked to develop the topic into a finished narrative, be sure to choose the one in which you are most interested. *Step 2:* Carefully review your prewriting notes for the selected topic. Make any additions or changes that you think will help to improve your story. Save your paper.

Assignment Checklist

Check your assignments for the following points:

   ✔ 1. Did you choose a topic that is suitable for a narrative—one that has a beginning, a middle, and an ending?

   ✔ 2. Did you identify a situation or a problem that must be settled before the end of the story?

   ✔ 3. Did you include only those characters who are involved in the actions of your story?

   ✔ 4. Did you make clear what the setting is?

   ✔ 5. Did you list the actions in chronological order?

14.2 Writing Your Narrative

Once you have a plan that satisfies you, write the beginning of your story and work through to the end. It is a good idea, when possible, to write the story in one sitting from the first word to the last. Once you have the whole story in front of you, you can revise and polish it into a finished narrative.

14.2a Writing the Beginning

The following suggestions will help you to write a beginning that will arouse the interest of your reader.

Strategies

1. *Begin your story in an interesting way.* In your first sentence, try to capture the attention of your readers at once. Often, as in the following example, you can begin with an action-packed sentence.

    WEAK   Anne opened the basement door and made a terrible discovery.

    BETTER   Anne yanked open the basement door, flicked on the lights, and shouted for help.

2. *Introduce the characters smoothly.* Mention the main characters and, as briefly as possible, tell who they are and how they are involved in your story.

    WEAK   This is a story about the time my friend and I were caught in a storm.

    BETTER   As my friend Jim and I started up the trail, we failed to notice the black clouds moving in over the valley.

3. *Briefly give the setting of the story*, telling where and when the actions of the story occur. Provide any details that will help your reader to understand what happens. However, do not give more information than is needed. For example, in the second example sentence in Strategy 2, the writer briefly gives the setting: on a trail in the valley. If the time is important in the actions that follow, the writer could add a sentence like this: "It was late afternoon, and we were not expected back at the campsite until just before sundown."

4. *Identify the situation or the problem.* Get to the point of the story as soon as possible by clearly identifying the situation or problem that must be settled before the end of the story. In the examples in Strategies 2 and 3, the situation has been identified as two friends hiking along a trail while being unaware of a threatening storm. The reader will expect the story to tell what happens to the two hikers in the developing storm.

The following paragraph begins the narrative that was written from the prewriting notes on page 383.

Model

The summer when I was eleven, I was forced to become a business tycoon. I desperately wanted the ten-speed, metallic-gray bicycle that sat in the window of Rooney's Bike Shop in the center of town. I was too young to get a real job, and no one was about to give me the bicycle. How was I ever going to come up with the money? It seemed hopeless.

In just a few sentences, the story begins to unfold. The writer arouses the reader's interest by referring in the first sentence to becoming a business tycoon at the age of eleven. The main character is introduced: the "I" who wants a ten-speed bicycle. The setting is shown to be summertime in a town. The problem—earning money to purchase a ten-speed bicycle—is soon identified.

Exercise 1 Prewriting: Story Beginnings Decide which story beginning in each of the following numbered pairs is more interesting. After each number on your paper, write the letter of the better story beginning.

1. a.   We had planned to have a street fair to raise money for our block association, but when we looked out the

window that morning, it was raining. Without the money from the fair, our block association could not survive.

b.   Rain! Buckets of it poured down, scattering the leaves and making deep puddles in the streets. It was the day of our street fair, a fund-raising event that we had been planning for weeks. Without it, our block association could not survive.

2. a.   The band director telephoned me the night before the concert. He said that Paco was sick and that I would have to play Paco's clarinet solo. I wondered if I could do it. After all, I had never practiced the solo part.

b.   The night before the band concert, our telephone rang. It was Mr. Ormond, the band director. He told me that Paco was sick and asked whether I would play Paco's clarinet solo. I had to say yes. In less than twenty-four hours, I had to learn an entire passage that I had never even practiced!

3. a.   There was one minute left in the league championship game, and the Cougars were trailing the Tigers 6-0. The Cougars had the ball on the Tigers' ten-yard line when Bill Major, the Cougars' captain, called a time-out.

b.   It was the league championship game. The Cougars were trailing when their captain called a time-out. That was certainly an exciting moment in the game.

Exercise 2   Writing: Story Beginnings   Read the following prewriting notes for the beginnings of three narratives. On your paper, write a beginning for one of the stories. The beginning should interest your reader, identify the situation, introduce the characters, and set the scene.

1. *Situation:* Teaching my dog, Brutus, to come when I call him
   Characters: Myself; my dog, Brutus
   Setting: Place—the kitchen. Time—Saturday morning

2. *Situation:* Getting to school on time after sleeping through the alarm
   Characters: Myself, my parents
   Setting: Place—our home. Time—fifteen minutes before the school bus is due to arrive

3. *Situation:* Trying to appear calm while watching a scary movie
   Characters: Myself, a friend from my new neighborhood
   Setting: Place—a movie theater. Time—late Saturday afternoon

14.2b Using Dialogue in Your Story

When you narrate a story, you tell what the characters do and what they say. You can tell what the characters say in either of two ways: (l) You can give their exact words. (2) You can summarize, or tell in your own words, what the characters say.

EXACT WORDS   Aunt Jane was there to meet me when I got off the bus in La Loma. "Susan," she said, "you'll have to help me to get the crop in."

SUMMARY   Aunt Jane was there to meet me when I got off the bus in La Loma. She told me that I would have to help her get the crop in.

When you give the exact words that your characters say, you are using **dialogue.** The following guidelines will help you to decide when to use dialogue in your stories.

Strategies

1. *Use dialogue to make your characters come alive.* For example, instead of telling your readers that a character is concerned about something, you can use the character's own words to show that concern.

   "Is everything all right, officer?" *Dad asked in a low voice.*
   "Everything is fine," *the police officer replied cheerfully.* "We found the lost wallet that you reported."

391

In the example, the words in italic type make clear not only *who* is speaking but also *how* he or she is speaking. When you use dialogue in a story, remember to include this kind of information.

2. *Use dialogue to tell some of the actions of your story.* Through dialogue, you can narrate part of your story in a way that is likely to interest your reader. The following dialogue is from a story about a group of hikers who discover a fire in the woods.

> "I think I smell smoke," said Jan. "Does anyone else?"
> "Someone must have a campfire," replied Laura without interest.
> "Well, let's take a look," insisted Jan with a worried frown. "The woods are pretty dry, and some campers can be careless."

Through dialogue the writer of this passage tells two actions of the story: (1) the girls smell smoke, and (2) they go to investigate the source of the smoke.

Dialogue, then, not only adds to the interest of your story but also tells some of the information that your reader needs to know. There are three basic rules for punctuating and paragraphing dialogue in a story.

Rule   Put the spoken words in quotation marks.

Rule   Start each sentence with a capital letter.

Rule   Begin a new paragraph each time the speaker changes.

See pages 216–218 for more information on punctuating dialogue (direct quotations).

Exercise 3   Revising: Dialogue   Each of the following sentences summarizes what someone said. On your paper, rewrite each sentence as it would appear in dialogue.

SAMPLE	Michael said that the movie did not sound very exciting.
ANSWER	"The movie doesn't sound very exciting," complained Michael.

1. At the surprise party, Lorraine said that she was truly surprised, not having suspected anything.
2. Ms. Robertson, my teacher, told us that the test would last only twenty minutes and that we had better get right to work.
3. Wally complained that if it got one degree hotter he was going to jump into a tub of ice water.
4. My mother said that the best way to be satisfied in life is to set a goal and work toward it.
5. Bill wondered aloud how long it would be before Halley's Comet passed the earth again.
6. Lindsay asked her friend Stuart if he would like to go to a concert that afternoon.
7. The aquarium guide said that the shark tanks could be found at the end of the hall.
8. Samantha told her brother that their parents had received some astonishing news from Aunt Jenny.
9. Suzi announced that she had won the blue ribbon for first place in the marathon.
10. Mr. Rich, the supermarket manager, said that I could exchange the dented cans of vegetables for ones that were undamaged.

Exercise 4 Writing: Dialogue Write a short dialogue that helps to bring alive the characters in one of the following situations. Use quotation marks, and make clear who is speaking in each sentence.

1. A teen-ager tries to explain to a friend why he or she must break a promise.
2. A student approaches a coach and asks to try out for a team.

3. Two friends disagree about something but eventually reach an understanding.

4. Two good friends say good-by on the day that one of them must move to another city.

14.2c Telling the Actions in Chronological Order

In your prewriting notes, you made a chronological list of the actions that occur in your story. As you write your story, you should follow the list, making any changes that seem appropriate. Remember that in a narrative of more than one paragraph, you must place each group of related actions in a paragraph of its own.

In the following model, the writer narrates the middle paragraphs of the story about the eleven-year-old who wants a bicycle *(page 389)*.

Model

I sat in the park across from Rooney's, daydreaming about how I would look sweeping through the neighborhood on that beautiful silver bike. Suddenly I remembered how my mother always says that if you really want something badly enough, you can usually find a way to get it. Then, for some reason, I noticed the whirring and clanging of the car wash on the corner. I saw the five-foot sign: "Car Wash—$4." What a joke! People paid four dollars for a five-minute car wash that left half the dirt on the car.

That was it! I would give custom car washes for five dollars. People would be willing to pay the extra dollar for a really careful job. Five into $175—that came to thirty-five cars. I knew at least thirty-five car owners in my neighborhood. What a great idea!

I raced home and wrote out an advertisement on a sheet of paper. Then I shook all the change out of my bank.

Rushing to the library, I made fifty copies of my advertisement:

Johnson's Custom Car Care
Personal Car Wash
Cleaned, Vacuumed, and Polished
Inside and Out
$5.00
Call Day or Night
Lee Johnson
555-6160

I delivered the advertisements to everyone I knew who owned a car.

From the very beginning, business was so good that I had a hard time keeping up. One afternoon, my sister Beth watched me as I frantically washed one car while another customer was parked nearby, waiting her turn. Suddenly, Beth asked, "Lee, would you like me to be your 'gofer'?"

"My what?" I said.

"Your 'gofer'," she repeated patiently. "You know—whenever you have to go for more cleaning supplies, I'll go for you. It will save you lots of time."

Eyeing her suspiciously, I said, "I'll have to pay you, of course."

"Of course," she said with a grin. "Fifty cents a car."

With Beth's help, I was soon averaging three cars a day. By the end of the second week, I had washed my thirty-fifth car. The next morning, as I settled down at the kitchen table, I added up fives, ones, and assorted coins three times. Each time, the total came to $125, not $175. Then it hit me. In my excitement I had forgotten all about expenses. I needed fourteen more cars to reach my goal. The only problem was that I had already washed every car in the neighborhood. My parents had made it clear that I should not approach strangers. Where would I find fourteen more car owners?

The writer tells the actions in chronological order, according to the prewriting notes *(page 384)*. Beginning with two paragraphs about the events that lead to Lee's decision to wash cars, the writer places in the next paragraph the actions related to the advertisement. Finally, after using dialogue to tell about Beth's offer to help, the writer skillfully builds to the high point—the discovery that Lee may not reach the goal of $175.

Exercise 5 Prewriting: Chronological Order Read the following topics and choose two. List in chronological order at least five actions for a true or a fictional narrative about each topic. End each list with the high point of the story. Save your papers.

1. An experience involving sports
2. A family outing
3. A time that you wanted something very much
4. A lost pet
5. A discovery

14.2d Writing the Ending

It is important to think carefully about how much to tell your reader after the high point of the story. One thing that you must do before the end of the story is to settle the situation or problem that you identified at the beginning. You may also briefly tell your reader what happens to the characters afterward or how the characters feel about what has happened to them.

This is the ending of the story about earning money to buy a bicycle.

Model

As I sat at the table, my mother came into the kitchen on her way to work. After one look at my face, she asked, "What's the matter, Lee?"

"Everything!" I said. Then I told her about my desperate need for fourteen more cars.

"Well," she said, "why don't you wash our car again? Then I'll ask some friends at work and have them call you."

Fourteen cars later, I finally reached my goal. Late one Saturday afternoon, I raced to Rooney's Bicycle Shop and got there just before it closed. I carefully counted out the $175. Never in my whole life had I felt so good about anything. I have the bicycle, but I still wash cars. Now I am saving for a racing bike.

In the ending the writer tells how Lee finally reaches the goal and buys the bicycle. The situation introduced at the beginning of the story is settled—in this case, successfully. The writer also briefly tells how Lee feels and what happens afterward: Lee still has the car-washing business and a reason for earning money.

Exercise 6 Writing: Endings Read the following notes, which outline the actions in a famous story. Write a good ending for the story.

1. A fox spies a crow sitting in a tree with a piece of cheese in its beak.
2. The fox decides to trick the crow into giving him the cheese.
3. The fox says good morning to the crow.
4. The crow ignores the fox.
5. The fox compliments the crow on its beautiful black feathers.
6. The crow looks at the fox.
7. The fox admires the crow's shiny beak.
8. The crow smiles at the fox but still holds fast to the cheese.
9. The fox says that such a beautiful crow must have a beautiful voice and he wishes that he could hear the crow sing.
10. The crow is overcome by the fox's flattery and . . .

Exercise 7 Writing: Endings Write an ending for one of the two narratives that you chose in Exercise 5 on page 396.

Assignment 1   Prewriting/Writing   *Step 1:* Think of something that happened to you or to someone you know. It should be a brief incident that you can narrate in a single paragraph. *Step 2:* Plan your paragraph by listing the actions of the story in chronological order. *Step 3:* Write a paragraph in which you narrate the incident.

Assignment 2   Prewriting/Writing/Revising   Plan and write a narrative of at least four paragraphs that tells the story outlined in the notes at the end of this assignment. Introduce the characters and present the setting at the beginning of your narrative. Identify the situation and be sure to settle it by the end of the story. Use your imagination to create the actions of the story and any dialogue between the two classmates. After finishing the story, revise it by using as a guide the Assignment Checklist on the facing page.

> *Situation:* A member of the basketball team persuades an unenthusiastic classmate to join the team.
> *Characters:* Two classmates who are also good friends
> *Setting:* Place—school. Time—early spring

Assignment 3   Prewriting/Writing/Revising   Plan and write a narrative of at least four paragraphs in which you tell about something that happened to you when you were very young. *Step 1:* Make notes about the characters, the setting, and the situation or problem. In your notes remember to list the actions in chronological order and to identify the high point of the story. *Step 2:* Using your notes as a guide, write the narrative. Be sure to write a strong beginning and a definite ending. *Step 3:* Revise your narrative.

Assignment 4   Prewriting/Writing/Revising   Plan and write a fictional narrative of four to twelve paragraphs on one of the following topics. Then revise your narrative.

1. A story about an animal
2. A story about winning or losing
3. A story about courage
4. A humorous story
5. A story that teaches a lesson

Continuing Assignment Writing/Revising Use your notes from the Continuing Assignment on page 387 to write your narrative. It should be no shorter than four paragraphs and no longer than twelve. *Step 1:* Write a beginning that will interest your reader. Identify the situation or problem that will be settled by the end of the story, and present the characters and the setting. Tell the actions in chronological order. Include dialogue, if possible. Bring your story to a definite conclusion. *Step 2:* Using the Assignment Checklist, revise your narrative. *Step 3:* Make a finished copy, following the suggestions on pages 229–230.

Assignment Checklist

Check your assignments for the following points:

✔ 1. Did you identify the problem or situation and present the characters and the setting at the beginning of your story?
✔ 2. Did you write a beginning that is likely to interest your reader?
✔ 3. Did you present the actions of the story in chronological order?
✔ 4. Did you place each group of related actions in a separate paragraph?
✔ 5. Did you include dialogue when appropriate?
✔ 6. Did you include a high point in the action?
✔ 7. Did you settle the situation or problem by the end of the story?
✔ 8. Did you proofread your narrative for correct grammar, usage, spelling, and punctuation?

Into the Past: Narrating a Historical Event

Situation: The Heritage Society is sponsoring a short story contest for students. The stories are to be based on well-known moments in American history. You have decided to tell the story of Washington's crossing of the Delaware River. You intend to narrate the story as if you were one of the soldiers who were with Washington. To plan your story, you made prewriting notes, some of which appear on the facing page. In the beginning of your story, you want to make clear the situation, to identify the setting and the main characters, and to arouse the interest of your readers. As you write the beginning of the narrative, you will keep in mind the following information.

Writer: you as a contestant

Audience: judges of the contest

Topic: Washington's crossing of the Delaware River

Purpose: to narrate the beginning of the story

Directions: To write your narrative, follow these steps.

   Step 1. Read the prewriting notes.
   Step 2. Begin by describing what it was like on the shore of the Delaware River. Emphasize the harshness of the weather, and mention the place and the time of day. Remember to write from the point of view of a soldier who was with Washington. Use the pronoun *I*.

(Continue on page 402.)

Prewriting Notes

BEGINNING

Situation: In a daring move, General George Washington and his army are about to cross the Delaware River and surprise the Hessian troops at Trenton, New Jersey.

Characters: General Washington, forty-six, commander of the Continental Army in the American Revolution

About 2300 soldiers, who are suffering from cold, fatigue, and hunger

Setting: Place: Pennsylvania, on the shore of the Delaware River
Time: Christmas night, 1776
Other details: patches of ice on the river, storm of driving sleet, snow on the ground, very cold, campsite with a few fires, rowboats lying by water's edge

Actions: 1. Washington assembles the men by the river and tells them to board the boats.
2. Washington boards a boat (with the narrator).
3. The boats begin the crossing.

Step 3. Using the notes about characters, tell who was there.

Step 4. In the next sentences, give the actual date and make clear the situation: a whole army is about to make a difficult crossing of a river in small boats.

Step 5. Now narrate the first action, using a direct quotation to make the story vivid.

Step 6. Narrate the second and third actions. Tell how you, the narrator, felt. Try to leave your readers in suspense.

Step 7. Reread your story beginning and revise it. To do so, ask yourself these questions: Did I tell about the situation, the setting, and the characters in such a way that my readers can easily imagine them? Did I narrate the actions clearly?

Unit Assignments

Assignment 1   Recall an incident that you witnessed. It should be brief enough to be told in a single paragraph. Narrate the actions in chronological order.

Assignment 2   Write a narrative of four to twelve paragraphs about an experience that taught you something or that impressed you in some way. For example, you might write about something that happened while you were baby-sitting. Include dialogue if you can.

Assignment 3   Write a fictional story of four to twelve paragraphs in which someone overcomes a difficulty. For example, you might write about someone who has to move to a new community. Be sure to settle the problem by the end of your story.

Assignment 4   Write a fictional narrative that is a modern version of a familiar story. The characters and the situation should be similar to those in the original, but they should fit into a present-day setting. For example, Paul Bunyan, the legendary lumberjack, might live in a modern city instead of in a lumber camp.

Assignment 5   Write a story about someone who succeeds in doing the seemingly impossible. For example, you might write about someone who makes a team even though he or she is new to the sport.

Revising Your Assignments

For help in revising a narrative, consult the Checklist for Revision on the last page of this book.

Unit Tests

Test 1

A. Number your paper from 1 to 5. Next to each number, write *True* if the sentence is true or *False* if it is false.

1. A story should have only one paragraph.
2. You should include many interesting people in your narrative even if they are not involved in the action.
3. In a fictional narrative, you make up the characters and the details about what happens to them.
4. You should try to capture your reader's interest at the beginning of your narrative.
5. When you summarize the words of your characters, you must use quotation marks.

B. Number your paper from 6 to 10. Next to each number, write the letter of the item that correctly completes the sentence. You will use all but one of the items.

a. dialogue d. setting
b. narrative e. ending
c. high point f. chronological order

6. A __?__ is a story about a true or an imaginary happening.
7. The __?__ is the time and place of the narrative.
8. When you present exact words of your characters, you use __?__.
9. You should present the actions of a narrative in __?__.
10. The __?__ of a narrative is the most exciting action.

C. Number your paper from 11 to 15. Next to each number, write the letter of the item that correctly answers the question.

11. Which of the following should you *not* do at the beginning of a narrative?
    a. Introduce the main characters
    b. Explain the setting

c. Identify the situation or problem

d. Tell how the situation or problem is settled

12. In which part of a narrative should you present the high point?

   a. In the beginning

   b. In the middle

   c. In the ending

   d. Anywhere in the story

13. Which of the following sentences introduces the setting of a story?

   a. The first day of my vacation was exciting.

   b. We entered the Mojave Desert at five in the morning, when it was actually cold.

   c. When the performance started, Norma had no idea how it would end.

   d. Jill was the leader of the two-day project to clean up the park.

14. Which of the following sentences contains dialogue?

   a. Marco exclaimed loudly that he did not want to go.

   b. During the concert, I quietly told Astrid that she should look at the left side of the stage.

   c. Breathing heavily, Gilbert claimed, "I know I can make it to the end of the race."

   d. Vivian warned Jack that the bicycle path by the river is bumpy.

15. Which of the following should you *not* tell your reader at the end of a narrative?

   a. What happened to one of the characters at an earlier time

   b. How the problem is settled

   c. What happens to the characters when the problem is settled

   d. How the characters feel about the solution to the problem

Test 2

Choose one of the Unit Assignments. Write the assignment as directed and hand it in to your teacher.

Writing a Report

Unit Preview

A **report** presents facts on a specific topic. It is based on information about your topic that you find by reading books, magazines, and newspapers about your topic. You collect the facts for your readers so that they can learn about the subject without searching for the information themselves.

The following two paragraphs begin a report about insect sounds.

The Voices of Summer

Summer days and evenings are filled with what seem to be the voices of thousands of insects, but, in reality, insects do not have voices. In fact, most species never make a sound. The insect chorus is made up of just a few species. Those insects make noise by rubbing their wings and legs together.

One of the most commonly heard insect sounds is the buzz or hum of dry insect wings vibrating against the air as the insect flies. As bees hover over flowers, their wings make a low, buzzing sound. Dragonflies have larger wings. Therefore, they produce a deeper tone. Mosquitoes make a high-pitched buzz because their wings are smaller and move faster.

Notice that the sample report is simple and direct. The topic is stated at the beginning, and every sentence presents information about the topic.

For Analysis   On your paper, answer the following questions about the opening paragraphs of the report on insect sounds.

1. What is the topic of the report?
2. Which sentence states the topic?
3. What is the topic of the second paragraph?
4. How is the second paragraph related to the first paragraph?

By answering questions about the opening paragraphs of one report, you have observed important characteristics of all reports. In this unit you will learn how to write a report. As you write, you will follow the three steps in the writing process. These steps are prewriting, writing, and revising.

15.1 Selecting and Limiting a Topic

The first step in planning a report is to choose your topic carefully. Then you must limit that topic so that you can cover it completely in your report.

15.1a Selecting a Topic

Sometimes your teacher will assign a topic for a report. At other times you will be asked to select a topic. If you select your own topic, choose one that is interesting to you. Because you will enjoy reading and writing about the topic, you will be able to write a more interesting report. Also, choose a topic that requires research. Reports are based on factual information that you find by reading. They are not based on your personal experiences.

The examples on the following page show original topics that cannot be researched and, therefore, are unsuitable for reports. The revised topics are suitable for reports.

UNSUITABLE TOPIC	Why I want to become a lawyer [cannot be researched]
REVISED TOPIC	Requirements for becoming a lawyer
UNSUITABLE TOPIC	My family's backpacking trip on the Appalachian Trail [cannot be researched]
REVISED TOPIC	The history of the Appalachian Trail

Exercise 1   Prewriting: Report Topics   Number your paper from 1 to 10. Rate each of the following topics. Then write *Suitable* or *Cannot be researched* after each number.

SAMPLE	Why I like the Olympics
ANSWER	Cannot be researched

1. My pet lizard
2. The eating habits of polar bears
3. Abraham Lincoln's Gettysburg Address
4. Why my grandparents like farm life
5. How I learned to play football
6. Our trip to Nova Scotia
7. The plants in Everglades National Park
8. Why I enjoy listening to the radio
9. How a telegraph works
10. The importance of regular exercise

15.1b Limiting a Topic

When you write a report, you need to cover your topic thoroughly. Thus, you must limit your topic to fit the size of the report. The report that you write will have a length of 200 to 450 words (two to three pages). The subject "Automobiles" is too large to be covered in a brief report. By limiting that topic to "Safety devices in automobiles," you can discuss the topic completely. In addition, having a limited topic will make finding good sources of information on your topic easier for you.

To limit your topic, ask yourself the following questions:

1. Can I limit my topic to one part of the general topic?
2. Can I limit my topic to one person, one group, or one example?
3. Can I limit my topic to a brief time period?
4. Can I limit my topic to one event or one place?

The following general topics have been limited so that they are suitable for brief reports.

GENERAL TOPIC   Bridges

LIMITED TOPIC   The Brooklyn Bridge [one example]

GENERAL TOPIC   Marie Curie

LIMITED TOPIC   Marie Curie's discovery of radium [one event]

Once you have limited your topic, test its suitability. You need to check how much information is available on your topic. Begin by looking in an encyclopedia. Next, check your library card catalog *(page 531)* for the location of books on your topic. To locate magazine articles on your topic, look in the *Readers' Guide to Periodical Literature (pages 538–539)*. The *Readers' Guide* lists articles by their subjects and their authors.

If you find too much information on your topic to cover it fully in two to three pages, you will need to limit your topic further. Also, if you cannot find at least two sources dealing with your topic, it may be too limited. If your topic seems too general or too limited, you do not have to reject it completely. The material that you found as you tested your topic may suggest some related topics that are better suited to a short report.

Exercise 2 Prewriting: Limited Topics Number your paper from 1 to 5. For each of the following pairs of topics, choose the topic that is limited enough for a report of two to three pages. Write the letter of the limited topic.

SAMPLE   a. French presidents
             b. Why Charles De Gaulle resigned as President
                of France

ANSWER   b

1. a. The new exhibit in the British Museum
   b. The history of England
2. a. Types of bears
   b. Why bears hibernate
3. a. Famous women in history
   b. Why Jane Addams started Hull House
4. a. Columbus's voyages to the New World
   b. Columbus's last voyage
5. a. How dogs can be trained to help disabled persons
   b. Types of dogs

Assignment Prewriting   *Step 1:* Choose five of the subjects from the list that follows. *Step 2:* For each, list a general topic that can be researched. *Step 3:* Limit each general topic to make it suitable for a report of two to three pages.

1. Animals
2. Famous musicians
3. Sources of energy
4. The human body
5. Inventions
6. Rivers
7. Farm products
8. Sports
9. Politics
10. Medicines

Continuing Assignment Prewriting   *Step 1:* On your paper, list five topics about which you would like to learn more. Then choose the three topics that interest you the most. *Step 2:* Limit each topic to make it suitable for a report of two to three pages. *Step 3:* Test your limited topics by finding sources about them. Choose one limited topic for which you have found at least three sources. Write down your topic. Save your paper.

Assignment Checklist

Check your assignments for the following points:

  ✔ 1. Did you select topics that interest you?

  ✔ 2. Did you choose topics that require research?

  ✔ 3. Did you limit your topics so that they can be covered in detail in two to three pages?

Check your Continuing Assignment for this additional point:

  ✔ 4. Did you find at least three sources that contain information about the topics?

15.2 Gathering Information

Once you have selected and limited your topic, begin gathering information about it. The first step is to list facts about the sources that you found in the library. The next step is to take notes on the useful information in those sources.

15.2a Preparing Source Cards

Prepare a source card for each possible source that you find for your limited topic. Use one three-by-five-inch index card for each source. The information that you include on the source card varies depending on the type of publication.

Encyclopedias. On your source cards, list the author's name (last name first) and then the title of the article (in quotation marks). If the name of the author is not given, begin with the title of the article. Next, list the name of the encyclopedia (underlined) and the year of the edition. The correct form and punctuation of the listing are shown in the following example.

> Dodson, Peter. "Dinosaur." <u>World Book Encyclopedia.</u>
> 1981 ed.

Books. List the author's name (last name first) and the title (underlined). Then list the city where the publisher is located, the publisher's name, and the date of publication. Note the form and the punctuation used in the following example.

> Horvath, Joan. <u>Filmmaking for Beginners.</u>
> New York: Lodestar Books, 1974.

Magazines and Newspapers. List the author's name if it is given (last name first), the title of the article (in quotation marks), the name of the newspaper or magazine (underlined), the date of publication, and the first and last page numbers on which the article appears (for example: pp. 4–6). If the article does not run on consecutive pages, list each page on which it appears (for example: pp. 18, 34). For newspaper articles only, list the section number before the page number. The following examples show the correct form and punctuation for magazine and newspaper source cards.

> MAGAZINE   "Climbing Among the Clouds." <u>National
> Geographic World</u>, June 1981, pp.
> 24–28.

> NEWSPAPER   Yang, Linda. "Snow Is a Friend of Dormant
> Plants." <u>New York Times</u>, 10 Feb.
> 1983, Sec. C, p. 10.

An example of a source card for a book appears on the following page.

Source Card

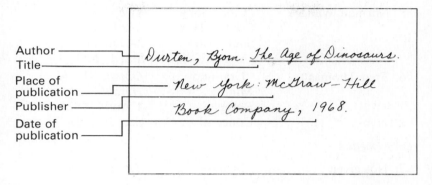

Author ——
Title ——
Place of publication ——
Publisher ——
Date of publication ——

Dursten, Bjorn. The Age of Dinosaurs.
New York: McGraw–Hill
Book Company, 1968.

Exercise 1 **Prewriting: Source Cards** Use the following information to write source-card listings. For this exercise write the listings on a sheet of paper. Be sure to list the information in the proper order and to punctuate it properly.

AUTHOR	TITLE	PUBLICATION FACTS
Books		
1. Ludwig Goldsheider	*Michelangelo: Paintings, Sculptures, Architecture*	Phaedon Press, Ltd. London, England 1964
2. Alistair Cooke	*Alistair Cooke's America*	Alfred A. Knopf New York 1977
Magazines		
3. George B. Schaller	"Pandas in the Wild"	*National Geographic* December 1981 pp. 734–749
4. Claudia Wallis	"Salt: A New Villain?"	*Time* 15 March 1982 pp. 64–71

Newspapers

5. Norman Wallace	"City's Song Contest Hits Sour Note"	*Crain's Chicago Business* 24 January 1983 Sec. 1, p. 9
6. Fred Thomas	"Uranium Mining Raises Concern"	*Omaha World-Herald* 1 April 1982 Sec. 1, p. 13

Encyclopedias

7. Not given	"Measles"	*The Columbia Viking Desk Encyclopedia* 1968 edition
8. Otto H. Siegmund	"Falconry"	*Merit Students Encyclopedia* 1981 edition

15.2b Taking Notes

You are now ready to prepare note cards from the sources that you listed on your source cards. The following suggestions will help you to take useful notes.

Strategies

1. *Skim each source.* Check whether each source covers your limited topic. If the source is a book, scan the table of contents and the index to see which sections might be useful. If the source contains material about your limited topic, read that information carefully.

2. *Write your notes on index cards.* When you have finished doing research and are ready to make an

outline, you will find it easier to work from index cards. Use either three-by-five-inch or four-by-six-inch index cards.

3. *Write notes on only one idea on each note card.* Then you can rearrange your note cards easily when you organize the ideas for your report. For example, if you are doing research for a report on the use of computers in schools, you may find a paragraph on their uses for teaching and their uses for testing. Even though this information is contained in a single paragraph, make one card for details about the use of computers for teaching and another card for details about the use of computers for testing.

4. *Summarize important information from each source.* In a summary you briefly state the author's point in your own words. (See Unit 19 for further information on writing a summary.) You may write a summary in phrases rather than in complete sentences.

5. *Write a subject heading in the upper left corner of each card.* Choose a word or a phrase that identifies the main idea of the note card. You can sort your cards by these headings when you organize your report.

6. *Write the author's name if it is given and an abbreviated title of the source in the upper right corner of each card.* This information will help you to identify the source if you need to check your information.

7. *Write the page number from which the information came on the bottom of each card.* This information, too, will help you to check your facts if necessary.

Review the example of a note card on the following page. The notes summarize a point made by the author.

Note Card

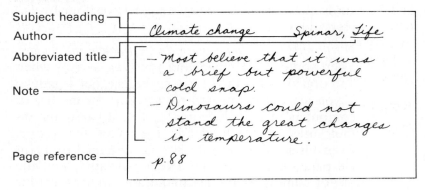

Subject heading —
Author —
Abbreviated title —
Note —
Page reference —

Climate change   Spinar, Life

— Most believe that it was a brief but powerful cold snap.
— Dinosaurs could not stand the great changes in temperature.

p. 88

Use the preceding example as a guide when you prepare note cards for your report.

Exercise 2   Prewriting: Note Cards   You are writing a report on the content of valuable metals in coins. Read the following passage. Then write a note card with the subject heading "Hoarding coins." The passage is from the article "Money" in the 1978 edition of *Compton's Encyclopedia*. No author was listed for the article.

> . . . People hoarded coins during President Van Buren's administration and during the Civil War. They did this because they were afraid paper money had lost its value. Coins, they thought, would always be valuable if only for the copper, silver, and gold in them. Soon there were almost no metal coins to make change. People began to have a great deal of trouble buying things, because they did not want paper money and there were few coins.

Assignment 1   Prewriting   Choose one of the following limited topics. Using materials in your library, write at least three source cards for a report on your topic.

1. Agriculture in Honduras
2. Prehistoric cave paintings
3. Glassmaking in Sweden
4. How bats navigate
5. How geysers are formed
6. Types of cargo ships

Continuing Assignment **Prewriting** You selected and limited a topic in the Continuing Assignment on pages 410–411. Now prepare source cards for at least three sources that contain information on your limited topic. Then prepare at least fifteen note cards from these three sources. Save your source cards and your note cards.

Assignment Checklist

Check your assignments for the following points:

✔ 1. Did you make a source card for each book, magazine, newspaper, or encyclopedia that you used?
✔ 2. Did you take notes on each source in your own words, summarizing what you read?
✔ 3. Did you limit the notes on each card to one idea?
✔ 4. Did you write a subject heading on each note card?
✔ 5. Did you write the author's name (if given) and an abbreviated title on each note card?
✔ 6. Did you write the page number on which the information is found on each note card?

15.3 Organizing Your Information

You are now ready to use your note cards to organize your written report. You will write a topic statement and make an outline. Your **topic statement** is a single sentence that presents the main idea of a report. An **outline** is a list of ideas arranged in a logical order. Your outline will serve as a guide when you write your report. The following steps explain how to write a topic statement and how to make an outline.

Procedure

1. *Separate your note cards into stacks according to their subject headings.* Combine stacks that have headings that are closely related.

2. *Choose the most important subject heading for each stack of cards.* These subject headings will become the main headings in your outline. Note that these headings are not complete sentences.

3. *Use your main headings and your note cards to write a topic statement.* Make sure that your topic statement presents the main idea of your report. The following is a topic statement for a report on why dinosaurs became extinct.

   Topic statement: Scientists can only suggest theories to explain why dinosaurs became extinct.

   Place your topic statement at the top of your complete outline.

4. *List your main headings in logical order.* The headings can be arranged in chronological order, spatial order, order of importance, or whatever order seems suitable for your topic. This list is your **rough outline.** The main headings for the report on dinosaurs could be arranged in order from the least probable theory to the most probable theory.

   Changes in the species
   Changes in geologic conditions
   Changes in climate

5. *Assign Roman numerals to the main headings in your rough outline.* Include "Introduction" as your first main heading and "Conclusion" as your last main heading.

6. *Review each stack of note cards separately.* Put cards with similar ideas together. Then put the grouped cards in a logical order. Use the main points in each stack of cards as the subheadings under each main heading of your outline. Place a capital letter before each subheading.

Study the form of the following complete outline for the report on dinosaurs.

Topic statement: Scientists can only suggest theories to explain why dinosaurs became extinct.

    I. Introduction
   II. Changes in the species
      A. Died of collective old age
      B. Shells on eggs too thin for survival
  III. Changes in geologic conditions
      A. Appearance of mountains
      B. Disappearance of tropical plants when swamps drained
  IV. Changes in climate
      A. Changes in environment and food supply
      B. Radiation effects from supernova
   V. Conclusion

Exercise   The Outline   On your paper, prepare an outline that develops the following topic statement. To prepare the outline, list the main headings and the subheadings in a logical order. Use Roman numerals and capital letters as required by the form of an outline.

Topic statement: The space shuttle is the first step in a new era of space travel.

Main headings:

Can be used many times
Takes satellites and experiments into orbit
Makes space colonies possible

Subheadings:

Allows inhabitants from colonies to travel to and from Earth
Saves money because it is reusable
Allows equipment and supplies for space colonies to be delivered
Has enough room for carrying experiments
Needs only minor repairs to heat shield tiles before reuse
Provides most economical way of launching satellites

Assignment Prewriting   Choose one of the following limited topics. On your paper, write a topic statement and then use it to prepare a rough outline. Include at least two main headings in addition to the introduction and the conclusion. You may consult reference books for information.

1. How crop rotation keeps the soil from wearing out
2. How a dry-cell battery works
3. How cable television can help people to learn
4. Why birds migrate

Continuing Assignment Prewriting   *Step 1:* Using the note cards that you made for the Continuing Assignment on page 417, write a topic statement and make a rough outline for your report. *Step 2:* Use your note cards to make a complete outline. Save your paper.

Assignment Checklist

Check your assignments for the following points:

✔ 1. Did you choose the most important main headings for your outline?
✔ 2. Did you use the main headings to write a topic statement?
✔ 3. Did you arrange the main headings in a logical order?

Check your Continuing Assignment for these additional points:

✔ 4. Did you use the points on your note cards as subheadings in your outline?
✔ 5. Did you make a complete outline with Roman numerals before main headings and capital letters before subheadings?

15.4 Writing Your Report

You are now ready to write your report. Once you have written the **first draft,** or first version, of your report, you will revise it. Then you will prepare a final copy.

15.4a Writing the First Draft

Your outline will guide you as you write your first draft. Include one paragraph for each of the main headings in your outline. Refer to your note cards and sources if you need more information. Be sure, however, to present all of the information in your own words.

The Introductory Paragraph

Your introductory paragraph is important because it is the first impression the reader has of your report. A good introductory paragraph will make the reader want to continue reading.

To write a strong introductory paragraph, you should follow these guidelines.

Strategies

1. *Capture the reader's interest.* Begin your report by telling why the topic is important, unusual, or memorable in some way.

2. *Present your topic statement.* Usually your topic statement is the last sentence of the introductory paragraph.

3. *Give any necessary background information* that the reader will need to understand the report. For example, include the time or place, the people involved, or the definitions of unfamiliar terms that are used in the report.

The Body

The body of your report presents points that explain your topic statement. Begin the first body paragraph with a topic sentence that includes the information in the second main heading (Roman numeral II) of your outline. Then follow the subheadings of your outline as you write the rest of the paragraph. All of the information in the paragraph should support the topic sentence. Repeat this procedure for the rest of the body paragraphs, using the remaining main headings and subheadings in your outline.

The Concluding Paragraph

Your concluding paragraph reminds your readers of what you have written and helps them to grasp the meaning of your report. The paragraph should be brief. Restate your topic statement from your introductory paragraph. Then briefly review the main points from the body of your report.

You can also make an observation about your topic in your concluding paragraph. For example, you could mention why the subject is important or what might happen in the future. Do not, however, raise any points that should have been covered in the body of your report.

Exercise 1   Writing: Introductory Paragraphs   Read the two introductory paragraphs that follow. Choose the paragraph that would be the better introduction to a report on thunder and lightning. On your paper, write one or two sentences to explain why you chose that paragraph.

1.   Lightning is just electricity. Everyone has seen lightning. The sudden heating of the air around the lightning causes the air to expand violently. Thunder is the vibration of the expanding air.

2.   Since time began, people have been amazed by lightning that flashes through the sky and thunder that crashes in the air. Ancient people thought that angry gods or evil spirits were speaking through these thunderstorms. We know today that lightning is electrical energy and that thunder is the sound created by air molecules vibrating after being super-heated by the electrical charge of the lightning bolt.

Exercise 2   Writing: Body Paragraph   Using your outline from the exercise on page 419 write a paragraph that covers the heading "Can be used many times."

Exercise 3   Writing: Concluding Paragraph   Using the outline that you made in the exercise on page 419, write a concluding paragraph for a report on the space shuttle.

15.4b Listing Your Sources

You must make a list of the sources of information that you used for your report. This list is important for two reasons. First, you must always give credit to the sources from which you learned new ideas. Second, you list your sources for readers who wish to consult them for more information.

Your list of sources should be the last page of your report. To prepare the page, begin by alphabetizing your source cards by the author's last name. If no author is given, use the first word in the title of a source. Ignore the articles *A, An,* and *The* at the beginning of a title. Then copy the information from your source cards. (To make sure that you listed the information correctly, see pages 411–413.) Double-space all lines in the list. Indent all lines five spaces except the first line. You may refer to the model on page 428.

Exercise 4   Writing: List of Sources   The following sources were used in a report about John Glenn, former astronaut and United States senator. Arrange the sources in alphabetical order. Then, on your paper, write the publication information in the proper order. Be sure to use the correct punctuation.

1. New York, E. P. Dutton, *The Astronauts: The Story of Project Mercury,* 1961, Martin Caidin
2. *The New York Times Magazine,* pp. 32–35, E. Kennedy, "John Glenn's Presidential Countdown," October 11, 1981

3. 1981 edition, "John Glenn, Jr.," *World Book Encyclopedia*
4. pp. 40–41, "Mr. America in the Senate," December 1975, P. Healy, *Saturday Evening Post*

Assignment 1   Writing   Write a first draft of an introductory paragraph for a report on elephants. Use the following topic statement and partial outline.

Topic statement: Elephants have several features that make them excellent work animals.

    I. Introduction
   II. Trunk
      A. Is flexible, enabling it to pick up logs and other objects
      B. Can pick up objects that weigh six hundred pounds
      C. Can push objects that weigh two tons

Assignment 2   Writing   Using the topic statement and the partial outline in Assignment 1, write a first draft of a body paragraph for a report on what makes elephants good work animals.

Continuing Assignment   Using the note cards, the topic statement, and the outline that you prepared for the Continuing Assignments on page 417 and page 420, write the first draft of your report. Its length should be from 200 to 450 words. Then prepare a source list for your report.

Assignment Checklist

Check your assignments for the following points:

    ✔ 1. Did you include a topic statement in your introductory paragraph?
    ✔ 2. Did you try to capture your reader's interest with your introductory paragraph?
    ✔ 3. Did you write a topic sentence for each body paragraph based on the appropriate main heading in your outline?

Check your Continuing Assignment for these additional points:

✔ 4. Did you develop each body paragraph using details from your outline and from your note cards?

✔ 5. Did you write a concluding paragraph?

✔ 6. Did you prepare a source list using the correct form and punctuation?

15.5 Revising and Finishing Your Report

Revising the First Draft

Revising involves rereading your first draft several times to look for ways to make it clearer or more interesting. If possible, put your first draft aside for several hours or even a day before you reread it. Then you can take a fresh look at it and more easily see where improvement may be needed.

Use the following strategies to revise your report.

Strategies

1. *Check your report against your outline.* Make sure that you followed your outline and be sure that you covered all the important points. If your outline does not work in certain places, however, you may depart from it. Make sure, also, that you did not include unnecessary information in the report.

2. *Check your sentences to make sure that they state your ideas clearly.* If necessary, combine short, choppy sentences *(pages 316–324),* or separate long, awkward ones *(pages 325–326).* Replace vague words with words that say exactly what you mean.

3. *Check your report for correct grammar, sentence structure, and word choice.* Correct any errors that you find.

4. *Proofread your report.* Correct any errors in punctuation, spelling, and capitalization. Make sure your sources are listed in the proper form.

After you have revised your first draft, you need to choose a title for your report. Your title should tell what the report is about and should capture the reader's interest. For example, the title "What Happened to the Dinosaurs?" is more interesting than "How Dinosaurs Became Extinct." Sometimes a key word or phrase from your report makes a good title. Avoid titles that are overly clever or humorous.

Preparing the Finished Report

The final step of preparing your report is to recopy or type the revised draft so that it has the best possible appearance. Follow the guidelines on pages 229–230 for preparing a finished paper. Then proofread your final copy to correct any mistakes that you may have made when you copied it.

Use the following final draft of the report on dinosaurs as a model for your final draft.

Model

```
                                    Marsha Gilbert
                                           Science
                                  November 16, 19__


             What Happened to the Dinosaurs?


       The prehistoric existence of dinosaurs was discovered

   in the early 1800s.  Since then, people have been

   fascinated by these mysterious creatures.  Their huge size

   and strange shapes make them seem even more fantastic than

   unicorns or dragons.  Scientists now know a great deal

   about these ancient monsters.  However, the greatest
```

mystery surrounding dinosaurs still remains. Scientists can only suggest theories to explain why dinosaurs suddenly became extinct.

Some experts think dinosaurs died naturally of collective old age. After 135 million years, dinosaurs might have failed to produce healthy offspring. Archaeologists have discovered that many of the last dinosaur eggs never hatched. These eggs had shells that were much too thin. The offspring did not develop healthy skeletons because the thin shells did not supply enough calcium. Obviously, a species that produces no offspring will disappear within a short time.

Some scientists believe that changes in the structure of the earth caused all the dinosaurs to vanish. Dinosaurs lived on flat plains or in swampy areas. Near the end of the dinosaur era, mountain ranges formed, causing the swamps to drain. The dinosaurs could not climb the rocks, and the tropical plants that they lived on disappeared. Therefore, the dinosaurs could not survive.

Perhaps the most interesting theory is that shortly before the end of the dinosaur era, the weather changed suddenly. Some scientists believe that a supernova, or exploding star, passed within one hundred light-years of the earth. The supernova gave off ten million times the amount of radiation that usually comes from the sun. The radiation caused the atmosphere to turn upside down, lowering the temperature greatly. The climate became much colder––not cold enough for an ice age, but cold enough to change the world in which the dinosaurs lived. Such a reduction in temperature chilled the huge bodies of the dinosaurs and killed the plants that they ate. When the plant-eating dinosaurs died from starvation, the meat-eaters lost their source of food as well.

Scientists have not yet agreed on what caused dinosaurs to become extinct. Some believe that dinosaurs died of collective old age. Others think that changes in the earth's structure caused dinosaurs to vanish. Still others feel that a change in the climate made it impossible for these giants to survive. Most of the evidence points to a change in the climate as the reason that dinosaurs died out. In the future, scientists may discover new evidence that will solve this mystery.

Sources page

Sources

Desmond, Adrian J. The Hot-Blooded Dinosaurs. New York: The Dial Press, 1976.

Dodson, Peter. "Dinosaur." The World Book Encyclopedia. 1981 ed.

Kurten, Bjorn. The Age of Dinosaurs. New York: McGraw-Hill Book Company, 1968.

Spinar, Z. V. Life Before Man. New York: Time-Life Books, 1972.

Exercise **Revising: Body Paragraphs** Number your paper from 1 to 5. Then read the following passage from the body of the first draft of a report on how animals use camouflage to protect themselves. Some of the numbered items need revision. On your paper, write the letter of the revision that will improve the sentence.

(1) Many animals use their color to hide from their enemies. (2) Their color blends with their environments so well that they cannot be seen. (3) A brown toad can hardly be seen. (4) When it sits on brown soil. (5) It is difficult to spot a gray-winged moth standing on gray bark. (6) Some animals play dead to fool their enemies. (7) Some animals change their color to blend with their surroundings. (8) Certain chameleons can change their color.

1. Sentences 1 and 2
   a. Combine the sentences: *Many animals rely on their color to hide them from their enemies because their colors blend with the colors of their environments so well that they cannot be seen.*
   b. Rewrite the sentences: *Many animals rely on their color to hide them from their enemies. Their colors blend with the colors of their environments so well that they cannot be seen.*

2. Sentence 3
   a. Combine the sentence with what follows it: *A brown toad can hardly be seen when it sits on brown soil.*
   b. Rewrite the sentence: *It is not easy to see a brown toad.*

3. Sentence 6
   a. Remove the sentence.
   b. Rewrite the sentence: *Some animals pretend to be dead in order to fool their enemies.*

4. Sentence 7
   a. Divide the sentence: *Some animals change their color. They blend with their surroundings.*
   b. Make no change.

5. Sentence 8
   a. Delete the sentence.
   b. Rewrite the sentence: *Certain chameleons can change their color to match gray rocks, brown soil, or green leaves.*

Assignment   Revising   Revise the first draft of the paragraphs that you wrote for Assignments 1 and 2 on page 424. Then prepare a final copy of those paragraphs.

Continuing Assignment   Revising   *Step 1:* Revise the first draft of the report that you wrote for the Continuing Assignment on page 424. *Step 2:* Prepare the final copy of your report. Submit your first draft, your final copy, and your outline to your teacher.

Assignment Checklist

Check your assignments for the following points:

✔ 1. Did you make sure that you stated all important ideas?
✔ 2. Did you check your report for correct grammar, usage, spelling, and punctuation?
✔ 3. Did you choose a title that is both informative and interesting?
✔ 4. Did you prepare a finished paper that is neat and free of errors?

15.6 Writing a Book Report

A **book report** has two purposes. First, it shows that you understand the book that you read. Second, it gives you a chance to express your ideas about the book. Writing a book report is similar to writing any report. That is, all book reports have an introductory paragraph, body paragraphs, and a concluding paragraph.

15.6a Book Reports About Fiction

Fiction includes novels, short stories, and plays. The writer of a fictional book creates the characters and events in the book. A book report about fiction describes the characters, the action, and the ideas of the story. Also, the writer of the book report expresses personal opinions or ideas about the book.

Before you begin to write your book report, take notes on what you have read. Your notes should include the names of the title and the author of the book. Also, take notes on the main characters and the important actions in the story. Use your notes as a guide when you write your report. Write in the present tense and follow these steps as you write.

Procedure

1. *Begin your introductory paragraph with a sentence that identifies the author and the title of the book.* This is the topic statement for your book report. In addition, mention what type of fiction the book is.

2. *Describe the main characters in the first body paragraph of your report.* You should focus your attention on the most important character.

3. *Write a brief summary of the important events in your second body paragraph.* Explain how the main characters react to those events.

4. *Give your opinion of the book in the concluding paragraph.* Be specific. You might answer the following questions: What was interesting or memorable about the book? Can you compare some event or person in the book to an event or person in your own life? Did you learn something new?

The following is a book report on *Island of the Blue Dolphins.*

Model

Scott Gerver
English
January 14, 19__

Island of the Blue Dolphins, by Scott O'Dell, won the
Newbery Award for outstanding literature in 1960.   It is
an adventure novel based on the experiences of a young
Indian girl who is stranded for eighteen years on an
island seventy-five miles southwest of Los Angeles.

Karana is the main character in the novel.   In her
Indian language, she is probably about "twelve or fourteen
summers old" when she has to learn to survive alone.   She
is very clever, as shown by her ability to build houses,
create weapons, trap animals, and build and repair canoes.
She is also kind and loving.   Rontu, an injured wild dog
that she nursed back to health, becomes her devoted
friend.   Karana is never discouraged and she never pities
herself.   Sometimes she is afraid of wild dogs, terrible
storms, or the enemy, but she always uses her intelligence
to overcome her fear.

The novel begins when Karana's people decide to leave
their island home because of the arrival of the hostile
Aleuts.   When her people set sail for the mainland
seventy-five miles away, Karana is accidentally left

behind. She is certain that they will return for her, so
month after month she watches for a boat. Karana learns
to survive despite her enemies. An Aleut girl becomes
Karana's secret friend. This friendship is the only human
contact Karana has. After eighteen years, she is
discovered by a missionary and goes with him to live the
rest of her life at the Mission of Santa Barbara.

I enjoyed reading Island of the Blue Dolphins.
Karana's adventures are exciting. The story is
suspenseful because there is always the chance that
someone might rescue her or that the Aleuts might discover
her. The story seems real because Karana tells it in her
own words. Karana is a remarkable person. I admire her
strength and courage and the way that she faces danger and
loneliness.

Notice that the writer does more than provide a description of the main character and the important events. The writer also explains why the book is exciting and why the main character is admirable.

Exercise 1 Prewriting: Organizing The following notes were taken for a book report on a work of fiction. Number your paper from 1 to 5. After each number, write *Introduction, Body,* or *Conclusion,* to identify the part of the report in which the note belongs.

1. *The Call of the Wild* is by Jack London.
2. Buck's struggles seem as important and as memorable as those of any human hero.

3. Buck is stolen from California and shipped to the gold rush region of the Klondike.

4. It is an adventure novel.

5. The dog hero, Buck, is proud, intelligent, and cunning.

15.6b Book Reports About Nonfiction

Nonfiction presents facts about real people, things, and events. Nonfiction can be divided into two groups: biography or autobiography and general nonfiction.

Biography and Autobiography

Biography is the story of a person's life written by another person. **Autobiography** is the story of a person's life written by that person. Both are nonfiction because they present the events in the lives of real people.

Just as you would do for a report about a fictional book, take notes on a biography or an autobiography before you begin to write your book report. You can use your notes as a guide for writing your report. Follow these steps when you write your report.

Procedure

1. *Begin your introductory paragraph by identifying the book and its author.* Tell whether the book is a biography or an autobiography. Include a sentence or two about why the subject of the book is important.

2. *Summarize two or three important events in the person's life.* Usually, it is best to place this summary in the first body paragraph. If more space is required, however, write one paragraph about each event. Tell why each event is important.

3. *Explain in detail why the person is noteworthy* in the next body paragraph. Tell why the person is important in a particular field or in history.

4. *Give your reaction to the book.* Discuss why you liked or did not like the book. Indicate whether you learned a great deal about the person from the book.

General Nonfiction

This category includes books on science, history, the arts, government, and so on. To prepare a report on a nonfiction book, take notes and refer to them as you write. Follow these steps.

Procedure

1. *Begin your introduction by identifying the book and the author.* Tell what type of general nonfiction the book is. Also, include a description of the subject.

2. *Explain two or three of the major ideas in the book.* Be brief; discuss only the most important ideas. You may discuss all of the ideas in one paragraph, or you may discuss each idea in a separate paragraph.

3. *Evaluate the book.* Give answers to some of the following questions: Does the author support his or her arguments with facts? Is the information presented in an interesting way? Did you learn something new about the subject?

Exercise 2   Prewriting: Organizing   The following notes were taken for a report about a nonfiction book. Number your paper from 1 to 5. After each number, write the part of a book report in which the information belongs: *Introduction, Body,* or *Conclusion.*

1. Describes the many people who visited North America before Columbus

2. Interesting because the author seems to answer every question that a reader might have
3. Strong evidence that the Vikings had settled on the continent long before the voyages of Columbus
4. *Who Discovered America?* by Patricia Lauber
5. Mentions earliest inhabitants, thought to have come across from Siberia on a "land bridge" perhaps fifty thousand years ago

Assignment 1   Prewriting   Choose a book of fiction that you have read recently. If the details are not fresh in your mind, skim the book again. Then take notes for a book report on the work.

Assignment 2   Writing/Revising   Using your notes from Assignment 1, write a first draft of your book report. Then revise the first draft of your book report. Make sure that your report includes all of the necessary information. Correct any errors in grammar, usage, spelling, and punctuation. Then prepare your final copy.

Assignment 3   Prewriting   Choose a topic or a person about which you would like to learn more. In the nonfiction section of your library, find a book that deals with this topic or person. Read the book. As you read, take notes for a book report.

Assignment 4   Writing/Revising   *Step 1:* Using your notes from Assignment 4, write the first draft of your book report. *Step 2:* Revise your first draft. *Step 3:* Write your final copy.

Assignment Checklist

Check your book reports for the following points:

✔ 1. Did you begin your book report with a sentence that identifies the title and author of the book?

✔ 2. Did you evaluate or give your opinion of the book in the last paragraph?

✔ 3. Did you check your book report for correct grammar, usage, spelling, and punctuation?

Check your book reports on works of fiction for these additional points:

✔ 4. Did you include a brief description of the main characters?

✔ 5. Did you provide a brief summary of the action?

Check your book reports on biographies and autobiographies for these additional points:

✔ 6. Did you present two or three important events in the person's life?

✔ 7. Did you explain why the person is important?

Check your book reports on general nonfiction for these additional points:

✔ 8. Did you describe the subject and explain how the author presents it?

✔ 9. Did you discuss the major points made by the author?

The First Electronic Computer: Preparing an Outline

Situation: The science museum in your community is preparing an exhibit of computers. The exhibit will include several old computers. To provide more information to visitors, the museum is producing a booklet of reports on the first computers. As a staff assistant at the museum, you have been asked to make an outline for the report on ENIAC, the first large electronic computer. In preparation for making the outline, you have found sources and made note cards from them. As you make your outline, keep in mind the following information.

Writer: you as a staff assistant at the museum
Audience: visitors to the computer exhibit
Topic: ENIAC, the first large electronic computer
Purpose: to make an outline for a report
Directions: To prepare your outline, follow these steps.

> *Step 1.* Read the note cards on the facing page that you prepared from sources on your topic.
> *Step 2.* On your paper, list the subject headings from the note cards. Remembering that more than one card may have the same heading, list each heading only once. Then arrange the headings in a logical order.
> *Step 3.* Using your main headings, write a topic statement for the report on ENIAC.
> *Step 4.* Using your main headings and note cards, write at least two subheadings for each main heading.
> *Step 5.* Using the main headings and subheadings that you have listed, prepare a complete outline. Place your topic statement at the top of the outline.

Problems with ENIAC   Alt, "Computers"

Because ENIAC had no separate
memory, it could store only
twenty numbers at a time.
Its small storage limited
the type of calculations
that it could do.

p. 491

How different from   Alt, "Computers"
earlier computers

- Used vacuum tubes, which are
electronic, rather than mechanical
and electric switches
- Contained 18,000 vacuum tubes

p. 491

Problems with ENIAC Sefor, History

Difficult to operate because
programmed by changing the
position of many wires
plugged into it.

p. 39

How ENIAC worked   Alt, "Computers"

Information was given to ENIAC
on punched cards, and answers
were returned in the same
way.

Calculations were made by
electronic circuits.

p. 491

Who built ENIAC   Eismann,
                Birth of Computers

- Designed by John W. Mauchly,
a physicist, and J. Presper
Eckert, an engineer
- Both scientists at the
University of Pennsylvania

p. 18

How different from Sefor, History
earlier computers

- When built in 1945, was the
fastest machine
- More than 1000 times faster
than earlier computers
- Could do up to 5000
calculations per second

p. 37

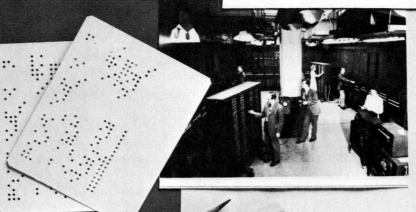

Unit Assignments

Assignment 1   Write a report about how a specific part of the human body functions. For example, you could write about how the eye, a muscle, the heart, or the skeleton works.

Assignment 2   Write a report about a famous person who lived in your community, state, or province. Check your library for sources of information on the person.

Assignment 3   Write a report about an endangered species. Include information on the following: What caused the species to become endangered? What is being done to protect this animal?

Assignment 4   Write a book report about a novel in which the events take place many years ago. Write about your reactions to the novel as well as the events and the characters that are presented in the book.

Assignment 5   Choose a nonfiction book about a subject or a person whom you have learned about recently. It could be a biography of a person whom you have read about, or a book about a topic that you are studying. Read the book and then write a book report about it.

Assignment 6   Write a report about a craft that interests you. For example, you could write a report about weaving, carving, or ceramics. Limit your topic to one aspect of the craft that you have chosen.

Assignment 7   Choose a nonfiction book about an invention or a person who made an important invention. Read the book and then write a book report about it. Include an explanation of why the invention is important.

Assignment 8 Write a report about a place that you would like to visit. Limit your topic to one aspect of that place. For example, you could write about the weather, the early history, or the government.

Revising Your Assignments

For help in revising a report, consult the Checklist for Revision on the last page of this book.

Unit Tests

Test 1

A. Number your paper from 1 to 5. Next to each number, write *True* if the sentence is true or *False* if it is false.

1. A report should be based on your personal experience.
2. As you read about your subject, you should take notes on what you have learned.
3. You should arrange the headings of your outline in a logical order.
4. At the end of a report, you should include a list of sources.
5. In a book report, you should not include your opinions about the book.

B. Number your paper from 6 to 10. Next to each number, write the letter of the term that correctly completes the sentence. You will use all but one of the items.

a. revise   d. nonfiction
b. fiction   e. outline
c. source   f. topic statement

6. A(n) __?__ is a book, an encyclopedia, a magazine, or a newspaper that you use to gather information about your topic.
7. A(n) __?__ tells a reader what you will discuss in your report.
8. You use your __?__ as a guide when you write your first draft.
9. When you __?__ your report, you review it to see whether you can make it clearer and more interesting.
10. In __?__ the characters are real, and the events actually happened.

C. Number your paper from 11 to 15. Next to each number, write the letter of the item that correctly answers the question.

11. Which of the following is an appropriate topic for a report?
    a. Animals that are found only in Australia
    b. My camping trip in a wildlife refuge
    c. How I learned to identify animal tracks
    d. Why I would like to work with animals

12. Which of the following should *not* be contained on a note card?
    a. The year that the work was published
    b. The author's name
    c. A subject heading
    d. A summary of the author's main points

13. Which of the following should you include in a finished report?
    a. Source cards   c. The rough outline
    b. Note cards   d. A source list

14. Which of the following is *not* true about a source list?
    a. It should be arranged in alphabetical order by the last names of the authors.
    b. Every line except the first line should be indented five spaces.
    c. It should contain the names of all the sources that you used to learn about your topic.
    d. Each entry should begin with the title of the book or article.

15. Which of the following is *not* contained in a book report?
    a. A sentence that identifies the author and the title of the work
    b. A brief description of the work
    c. A list of other works by the same author
    d. An explanation of your reaction to the work

Test 2

Choose one of the Unit Assignments. Write the assignment as directed and hand it in to your teacher.

Writing Letters

Unit Preview

Knowing how to write a letter is a valuable skill. It will help you to convey news to someone far away. Knowing how to write a letter will also help you to make purchases accurately or receive information promptly.

Read the social letter on the next page. Notice how it expresses friendship and gives the reader interesting news about the activities of the writer.

For Analysis   On your paper, answer the following questions about the social letter.

1. What is the purpose of the letter?
2. How does the letter begin?
3. What sorts of things does the letter mention?
4. How does the letter end?
5. Where does the writer live?

In this unit you will learn how to write both social letters and business letters. One kind of social letter that you will learn to write is the thank-you note. You will also learn to write a business letter to make a request and to place an order. As you write your letters, you will use the three steps of the writing process: prewriting, writing, and revising.

1021 Garrison Avenue
Des Moines, Iowa 50321
September 16, 19___

Dear Tim,

Do you remember how I fussed about moving from Wilson Middle School to McLean? Well, I was wrong. McLean is great! We have band tryouts later this week, and I have been practicing my clarinet for hours at a time. Fortunately, no one has complained. I'm a little nervous about the tryouts because there are so many good musicians at McLean. I'll let you know if I make it. Wish me luck.

Do you remember Ruthie Samuels, my next-door neighbor? Well, I took some pictures of her during our Bike-a-thon fund-raiser. I will send you some as soon as they are developed. She rode the whole thirty miles and raised almost fifty dollars!

Are you still planning to try out for the track team? If so, I hope you make it. Let me know if you'll be able to come over for the Thanksgiving game this year. We're all looking forward to that.

Sincerely,
Theresa

16.1 Writing Social Letters

A good way to keep in touch with a distant friend or relative is to write a social letter.

16.1a Form and Content

Show consideration for your reader by taking the time to see that your letter follows correct form.

Parts of the Social Letter

Heading.   Write the heading in the upper right corner of your letter. The heading consists of your street address, the city, state, and ZIP code and the date. If you have an apartment number, rural-route number, or post-office box number, include them.

Salutation.   The salutation is your greeting. Always follow the salutation of a social letter with a comma.

Body.   The body of the letter is its message. Be sure to use paragraphs when writing the body of a social letter. Make your letter friendly and cheerful. Do not give the impression that you are writing because you have to or because you have nothing better to do.

Complimentary Close.   Write the complimentary close below the last paragraph. Use phrases such as *Yours truly, Sincerely, Love,* or *Affectionately.* Follow the complimentary close with a comma.

Signature.   The signature is your name. Write it below the complimentary close.

Use the following strategies when writing social letters.

Strategies

1. *Use unlined, light-colored paper and an envelope to match, and write in blue or black ink.*
2. *Center your letter on the page,* using margins of about one inch.
3. *Write neatly and clearly.*
4. *Write as if you were speaking to your reader.* You may use informal language and contractions.
5. *Keep your reader in mind as you write.* Make your letter cheerful and informative, but not gossipy. Answer any questions that your reader may have asked you in a previous letter.
6. *Ask questions that your reader can answer.*

Addressing the Envelope

Write the address of the person who will receive the letter on the front of the envelope, just below the center. The address has three lines: the person's name, the exact street address, and the city, state, and ZIP code. Always use a title such as *Mr., Mrs., Ms.,* or *Miss* with a person's name. In the upper-left corner, write your return address: your name, street address, city, state, and ZIP code. Do not include a title with your name.

Exercise 1 Prewriting: The Social Letter On your paper, answer these four questions about the following social letter.

1. What parts of a social letter are missing?
2. What error in punctuation has Tony made?
3. What is wrong with the form of the body of the letter?
4. What is wrong with the contents of the body of the letter?

> Dear Andrew,
>
> How are you? I'm fine, I guess. Mother said I have to write this letter tonight or she will never let me come to visit you again.
> I have some bad news. In the fancy skating exhibition last week, another student in my class got on the rink and made me break my routine. You see I have not been having a very good time.
> Since I can't think of anything more to write about, I'll close.
>
> Tony

Exercise 2 Writing/Revising: The Social Letter
Using your answers from Exercise 1, rewrite the preceding letter so that it is correct in form and content. Add any details that you think are necessary.

16.1b The Thank-You Note

Whenever someone sends you a gift or does something especially thoughtful for you, show your appreciation by writing a thank-you note. A thank-you note is a brief expression of gratitude. Study the following example.

> 1302 Locust Street
> Andarko, Oklahoma 73005
> June 16, 19—
>
> Dear Aunt Ruth,
>
> Thank you for the baseball glove you sent me for my birthday. Mother likes my present, too, because she says now she won't have to listen to Joey complain when I use his. You have made my thirteenth birthday special for all of us.
>
> Love,
> Malcolm

A thank-you note is also appropriate for expressing your appreciation whenever you have been a guest in someone's home.

Use the following strategies when writing thank-you notes.

Strategies

1. *Include the five parts of a social letter in your thank-you note.*

2. *Write your thank-you note promptly.*

3. *Mention specifically the gift or favor that you received.* Include details.

4. *Mention one or two highlights of your visit when you write a thank-you note.*

5. *Check your note for correct grammar, usage, spelling, and punctuation.* The care with which you write a thank-you note is a measure of the respect that you show your reader.

Exercise 3 Prewriting: The Thank-You Note   On your paper, write the numbers of the statements that you would likely use in a thank-you note to your relatives. There are some statements that you would not use.

1. My sister had a piano recital last week.
2. It is very easy to carry, and quite strong.
3. Thank you both so much for the new guitar case.
4. My friend Yvonne has one with silver stitching.
5. More important, I'll be able to bring it when I visit you!
6. Now I can take my guitar with me wherever I like.
7. One place where I'd like to go is Quebec.
8. Thanks again. You've both played an important part in my musical career!

Exercise 4 Writing: The Thank-You Note   On an unlined sheet of paper, write a thank-you note, using the statements that you selected from Exercise 3. Use your own address for the heading. Add any information that you feel is needed to complete the note.

Assignment 1   Writing   *Step 1:* A relative from out of town has sent you a photograph album for your birthday. On a sheet of unlined paper, write a brief thank-you note. Be sure to include all the parts of the social letter. *Step 2:* Draw an envelope on your paper, and address it to your relative.

Assignment 2   Writing   *Step 1:* On your paper, make notes for a letter that you will write to a friend or relative whom you have not seen for a while. Make notes on news and events that you think will interest your reader. *Step 2:* On a sheet of unlined paper, write a social letter based on your notes. Be sure to include all the parts of a social letter, with correct capitalization and punctuation. *Step 3:* Draw an envelope on your paper, and address it to your friend. Include your return address.

Assignment Checklist

Check your assignments for the following points:

  ✓ 1. Did you center your letter on the page?
  ✓ 2. Did you include all the information needed in the heading?
  ✓ 3. Did you capitalize the salutation correctly and follow it with a comma?
  ✓ 4. Did you write the body in paragraphs?
  ✓ 5. Did you include an appropriate complimentary close and sign the letter?
  ✓ 6. Did you proofread your letter for correct grammar, usage, spelling, and punctuation?
  ✓ 7. Did you correctly address the envelope that you drew?
  ✓ 8. Did you write a complete return address in the upper left corner of the envelope on your paper?

16.2 Writing Business Letters

Many letters that you write will be for business reasons. You may want to make a request or to place an order. When doing so, make sure that your letters are neat, courteous, and clearly written.

16.2a Form and Content

Parts of the Business Letter

Heading. Place the heading at the top of the page, in the left-hand or right-hand corner, depending on which style you use (*page 452*). The first line is your street address, with your apartment number, if you have one. It can also be your rural route and box number. The second line of the heading is your city, state, and ZIP code. The third line is the month, the day, and the year.

Inside Address. The inside address is the same address you will put on your envelope. It is placed at the left-hand margin of your letter. The first line is for the name of the person, the business, or the organization to whom you are writing. The next line is the street address or box number. The last line gives the city, state, and ZIP code.

Salutation. The salutation is the greeting. If you do not know the name of the person to whom you are writing, use the salutation *Dear Sir or Madam*. Always follow the salutation of a business letter with a colon.

Body. The body of your letter contains your purpose for writing. State your purpose clearly. Give complete information. If you are enclosing a stamped, self-addressed envelope, mention that fact in the body of your letter. Be brief, specific, and courteous. Leave one line of space between the paragraphs in your letter.

Complimentary Close. The complimentary close may be written to the right of the center of the page or at the left margin. Use a phrase such as *Yours truly* or *Sincerely yours* followed by a comma. Capitalize only the first word.

Signature. The signature is your name. Write it in longhand under the complimentary close. Print or type your name beneath the handwritten signature.

Forms of Business Letters

Business letters are written in one of two forms: the block style or the modified block style. In the **block style**, write the heading at the left margin. Do not indent the paragraphs. Also write the complimentary close and your name at the left margin. Use the block style only when you are typing your letter. The letter on page 455 is written in the block style.

In the **modified block style,** place the heading, complimentary close, and signature on the right. You can either indent paragraphs or begin them at the left margin. The letter on page 457 is written in the modified block style.

Addressing the Envelope

Write the address slightly below the center on the front of the envelope. The address should be the same information that you used in the inside address. However, on the envelope use the correct Postal Service abbreviation for the state (*page 205*).

In the upper left corner of the envelope, write your return address. The first line should have your full name. The second line is for your street address. The third line is for your city, state, and ZIP code. Use the Postal Service abbreviation for your state.

Folding and Inserting the Letter

Follow the steps shown in the diagrams for folding letters for long and short envelopes.

Procedure

Long Business Envelopes

1. With the letter face up, fold the bottom of the letter up, a little less than one third of the way.
2. Fold the top down, leaving ½ inch at the bottom.
3. Put the letter in the envelope, with the last fold in the bottom of the envelope.

| STEP 1 | STEP 2 | STEP 3 |

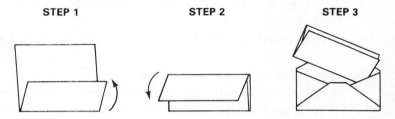

Short Business Envelopes

1. With the letter face up, fold the bottom of the letter up to about one half inch from the top.
2. Fold from right to left about one third of the way.
3. Fold the left side over to within ½ inch of the right side.
4. Put the letter in the envelope, with the last fold first.

| STEP 1 | STEP 2 | STEP 3 |

| STEP 4 | STEP 5 | STEP 6 |

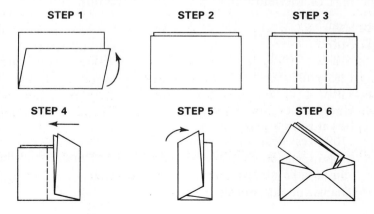

Use the following strategies when writing business letters.

Strategies

1. *Use unlined paper measuring 8½ inches by 11 inches.*
2. *Use black or blue ink.* Type your letter, if possible.
3. *Make sure the heading and the inside address have the correct information.* Your name does not appear in the heading.
4. *Make sure the salutation is suitable and that a colon follows it.*
5. *Be neat.* You want to make a good impression on your reader.
6. *Do not use slang or contractions.*
7. *Check your letter for correct grammar, usage, spelling, and punctuation, as well as for completeness.*
8. *Make sure the complimentary close is suitable and that a comma follows it.*
9. *Address the envelope carefully.* Be sure that it is easy to read. Also, check to see that the return address in the upper-left corner is correct and complete.

Exercise 1   Prewriting: Parts of Business Letters
Number your paper from 1 to 5. After each number, rewrite the part of the letter that is shown, correcting all errors.

1. Dear Sir
2. April 8, 19—
   Ripley Ohio 45167
   1310 Westover Ridge
3. Truly
4. Hudson City New Jersey 07307
   Edwards Stamp Company
   1100 West Brunswick Avenue
5. Please send me your free spring catalogue. I understand that you pay the postage.
   Thank you very much.

16.2b The Request Letter

When you write to request information or a favor, you write a **request letter**. Begin your letter by stating your purpose. Give all the necessary background information, and state clearly the details of your request.

1107 Brant Road
Portland, Oregon 97231
April 10, 19__

Director
Expeditions, Incorporated
723 Broadway East
Seattle, Washington 98102

Dear Sir or Madam:

    I am the president of the Ecology Club at Bertha Dean Junior High School. Each year we plan an outing for our members.
    Recently I read in The Portland Overlander that you offer a student field trip that is especially planned for picture-taking.
    Please send me whatever information you have about the photographic expedition. We will also need information about overnight accommodations for approximately twenty-five persons.
    We plan to take our trip during the last week of May, so I would appreciate a prompt reply. I have enclosed a self-addressed, stamped envelope.
    Thank you very much.

Sincerely yours,

Coleman Ross

Coleman Ross
Class Secretary

The request letter on the preceding page gives all the necessary information in a courteous manner.

Use the following strategies when writing request letters.

Strategies

1. *Identify yourself and make your purpose clear.*
2. *Furnish background information.*
3. *Give exact details about what you want.*
4. *Conclude with a courteous statement.*
5. *Check your letter carefully for errors in grammar, usage, spelling, and punctuation.*
6. *Check your letter for errors in form.* Choose either the block or the modified block style and use the same style throughout.

Exercise 2   Writing: The Request Letter   On a sheet of unlined paper, prepare a letter requesting information. *Step 1:* Use your own address for the heading. *Step 2:* Use the following inside address: Museum Director, Midwest Native American Center, Incorporated, 650 North Seneca, Wichita, Kansas 67203. *Step 3:* Write a suitable salutation. *Step 4:* Request information about a pottery exhibit that will be at the museum next month. *Step 5:* Finish your letter with a courteous statement. *Step 6:* Write a suitable complimentary close, and sign your name.

Exercise 3   Writing: The Envelope   *Step 1:* On your paper, draw a long business envelope for the letter in Exercise 2, and address it correctly. *Step 2:* Neatly fold your letter to fit the envelope.

16.2c The Order Letter

When you are ordering an item through the mail, you may sometimes have to write the kind of business letter known as an **order letter**. Study the following example.

```
                        701 Dupont Lane, Apartment 106
                        White Plains, Georgia 30678
                        September 30, 19__

Dixon Science Supplies
2124 Lexington Avenue
New York, New York 10010

Dear Sir or Madam:

     I wish to order the following items from
your catalogue, number 8210.

Quantity      Number     Item              Price
    1          7147      15X Refractor     $10.95
                         Telescope Kit
                                           _____
                         Shipping and        3.00
                         handling
                                           _____
                         Total            $13.95

     I have enclosed a money order for $13.95
to cover the cost of the item and the
handling charges.

     Thank you.

               Yours truly,

               Deborah Baltzly
               Deborah Baltzly
Enclosure
```

Use the following strategies when writing order letters.

Strategies

1. *Mention where you saw the item advertised.* If you are ordering from a catalogue, give the date or number.

2. *Furnish all necessary information.* List the name, quantity, number, and cost of each item that you wish to order. Often, you will need to give color and size or other kinds of information.

3. *State how you will pay for the item.* Do not enclose cash. Send a money order.

4. *Write the word* Enclosure *at the bottom-left margin if you have placed your payment in the envelope.*

Exercise 4   Prewriting: The Order Letter   On your paper, write the numbers of the statements that you would include in an order letter for sweatshirts. There are some statements that you will not use.

1. Please note that one is in a medium size with a Philadelphia Eagles logo and the other is in a small size with a Los Angeles Rams logo.

2. My brother likes the Eagles, and I like the Rams.

3. The catalogue number and price of each item are listed below.

4. Number 41 G 4803 5M $8.99
   Number 41 G 4803 11S $8.99

5. Do professional football players actually wear sweatshirts like these?

6. I would like to order two items from your fall *Sports World* catalogue.

7. Both styles come with a hood.

8. Postage and handling $1.70
9. They will certainly come in handy when we are outside in cold weather.
10. Enclosed please find a money order for $19.68.

Assignment 1 Writing   Your science class is studying the causes of weather. The class would like to have a local television weather reporter come the school and speak about meteorology. You have volunteered to write the request letter. Address your letter to a local television station.

Assignment 2 Writing   Make up a name and address of a company that sells exercise equipment. Using that address, write an order letter for a set of junior barbells. The item that you want is called Gravi-Grips, model number 227-08J, made by The Reliant Company. They cost $9.95 a pair. The total weight is twenty-five pounds, and the shipping cost is $8.50.

Assignment Checklist

Check your assignments for the following points.

✔ 1. Did you follow either the block style or the modified block style throughout the letter?

✔ 2. Did you include all the parts of a business letter?

✔ 3. Did you state clearly your purpose for writing?

✔ 4. Did you give all the necessary information in your request letter?

✔ 5. Did you give all the necessary information about the items you wished to order: the quantity, the catalogue number, the name, size, price, and shipping and handling charges?

✔ 6. Did you check your letter for correct grammar, usage, spelling, and punctuation?

✔ 7. Did you address your envelope accurately?

Computer Camp: Writing a Letter

Situation: You plan to spend two weeks of your summer vacation at a computer day camp and hope that your cousin, who lives in a nearby town, will also want to go. In a social letter, describe the camp and ask your cousin to go with you. As you write your social letter, keep in mind the following information.

Writer: you as a person interested in computers
Audience: your cousin in a nearby town
Topic: a computer day camp
Purpose: to invite your cousin to attend the camp with you

Directions: To write your letter, follow these steps.

Step 1. Read the information on the following page from the Camp Computech brochure.

Step 2. Using the correct format for a social letter, write a letter of three paragraphs. In the first paragraph, explain why you want to go to Camp Computech for two weeks. Ask your cousin to go with you. In the second paragraph, describe the activities at Camp Computech. In the third paragraph, suggest that your parents and your cousin's parents can take turns driving you and your cousin to and from camp.

Step 3. Address an envelope to your cousin.

CAMP COMPUTECH

Are you interested in computers? Are you between the ages of 7 and 15? If so, Camp Computech is for you. Spend two weeks this summer at Camp Computech on Lake Windsor. Make new friends while you learn the latest in computer technology.

Camp Computech

■ develops your computer literacy

■ teaches you programming in BASIC and Logo

■ provides hands-on training on individual computers with video display screen (CRT) and keyboard

■ has a student-faculty ratio of 10–1

Activities are scheduled Monday through Friday from 9:30 A.M. to 4:30 P.M. Lunch is provided.

Unit Assignments

Assignment 1   You have moved to another town or city. Write to a friend about your new home. Give details of your house or apartment, your neighborhood, what you do during and after school, and other details of interest to your friend. Be sure to ask questions that your reader can answer in a letter to you.

Assignment 2   Assume that you have returned to your home after a visit to a friend who lives in another state. Write a thank-you note to show your appreciation for your friend's hospitality. Remember to mention your friend's family.

Assignment 3   Order two copies of the special anniversary issue of the magazine *California Today,* $3.95 each, postpaid. The address is *California Today,* 205 Barrington Plaza, 11700 Wilshire Boulevard, Los Angeles, California 90025.

Assignment 4   Order the following posters from *New Mexico Magazine,* Santa Fe Memorial Building, Santa Fe, New Mexico 87503: "A Shepherd and His Flock," by Gerald Cassidy, "One of New Mexico's Old Missions," by Gerald Cassidy, and "New Mexico in the Winter," by Tom Lea. The posters are $2.50 each. Add 75 cents postage for each poster.

Assignment 5   You are interested in coin collecting as a hobby, but you are not certain which coins you should acquire to start your collection. Write a letter to a local coin shop requesting information about which pennies, nickels, dimes, and quarters are collectors' items. Also request information on how to recognize collectible coins. Make up a name and address for the store, but use your own return address.

Assignment 6   Your science club is interested in visiting a science museum in a nearby city. Write a letter to the publicity director of the museum. Request information on the museum's hours and admission rates. Also request information on special events at the museum during the next month. Make up the name of the publicity director and the address of the museum, but use your own return address.

Assignment 7   A friend has given you a record album for your birthday. Write a thank-you note to express your gratitude. Mention the record by name and state why you like the record.

Assignment 8   The members of your bicycle club would like information on how to care for their bicycles. As secretary for the club, write a letter to a local bicycle store requesting the names of good books for them to consult. Make up the name and address of the store, but use your own return address.

Revising Your Assignments

For help in revising a letter, consult the Checklist for Revision on the last page of this book.

Unit Tests

Test 1

A. Number your paper from 1 to 5. Next to each number, write the letter of the item that is best suited to a social letter.

1. a. I can't think of anything to write, but here goes.
   b. Hello there, I'm fine. How are you?
   c. Aunt Alice told us that your picture was in the paper.

2. a. Dear Uncle Jim,
   b. Dear Ms. Walton:
   c. Dear Margaret,

3. a. You misspelled three words in your last letter.
   b. Our cousins came over that night and told us about their trip to Knoxville.
   c. This is to thank you for the book, even though I already have a copy.

4. a. Yours truly,
      Julie
   b. Very sincerely yours,
      Mr. Benjamin Forbes
   c. Your good old buddy,
      Fred Howard

5. a. Sorry I haven't written sooner, but I haven't had time.
   b. I thought you'd like to hear about the new trick our spaniel Macbeth learned in obedience school.
   c. Nothing ever happens around here.

B. Number your paper from 6 to 10. Next to each number, write the letter of the word or phrase that completes each statement correctly.

6. A salutation in a business letter is followed by a __?__.
   a. colon
   b. comma
   c. period

7. In a request letter, you will __?__.
   a. demand an immediate reply
   b. make a courteous statement about what you want
   c. make some friendly comments about your family

8. One part of the business letter not found in the social letter is __?__.
   a. heading
   b. inside address
   c. return address

9. A suitable complimentary close for a business letter is __?__.
   a. Yours as ever
   b. Your friend
   c. Yours truly

10. When you place an order, it is best to make your payment by enclosing __?__.
    a. cash
    b. a money order
    c. a self-addressed envelope

C. Number your paper from 11 to 15. Next to each number, write the letter of the item that correctly completes the following sentences about business letters. You will use all but one of the items.

a. Dear Sara,   d. Printed
b. Writer's name   e. Right
c. Inside address   f. Dear Sir or Madam:

11. In the modified-block style, place the heading to the __?__ of the center.

12. In the signature, the name of the writer should be both handwritten and __?__.

13. The heading of a business letter is different from the return address because it does not include the __?__.

14. The address on a business envelope is the same as the __?__.

15. One correct salutation for a business letter might be __?__.

Test 2

Choose one of the Unit Assignments. Write the assignment as directed and hand it in to your teacher.

Part Three

Related Skills

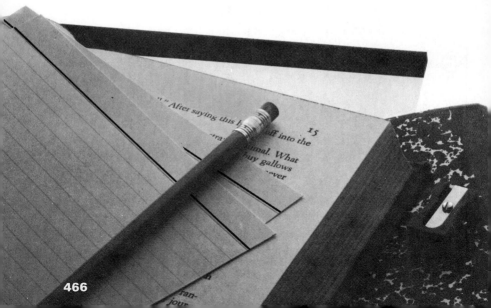

466

In Part Three you will learn and practice a variety of skills that are related to writing. By developing your spelling and vocabulary skills, you will directly improve your writing. Speaking skills will aid you in giving oral presentations. Learning better ways to study, to listen, and to use the library will help you to gather information to use in your writing and in your speaking.

By studying the information and strategies in these units, you will develop skills that will be useful for many activities in school and outside. By referring to the units often, you will find many ways to apply these skills.

Unit 17

Spelling Skills

Some words are easy to spell; others are not. Everyone has trouble with at least a few words. Your goal should be to master the words that you misspell frequently by applying the methods and the rules that are presented in this unit.

Before you begin to read this unit, think about your answers to these questions:

1. Do you use spelling rules and their exceptions to choose the correct spelling of a word?
2. Do you pronounce words carefully?
3. Do you think carefully about what words look like?
4. Do you create memory aids for troublesome words?
5. Do you know how to use a dictionary to find the correct spelling of a word?
6. Do you proofread everything that you write to make sure that you have spelled words correctly?

If you answered yes to all six questions, you are probably a good speller. This unit will show you a number of ways to develop your spelling skills.

17.1 How to Study Spelling Words

Use the following steps to study a particular word that you wish to learn to spell.

Procedure

1. *Look* at the word carefully.

2. *Pronounce* the word. If it has more than one syllable, say the word slowly—syllable by syllable. Note the sound that each letter spells or helps to spell.

3. *Write* the word without looking at your book. Pay special attention to the trouble spots.

4. *Check* your spelling against your book.

5. *Write the word once more* if your spelling is correct. If it is incorrect, take careful note of the part of the word that you misspelled. Then start over again with Step 1.

17.2 Spelling Rules

17.2a Making Nouns Plural

A **singular noun** (*page 144*) names one person, place, thing, or idea. A **plural noun** (*page 144*) names more than one person, place, thing, or idea. You can develop your spelling skills if you learn the rules for writing plural forms.

Regular Plurals

The plurals of most nouns are formed by adding *-s* or *-es* to the singular form.

Rule Form the plural of most nouns by adding *-s* to the singular form.

strap	book	helicopter
straps	books	helicopters

Rule Form the plural of a noun that ends in *s, x, z, ch,* or *sh* by adding *-es* to the singular.

kiss	box	buzz	arch
kisses	boxes	buzzes	arches

Rule Form the plural of a noun that ends in *o* preceded by a vowel by adding *-s* to the singular.

radio	shampoo	rodeo
radios	shampoos	rodeos

Rule Form the plural of a noun that ends in *ay, ey, oy,* or *uy* by adding *-s* to the singular.

bay	turkey	convoy	guy
bays	turkeys	convoys	guys

Some nouns that end in *y* change their spelling before adding *-es.*

Rule Form the plural of a noun that ends in *y* preceded by a consonant by changing *y* to *i* before adding *-es.*

ferry	army	courtesy
ferries	armies	courtesies

Rule Form the plural of most nouns that end in *f* or *fe* by adding *-s* to the singular.

safe	roof	chief
safes	roofs	chiefs

Some nouns that end in *f* or *fe* change their spelling before adding *-es.*

shelf	loaf	wife	thief
shelves	loaves	wives	thieves

Rule Form the plural of a proper noun by adding *-s* or *-es* to the singular.

Gary Rankin and Gary Liu	Tom and Lois Duffy
the two Garys	the Duffys

Irregular Plurals

The following are examples of some kinds of irregular plurals. You should memorize the correct irregular forms. Whenever you are in doubt, however, check the correct spelling in a dictionary.

1. Nouns that end in *o* preceded by a consonant.
   For some of these nouns, add *-s* to the singular.

soprano	ego	photo
sopranos	egos	photos

   For some others, add *-es* to the singular.

tomato	torpedo	hero	veto
tomatoes	torpedoes	heroes	vetoes

   For certain of these nouns, it is correct to add either *-s* or *-es* to the singular.

cargo	tornado	volcano
cargos	tornados	volcanos
cargoes	tornadoes	volcanoes

2. Nouns that do not add *-s* or *-es* to form the plural.

tooth	man	mouse	ox
teeth	men	mice	oxen

3. Nouns that are the same in both the singular and the plural.

cattle	deer	Chinese

Compound Nouns

Rule Form the plural of a compound noun that is written as one word by changing the last word in the compound to its correct plural form.

motorboat	stopwatch	godchild
motor**boats**	stop**watches**	god**children**

Rule Form the plural of a compound noun that is hyphenated or written as separate words by changing the most important word to its correct plural form.

| daughter-in-law | field mouse | head of state |
| daughters-in-law | field mice | heads of state |

Assignment 1   Rules for Plurals Write the plural form of each of the following singular nouns by applying one of the rules in Section 17.2a. Use each plural noun in a sentence of your own.

1. branch
2. potato
3. comedy
4. foot
5. moonbeam
6. father-in-law
7. Jones
8. piano
9. corps
10. pulley
11. radio
12. piece

Assignment 2   Noun Plurals In one of your other textbooks, find ten singular nouns. On your paper, write the plural of each noun. Then use each plural noun in a sentence.

17.2b Adding Endings

You have just studied the rules for adding the plural endings -*s* and -*es* to nouns. The rules that follow will help you to add other endings to nouns and to words used as other parts of speech. (See also Unit 18.)

Doubling the Final Consonant

The following rules apply only when you are adding an ending that begins with a vowel—for example, -*ing*, -*est*, -*ance*.

Rule Double the final consonant if the word has only one syllable and ends with a single consonant preceded by a single vowel.

fun	map	bus	sit
funny	mapped	bussing	sitting

Rule Double the final consonant if the word (1) has more than one syllable, (2) ends with a single consonant preceded by a single vowel, and (3) is stressed on the final syllable.

occur	admit	compel
occurring	admittance	compelling

To apply these rules, you must carefully study the base word. Then ask yourself the following questions:

1. Is the base word a one-syllable word or a word that is stressed on the final syllable? The words _fun_ and _occur_ meet this test. The word _open_ does not, for it is stressed on the first syllable.
2. Does the base word end in a single consonant? The words _fun_ and _occur_ meet this test. The words _help_ and _report_ do not, for each ends in two consonants.
3. Is the final consonant in the base word preceded by a single vowel? The words _fun_ and _occur_ meet this test. However, the words _look_ and _repeat_ do not, for each has two vowels before the final consonant.

Dropping the Final _e_

Rule If a word ends in silent _e_, drop the final _e_ before adding an ending that begins with a vowel.

use	line	fame	file
usage	lining	famous	filing

Rule   If a word ends in silent *e* preceded by *c* or *g,* keep the final *e* when adding an ending that begins with *a* or *o.*

enforce	courage	damage
enforceable	courageous	damageable

Rule   For most words that end in silent *e*, keep the final *e* when adding an ending that begins with a consonant.

	late	fine	encourage
	lately	fineness	encouragement
BUT	true	argue	nine
	truly	argument	ninth

Changing Final *y* to *i*

Rule   For most words that end in *y* preceded by a consonant, change the *y* to *i* before adding any ending except *-ing.*

	angry	try	try
	angrily	tried	trying
BUT	dry	shy	
	dryly *or* drily	shyness	

Rule   If a word ends in *y* preceded by a vowel, you usually do not change the *y* to *i* before adding an ending.

	joy	obey	pray
	joyful	obeying	prayed
BUT	day	pay	
	daily	paid	

Assignment 3   Adding Endings   On your paper, write the words that are formed by adding the endings in parentheses to the listed words. Write a sentence for each new word.

1. rebel (*-ing*)
2. move (*-ing*)
3. trace (*-able*)
4. happy (*-ness*)
5. manage (*-ment*)
6. fry (*-ed*)

17.3 The *ie/ei* Pattern

The following rules establish a pattern for using *ie* and *ei*.

Rule When the vowel combination has the long *e* sound (as in *belief*), usually write *ie* except after *c*. After *c*, write *ei*.

field	niece	BUT	leisure
grief	deceit		species

Rule When the vowel combination has the long *a* sound (as in *weigh*), always write *ei*.

vein   neighbor   sleigh   freight

Rule When the vowel combination does not have the long *e* sound, usually write *ei*.

	sovereign	heifer	counterfeit
BUT	friend	sieve	glacier

Assignment *ie/ei* On your paper, write the following words, completing each blank with *ie* or *ei*. Then use each completed word in a sentence.

1. bel_?_f
2. w_?_ght
3. _?_ther
4. br_?_f
5. forf_?_t
6. rec_?_pt
7. f_?_nd
8. n_?_gh
9. sh_?_ld
10. rel_?_ve
11. ch_?_f
12. gr_?_ve

17.4 Spelling What You Hear

How you pronounce a word can affect how you spell it. Here are some pronunciation problems that often lead to misspellings.

Extra Syllables. Do you pronounce *film* with one syllable or two? Do you pronounce *laundry* with two syllables or three? Adding syllables can result in extra letters that do not belong in a word. This kind of error can occur in the words listed below. The number in parentheses tells how many syllables the word has.

athletics (3)   drowned (1)   helicopter (4)   burglar (2)

Omitted Sounds. Do you pronounce the *t* in *sentence*? Do you pronounce the *n* in *government*? People sometimes misspell a word because they omit a sound when they pronounce the word. The words in the list below are examples of words from which sounds are sometimes omitted.

candidate   probably   attract   landlord

Transposed Sounds. When you pronounce *relevant,* do you say "RELevant" or "REVelant"? People sometimes misspell a word because when they pronounce it they transpose some of the letters. The list below shows examples of words in which the sounds are sometimes transposed. Be sure that you pronounce and spell the underlined letters in the right order.

prevent   perform   prescribe   introduce

Assignment   Spelling and Pronunciation   Use a dictionary to check your pronunciation of the following words. Then write each word in a sentence.

1. athlete   3. boundary   5. cavalry   7. helicopter
2. disastrous   4. strictly   6. modern   8. library

17.5 Spelling What You See

The following explanations describe some other common causes of misspellings.

Homophones. Do you write "I'll *meat* you" when you mean "I'll *meet* you"? **Homophones** are words that have the same pronunciation but different spellings and meanings. The only way to master these sound-alike words is to fix their meanings and spellings firmly in your mind. Be sure that you know the meaning and spelling of each word in the following list of frequently confused homophones.

aisle, isle	grate, great	patience, patients
all ready, already	hoarse, horse	principal, principle
altar, alter	it's, its	scene, seen
brake, break	lead, led	their, there, they're
cent, scent	lessen, lesson	to, too, two
die, dye	miner, minor	weak, week
fair, fare	passed, past	your, you're

Words Often Confused.   Do you *accept* an invitation, or do you *except* it? Some words are not homophones but are similar enough in sound or spelling to cause confusion. The following list includes some commonly confused words.

breath, breathe	conscience, conscious	loose, lose
clothes, cloths	desert, dessert	than, then

Overlooked Letters.   Do you sometimes forget about the *k* in *know* or the second *t* in *stretch*? Some people overlook letters that help another letter spell a sound. When you spell the following words, pay attention to the underlined letters.

hand<u>s</u>ome	me<u>a</u>nt	vege<u>t</u>able	colum<u>n</u>

Assignment Spelling and Meaning   Use your dictionary to write simple definitions for four sets of homophones and for two pairs of commonly confused words from the preceding lists. Then use each word in a sentence.

SAMPLE   cereal, serial

ANSWER   <u>Cereal</u> is a food made from grain.
<u>Serial</u> describes things arranged in a series.
Frank ate hot <u>cereal</u> every morning.
Lassie was once a popular television <u>serial</u>.

17.6 Other Spelling Helps

This section suggests some strategies that will further help you to develop your spelling skills. It also provides (1) help for finding dictionary entries for words that you do not know how to spell and (2) a list of twenty-five frequently misspelled words.

Strategies

1. *Keep a list of troublesome words.* Whenever you make a mistake in spelling, write the word correctly in a special section of your notebook. This will be your personal spelling list. At least once a week, study your list by following the steps on page 469.

2. *Think carefully about how words are pronounced and written.* Pay special attention to the problems discussed on pages 475–477.

3. *Make up memory aids.* There are a number of ways to help yourself remember the trouble spots in a word. Here are some examples:

   There is **a rate** in *separate.*
   Can a **liar** be *familiar* with the truth?

4. *Proofread your written work.* Be alert not only for misspellings but also for careless handwriting that makes the spelling unclear. For example, avoid *o*'s that look like *a*'s and uncrossed *t*'s that look like *l*'s.

The Dictionary as a Spelling Aid

Whenever you are unsure of the spelling of a word, use a dictionary (*Unit 18*). Remember that most dictionaries include as part of the entry those forms that involve a doubled final consonant and a dropped final *e.*

To find a word that you cannot spell, you have to be familiar with the different spellings for consonant and vowel sounds. The following lists show different spellings for some of the sounds that occur at the beginning of words.

CONSONANT SOUNDS	OTHER SPELLINGS
f, as in *fast*	*ph,* as in *physician*
j, as in *joke*	*g,* as in *gem*
k, as in *keep*	*c,* as in *cat; ch,* as in *character*
n, as in *now*	*gn,* as in *gnaw; kn,* as in *knee; pn,* as in *pneumatic*
r, as in *ripe*	*wr,* as in *wrestle*
s, as in *sell*	*c,* as in *cereal; ps,* as in *psychology*

VOWEL SOUNDS	OTHER SPELLINGS
a, as in *ape*	*ei,* as in *eighth*
e, as in *entrance*	*a,* as in *any*
i, as in *in*	*e,* as in *erasing*
yoo, as in *use*	*yu,* as in *yule; you,* as in *youth*

Frequently Misspelled Words

The following list contains twenty-five words that you probably use often in your writing. Use the steps on page 469 to study the spelling of these frequently misspelled words.

absence	develop	mischievous
advise	different	pastime
all right	doesn't	secretary
answer	familiar	surprise
appearance	generally	vegetable
athletics	grammar	Wednesday
calendar	interesting	woman
certain	losing	written
describe		

Assignment **Frequently Misspelled Words** On your paper, write sentences in which you use ten of the frequently misspelled words in the preceding list. You may use more than one of the words in the same sentence. Underline each word from the list that you use in your sentences.

Unit 18

Vocabulary
Skills

The words that you use when you communicate make up your **vocabulary.** Your vocabulary includes the words that you use when you speak and write and the words that you understand when you read and listen. Adding words to your vocabulary will help you to express your ideas in a more precise and interesting way. It will also expand your understanding of what you read and hear.

18.1 How to Learn New Words

This unit will provide you with strategies for increasing your vocabulary. The sections that follow will help you to add words to your vocabulary by using context clues, word parts, word choices, and the dictionary.

Strategies

1. *Keep a vocabulary notebook.* In your notebook list unfamilar words that you read or hear.

2. *Use a dictionary to find the meanings of unfamiliar words.* Write the meanings next to the words on your list. Write a sentence or two using each word in a way that conveys its meaning.

3. *Review the words in your notebook* from time to time to remind yourself of their meanings.

4. *Use the words in your conversation and writing* and be on the alert for them when you read and when you listen.

5. *Add prefixes and suffixes to the words on your list and to words that you already know.* Forming new words from familiar words is a simple way of expanding your vocabulary.

18.2 Learning Words from Context

You can always use your dictionary to find the meaning of an unfamiliar word. You can also discover the meaning of a word from the words around it. The surrounding words that give meaning to a word are called its **context.**

In this section you will learn about three things to look for when you are trying to determine meaning from context: (1) context clues, (2) synonyms, and (3) examples.

Context Clues.   Look for clues to the meaning of the unfamiliar word. In the following sentence, notice how the word *overflowed* provides a clue to the meaning of *inundate*.

The river overflowed its banks and threatened to *inundate* the countryside.

The more familiar word *overflowed* tells you that the word *inundate* probably means "to cover with water."

Synonyms.   Sometimes the context includes a synonym (*page 486*) for an unfamiliar word. If you know the meaning of the synonym, you can usually figure out the meaning of the unfamiliar word.

The *goober* is no ordinary peanut.

In this sentence the synonym *peanut* provides a meaning for the word *goober.*

Examples.   Some writers use examples to explain an unfamiliar word or idea. When you know the kinds of things that a word refers to, you can usually figure out the meaning of that word.

> That pony is very *tractable;* for instance, he never objects to being led or to learning new tricks.

From the examples of how the pony acts, you can guess that *tractable* means "obedient" or "easily managed."

The following words often signal that examples follow:

as	such	for instance
like	especially	for example

Assignment   Using Context   Read the paragraph that follows, paying special attention to the words in italic type. Use the context to determine the meaning of each of these words. Check the meanings in your dictionary. Write each italicized word and its meaning on your paper.

> The subway train, its sides covered with a jumbled scrawl of *graffiti,* pulled into the station. With a feeling of *apprehension,* we fearfully made our way into the front car. We could hardly breathe and were afraid we would soon be *asphyxiated.* At our stop, we left our *subterranean* prison, vowing never to travel underground again.

18.3 Getting Meanings from Word Parts

Another way to increase your vocabulary is to become familiar with the meanings of word parts. A word consists of a base word, to which may be added a prefix, a suffix, or both. The word *unmovable,* for example, is made up of the prefix *un-,* the base word *move,* and the suffix *-able.*

Prefixes.   A **prefix** is a letter or a group of letters added at the beginning of a base word to make a new word. When you add a prefix, the spelling of the base word does not change.

A prefix usually does change the meaning of the base word. For example, the prefix *un-* means "not." When *un-* is added to a base word, the new word usually has a meaning opposite to that of the base word.

un- plus *kind* = *unkind* (not kind)

Here are some common prefixes and their meanings:

PREFIX	MEANING(S)	EXAMPLES
ante-	before	anteroom, antedate
anti-	against	antiwar, antislavery
dis-	not	disagree, disown
in- (il-, im-, ir-)	not	inactive, illegal, immature, irresponsible
mis-	wrong	misspell, misquote
post-	after	postdate, postwar
pre-	before	predate, prewar

Suffixes. A **suffix** is a letter or a group of letters added at the end of a base word. A suffix sometimes changes the meaning of the word to which it is added. Most suffixes also change the part of speech of the base word. Like prefixes, suffixes have meanings that you can find in your dictionary.

Noun suffixes. Certain suffixes are used to make nouns from verbs or adjectives. If you know the meaning of the base word, you can figure out the meaning of the new word.

SUFFIX	MEANING(S)	EXAMPLES
-ance	action, quality, condition	attendance
-er	the person or thing performing the action indicated by the verb	writer
-ment	product, means, action, state	arrangement
-ness	state, quality, or condition of being	kindness
-or	the person or thing performing the action indicated by the verb	actor

Verb suffixes. Certain suffixes are used to make verbs from nouns or adjectives.

SUFFIX	MEANING(S)	EXAMPLES
-ate	make, apply, do	originate
-en	make, become	brighten
-fy	make or form into	beautify
-ize	make, make into, cause, cause to be	apologize

Adjective Suffixes. Certain suffixes are used to make adjectives from nouns or verbs.

SUFFIX	MEANING(S)	EXAMPLE
-able	capable of, inclined to	suitable
-ous	possessing, having, full of	nervous
-some	being, tending to be	fearsome
-y	full of, like	dusty

Adverb suffixes. Many adverbs are formed by adding the suffix *-ly* to an adjective.

ADJECTIVE	soft	careless	fortunate
ADVERB	softly	carelessly	fortunately

Suffixes and Spelling.   When you add a suffix to a base word, apply the rules for (1) doubling or not doubling the final consonant (*pages 472–473*), (2) dropping or keeping the final *e* (*pages 473–474*), and (3) changing *y* to *i* (*page 474*).

suit	regret	nerve	beauty
suitable	regrettable	nervous	beautify

When you add the suffix *-ly* to a word ending in *l*, remember to keep both *l*'s. When you add the suffix *-ness* to a word ending in *n*, remember to keep both *n*'s.

hopeful	thin
hopefully	thinness

Assignment 1 Prefixes On your paper, use the prefixes listed on page 483 to form a word to replace the blank in each of the following sentences. Use each new word in a sentence of your own.

> SAMPLE   A person who is not competent is __?__.
> ANSWER   incompetent
>   He felt incompetent when he tried to repair the bicycle.

1. To keep a car from freezing, motorists use __?__.
2. A chamber that comes before another room is an __?__.
3. Behavior that is not appropriate is __?__.
4. An object that is not movable is __?__.
5. When you put something in the wrong place, you __?__ it.
6. Someone who takes advanced courses after graduating from college is a __?__.
7. Handwriting that is not legible is __?__.
8. An interview that takes place after a game is a __?__ interview.

Assignment 2 Suffixes On your paper, use one of the suffixes listed on pages 483–484 to change each of the words in italic type to the indicated part of speech. Use each new word in a sentence.

> SAMPLE   Change the noun *length* to a verb.
> ANSWER   lengthen
>   Tomorrow I'm going to lengthen my skirt.

1. Change the adjective *pure* to a verb.
2. Change the adjective *good* to a noun.
3. Change the noun *peril* to an adjective.
4. Change the adjective *faithful* to an adverb.
5. Change the verb *refrigerate* to a noun.

Assignment 3 Suffixes and Spelling On your paper, practice your spelling skills by adding the indicated suffix to each of the following words. Use each new word in a sentence.

1. worthy (-ness)	6. pay (-ment)
2. forget (-able)	7. blot (-er)
3. careful (-ly)	8. taste (-y)
4. pave (-ment)	9. bake (-er)
5. bag (-y)	10. run (-er)

18.4 How to Choose the Best Word

The number of words in the English language is estimated by some to be over one million. Most words have more than one meaning, and no two words mean exactly the same thing. As you add to your vocabulary, always try to use the word that expresses exactly what you want to say. Choosing the best word will make what you say and write interesting and easy to understand.

The following will help you to choose the best word. To do so, you need to become familiar with synonyms and their meanings and to become aware of the difference between the connotation and the denotation of a word.

Synonyms

Synonyms are words that have similar meanings. Synonyms help you to express your ideas in a variety of ways; they also help you to make important distinctions in meaning. For example, the prepositions *under, below,* and *beneath* are synonyms. However, you would not say that someone was "beneath legal age" or that you live "below a system of democracy." In both examples the word *under* is the best choice.

To help you see the differences between synonyms, many dictionaries include paragraphs that explain shades of meaning. A synonym paragraph following the word *gaze* might look like this:

> **Synonyms:** *gaze, stare, gawk, glare.* These verbs generally mean to "look at someone or something long and steadily." To *gaze* is to look at someone or something for a long time with wonder, fascination, awe, or admiration. To *stare* emphasizes the steadiness of one's look, usually with curiosity or boldness. To *gawk* is to stare stupidly or foolishly. To *glare* is to fix someone with a hard or unfriendly look.

Use the synonym paragraphs in your dictionary (*page 490*) whenever you need to choose the right word.

Connotation and Denotation

Many words have two kinds of meanings. For example, look up the word *friend* in your dictionary. The definitions listed are the **denotation** of the word. When *friend* is used in a sentence, however, it takes on feelings and associations from the context of the sentence. These feelings and associations give the word its **connotation.**

Notice the different connotations of the word *friend* in the following sentences.

> She is a *friend* of the arts. [*Friend* in this sentence means a supporter of the arts.]
>
> She told her secret to her best *friend*. [*Friend* in this sentence means a trusted associate.]

You can often see the difference between connotation and denotation in the synonyms given for a word. For example, each of the following synonyms for *car* carries a different connotation: *automobile, motorcar, hardtop, limousine, heap, jalopy.*

You can detract from the effect of what you say or write by using a word that carries an unintended connotation. For example, to refer to someone's prized automobile as a *heap* might be embarrassing. To call the family's economy car a *limousine* would be an overstatement.

Assignment 1   Synonyms   Use the information in the synonym paragraph on page 487 to complete each of the following sentences with the past form of the verbs *gaze, stare, gawk,* or *glare.*

1. We __?__ at the sky, hoping to see a falling star.
2. When I took out my jigsaw puzzle on the bus, everybody __?__ at me.
3. The customer __?__ at me when I spilled coffee on his newspaper.
4. The clowns __?__ at the elephants and pretended to be frightened by them.

Assignment 2   Connotation   On your paper, write the following word pairs. For each pair, put a check after the word that usually has the more positive connotation. Write a sentence using each of the words that you checked.

1. bold—reckless
2. flatter—praise
3. thrifty—stingy
4. cautious—fearful
5. relaxed—lazy
6. slim—skinny

18.5 Using the Dictionary

Throughout this unit, you have been referred to your dictionary as a source for increasing your vocabulary. To find information about a word, you must first know how to use your dictionary.

Locating a Word

The Entry Word and the Entry.   The words listed in a dictionary are called **entry words.** Centered dots or hyphens

word show the number of syllables in the word. The entry word and the information that follows it are called the **entry.** The entry words are listed in alphabetical order. Words beginning with the same letter are alphabetized according to the second letter, the third letter, and so forth. For example, you will find *town* before *trace* and *trace* before *trade.* Hyphens, spaces, and apostrophes do not affect the alphabetical order of words.

Guide Words. The words in boldface type at the top of a page are **guide words**. The first guide word is the same as the first entry word on the page. The second guide word is the same as the last entry word. All of the entry words that fall alphabetically between the two guide words are on that page. For example, the words *fun, function,* and *fungus* would be on a page with the guide words *fumigate* and *funny.*

Using a Pronunciation Key

Pronunciations. A dictionary also shows how to pronounce a word. The pronunciation is usually shown immediately after the entry word. Pronunciations are set off with parentheses, brackets, or bars. Dots or hyphens are usually used to separate the syllables in a word.

dis·con·nect (dĭs′-kə-nĕkt′)

The degrees of loudness, or stress, with which the syllables in a word are spoken are indicated by special symbols. For example, in the pronunciation for *disconnect* the unmarked syllable, (kə′), has the weakest stress. The third syllable, (nekt′), has the strongest, or primary, stress—indicated by a mark in boldface type after the syllable. The first syllable, (dĭs) has the secondary stress—indicated by a lighter mark.

At the beginning of most dictionaries, you will find a complete key to the pronunciation symbols. A shortened key often appears on each page or each pair of facing pages.

Parts of a Dictionary Entry

Definitions.   Many English words have three or four different meanings. In most dictionaries, the different meanings are numbered. Letters may also be used to indicate meanings closely related to the numbered definition. Often an example is given to show the sense of a word in a particular context.

Parts of Speech.   An abbreviated part-of-speech label appears in the entry, usually following the pronunciation.

      dis·con·nect (dĭs′-kə-nĕkt′) *v.*

The following abbreviations are used in most dictionaries to indicate the eight parts of speech:

n.	noun	*conj.*	conjunction
adj.	adjective	*prep.*	preposition
adv.	adverb	*v.*	verb
pron.	pronoun	*interj.*	interjection

The abbreviations *sing.* and *pl.* are used to indicate singular and plural forms.

Synonyms.   On page 487 you studied an example of a synonym paragraph for the entry word *gaze.* Most dictionaries include synonym paragraphs for selected words and provide a cross-reference at the entry for each synonym. In this case, the cross-reference for the entry word *stare* would be "See Synonyms at **gaze.**"

Usage Labels.   Most dictionaries explain the correct usage of certain words. Three examples of common word categories are *Nonstandard, Informal,* and *Slang.* Such labels are explained in detail in the introduction to the dictionary.

Homographs.   Sometimes two or more entry words are spelled exactly alike. Words that are spelled alike but have different meanings or functions are called **homographs.** Homographs are usually identified by a small raised numeral either before or after the entry word.

Changes in Form. In English there are three major changes in the form of a word: (1) a change in the form of a noun to show its plural, (2) a change in the form of a verb to show its principal parts, and (3) a change in the form of an adjective or adverb to show degrees of comparison. In most dictionaries, these changes in form are shown after the part-of-speech label.

> **dis·con·nect** (dĭs′-kə-nĕkt′) *v.* -nected, -necting, -nects

The entry for the regular verb *disconnect* gives the past form, the present participle, and the singular form. The past participle form is usually given for irregular verbs only.

Assignment 1 Using the Dictionary Spend an hour looking through the dictionary that you use for your schoolwork. Be ready to discuss in class how your dictionary presents the information listed on pages 488–491. For example, consider the answers to these questions: Are the pronunciations enclosed in parentheses? What pronunciation symbols are used? How are degrees of stress shown? Are synonym paragraphs included?

Assignment 2 Improving Your Vocabulary In a newspaper or magazine that is known for being written well, find at least two interesting articles. In the articles find at least five words that are new to you. Add these words to your vocabulary by following the strategies on page 480–481.

Unit 19

Study Skills

To study well, you should know how to locate information, how to read effectively, and how to take good notes. This unit will help you to learn these skills.

19.1 Reading Skills

19.1a Parts of a Book

Knowing the major parts of a book can help you to find information quickly and easily.

Table of Contents. The **table of contents** is located at the front of a book. It lists the titles of units and chapters and their subdivisions. It also lists the page numbers on which units, chapters, and subdivisions begin.

The following example is part of a table of contents.

Index.   The index is located at the back of a book. It is an alphabetical list of main entries for all persons, places, things, and ideas covered in the book. Some main entries in an index may also have subentries, as shown in the following example. The words *See* and *See also,* which sometimes appear in a main entry, refer you to other main entries on the same topic.

In the following example of an index main entry, *p* indicates that a picture appears on that page.

Main entry ⎤
Subentry ———   Architecture, of 1893, *p* 561; modern, *p* 545, 562,
Related main   *p* 711, *p* 712. *See also* Houses
entry ⎦

Use the following strategies to locate information in a book.

Strategies

1. *Skim the table of contents* for a general idea of the subjects covered.

2. *Read unit or chapter titles* and subdivision titles to see if the information that you need is listed.

3. *Skim the index* if the information that you need is not listed in the table of contents.

4. *Use the index to find the numbers of pages* that refer to the specific person, place, thing, or event for which you want information.

Subheadings.   Subheadings are words, phrases, or sentences that summarize the text that follows them. They are usually set apart from the chapter title and text by such devices as capital letters, boldface or italic type, or color.

Illustrations.   Many books include illustrations, study aids such as maps, diagrams, charts, tables, and graphs.

Maps show large or small areas of the earth's surface. Some maps show countries, cities, mountains, rivers, lakes, forests, deserts, or roads. Other maps include information on population size, annual rainfall, and other items of interest. Most maps have a key to explain the symbols that they use, such as a scale of miles to help you compute distances.

Diagrams show how objects are put together and how they work. Diagrams, which are usually labeled to show parts or steps, can also show you how to make or do something.

Charts and **tables** give detailed information that is usually presented as numbers arranged in labeled columns.

A **graph** demonstrates changes that occur over a period of time. For example, a graph might show how many inches of rain fell per month over a period of several months.

Assignment 1   Parts of a Book   Read the following portion of a table of contents. Then, on your paper, write the chapter titles and page numbers where you would find the answers to the questions that follow.

Unit   3   New Nations Are Born as the New World Shakes Off European Rule   **124**

7   How Were the English Colonists Governed?   **126**

8   The American Colonists Resist Strict Control by England   **139**

9   The Thirteen English Colonies Win Their Independence   **155**

10   The Spirit of Independence Affects Canada and Latin America   **184**

1. Why did England and the colonists disagree?
2. How did America's independence change the world?
3. What points were made in the Declaration of Independence?
4. How did England control the colonies?

Assignment 2 Parts of a Book   Read the following main entry from an index. Then, on your paper, write the subentry and the number of the page where you find the answers to the questions that follow the entry.

> Manufacturing, colonial, 134; encouraged by War of 1812, 252; in 1840s, 260-261; in 1850s, 262; develops in Northeast, 268-271; new methods in, 460-462. *See also* Factories; Industry

1. How manufacturing developed between 1840 and 1850
2. Products manufactured during the colonial period
3. The new methods that developed in manufacturing
4. Other main entries to look for in the index

Assignment 3 Illustrations   From your social studies, science, or mathematics textbook, find a map, a chart, a diagram, and a graph. On your paper, explain what information is presented in each illustration.

Assignment 4 Subheadings   On your paper, copy three subheadings from your social studies, science, or mathematics textbook. Beside each, tell what device is used to separate the subheading from the text around it. For example, you might point out that rules are given in color.

19.1b Reading Effectively

The ability to read effectively is an important study skill that will help you in all areas of your schoolwork.

SQRRR Method.   The SQRRR reading method helps you to analyze and to remember what you have read. **SQRRR** stands for *Survey, Question, Read, Recite,* and *Review.* The following selection is used to show you how to use this method.

First, read this selection.

England Tries to Tighten Control over the Colonies

England considers new plans for its colonies.

In London at the close of the French and Indian War in 1763, Prime Minister George Grenville addressed his companions in words like these: "Gentlemen, a great war was just ended. Victory has brought us a vast territory in America. Today England is the proud ruler of the greatest empire in the world."

Grenville puts into effect a new program for the colonies.

Grenville and the British government took steps to tighten their control over the American colonies.

1. *The Proclamation of 1763.* In 1763 Grenville issued a proclamation stating that no settlements were to be made west of the Allegheny Mountains except by special permission. All trade with the Indians would be closely controlled by the British government. To guard the frontier, Grenville suggested sending ten thousand British troops to the American colonies.

2. *Strict enforcement of the Navigation Acts.* Grenville realized that greater profits would go to English merchants and manufacturers if smuggling could be stopped. More taxes would also be collected. He sent officers to America to search for smugglers and to punish lawbreakers.

3. *The Stamp Act.* Finally, to raise more money in the colonies, Parliament passed the Stamp Act in 1765. This law required that stamps sold by the British government must be placed on many items, such as newspapers and calendars.

Using the passage that you have just read, follow these steps of the SQRRR method.

Survey.   Read all the titles and subheadings, and the terms in color, boldface, or italic type. Then look at the illustrations. Finally, read summary paragraphs or lists. A survey of the selection that you just read tells the following:

The topic is how England tries to tighten control over the thirteen colonies. (chapter title)

England has plans for the colonies, and Grenville begins a new program. (subheadings)

New programs are the Proclamation of 1763, the Navigation Act, and the Stamp Act. (italic type)

Question. Think of questions that might be answered by reading the selection. Base your questions on the survey that you did in the first step. The following questions are based on the sample selection:

What were England's plans for its colonies?

Who was Grenville?

What was the Proclamation of 1763?

What were the Navigation Acts?

What was the Stamp Act?

How were the laws enforced?

Read. Read the selection to try to answer your questions. If it helps you to remember the questions, write them out and take notes on the answers. Watch for important information that may not be included in your questions and answers.

Recite. After reading the selection, answer each question in writing or by reciting silently or aloud. Think of new questions for information that you did not include before. Write or recite the answers to these questions.

Review. Ask yourself the questions again and review the answers. Try to review within twenty-four hours of your first reading. Review first without looking at your notes or at the selection. Then check your answers. Continue reviewing until you can answer each question correctly. Refer to the selection as necessary to clarify points that still confuse you.

Assignment 5   SQRRR Reading Method   Use the Survey, Question, Read, Recite, and Review method to study the following selection. Then, on your paper, write the letters of the correct answers to the questions after the selection. There is more than one correct answer for each question.

The English Go to the New World

By the early 1600s, the English began to take an interest in founding colonies of their own in North America. In spite of the hardships and dangers of travel to America, they left for a better life.

The Settlers Sought Freedom

America meant freedom to earn a better living.   Most of the English people had once been farmers. They had rented land from wealthy landowners and raised crops, but there came a time when the landowners could make more money by raising sheep and selling the wool to be made into clothing. Consequently, the landowners fenced off much of the farmland and made it into pastures for the sheep. Only a few people were needed to tend the large flocks.

Large numbers of people were without homes or jobs. The New World offered these people a chance to make a better living.

America meant greater freedom to own land.   In England in the early 1600s, there were many people who could never hope to own land. Land belonged chiefly to the upper class. In the New World, there was plenty of land for everyone. Even poor people could become landowners in America.

America meant freedom of religion.   In Europe in the 1600s, people were not free to worship as they wished. In England the people were supposed to accept the king as the head of the Church of England. They were expected to attend the services of this church, to agree to its teachings, and to give money for its support. Many English people objected to these religious restrictions. They wanted to go to America to worship as they pleased.

America meant freedom to share in government. The people of England during the 1600s were not satisfied with their government. King James and King Charles thought that their subjects should accept without question whatever the king wanted. Many English people believed that they were losing their rights under such a government. If they went to the colonies in America, they might participate in their own government. They were willing to trade the comforts of their old homes for freedom in a new land.

1. After you survey the selection, which of the following statements can you make?
   a. The English wanted to go to North America in the 1600s.
   b. They left England because they did not like raising crops.
   c. In America, they would have a chance for a better living.
   d. Hardships and dangers faced travelers sailing to America.
   e. America offered the English greater freedom to own land, to worship, and to share in government.

2. Which of the following questions would you ask yourself after surveying the selection?
   a. Why were the English seeking a better life?
   b. What were the conditions in England in the 1600s?
   c. How would the English travel to America?
   d. Who was king? What rules did he enforce?
   e. Why did the English not own land?
   f. How did the English feel about their part in government?

3. Which of the following answers will help you to remember important information in the selection?
   a. In the 1600s, people in England were homeless and jobless.
   b. There was little opportunity to own land in England.
   c. People had to accept the king as head of the church.
   d. People wanted more voice in their government.
   e. The English went to America on ships.
   f. The English went to America to find freedom.

19.2 Note-Taking Skills

The ability to take good notes is important because it will enable you to study more efficiently. Because note taking is a selective process, you will learn to determine what is important. You will also find that writing something down will help you to remember it.

19.2a Taking Notes from Textbooks

You will do most of your note taking in school from textbooks. Before taking notes on a selection, read the entire selection through. Then use the following strategies to take notes.

Strategies

1. *Write your notes in your own words.*

2. *Use words and phrases, not complete sentences.* Use mostly nouns and verbs. Omit articles (a, an, the). Use adjectives and adverbs sparingly.

3. *Use abbreviations and symbols when possible.*

4. *Pay close attention to words in boldface and italic type, in quotation marks, or in another color in order to determine what is important.*

5. *Watch for words and phrases that signal main points.* Examples include *first, then, finally, in summary, in conclusion, most important, more important, the reason for, the causes of, the result was, for instance,* and *for example.*

6. *Separate your notes from different classes.*

7. *Review your notes shortly after you write them.*

8. *Write your notes in ink.* Notes in pencil will fade or blur.

Assignment 1 Note Taking On your paper, copy the following passage and underline the important words to include in notes. Follow the strategies that you just read on page 500.

Some of our decisions are made in the marketplace, where we buy goods and services. As consumers, we have to make decisions because there may be no limit to what we would like to buy, but there are very real limits to what we can afford. Our **wants** are unlimited, but our **resources** are limited. We must decide, therefore, which goods or services we need or want most. In doing so, we also decide which goods and services we are willing to do without.

Suppose you want some new jeans and have just enough money to buy a pair. Suppose you would also like to have a few new tapes for your cassette player. Your wants are greater than your resources, so you must make a decision. You think about how much pleasure each alternative will give you and what it will cost you.

Assignment 2 Note Taking On your paper, write notes for the passage in Assignment 1. Use the words that you underlined.

19.2b Taking Notes from Encyclopedias

Encyclopedia articles are different from textbook units because each article explores and explains a separate topic, while units in a textbook are presented in a particular order and usually relate to each other in a specific way. An encyclopedia article gives complete, detailed information. Often, articles are very long. You may want to take notes on one topic in an article or on an entire article. When taking notes, choose the information carefully. Read each paragraph to identify key ideas.

When taking notes from an encyclopedia, follow the strategies you learned on page 500. In addition, pay attention to indented lines, lists, subheadings, illustrations, and captions. Also refer to any related articles that pertain to your topic. Special information in either an encyclopedia or a textbook may include definitions, pronunciations, dates, foreign words, and related topics.

Assignment 3   Taking Notes from Encyclopedias
On your paper, copy the following paragraph and underline the important words.

NURSES. Although most nurses work in hospitals taking care of patients who are ill, injured, or recovering from surgery, some nurses work in places other than hospitals. For example, visiting nurses work in the homes of sick or injured persons. Some nurses assist in the offices of doctors and dentists. Still others work in medical clinics in schools, in stores or factories, in the armed services, and on ships and trains. Nurses are found wherever their skills are needed: in cities, small towns, and the farm areas in all parts of the world.

In addition to caring for the sick and injured, nurses may also teach adults and children how to practice preventive medicine in order to protect themselves from illness and accidents. Nurses who have had advanced training may also teach in schools and colleges of nursing, where they train other people to become professional nurses.

The two main kinds of nurses are professional and practical nurses. *Professional nurses,* also called registered nurses, are graduates of two-year junior college programs, hospital programs of two or three years, or college programs of four or five years. *Practical nurses,* who complete a training program that usually lasts for one year, perform duties that leave professional nurses free for work that requires more preparation and skill.

Hospital Nurses. Most professional nurses serve as *general-duty* nurses in hospitals, working with doctors to speed a patient's recovery. They may work in an operating room as an important member of a surgical team, or in recovery areas where they administer prescribed medicines and treatments to patients, or in the nursery where they care for newborn infants. General-duty nurses may also assist in giving blood transfusions and in teaching patients how to care for themselves. They also report to the attending physician any change in a patient's condition.

Assignment 4 Note Taking   On your paper, write notes for the paragraph in Assignment 1. Use the words that you underlined.

Unit 20

Listening Skills

20.1 Why Learn Listening Skills?

Good listening is as important as good speaking. It is a skill that you can practice and learn. When you really listen, you pay close attention and think about what you are hearing. In this unit, you will learn how you can become a better listener.

Different occasions call for different ways of listening. When you listen to a teacher explain a complicated assignment, you are **listening for information**. When you listen to a commercial for a new product and try to decide whether you should buy it, you are practicing **critical listening**. When you listen to a friend describing a funny incident, you are engaged in **conversational listening**. Sometimes you may combine these ways of listening.

Each kind of listening requires a particular approach on your part. Whenever you listen, you have a purpose. In the preceding examples, your purpose would be to understand the assignment, to judge the new product, or to enjoy and respond to your friend's story.

Listening for information, critical listening, and conversational listening all require you to be an active listener. You need to put effort into your listening and to think about what you are hearing.

Passive listeners, in contrast, do not work at listening. They let their minds wander and do not hear all that is said. They do not make an effort to understand and weigh information.

As an active listener, you are more likely than a passive listener to be able to tell the difference between fact and fiction. You can distinguish between reliable and unreliable information and between information that sticks to the point and information that wanders.

Assignment Listening With all activity in the classroom stopped for five minutes, listen carefully for all the sounds that you can identify. On your paper, list each sound, and state what it is, if possible. At the end of the five minutes, compare your list with those of your classmates.

20.2 Getting Ready to Listen

A good listener starts with a positive attitude. You should plan to learn and understand as much as you can. You should prepare yourself so that you will be ready to listen actively and effectively.

20.2a The Setting

Before you begin to listen to a speaker, it is important that your surroundings be comfortable. You should be settled and free to concentrate. In a conversation with a friend, look at the person who is speaking, and avoid being distracted by activities taking place around you.

In listening to a more formal presentation, such as a speech, use the following strategies to improve your setting for listening.

Strategies

1. *Be early or on time.* Give yourself enough time to prepare and settle down before the presentation begins.

2. *Have your materials ready ahead of time.* If you plan to take notes, have your pencil and paper ready. Put away any books and other materials that you will not need.

3. *Sit in a comfortable but alert position.* Watch the speaker, not the people around you or what is going on outside.

4. *Listen politely and quietly.* Avoid distracting habits such as tapping your pencil. Shuffling papers, waving to other members of the audience, whispering, and so forth can disturb the speaker, other listeners, and yourself.

5. *Concentrate on what is being said, and put aside other thoughts.*

20.2b Questions to Ask Yourself Before Listening

You will probably get more benefit from listening if you know something ahead of time about the subject and about the speaker. Prepare for active listening by asking yourself questions like the following:

1. What is the topic of the speech? What do I already know about it?
2. Who is the speaker? What special knowledge or experience does the speaker have on the subject?
3. What is the speaker's purpose? Is it to inform, to persuade, or to entertain?
4. What is my purpose as a listener? Is it to obtain information, to make a decision or form an opinion, or to be entertained?
5. Do I have a positive attitude? Is my mind open to new ideas and opinions?

Assignment 1 Active Listening On your paper, write a sentence or two for each situation listed, telling why it is important for each person to be an active listener.

1. A student asks a librarian for help in locating a book.
2. Two friends plan a picnic.
3. A school nurse tends to a student's injured ankle.
4. A traveler asks a police officer for directions.
5. A guide explains the plans for a hiking trip.

Assignment 2 Kinds of Listening On your paper, write the kind of listening that you would need to do in each of the following situations. State whether it requires listening for information, critical listening, or conversational listening. You may give more than one answer for some items.

SAMPLE   A reviewer on the radio describes and recommends a movie.

ANSWER   Listening for information; Critical listening

1. A friend describes a funny incident during lunch.
2. A civic leader proposes a change in a law.
3. Your science teacher explains an assignment.
4. A neighbor asks you to babysit.
5. Your principal gives a speech about a new dress code.
6. A relative calls to wish you a happy birthday.
7. You and a friend plan a summer project.
8. You and a favorite teacher discuss your plans for the future.

20.3 What to Listen For

When you travel along an unfamiliar road, you look for signs that tell you where you are, how far it is to the next town, and so on. A good speech is like a well-marked road. The speaker uses certain kinds of words and phrases to guide you and to let you know what lies ahead. A good listener, like a good driver, remains alert and watches for signs and signals.

You understand better what you hear when you know the speaker's purpose and how the speech is organized. You also need to recognize the main ideas in the speech, how they relate to one another, and what facts or details support them. You can learn to listen for these points and for the signs and signals that will guide you.

Listen for the Speaker's Purpose

A speaker's purpose may be to inform you about something, to persuade you to change your opinion or take some action, or to entertain you. Early in the speech, listen for statements that tell exactly what the speaker plans to do.

EXAMPLE	PURPOSE
"Here is a report on the committee's work."	To inform you about what the committee has done
"Let me present the reasons why you should vote for Marcus."	To persuade you to vote for Marcus
"I want to tell you about the time I played an April Fool's joke that backfired."	To entertain you with a story

Listen for the Method of Organization

In listening for the speaker's purpose, you should also listen for statements that tell you how the speech is organized. For instance, if a speech topic is to be divided into two or more parts, using topical order, the speaker may say so early in the speech, as this speaker does.

Plants can be divided into two major groups: those that make seeds and those that do not.

Some speeches are organized by chronological order, or time order. They start with events that happened longest ago and proceed to events that happened most recently. Sometimes a speech may start in the present and move in reverse order to events in the past.

A speech or demonstration that gives a set of steps or directions may also be organized in chronological order. Listen for signals that the speaker has used this method, as in these examples:

I will outline the life of Thomas Jefferson, who was born in 1743.

Let us start with today's horses and trace their use as far back in history as we can.

I will present and explain the steps for making a box kite.

Another method for organizing a speech is by spatial order. A speaker may use this method when describing a place or telling how objects are located in relation to one another. Here are two examples:

> The town of Sharplesville is laid out like a giant crescent.
> Here is what you will see as you walk through the dinosaur hall at the museum. The first case to your right as you enter contains . . .

Some speeches present problems and then offer solutions to them. If the speech you are listening to is organized by this method, the speaker will usually use words like *problem, solution,* and *answers* in telling what the speech will be about. For example,

> Noise pollution has become a serious problem in our school.
> Let us look at some of the answers that have been suggested for improving national elections.

Listen for Signals and Transitions

Certain phrases alert you to what follows in a speech. Phrases like the following tell you that the speaker is about to state the purpose.

> My purpose is to show . . .
> I would like to tell you about . . .
> Today I will explain . . .

Other phrases are signals that the speaker is about to reveal the method by which the speech is organized. For instance,

> This topic has three important parts.
> We need to find a solution to the problem of . . .

Speakers also give signals about what they consider most important in their speeches, as in these examples.

A major issue is . . .

A vital point to remember is . . .

In some cases, speakers provide background information that will help you to understand the points they want to make. Listen for signals like these:

Here is how this problem came about.

Let me explain how the present situation developed.

Speakers frequently give summaries at the end of a speech to help you remember the main points. A summary is a brief review of the main ideas in a speech. Sometimes a speaker will also give a brief summary in the main part of the speech as a review before going on. Be alert for signals that a summary is coming.

To summarize . . .

Let me review briefly . . .

Before going on, I will quickly review . . .

Transitions mark changes from one idea to another, or from one part of a speech to another. Listening for transitions helps you to understand how the idea that you will hear next is related to what the speaker has already said.

TRANSITIONAL WORDS AND PHRASES

after	besides	instead
another	first	most important
as a result	in addition to	next

Transitions are often related to the method in which a speech is organized. Study the transitions on the following page.

METHOD OF ORGANIZATION	TRANSITION
Topical order	The second point to think about
	Another important item
Chronological order	First; next; then
	The following day
	Some years later
Spatial order	Continuing in the same direction
	Next you come to
Problem-and-solution order	Another approach that has been tried
	Now that we understand the problem, let's look at some possible solutions.

Listen for Main Ideas

Some statements that are made in a speech are more important than others. You cannot expect to remember every bit of information that you hear in a speech. You will want to know which points are most important so that you can remember them.

The speaker will usually give you signals that help you to know what the main ideas are. Some of the signals and transitions that you have already learned about can guide you in listening for these key points.

A major issue is . . .

An important point is . . .

Knowing the method by which the speech is organized can also help you in listening for key points. If the speaker tells you that there are three parts to the topic, for example, you know that you should listen for three main ideas. If you know that the speaker will describe a problem and suggest a solution, you know that you should listen for a statement of the problem and a statement of the suggested solution.

When the speaker signals a summary, you know that the key points will probably be repeated. Listen carefully to the summary to be certain that you have correctly identified the main ideas.

Taking Notes

Taking notes helps you remember what you have heard. When you take notes, you have to pay close attention to the speaker and not let your mind wander or be distracted. You have to think about what you are hearing at the same time that you are listening to it.

At the start of a speech, before you begin to take notes, listen for a few moments to get a sense of the speaker's direction. Then begin taking your notes. Use these strategies.

Strategies

1. *Jot down the speaker's purpose, the main ideas, and other important information.* If you have trouble identifying any of these points, make a note about that problem.

2. *Jot down any questions* that occur to you or any points you disagree with or do not feel sure about.

3. *Keep your notes brief and specific.* Do not try to write down everything you hear. Your notes are meant to remind you of key points and important details.

4. *Keep your notes neat.* Write clearly so that you will be able to understand your notes later.

5. *Look over your notes when the speaker summarizes* to be sure that you have included the most important information.

Listen for Supporting Details

A good speaker should provide facts and information to support each main idea. Listen carefully to this supporting material to help you understand the main ideas. This material may also help you decide whether you agree or disagree with what the speaker is saying.

Depending on the speech topic, you may make notes about many supporting details or only a few. For example, if you are taking notes about instructions or a demonstration, you will need to include all of the steps. If you are taking notes on a report, you will need to write down only the details that will help you to understand and remember the main ideas.

Assignment 1 Listening for Main Ideas   Your teacher will read aloud to the class an article or a short story, but not its title. You should listen carefully without taking notes. After listening to the reading, write on your paper a title for the article or story and a brief summary of the main ideas. Then compare your responses with those of your classmates.

Assignment 2 Taking Notes   Listen to a ten-minute portion of a television or radio newscast. As you listen, take notes in your notebook or on separate paper, using the strategies given on page 513. Bring your notes to class. Be prepared to explain how you decided what to include in your notes.

20.4 Being a Responsive and Courteous Listener

One way to respond to a speaker is by polite attention. When you listen quietly and alertly, you are showing courtesy to the speaker. Sometimes you may be able to applaud or to thank the speaker afterward.

Often you will have a chance to ask questions or to make comments. Jot down questions or comments in your notes and save them until the speaker finishes the presentation.

There are various kinds of questions that you might want to ask. If you think that you may not have understood something in the speech, you can ask the speaker to explain it or to give more information. You may also ask for suggestions about what you might do or how you could learn more about the topic.

Comments should relate directly to the speech. Ask yourself whether what you plan to say will interest other listeners as well.

Keep your question or comment brief and to the point. Speak up in a clear, strong voice. Others may be able to hear you better if you stand, especially if you are part of a large audience. Remember to be polite and to thank the speaker for responding.

Do not be afraid to ask questions. The speaker's goal is to have you understand the topic. He or she can achieve that goal only if you are an active and responsive listener.

Assignment Responsive Listening Listen to a report or a speech on radio or television. You may choose an extended news report, a political speech, an editorial, or an analysis. As you listen, jot down on your paper any questions or comments that you would bring up if you could respond to the speaker in person. Bring your paper to class.

Unit 21

Speaking Skills

21.1 Speaking to a Group

Often you have to speak to a group of people. The group may be large or small. Your speech may be long or short. In any case, your goal in speaking is always to communicate. You want your listeners to understand what you are telling them.

In this unit you will learn basic steps that will help you to speak effectively before a group.

21.1a Formal and Informal Speeches

A speech may be either **formal** or **informal.** To decide whether a speech is formal or informal, you should consider the occasion, the purpose, and the audience. In this book the word *speech* refers to any kind of prepared talk that you give before a group. Here are some examples of formal and informal situations for speeches:

FORMAL   A police officer addresses a school assembly about bicycle safety rules.

The mayor speaks to local business leaders about your community in the coming decade.

You speak to a sixth-grade class to tell the students what seventh grade is like.

INFORMAL A police officer gives a group of bike riders directions to the park.

The mayor of your town answers reporters' questions while leaving the building.

You contribute to a class discussion in social studies.

In speaking before a group, you may be giving instructions, making announcements, or giving oral reports, depending on the occasion. The following are examples of the kinds of speeches you may need to give:

INSTRUCTIONS You instruct your scout troop on how to build a campfire.

You show your math class how to plot numbers on a graph.

ANNOUNCEMENTS You announce soccer tryouts to a school assembly.

You announce to members of an organization the names of newly elected officers.

ORAL REPORTS You report to your class on a science experiment.

You report to the school board on the results of a survey.

21.1b Purposes of Speaking

As a speaker, you will have different purposes at different times. The three main purposes of speaking to a group are to **inform,** to **persuade,** and to **entertain.**

In thinking about your purpose, you need to think about your listeners. All the decisions that you make in planning your speech should be made with your audience in mind.

Speaking to Inform. When your purpose is to inform, you want to increase your listeners' knowledge about your subject, as in these cases.

> You explain photosynthesis to your science class.
>
> You announce the day's activities over your school's public-address system.

Speaking to Persuade. When your purpose is to persuade, you want to change your listeners' minds or cause them to take some action. Consider these examples:

> You explain to a student assembly why your school should help to support the local animal shelter.
>
> You encourage members of the basketball team to contribute toward a gift for the coach.

Speaking to Entertain. When your purpose is to entertain, you simply want your listeners to enjoy hearing what you say. Some speeches to inform or to persuade also include entertaining moments. Other speeches, such as the following, are designed only to entertain.

> You tell the History Club members a funny story about Abraham Lincoln.
>
> You speak in class on the subject "The Most Surprising Moment in My Life."

Assignment   Purpose and Audience   For each topic listed, write down what the purpose would be and who would be a suitable audience. Discuss your answers in class.

1. Why we should put more bike racks outside our school
2. How to develop your own photographs
3. A funny fishing story
4. Black holes in space
5. The best person to be president of the Gymnastics Club

21.2 Planning Your Speech

In making any kind of speech, take one step at a time. You will find the project easier if you work according to a plan. The following steps make up the process of preparing and giving a speech:

1. Selecting a topic
2. Limiting a topic
3. Gathering information and developing ideas
4. Organizing your speech
5. Preparing and rehearsing your speech
6. Delivering your speech

Each of these steps will help you plan your speech and deliver it well. Giving time and thought to each step in the process makes the later ones easier.

21.2a Selecting and Limiting Your Topic

You may decide to give a speech about a subject such as robots, weather, or movies. Of course, you cannot tell in a short speech all there is to know about any subject that is so broad. You would not be able to cover your subject well.

In selecting a speech topic, you must decide what part of your subject you want to cover. Then you need to limit your topic to make it narrow enough for you to cover well.

SUBJECT	SPEECH TOPIC
Robots	How robots are used in industry today
Weather	How to use a barometer
Movies	Special effects in two recent space movies

When you limit your topic, you should think about your purpose, your audience, and your time limit. You need to limit your topic to fit the occasion.

Stating Your Purpose

Your **general purpose** is either to inform, to persuade, or to entertain. Think about your general purpose when you select and limit your topic. For instance, you may decide to speak on scouting. You could inform your listeners about the history of scouting. You could try to persuade them to join scout troops. You could entertain them with stories of your experiences as a scout.

Your **specific purpose** tells exactly what you want to do in your speech. Here are some other examples.

GENERAL PURPOSE	SPECIFIC PURPOSE
To inform	I want my audience to learn why leaves turn color in the fall.
To persuade	I want my audience to agree that we should have a School Clean-Up Day.
To entertain	I want my audience to be amused by my experiences in teaching my parakeet to talk.

After thinking about your subject, your audience, and your time limit, state your specific purpose clearly in one sentence. You will not make this statement in your speech, but having it in mind will help you as you plan.

Knowing Your Audience

In deciding on a speech topic and a specific purpose, you have to think carefully about your listeners. Ask yourself the following questions:

1. Who are my listeners?
2. Will they be interested in my topic?
3. What do they already know about this topic?
4. What do I want my audience to learn, to think, or to do?

You do not want to give your listeners information that they already have. You do not want to ask them to do something that they already plan to do. For instance, you might speak at a school assembly on why it would be a good idea for the school to have a field day. This would not be a good topic for a speech to the Field Day Committee, however. A better topic for that speech might be how to plan such an event.

Knowing Your Time Limits

The amount of time that you have to give your speech is an important factor in limiting your topic. You can plan to cover a broader or narrower topic once you know how long your speech will be. Knowing your time limit will also help you to decide on the amount of information and ideas that you need to gather.

Assignment 1   Selecting and Limiting Your Topic

Step 1: On your paper, write a limited speech topic for each of the following subjects. Make each of your topics suitable for a five-minute speech to your English class. *Step 2:* For each of your topics, write a general purpose and a specific purpose. Save your paper.

1. An interesting experience that you have had
2. A subject that you already know about or that you want to know about
3. An idea that you want others to support

21.2b Gathering Information and Ideas

Gather material for a speech as you would for a written report (*pages 411 – 412*). Depending on your topic and your purpose, there are a number of sources that you can use.

For some kinds of speech topics, an important source of information is your own knowledge and experience. For many topics, though, you will have to obtain information from books, articles, and other sources. You might interview someone in person or over the telephone. Radio, television, and films can also be good sources of information.

For some topics, you may have to give background information. Historical facts and descriptions might help your listeners to become more familiar with your subject. You may also need to include examples and explanations.

When you make a statement in a speech, you must be able to support it. Supporting material includes quotations, experts' opinions, survey results, and related facts.

Remember that your listeners cannot stop, as readers can, to look up words that they do not understand. If you use a term that may not be familiar to your listeners, give a definition of that term.

All the information that you use in your speech should be clear and complete. The evidence you give should be accurate, and all information should be directly and clearly related to your topic. Be sure that you have carefully thought through your information and included your own ideas about it.

Assignment 2   Gathering Information   Select one of the speech topics and your specific purpose that you wrote for Assignment 1 on page 521. *Step 1:* List the ideas and information that you already have about your topic. *Step 2:* List the kinds of information you need to gather about the topic. Then list all the sources you can think of that might provide the information you need. *Step 3:* Find the necessary information. Take clear, complete notes (*pages 500–502*). Be sure to write down where you obtained each piece of information. Save your notes.

21.3 Organizing Your Speech

Like a written report, a speech or an oral report should have an introduction, a body, and a conclusion. As you organize your material, make an outline (*pages 417–419*) that includes main headings, subheadings, and specific pieces of information. An outline will help you to present your material clearly. Your listeners will be able to follow your thoughts and to remember what you tell them, because you will present your material in an order that makes sense.

The Body of Your Speech

Most of the important information in your speech will be presented in the body. Therefore, you should organize that part of your speech first. As you begin to work on your outline, keep in mind your audience and your time limit.

The main headings in your outline are the main ideas in your speech. The subheadings are facts, reasons, and other supporting material. The number of main headings depends on your purpose, your audience, and the length of your speech.

There are a number of ways to organize the body of your speech. A few are explained here.

When your topic can be divided into separate parts, you can arrange your main headings in topical order, as in this example.

Three types of gymnastics events are vaulting, uneven bars, and floor exercises.

When your topic involves a set of steps or a series of historical events, you can arrange your headings in chronological order, or time order.

I will talk about the invention of movies, the development of sound movies, and the introduction of color.

When your speech describes a place or tells how objects are located, you can arrange your headings in spatial order.

Here is a good way to lay out a small vegetable garden.

When you are describing a problem and considering solutions, you can arrange your headings so that the first main heading describes the problem. Each of the other main headings describes one of the solutions that you will talk about.

People have suggested different solutions to the problem of raising money for club activities.

The Introduction

When you have decided what to include in the body of your speech and have made an outline, you are ready to write your introduction. The opening sentences of your speech are very important. In your introduction, you have several purposes. Use the following strategies to accomplish them.

Strategies

1. *Get the attention of your listeners.* Open your speech in a strong and interesting way. Make your audience want to listen to you. A question, a quotation, and a startling or funny fact are some of the ways that you can begin a speech.

2. *Make your topic sound interesting.* Show your audience that the topic matters to them and that they will gain something by listening to you.

3. *Tell what you are going to talk about.* Let your listeners know what your limited topic is.

4. *Let your audience know how the speech will be organized.* Your listeners will then know what to expect and be able to follow your speech easily. Give signals (*page 510*) to help your listeners.

The Conclusion

Different kinds of speeches need different kinds of conclusions. If your purpose is to inform, you may end your speech by summing up or reviewing the main points. If your purpose is to persuade, you may end your speech with a call to action or a strong restatement of your opinion. If your purpose is to entertain, you may end your speech with a story or a question.

Your conclusion, like your introduction, should be both strong and interesting. It should also be suitable for your topic, your purpose, and your audience.

Helping Your Audience to Listen

Listening is different from reading. You have to help your audience to follow and understand your speech. Use signals and transitions (*pages 510–512*) to let your listeners know what to listen for, what your main points are, and when you are presenting supporting material.

Remember that listeners, unlike readers, cannot go back to look over something that they did not understand. Explain important points, and summarize your ideas occasionally.

Long, complicated sentences are hard for listeners to understand. Use clear sentences that are long enough to be interesting but short enough to be easily understood. Make your points directly, and do not stray from the outline that you have prepared.

Assignment Organizing Your Speech Use your statement of specific purpose and the notes that you made for Assignments 1 and 2 on pages 521 and 522. *Step 1:* Make an outline to organize your material into main headings, subheadings, and supporting details. *Step 2:* Write an introduction and a conclusion for your five-minute speech. Save your papers.

21.4 Delivering Your Speech

Most speakers feel nervous before going in front of an audience. If you are well prepared, however, you will be less nervous and do a better job.

Preparing to Deliver Your Speech

There are two important ways that you can prepare for delivering a speech. Making note cards and rehearsing will help you to feel more confident and relaxed. These preparations will lead to a smooth and effective presentation that you will be proud to give.

Note Cards.   Giving a memorized speech or reading a speech word for word makes it hard to speak naturally. If you use note cards, you will be able to look at your audience and speak more comfortably.

When making note cards, do not write complete sentences. Write words and phrases that will remind you of your main points. Each card should contain no more than one main point, with its subheadings and supporting details. You may want to write in different colors to separate major points, subheadings, and details.

Besides key words and phrases, write down any material that you need to remember exactly, such as names, dates, numbers, and quotations. Write clearly and do not crowd your notes. You will need to read them easily. Number your note cards so that you can keep them in order.

Rehearsing.   You will feel much less nervous if you spend enough time rehearsing your speech. You will become familiar with what you are going to say and feel comfortable using your note cards.

Rehearse your speech aloud several times, referring to your note cards. Use a tape recorder if one is available. Ask a friend or a relative to listen to your speech and to make suggestions. Practice looking at your audience.

If you get mixed up or forget what you want to say, make changes on your note cards. Rehearse until you think that your speech goes smoothly.

Presenting Your Speech

The way you present your speech affects how well your listeners understand your message.

Speak loudly enough for every person in the room to hear you. Speak more slowly than you would in ordinary conversation, but try to speak in a natural way. Think about what you are saying and let your voice and your facial expressions show your feelings.

Stand straight when you speak, but not stiffly. Like your voice, your posture should be natural and relaxed. Gesture with your hands when it fits what you are saying.

It is important to look directly at the people to whom you are speaking. Look around the room at your listeners, not at the floor or the wall. Make eye contact with members of your audience.

Assignment Delivering Your Speech Use your notes, outline, introduction, and conclusion from the Assignment on page 525. *Step 1:* Prepare note cards for your speech. *Step 2:* Rehearse your speech several times and make any needed improvements in your notes. *Step 3:* Deliver your five-minute speech to your English class.

Unit 22

Library Skills

You can find good books to read and information that you need for class reports in your school library or public library. This unit will help you learn to use library resources efficiently.

22.1 How to Locate Books

Fiction

Books in the fiction section of the library are arranged alphabetically by the last names of the authors. If two or more authors have the same last name, the books are arranged alphabetically by their first names. For example, books by Nathaniel Benchley come before those by Robert Benchley.

All books by the same author are placed alphabetically by title. For example, Nathaniel Benchley's book *Beyond the Mists* would come before his book *Bright Candles*.

The words *A, An,* and *The* are not used when arranging books alphabetically.

Nonfiction

In 1876 a librarian named Melvil Dewey created a simple system for arranging nonfiction books. It is called the Dewey decimal system and is still used by many libraries.

Dewey divided nonfiction into ten subject groups and gave each group a number. The ten groups are numbered from 000 to 999. Every nonfiction book can be placed in one of the ten groups. Note that poetry and plays are also included.

The Dewey Decimal System

000–099 General Works	Includes encyclopedias, almanacs, and newspapers
100–199 Philosophy	Includes philosophy and psychology
200–299 Religion	Includes the Bible and mythology
300–399 Social Sciences	Includes government, economics, law, education, and folklore
400–499 Language	Includes dictionaries, grammar, and foreign languages
500–599 Science	Includes mathematics, physical and biological sciences, and geology
600–699 Technology	Includes agriculture, business, engineering, and medicine
700–799 Fine Arts	Includes art, music, films, photography, and sports
800–899 Literature	Includes plays, essays, and poetry
900–999 History	Includes history, geography, travel, and collective biography

The numbered groups are subdivided to identify specific subjects. For example, 900–999 includes all books about history. Books about United States history are numbered 973. All books about the Civil War in the United States are numbered 973.7. They are arranged alphabetically by author.

You need not learn the Dewey decimal system, for a copy of it is usually posted in the library. However, remembering that books are arranged by this system can make it much easier for you to locate them.

Biography

Books about people are found in a special section marked **Biography.** These books are arranged alphabetically by the last name of the person who is the subject of the biography. For example, a book about John Hancock would come before one about Henry Hudson. Several books about the same person are arranged alphabetically by the last names of the authors.

Books that contain biographies of more than one person are called **collective biographies.** They have a Dewey classification in the 920s.

Assignment 1   Classifying Fiction   On your paper, list the following titles in the order that you would find them in the fiction section of the library.

1. *Sing Down the Moon,* by Scott O'Dell
2. *A Wrinkle in Time,* by Madeline L'Engle
3. *Island of the Blue Dolphins,* by Scott O'Dell
4. *Portrait of Margarita,* by Ruth Arthur
5. *Mystery and More Mystery,* by Robert Arthur
6. *A Tale of Two Cities,* by Charles Dickens

Assignment 2   Classifying Nonfiction   On your paper, write the Dewey class number for each of the following subjects.

> SAMPLE   Native American paintings
> ANSWER   700–799

1. An encyclopedia for young children
2. Poetry
3. Engineering
4. Music in the nineteenth century
5. An English-Chinese dictionary

CURRICULUM RESOURCES CENTER
R. I. COLLEGE · MANN HALL
600 MT. PLEASANT AVE.
PROVIDENCE, R.I. 02908

22.2

The Card Catalog

Assignment 3 Classifying Biography On your paper, list the following titles in the order that you would find them in the Biography section of the library.

1. *The Diary of Nina Kosterina,* by Nina Kosterina
2. *Robert Frost,* by Norman Richards
3. *Genghis Khan,* by Robert N. Webb
4. *Langston Hughes: A Biography,* by Milton Meltzer
5. *Teacher of the Blind: Samuel Gridley Howe,* by K. Wilkie
6. *Invincible Louisa,* by C. Meigs (about Louisa M. Alcott)

22.2 The Card Catalog

The **card catalog** is a set of drawers containing three-by-five-inch cards with information about all the books in the library. The drawers are labeled in alphabetical order.

Cards for nonfiction titles have a call number in the top-left corner of each card. Cards for fiction books do not have call numbers. The letters FIC or the author's initials in the top left corner show that a title is fiction. To find a book of fiction, you would look by letter according to the author's last name.

Every book in a library has an author card and a title card. A nonfiction book has a subject card as well. Each card tells you the author's name, the title of the book, the publisher, and the year in which the book was published. Cards for nonfiction books usually include the number of pages. Any illustrations, maps, and biographies can also be noted on the card. Some cards have brief summaries of the books.

Author Cards. An **author card** is filed alphabetically by the author's last name. The name appears beside the call number or the letters *FIC*. Each book by the same author has a separate card. Author cards are helpful when you want to know what books by an author are found in your library.

Author Card

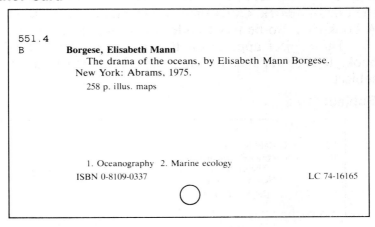

551.4
B   **Borgese, Elisabeth Mann**
               The drama of the oceans, by Elisabeth Mann Borgese.
           New York: Abrams, 1975.
               258 p. illus. maps

               1. Oceanography   2. Marine ecology
           ISBN 0-8109-0337   LC 74-16165

Title Cards. The **title card** is filed alphabetically by title. The title is given beside the call number (or FIC) above the author's name. Title cards are especially helpful when you do not know the name of a book's author.

Subject Cards. A **subject card** is used to locate books about a certain subject. Subject cards are placed alphabeti-

Title Card

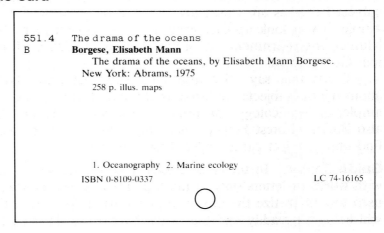

551.4   The drama of the oceans
B   **Borgese, Elisabeth Mann**
               The drama of the oceans, by Elisabeth Mann Borgese.
           New York: Abrams, 1975
               258 p. illus. maps

               1. Oceanography   2. Marine ecology
           ISBN 0-8109-0337   LC 74-16165

cally by the subject in the card catalog. Each subject card lists the title of a book. Often there are several cards for a subject. A book can also be listed under more than one subject.

The subject appears on the first line. The title of the book, the author's name, and the call number follow the subject.

Subject Card

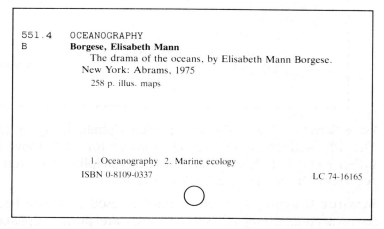

```
551.4    OCEANOGRAPHY
B          Borgese, Elisabeth Mann
                 The drama of the oceans, by Elisabeth Mann Borgese.
           New York: Abrams, 1975
               258 p. illus. maps




               1. Oceanography  2. Marine ecology
           ISBN 0-8109-0337                        LC 74-16165
```

Cross-Reference Cards. Cards that refer you to other subject headings are called **cross-reference cards.** For example, if you look up City Manager, the card may say "See Municipal Government." You then look under *M* for Municipal Government.

Cards that say "See also" tell you that other books about related subjects are listed under other headings. For example, under Ecology you might find a card that says "See also Botany, Forest Ecology, Seashore Ecology." You would find other subject cards under these headings.

Guide Cards. In the card catalog, you will see some cards with words or letters only at the top. These **guide cards** are used to alphabetize the file or to give other information that will help you readily find the cards that you are looking for.

Assignment   Card Catalog   On your paper, list the author, title, and the call number for a book on each of the following subjects. Use the card catalog in your library.

1. A book about French cooking
2. A book about Australia
3. *The Pushcart War*
4. A book of short stories about dogs
5. A book about the life of Edmund Hillary
6. A book by Robert Louis Stevenson

22.3 General Reference Books

Dictionaries

Dictionaries contain information in addition to word meanings. They give pronunciations, spellings, usage notes, word origins, and many other facts. Some dictionaries also include slang words, foreign words, and the names of important people and places.

A desk dictionary is **abridged.** It is smaller and contains fewer words than the **unabridged** dictionary, which has thousands of pages and is usually kept in a library.

Dictionaries are organized alphabetically. The guide words at the top of each page show you the first word and the last word on the page. Use these guide words to help you locate words quickly.

Many libraries also contain special dictionaries of synonyms, slang, foreign languages, sports, and music.

Assignment   Dictionaries   On your paper, write the answers to the following questions. Use an abridged or unabridged dictionary to find the information.

1. Find *domain*. What are the guide words for the page?
2. What are two meanings for *Jacob's ladder*?

3. Find another spelling and two pronunciations for *doggerel*.
4. What are the plurals for *rhombus*?
5. Use each meaning for *mammoth* in a sentence.
6. Write the words for the following abbreviations:
   a. T.V.A.   b. pd.   c. D.V.M.   d. Cdr.   e. dict.

Encyclopedias

An **encyclopedia** is a set of reference books that contains information on hundreds of subjects. The articles are arranged in alphabetical order and include illustrations, charts, maps, and diagrams.

The index is a guide that helps you to find topics in the encyclopedia. It lists the volume and page number for each main topic and all related topics. The index may be contained in a separate volume, or within each volume.

These encyclopedias can be found in most libraries:

Compton's Encyclopedia and Fact Index
The Encyclopedia Americana
The New Encyclopoedia Britannica
The World Book Encyclopedia

Assignment Encyclopedias On your paper, write the answer to each of the following questions. Use a current encyclopedia to find the answers. Use the index for the encyclopedia when necessary.

1. The Roman god Jupiter is the same as which Greek god?
2. Who invented the elevator? When?
3. How is quartz used?
4. How long does it take Halley's comet to go around the sun?
5. Who was Enrico Caruso?
6. What are natural resources?

Almanacs and Yearbooks

Almanacs and **yearbooks** are published annually. They contain current facts on topics such as government, sports, world events, and space exploration. Use the index to find topics.

The following are frequently used almanacs:

The World Almanac and Book of Facts
The Information Please Almanac
Guinness Book of World Records
The Hammond Almanac of a Million Facts, Records, Forecasts

Assignment   Almanacs   On your paper, write the answers to the following questions. Use a current almanac to find the answers.

1. What is the principal language of Brazil?
2. Which planet has the most satellites?
3. What is the population of Annapolis, Maryland?
4. What baseball team won the National League pennant in 1960?
5. What country is the smallest in square miles?

Atlases and Gazetteers

An **atlas** is a collection of maps and related geographical information. Some maps show information such as natural resources or climate. Charts, tables, and diagrams are also used in an atlas to give data about geographical subjects.

Atlases commonly found in libraries include:

Ambassador World Atlas
World Book Atlas
Rand McNally Cosmopolitan World Atlas
National Geographic Atlas of the World

A **gazetteer** is a dictionary of geographical names with a pronunciation, location, and brief summary of facts for each entry. *Webster's Geographical Dictionary* is one such book. Many atlases include gazetteers.

Assignment Atlases and Gazetteers On your paper, write the answers to the following questions. Use a current atlas or gazetteer to find the information.

1. In what part of Australia do most of its citizens live?
2. What is the area of Denmark in square miles?
3. What is the meaning of *maa*? What language is it from?
4. In which state of the United States is Falls Church?
5. What is the largest city in Africa?
6. Look at a land-use map for Minnesota. What does it show?

22.4 Biographical Reference Books

References that are published every month or every year are good sources to consult when you need information about living persons. *Current Biography,* a monthly publication, tells about people in the news. *The Current Biography Yearbook* is a collection of a year's issues. Other useful books describing important people include *Who's Who in America, Who's Who in the World, Who's Who Among Black Americans,* and *Who's Who of American Women.*

Assignment Biographical References On your paper, write two or three sentences about each of the following people. Use biographical reference books to obtain the information.

1. I. M. Pei
2. Leontyne Price
3. Sandra Day O'Connor
4. Andrew Young
5. Andrew Wyeth
6. Tenley Albright

22.5 The *Readers' Guide to Periodical Literature*

Magazines are a good source of up-to-date information about topics such as government, science, and sports. The *Readers' Guide to Periodical Literature* is an index of articles from almost two hundred magazines. Articles are listed alphabetically by subject and by author's name.

The subject and author entries are in dark type and capital letters. Each entry includes the title, the author's name,

A Portion of a *Readers' Guide* Page

Subject entry — **MOUNT LOGAN climbs.** See Mountaineering

MOUNT MCKINLEY National Park

Article title — Disneyland North. M. Frome. il Nat Parks & Con Mag 54:4-6 F '80

Author — Skiing a distant circle. G. Rowell. il Sierra 65: 23-5+ Ja/F '80

MOUNT RAINIER climbs. See Mountaineering

MOUNT ST HELENS (volcano). Washington (state) See Volcanoes

MOUNT SHASTA. See Shasta, Mount

MOUNT VERNON, N.Y.
Education

"See" reference — *See* Education–New York (state)

MOUNT VESUVIUS. See Vesuvius

MOUNT WASHINGTON. See Washington, Mount

MOUNT WILSON Observatory. See Astronomical observatories

Author entry — **MOUNTAIN, David C.**
Changes in endolymphatic potential and crossed olivocochlear bundle stimulation alter cochlear

Magazine title — mechanics. bibl f il Science 210:71-2 O 3 '80

MOUNTAIN climbing. See Mountaineering

MOUNTAIN ecology
Highlands and islands: ecosystems in danger. F.

Volume and page numbers — Di Castri and G. Glaser. il UNESCO Courier 33:6-11 Ap '80

Date of issue — Life on a rock ledge [Vermont's Wheeler Mountain] W.H. Amos. il Nat Geog 158:558-66 O '80

MOUNTAIN flying. See Aviation-Mountain flying

MOUNTAIN goat hunting. See Rocky Mountain goat hunting

MOUNTAIN gorillas. See Gorillas

MOUNTAIN lions. See Pumas

MOUNTAIN sheep
Bighorns are back! [national parks] H. E.

Illustration — McCutchen. il Nat Parks & Con Mag 54:12-15 S '80

the name of the magazine, the volume number, the pages on which the article appears, and the date of the magazine. Whether the article contains illustrations, maps, and photos is also indicated.

Assignment 1 *Readers' Guide* In the *Readers' Guide,* find entries on two of the following subjects. On your paper, copy the complete entry for both articles.

1. cats
2. water pollution
3. a popular movie
4. an opera singer
5. a scientific discovery
6. your favorite sport

Assignment 2 **Reference Books** On your paper, indicate which of the following references you would use to find each piece of information.

Card catalog
Dictionary
Encyclopedia

Almanac or yearbook
Atlas or gazetteer

Readers' Guide
Current Biography

1. The best route from your community to Mexico
2. The abbreviation for *ante meridiem*
3. A magazine article about hot air balloons
4. The life of a popular country singer
5. The eating habits of koala bears
6. A recent winner of the Westminster Dog Show

Unit 23

Test-Taking Skills

23.1 Preparing for a Test

The best way to perform well on a test is to be well prepared. This unit will help you learn how to prepare for a test. You will also learn skills to help you answer specific kinds of test questions.

Place and Time for Studying. Find a quiet, comfortable place to study for a test. Choose a spot where you will not be bothered by others. Remember that you will study better if you do not watch television or listen to music.

Set aside a special time to study. The best time is one when you are feeling rested and alert, and when you are least likely to be interrupted. Plan your time so that you have periods of study with short breaks between them. You should probably not study for more than half an hour at a time without a break.

A study kit that you can keep in or take to your study place is helpful. It should contain all the tools that you are likely to need for studying: paper, pencils, pens, ruler, drawing compass. You may also want to include a clipboard and a dictionary. With this kit available, you will not have to waste time looking for these items.

Emphasis of Studying. Before a test, your teacher may suggest that you review certain pages or chapters in your textbook. Pay special attention to those pages or chapters when you study. You should also carefully review all unit or chapter summaries. Be sure that you understand and can explain all words and phrases in boldface or italic type.

In addition to studying your textbook, you should look over your class notes and assignment sheets. The points that are covered in assignments and class notes are often important to know for a test.

Active Studying.   To prepare well for a test, you should do more than just read over the material. Instead, you should actively study the test material as thoroughly and effectively as you can. For example, before you begin to study, spend a few minutes thinking about the material that the test will cover. What facts and concepts do you remember from class discussions and from homework assignments? How do they relate to each other and to the general subject? Taking a few minutes to organize your thoughts is the first step in active studying.

Now read over your textbooks, your notes, and your assignments. As you study, think of questions that might be asked on the test and jot them down. After you finish reviewing, ask yourself the questions that you have written. Look back to check any answers that you are not sure of. Study your questions until you can recite all the answers from memory.

On the day of the test, you can use the following strategies to help you perform well.

Strategies

1. *Bring with you all the materials that you will need,* such as pens, pencils, paper, and a ruler.

2. *Listen well to oral instructions, and read all directions carefully.* A single word in a test item or set of directions can make a big difference. "Answer Parts A *and* B" is not the same as "Answer Part A *or* B."

3. *Follow directions exactly.* If you are asked to give three names, do not waste time giving more than three.

4. *Keep track of time.* Allow time for each question.

5. *Come to school rested and alert* on the day of the test. A good night's sleep and a good breakfast will help you to feel your best and to do your best.

6. *Relax.* Most people feel nervous before a test, but good preparation will help you to be confident.

Assignment   Preparing for a Test   The following sentences tell how a student might prepare for a test. On your paper, write *Good study habit* or *Poor study habit* next to the number of each statement.

1. Study at the same time every day.
2. Study in a quiet, comfortable place.
3. Study for long periods of time without taking a break.
4. Play soft music to help you relax.
5. Jot down questions that you think might be on the test.
6. Pay special attention to terms in boldface or italic type in your textbook.
7. Study your class notes and assignment sheets, as well as your textbook.
8. Stay up late studying the night before the test.
9. Skip breakfast on the day of the test so that you will have more time to study.
10. Skim directions in order to save as much time as possible for answering the test questions.

23.2 Taking a Test

The types of questions that you may have to answer on tests are objective, short answer, and paragraph. Your answer to an objective question may be a single word or a phrase. For a short-answer question, you will fill in one or more blanks, or you will write one or two sentences. Your answer to a paragraph question will consist of one or more paragraphs.

Objective Questions

The three types of objective questions are true-false, multiple choice, and matching. You will use different tactics to answer each of these three types of test questions.

True-False Statements. A true-false test consists of a set of statements. You must indicate if each statement is true or false. Here is an example of a true-false statement that might appear on a test:

> It usually snows during each month of the year in the United States.

Use the following strategies when taking true-false tests.

Strategies

1. *Read every word carefully.* A single word can change the meaning of a statement.

2. *Look for words that mean there are no exceptions.* They include *only, all, always, no,* and *never.*

3. *Look for words that mean that the statement can be true even if there are exceptions to it.* These words include *usually, most, many, some, sometimes,* and *may.*

4. *Study all key words* before you decide on your answer.

5. *Study all parts of the statement.* If any part of the statement is untrue, the whole statement is false.

Look again at the example of a true-false item. Notice the word *usually*. This word means that the statement can still be true even if there is a month with no snow. Because it snows in Alaska every month, the statement is true.

Multiple-Choice Questions.   A multiple-choice question includes several possible answers. You must choose the one that is correct. Here is an example:

Which one of the following place names comes from a Native American language?

a. Fairfield   c. Mississippi
b. Lafayette   d. San Jose

Use the following strategies when you answer multiple-choice questions.

Strategies

1. *Read the question carefully.*

2. *Read all of the choices before you choose an answer.*

3. *Eliminate the choices that you know are wrong.* Then decide which of the answers that are left is the best one.

4. *Do not make wild guesses.*

Now look again at the multiple-choice example. If you are not sure of the answer, you can try to eliminate some of the choices. *Fairfield* is formed from two common English words. There are two clues that show *San Jose* is Spanish. *San* is the Spanish word for *saint,* and *Jose* is the Spanish name for Joseph. You may also know that *Lafayette* was the name of a French general who fought in the American Revolution. The only choice left is *Mississippi,* which is correct.

Matching Questions.   A matching test item consists of two sets of information. You must match each item in the first set with an item in the second. The two lists may not always contain the same number of items. There may be items in one set that you do not use or items that are used more than once. Here is an example of a matching test item:

Match the colors in the right column with the terms in the left column. You will not use one of the colors.

_?_	1. canary	a.	brown
_?_	2. tomato	b.	green
_?_	3. emerald	c.	purple
_?_	4. lilac	d.	red
		e.	yellow

Use these strategies to answer matching questions.

Strategies

1. *Read the directions carefully.* There may be items that you will not use or that you will use more than once.

2. *Read both sets of information before writing an answer.* Try to see how the items in the two sets are related.

3. *Match first the items of which you are sure.*

4. *Try to find clues in the items that are left.* Suppose that on a test, you have not been able to match the term *inventor of dynamite.* If the choices that remain are *Alfred Nobel* and *Stockholm,* you know that *Alfred Nobel* is the correct choice. The *inventor* of something must be a person, not a place.

Look again at the example matching question. You should have no difficulty matching some of the items. If you know that a canary is yellow and that an emerald is green, you can match those items. If you also know that a tomato is red, you can match these.

Checking off the three colors that you have used, you see that only brown and purple remain. You may know that a lilac is a kind of flower that is either white or purple. Because the lilacs are not brown, *purple* is the correct answer.

Assignment 1   Objective Questions   On your paper, write *True* for each true statement and *False* for each false statement.

1. Three types of objective questions are true-false, multiple choice, and matching.
2. If any part of a statement is true, then the whole statement is true.
3. If any part of a statement is false, then the whole statement is false.
4. You can sometimes find the answer to a multiple-choice question by eliminating answers that you know are wrong.
5. In matching questions, you should always use every item.

Assignment 2   Objective Questions   On your paper, write the answers to the questions that follow the true-false statement.

Sedimentary rocks can contain plant and animal fossils.

1. What word in the statement means that there can be exceptions? What are other key words?
2. Is it necessary to know the meaning of the word *fossils* in order to answer this question? Explain.
3. If you know that limestone, a sedimentary rock, often contains fossil shells, can you therefore say that the statement is true? Explain.

Assignment 3   Objective Questions   On your paper, write the answers to the questions that follow the multiple-choice question. Do not answer the multiple-choice question itself.

What kind of punctuation is placed at the end of a sentence to make it stand out for special attention?

a. apostrophe   c. exclamation point
b. colon   d. question mark

1. Is it necessary to read the answer choices before you decide on the correct one? Why or why not?

2. If you know that one or more of the choices is never placed at the end of a sentence, can you eliminate that answer or those answers? Explain.

3. If you can only eliminate two of the choices, explain what you should do next.

Assignment 4   Objective Questions   On your paper, write the answers to the questions that follow the matching question. Do not answer the matching question itself.

   __?__ 1. spaghetti   a. German
   __?__ 2. chili con carne   b. French
   __?__ 3. bouillon   c. Spanish
   __?__ 4. sauerkraut   d. Russian
                                                e. Italian

1. What do the terms in the first column have in common?

2. What do the terms in the second column have in common?

3. What is the next step that you should take after reading all the items in both columns?

Short-Answer Questions

Like objective questions, short-answer questions test your recall of facts. However, you have to write the answers to short-answer questions yourself.

Some short-answer items, called fill-in-the-blank, are sentences containing one or more blanks for which you must supply the missing word or words. Here is an example:

If the subject of a sentence is plural, the verb in the sentence must be __?__.

Use the following strategies when answering fill-in-the-blank questions.

Strategies

1. *Read the sentence carefully.* Some of the words will give you clues about the answer.

2. *Try to write an answer for every blank.* Tell what you know. For example, if you cannot remember the term *dicotyledon,* write *plant with two seed leaves.*

3. *Write neatly.* You will not receive credit if your answer cannot be read.

Look again at the fill-in-the-blank example. The sentence suggests that a plural subject needs a specific kind of verb. If you remember that the subject and verb must agree in number, you can determine that the correct answer is *plural.*

Other short-answer questions ask you to provide certain information, usually in one or two sentences. Here is an example:

In what century and by whom was the telephone invented?

Use the following strategies when you answer short-answer questions that require sentence answers.

Strategies

1. *Read the question carefully.* Look for key words that give you clues about the answer. Note also whether you need to supply more than one fact.

2. *Give the best answer that you can.* Write what you know, even if you are not sure that your answer is correct.

3. *Write your answer in complete sentences,* unless the directions tell you not to. Use the words of the question in your answer. For example, if you are asked "What was Mark Twain's real name?" begin your answer "Mark Twain's real name was. . . ."

Look again at the example of the short-answer question on page 548. Notice that it requires two facts for a complete answer: the century when the telephone was invented, and the name of the inventor. You know that there were no telephones in George Washington's time. Therefore, they must have been invented in the nineteenth or twentieth century. If you are not sure which answer is correct, choose the one that seems best.

The inventor's name is still associated with telephone companies today. The correct answer is "The telephone was invented in the nineteenth century by Alexander Graham Bell."

Paragraph Questions

Paragraph questions may require both recall of specific information and general knowledge of a subject. You will usually be asked to write one or more paragraphs in which you *describe* by giving details or *explain* by giving reasons. Look at the following examples.

Explain President Roosevelt's Good Neighbor Policy.
Describe the process through which a bill becomes law.

Use the following strategies when answering paragraph questions.

Strategies

1. *Read the directions carefully and make sure that you understand what you are to do.* Sometimes you may be given a choice of questions to answer. If so, read all of the questions before you choose.

2. *Allot the time that you will spend on each question according to the number of points that it is worth.* You should spend more time on a question worth twenty-five points than on one worth fifteen. Sometimes all questions have equal value. Then, apportion your time according to how detailed your answer must be.

3. *Start with the question that you know the most about.*

4. *Jot down on scratch paper any names, dates, facts, or formulas required in your answer,* and arrange them in appropriate order or in outline form. For example, if you were to describe the process through which a bill becomes law, you might number your scratch paper from 1 to 10, and, beside each number, make brief notes on what happens at that step. You could also use your notes to make sure that you have not left out a step.

5. *Be specific in your answer, but do not pad it with unrelated details.*

6. *Reread your answer to make sure that you have made no errors in grammar, usage, spelling, or punctuation.*

Assignment 5 Short-Answer Questions On your paper, write answers to the questions that follow the fill-in-the-blank test item.

The Rio Grande forms part of the border between the ___?___ and ___?___ .

1. What are the key words in the sentence?
2. Why is the word *the* before the first blank a clue?
3. If you know that *rio* is a Spanish word for *river,* could this help you to answer the question? Explain.

4. If you know what belongs in one blank, should you guess an answer for the other blank? Explain.

Assignment 6   Short-Answer Questions   On your paper, write the answers to the questions that follow the short-answer item. Do not answer the short-answer question itself.

What states are part of the Corn Belt in the United States?

1. How do you know that you must supply more than one answer to this question?
2. If you remember the name of only one state that is part of the Corn Belt, what should you do?

Assignment 7   Paragraph Questions   In one of your textbooks, find a question that requires an answer of one or more paragraphs. On your paper, answer the question, using the strategies that you learned on pages 549–550.

Index

Abbreviations: capitalizing, 199, 200, 204–205; periods after, 208; Postal Service, 205, 446, 447, 451, 452

Abridged (desk) dictionary, 534

Action verbs: defined, 15; direct objects after, 101–102; distinguishing from linking verbs, 18

Adjective phrases: defined, 71; placement of, 72

Adjectives: answering *Which? What kind? How many?*, 29–30; articles, 30; commas with, 30, 31; comparison of, 171–172; defined, 29; demonstrative pronouns used as, 36; diagraming, 115; distinguishing from adverbs, 43–44; ending in *-ly*, 43; indefinite pronouns used as, 36; interrogative pronouns used as, 36; after linking verbs, 31, 105; nouns used as, 34–35; placement of, 31–32, 329; possessive pronouns used as, 36, 168; prepositional phrases used as, 71–72; proper, 33

Adjective suffixes, 484

Adverb phrases: defined, 74; placement of, 75

Adverbs: answering *How? When? Where? How often? To what extent or degree?*, 38; comparison of, 175; defined, 38; diagraming, 115; distinguishing from adjectives, 43–44; distinguishing from prepositions, 55; modifying adjectives, 41; modifying adverbs, 42; modifying verbs, 38, 39–40; *not, never,* 39; placement of, 40, 41, 329; prepositional phrases used as, 74–75

Adverb suffixes, 484

Agreement of pronouns and antecedents: antecedents joined by *and,* 159–160; antecedents joined by *or, nor,* 160; collective nouns as antecedents, 161; in gender, 161–162; indefinite pronouns as antecedents, 160–161; in number, 159–161; in person, 163–164; plural antecedents, 159; singular antecedents, 159

Agreement of subjects and verbs: auxiliary verbs, 146; collective nouns, 154–155; compound subjects, 150–152; after *Here, There,* 149; indefinite pronouns, 152–154; interrupting phrases, 148; *I, you,* 147; nouns ending in *-s,* 155; plural subjects, 146; in questions, 149; singular subjects, 146; titles, 156; verb phrases, 146; words of amounts and time, 156–157

Almanacs, 536

Alphabetical order: in card catalog, 531–533; in dictionary, 489, 533; in encyclopedias, 535; in library, 530; in *Readers' Guide to Periodical Literature,* 538

Antecedent: agreement of pronouns with, 158–164; defined, 9, 158

Apostrophe: in contractions, 220; to form plural of letters, numbers, etc., 220; to show possession, 34–35, 219–220

Articles: defined, 30; in titles, 200, 202

Atlases, 536

Audience: in speaking, 517–518, 520–521, 525; in writing, 249, 250, 251, 252, 269–270

Author card, 531

Autobiography: book reports about, 434–435; defined, 434

Auxiliary (helping) verbs: agreement with subjects, 146; *be* as, 20, 131, 132, 134, 145; defined, 19; *do* as, 20, 145; *have* as, 20, 132, 134, 140, 141, 145; list, 20; singular and plural forms, 145;

in verb phrases, 19–21, 146; *will,*
shall as, 142

Be: as auxiliary verb, 20, 131, 132,
134; as linking verb, 17, 20
Biographical reference books, 537
Biography: book reports about,
434–435; defined, 434; locating
in library, 530
Body: of business letter, 451; of
report, 421; of social letter, 446;
of speech, 523–524
Book reports, 430–435
Business letters: block style, 452;
body, 451; complimentary close,
452; envelope address, 452;
folding and inserting, 452–453;
heading, 451; inside address,
451; modified block style, 452;
order letter, 457–458; Postal
Service abbreviations in,
451–452; request letter, 455–456;
salutation, 451; signature, 452;
strategies for writing, 454, 456,
458

Call number, 533
Capitalization: of the abbreviations
A.D., B.C., A.M., P.M., 204; of
abbreviations in titles of persons,
199, 200; of compass points,
201; of family-relationship
words, 199; of first word of
direct quotation, 197; of first
word of line in poem, 198; of
first word of sentence, 197; of
initials, 199; of interrupted
quotation, 197; of languages,
201; of names of days, months,
201; of names of gods of
mythology, 200; of names of
heavenly bodies, 201; of names
of historical events, periods,
awards, documents, 202; of
names of holidays, special days,
special events, 201; of names of
organizations, 202; of names of
people, 199; of names of ships,
trains, planes, etc., 203; of

names of structures, 202; of new
sentence in quotation, 198; of
personal and official titles,
199–200; of place names, 200; of
Postal Service abbreviations,
204–205; of the pronoun *I,* 204;
of proper adjectives, 33; of
proper nouns, 4–5, 199–203; of
school subjects, 202; of titles of
books, movies, etc., 202; of trade
names, 203; of words naming
races, tribes, nationalities, 201
Capital letters, in outline, 418
Card catalog, 409, 531–533
Case. *See* Pronoun case.
Characters: describing, in book
reports, 431; in narratives, 380,
382, 388, 391
Charts, as study aid, 494
Chronological order: defined, 297;
in explanations, 342, 348, 349; in
narratives, 380, 383, 394–396;
revising for, 314
Closing. *See* Complimentary close.
Collective nouns: agreement of
verbs with, 154–155; as antecedents, 161; defined, 6, 154; list,
6
Colon, 215–216, 451–454
Comma: with adjectives, 30, 31; to
avoid confusion, 212; after
closing of letter, 213, 446, 452,
454; before coordinating conjunction, 107, 212; with dates
and addresses, 213; with direct
address, 213; after interjections,
60, 211; after introductory
expressions, 211–212; after prepositional phrases, 211; with
prepositional phrases in a series,
211; and quotation marks, 218;
in run-on sentence, 111; after
salutation of social letter, 213,
446; to separate sentence parts,
212–213; in a series, 210–211;
with title or degree, 213; after
Yes, No, 211
Common nouns: defined, 4
Comparative degree: of adjectives,
171, 172; of adverbs, 175;
defined, 171

Comparison: of adjectives, 171–172; of adverbs, 175; comparative degree, 171, 172, 175; degrees of, 171, 175; double, 177; with -*er*, -*est*, 171–172, 175; irregular, list, 172, 175; with *less, least*, 172, 175; with *more, most*, 172, 175; positive degree, 171, 172, 175; superlative degree, 171, 172, 175

Complements: after action verbs, 101–102; in complete predicates, 101–102, 103–105; compound, 102, 104, 105; defined, 101; diagraming, 117–118; direct objects, 101–102, 166; kinds, 101–102, 103–105; after linking verbs, 103–104, 105; predicate adjectives, 105; predicate nominatives, 103–104, 165; subject, 103–105

Complete predicate: defined, 96

Complete sentence: defined, 109; in paragraphs, 289, 294; writing, 109–112

Complete subject: defined, 95

Complimentary close: in business letter, 452; in social letter, 213, 446

Compound complements, 102, 104, 105

Compound direct objects: defined, 102; diagraming, 121

Compound nouns: defined, 5; hyphenating, 5–6, 222; spelling plurals, 471–472

Compound numbers, hyphens with, 223

Compound predicate: combining sentences by using, 318–319; defined, 92; diagraming, 120

Compound predicate adjectives: defined, 105; diagraming, 121

Compound predicate nominatives: defined, 104; diagraming, 121

Compound prepositions: defined, 52; list, 52

Compound sentence: combining simple sentences into, 320–321; coordinating conjunction in, 107, 212; defined, 107; diagram-

ing, 122; punctuating, 107, 212, 214–215; semicolon in, 107, 214

Compound subject: agreement of verb with, 150–152; combining sentences by using, 316–317; defined, 91, 150; diagraming, 119; pronouns in, 166

Conciseness, revising for, 325–328

Concluding paragraph: in book reports, 431; in reports, 422

Concluding sentence: defined, 280; in descriptions, 367; writing, 301–302

Conclusion, of speech, 525

Conjugation, of verbs, 138–139

Conjunctions: connecting groups of words, 58–59; connecting individual words, 57; coordinating, 57, 58–59, 91, 92, 107, 212; defined, 57; in titles, 200, 202

Connotation, 487–488

Context clues, 481

Contractions, apostrophe in, 220

Coordinating conjunctions: comma before, 107, 212; in compound predicates, 92, 318; in compound sentences, 107, 212, 320; in compound subjects, 91, 317; defined, 57

Coordination, revising sentences by, 316–321

Cross-reference card, 533

Dash, 224

Declarative sentence: defined, 85; diagraming, 114; placement of subject and predicate in, 98; punctuating, 85, 207

Definite article, defined, 30

Definitions, in dictionary, 490

Demonstrative pronouns: as adjectives, list, 36; defined, 13

Denotation, 487–488

Describing, 358–379. *See also* Descriptions.

Descriptions: concluding sentences in, 367; descriptive words in, 363–364, 370–371; of persons, 369–371; of places, 367–368; sensory details in, 359–361, 367,

Homographs, 491
Homophones, 476–477
Hyphen, 222–223

Illustrations, as study aid, 493–494
Imperative sentence: complete predicate in, 98; defined, 85; diagraming, 114; punctuating, 85–86, 208, 209; subject understood, 86, 99
Indefinite articles: defined, 30
Indefinite pronouns: as adjectives, list, 36; agreement of verbs with, 152–154; as antecedents, 160–161; defined, 13; list, 13, 153, 160; plural, 153, 160; singular, 153, 160; singular or plural, 153–154, 160–161; as subjects, 152–154
Index: for encyclopedia, 435; as study aid, 493
Indirect quotation: defined, 217
Infinitive: defined, 131
Information, locating, 493
Initials: capitalizing, 199; period after, 208
Inside address, in business letter, 451
Interest inventory, prewriting, 241
Interjections: comma after, 60, 211; defined, 60; exclamation point after, 60, 209; list, 60–61
Interrogative pronouns: as adjectives, list, 36; care of, 168–169; defined, 13
Interrogative sentence: defined, 85; diagraming, 114; placement of subject and predicate in, 98–99; punctuating, 85, 209
Introduction, to speech, 524
Introductory expressions, comma after, 211–212
Introductory paragraph: in book report, 431, 434, 435; in report, 421
Irregular comparisons, 172, 175
Irregular plurals, 471
Irregular verbs: defined, 134; principal parts of, 134–136
Italics, 220, 225

Letters. *See* Business letters, Social letters.
Library skills, 528–539
Linking verbs: adjective after, 31, 105; defined, 17; distinguishing from action verbs, 18; forms of *be* as, 17, 20; lists, 17; pronouns after, 17, 103–104, 165; subject complements after, 103–104, 105
Listening, 504–515: active, 504–505; conversational, 504–505; courteous, 514–515; critical, 504–505; for information, 504–505; for main ideas, 512–513; for method of organization, 509–510; passive, 505; questions before, 506–507; responsive, 514–515; setting for, 505–506; for signals and transitions, 510–512; for speaker's purpose, 508–509; strategies for, 506; for supporting details, 513–514
Lists, prewriting, 245–246

Main headings, in outline, 418
Main verb: *be, do, have* as, 20; defined, 19
Manuscript form: guidelines for, 229–230; for report, 426–428
Maps, as study aid, 494
Masculine pronouns, 11, 162
Matching questions, 544–546
Mechanics: rules of, 196–235
Misplaced modifiers, 178–179
Modifiers: adjectives, 29–36; adverbs, 38–44; correct use of, 171–179, 364; diagraming, 115; expanding sentences with, 266; misplaced, 178–179; placement of, 178–179; prepositional phrases, 69–75
Multiple-choice questions, 544

Narrating, 380–405. *See also* Narratives.
Narratives: actions of, 383–384, 392, 394–396; characters in, 380,

382, 388, 391; choosing topic for, 381–382; chronological order in, 380, 383, 394–396; ending of, 396–397; high point in, 380, 383, 384, 396; planning, 381–384; prewriting notes for, 383–384; setting in, 381, 382, 388; situation in, 383, 384, 389; strategies for beginning, 388; using dialogue in, 391–392

Neuter pronouns, 11, 162

Nominative case, 165

Nonfiction: book reports about, 434–435; locating in library, 528–530

Note cards: for reports, 414–416; for speeches, 526

Notes, prewriting, 240, 241, 242–243, 245, 246–247, 252

Note taking: for book report, 431, 434, 435; from encyclopedias, 501–502; for report, 414–416; strategies for, 500, 513; from textbooks, 500

Nouns: as adjectives, 34–35; collective, 6; common, 4–5; compound, 5–6, 222, 471–472; defined, 3; ending in *s,* agreement of verbs with, 155; after linking verbs, 103–104; plural, 469–472; possessive, 34–35, 219–220; proper, 4–5, 199–203, 470; using concrete, 262; using specific, 363

Noun suffixes, 483

Number: agreement of pronouns and antecedents in, 159–161; agreement of subjects and verbs in, 144–147; of auxiliary verbs, 145; defined, 144; determining, 150–157; of indefinite pronouns, 152–154, 160–161; of nouns, 144; of personal pronouns, 11, 12, 144; plural, defined, 144; singular, defined, 144; of subjects, 146; of verbs, 145

Numbers, in writing: with *and,* 227; at beginning of sentence, 227; compound, 223; in dates, street numbers, room numbers, etc., 227; in expressions of time, 227; italics used for, 225

Objective case, 165, 166

Objective tests, 543–546

Objects: direct, 101–102, 117, 121, 166; of prepositions, 54, 69, 102, 166

Order letter, 457–458

Organization: of paragraphs, 296–298; revising, 314

Outlining, 417–419

Paragraph questions, 549–550

Paragraphs, 278–309: chronological order in, 297; concluding sentence, 280, 301–302; defined, 279; developing, 293–299; indenting, 217, 230; limiting topic for, 283–284; listing and choosing details for, 285–286, 290–291, 294; planning, 283–286; revising, 311–315; selecting topic for, 283; to show change of speaker, 217; spatial order in, 297; supporting sentences, 279–280, 293–295, 296–298; topic sentence, 279, 280, 288–291; transitional words and phrases in, 297–298; unity in, 280–281, 294

Part-of-speech labels, in dictionary, 490

Parts of speech, 2–21, 28–44, 50–61. *See also* Adjectives, Adverbs, Conjunctions, Interjections, Nouns, Prepositions, Pronouns, Verbs.

Past perfect tense, 141

Past tense, 141

Period, 85, 207–208

Personal pronouns: agreement with antecedent, 158–164; case, 165–168; chart, 11–12; defined, 10; feminine, 11, 162; gender, 11, 161–162; masculine, 11, 162; neuter, 11, 162; number, 11, 12, 159–161; person, 10, 12, 163–164; plural, 11, 12, 159; possessive, 11–12, 36, 167, 168, 220; singular, 11, 12, 159

Person, of pronoun: agreement with antecedent in, 163–164;

Acknowledgments (continued)

From "The Wishing Well" by Phillip Bonosky. Reprinted by permission of the author.   From *When the Legends Die* by Hal Borland. (J.B. Lippincott Co.) Copyright © 1963 by Hal Borland. Reprinted by permission of Harper & Row, Publishers, Inc., and Barbara Dodge Borland.   From "Money" in *Compton's Encyclopedia* © 1983 by Encyclopaedia Britannica, Inc. Reprinted by permission of Encyclopaedia Britannica, Inc.   From "Time, You Old Gypsy Man" from *Collected Poems* by Ralph Hodgson. Reprinted by permission of Macmillan Publishing Company, Inc., and Macmillan, London and Basingstoke.   From "The Sea Girl" from *Love in Winter* by Kim Yong Ik. Reprinted by permission of the author.   Adapted from page 7 in *Consumer Action* by John S. Morton and Ronald R. Rezny. Copyright © 1978 by Houghton Mifflin Company. Used by permission.   From *Readers' Guide to Periodical Literature.* Copyright © 1980, 1981 by The H.W. Wilson Company. Material reproduced by permission of the publisher.   From *Beastly Neighbors* by Mollie Rights. Copyright © 1981 by The Yolla Bolly Press. Reprinted by permission of Little, Brown and Company.   Adapted from pp. 97–99 and 169–171 in *This Is America's Story* by Howard B. Wilder, Robert P. Ludlum, and Harriet McCune Brown. Copyright © 1983 by Houghton Mifflin Company. Used by permission.   From *This Is America's Story* by Howard B. Wilder, Robert P. Ludlum, and Harriet McCune Brown. Copyright © 1978 by Houghton Mifflin Company. Reprinted by permission.   Adapted from *The World Book Encyclopedia.* © 1983 World Book, Inc. Used by permission.

Student sample by Jackie McCoy from *Rainbow Bridge,* Spring 1977, Volume 1, Woodbridge Senior High School, Woodbridge, Virginia.

Credits

Cover concept, book design, and art production: Ligature Publishing Services, Inc.

Photos
Carl Corey: cover, viii–1, 236–237, 466–467
James L. Ballard: 257, 275, 305, 335, 353, 375, 401, 439, 461
Page 257 (right): Courtesy the House of Collectibles, Inc.   Page 305 (left): United Press International   Page 305 (right): United Press International   Page 375: Smithsonian Institution   Page 401: *General Washington on White Charger,* American School National Gallery of Art, Washington. Gift of Edgar William and Bernice Chrysler Garbisch   Page 439: Courtesy of Sperry Corporation

Checklist for Revision

As a guide in revising your writing, consider the following questions:

✔ 1. Did you cover your topic thoroughly?

✔ 2. Did you remove any information not directly related to your topic?

✔ 3. Did you include a topic sentence or a topic statement?

✔ 4. Did you present your information in a logical order?

✔ 5. Did you use transitional words and phrases to emphasize the order of your ideas?

✔ 6. Did you write an appropriate conclusion?

✔ 7. Did you use words and details that are suitable for your audience?

✔ 8. Did you achieve your purpose for writing?

✔ 9. Did you vary the length and structure of your sentences?

✔ 10. Did you use accurate and precise words?

✔ 11. Did you use the correct forms for reports and letters?

✔ 12. Did you avoid using sentence fragments, run-on sentences, and other incorrect sentence structures?

✔ 13. Did you use correct usage, spelling, punctuation, and capitalization?

✔ 14. Did you carefully proofread your finished copy?